Sustaining In Battle...

Breaking through the Storms

Volume One

Jolene McCall

Sustaining in Battle... Breaking through the Storms
Copyright © 2016 by Hori-Son Press

Printed in the United States of America

Cover Art by Lynn H. Pellerin

ISBN 978-1-938186-03-5

SAN 920-251X

Throughout this book, the name satan has deliberately not been capitalized. To capitalize a name would be proper grammar, and it also shows respect to that person. Since, I have no respect for satan or any demonic force of that nature, I choose to be grammatically incorrect and refrain from capitalizing his name.

Acknowledgements

To my Heavenly Father, this has been such a long road traveled. I have grown so much but only to realize just how little I really know; however, I have learned to let go and trust! I thank you Lord that you are patient with me and that you have loved me through all my tests and trials, not giving up on me. I feel blessed that you have placed me in a ministry where I have the privilege to minister to those you send on a weekly basis. Even when I feel so inadequate, you always come through and amaze me. My prayer today Lord is that each and every person that reads these words within this book, will see the need to seek you that much more. Forgive me Lord when I fall short and carry me through those tough storms when I am weak.

To my beloved grandchildren, there is nothing more precious than the gifts which come all bundled up from heaven above. I feel so blessed for each and every one of you. I believe that God has something great instore for all of you and that you find your place as you grow and mature in our Father's love. Be slow to anger, fast to forgive, find that within others to love, and seek Jesus with your whole heart. Never give up and continue running the same race in which Paul ran all the while keeping your feet planted on that narrow path which most will never travel. I love you with my whole heart! You are my heart!

To my new grandson, a special recognition to Cooper Lee, my newest grandson. Your smile lights up the sky even when there are storms all around. You are so precious and special. I love you with my whole heart and pray that you grow up to be in God's perfect will.

Table of Contents

Chapter One
Intro into Bootcamp

What makes a Christian unique? Or, should we say what <u>should</u> make a Christian unique? When we become engaged within the boundaries of our church home, far too often we are able to look around and see defeat among the Christian community. If the majority of Christians are living defeated, what needs to happen in order to see victory among God's people? I began a study some time ago realizing that those I minister to are often facing situations that seem hopeless. Many years ago, I was blessed in my walk with God to learn about Spiritual Warfare and was able to see that many today do not realize we are walking in a time of evil which requires us to engage in the Army of God. Following the calling of my Father, I had begun a prayer group a few years back after hearing the words, *"Jolene, go and teach my people to pray."* The teaching and revelation which God began to pour into me led to this book and what I call, *"Boot Camp."*

As I spent time ministering to those desiring to enrich their prayer life, I saw the need to understand just what Spiritual Warfare is and why it is important to line up our lives as one who is walking in battle at all times. In studying, God began to show me many similarities of those who go off to boot camp in the armed services and those who are enlisting to run this race with Christ.

Hebrews 12:1 (Amp) ¹THEREFORE THEN, since we are surrounded by so great a cloud of witnesses [who have borne testimony to the Truth], let us strip off and throw aside every encumbrance (unnecessary weight) and that sin which so readily (deftly and cleverly) clings to and entangles us, and let us run with patient endurance and steady and active persistence the appointed course of the race that is set before us,

1

If we are to be running the race that God has set before us, we should assume that we have to be in shape in order to finish this race to the end.   After studying the many similarities of a true military soldier, I enlisted my prayer group in a *"Spiritual Boot Camp."* We began this journey together, as we studied Truth in His Word, all the while seeking God to show ourselves approved. You too can begin your journey today as you enlist in the army of the Most High God!

2 Timothy 2:15 (Amp) [15]*Study and be eager and do your utmost to present yourself to God approved (tested by trial), a workman who has no cause to be ashamed, correctly analyzing and accurately dividing [rightly handling and skillfully teaching] the Word of Truth.*

Here is the great news – as you grow in this, you will also grow in strength.   You will realize the power given to God's children through the anointing of the Holy Spirit and in the name of Jesus, is for all who call themselves a child of the Most High God.   I believe it is time for all of God's children to take their rightful place in God's Army, equipping themselves with the full armor in order to begin taking back everything the enemy has stolen.

The Whole Armor of God

Ephesians 6:10-11 (ESV) The Whole Armor of God

[10]*Finally, be strong in the Lord and in the strength of his might.* [11] *Put on the whole armor of God, that you may be able to stand against the schemes of the devil.*

We will only be strong if we walk with the Lord.   We will only be able to overcome any and everything through Christ not through

2

ourselves. Paul tells us to put on the whole armor of God to be able to stand against satan. Paul knew there was a spiritual battle, and we will lose this battle if we are doing it in ourselves. Listen closely to what I am saying – we will lose this battle if we do not stay fully clothed with the whole armor of God and if we do not allow God to fight our battles. What does that mean? That means that we cannot do it in ourselves but only in and through Jesus Christ who gives us our strength. For when we are weakest, then we are strong.

2 Corinthians 12:10 (Amp) *[10]So for the sake of Christ, I am well pleased and take pleasure in infirmities, insults, hardships, persecutions, perplexities and distresses; for when I am weak [in human strength], then am I [truly] strong (able, powerful in divine strength).*

The strength we will learn to rely upon is not in physical strength but rather in spiritual strength. This is the divine strength to which Paul is referring. For God chooses those which the world looks at as weak as we see in 1 Corinthians below. Therefore, it does not matter what your physical strength is because God is going to transform you into His army to walk among those strongest spiritually. This begins with realizing there is nothing we can do within ourselves to walk victorious but only through Christ.

1 Corinthians 1:27 (Amp) *[27][No] for God selected (deliberately chose) what in the world is foolish to put the wise to shame, and what the world calls weak to put the strong to shame.*

In 2 Chronicles, chapter 25 below, we will look at Amaziah who was king of Jerusalem during this time. As the story goes, Amaziah did what was pleasing in the Lord's sight most of the time; however, he had decided to form an army and also to hire additional men from Israel. This was not in God's plan. We see in

3

verse 7 and 8, a man came to warn him that God had the power to either help him or trip him up.

2 Chronicles 25:7-8 (NLT) [7] *But a man of God came to him and said, "Your Majesty, do not hire troops from Israel, for the LORD is not with Israel. He will not help those people of Ephraim!* [8] *If you let them go with your troops into battle, you will be defeated by the enemy no matter how well you fight. God will overthrow you, for he has the power to help you or to trip you up."*

Here is the deal – when we make decisions to do things our way not God's, what we are really saying is this, *"God, I think I will fight this battle without you this time!"* God will either fight our battles with us, or we will fight them alone. We make the choice every day to either do it in ourselves or allow God to fight for us. That is why it is important that we clothe ourselves with the full armor of God for many reasons which we will learn, but the main thing is that we are doing it God's way not ours.

Paul also noted in verse 11 of Ephesians 6 below, that we must be able to stand against the schemes of the devil. We sometimes get so caught up in fighting our own battles that we cannot seem to understand how to let go and to just stand. However, if we are going to win our battles, we must know that we are **able** to stand. You cannot win a battle if you are continually being knocked off your feet, continually missing the mark and having to get back up again and again. Why is it that we cannot just stand? Why is it that we cannot just refuse to be moved by circumstances and just stand? Many times, it is because we cannot be quiet! Listen to what I am saying. Our mouth will get us into trouble because instead of standing on what God's Word says, we have to get the last word in. We have to make sure our opponents understand and agree with our point of view. Have you ever heard the saying,

4

"It is okay to agree to disagree"? Most of us have heard that and it is perfectly alright as long as the other person understands that **we** can disagree with them but don't turn it the other way around. We need to understand that our wisdom falls very short of the wisdom of God. We need to understand that it is perfectly alright that everyone does not agree with us. We also need to understand that we do not have to agree with everyone else. Until we understand both of those scenarios, we are going to miss it. When we are wrong and refuse to see this, God will allow us to go into battle alone. We better make certain that our pride does not stand in the way of agreeing with what God's Word says because that settles it right there. This does not mean that we try to force our beliefs and philosophies down other people because that is not showing others love the way God loves. Just because we interpret the Word of God to mean one thing and someone else sees it another way, does not mean we are right. There have been times in my walk that I felt I was right based on Scripture; however, instead of me missing the mark and losing my peace by trying to prove a point or show someone else where I felt they were missing it, I went to God and prayed. I have asked God many times to show me if I was wrong. If I was right, I have prayed for God to show the other person. You see, I believe first we have to understand that we are not all that. It does not matter how long you have studied God's Word or if you have a theology degree, if God has not opened your eyes to the truth in every area, you will miss it. None of us know all the revelation there is to know because God is the one who reveals His revelation in His timing and to whom He chooses. Nevertheless, do not seek man for your spiritual growth but instead seek the *"Author and Finisher"* of the Word Himself. It is also not our place to play God over someone. When I have taken it to God, many times He has shown me where I was wrong. Now isn't it better to receive the truth from God instead of getting all upset and bringing stress and

anxiety into your life when God can settle it right there. If I am wrong, I want to know I am wrong so I can get my thinking right. I do not want to go through life missing it over major things or even minor things for that matter. It continues in Ephesians saying, stand your ground and having done all stand. We do what we can and then we stand. We fall because we refuse to let it go. We are told to just stand. If you know that you are doing what God has called you to do and the circumstances are against you, just stand! If the tests and trials come, just stand!

Ephesians 6:13 (Amp) *[13]Therefore put on God's complete armor, that you may be able to resist and stand your ground on the evil day [of danger], and, having done all [the crisis demands], to stand [firmly in your place].*

Many times, we will miss our miracles because we refuse to just stand and wait upon the Lord. I sometimes get to the place that I just give it to God, *"Lord, I have done all I know to do and there is nothing more I can do – it is your battle, not mine!"* If the promises in God's Word are for me and I believe I am doing what He has called me to do, I am putting all my cares and concerns back on Him. I am refusing to pick them back up. That is giving it to God and that is what we are to do. However, once we know that we have clothed ourselves with the armor and it seems that we are not winning, we give up. Do not give up, clothe yourself and refuse to move – stand firm. We cannot always see those things which are in the spiritual realm; therefore, we need to remain standing and speak faith, *"God, I am standing on Your Truth and will not be moved; I am waiting and expecting my miracle to come through."* Faith is speaking what you cannot see. It's that simple.

In looking into what Paul was trying to teach the disciples, we must see that putting on the whole armor of God is just that. We cannot just put on some of it! Think about when men and women go to battle, does our government send them off to fight for our country half prepared? No, men and women are sent to boot camp in order to make sure they are fully equipped. We do not want to lose the battle; therefore, when we send men and women to fight for our country, we do our part to prepare them. We want to know that our government has done everything possible so that they can win the fight with few losses, right? God has done the same for us. He has done His part for us to be well prepared and fully clothed to go into this battle unscathed, unharmed, winning our battles, overcoming our circumstances, triumphing over our enemy, having authority over our jobs, our finances, our families and loved ones, our health, etc. If we are not winning, then we are not getting the training we need which will be thoroughly breaking down what Paul was trying to communicate to the disciples. Do not walk this walk alone and in making this decision, now is the time to begin your walk on the winning side.

Preparing for War

How do soldiers prepare for war? There is basic training and there is boot camp. If you study basic training according to the US Army or if you have ever been in the services at all, soldiers begin as infantrymen before they are ever recruited to a different level within the army. A Marine must first make it through what they call *"The Crucible"* before they leave boot camp for more advanced training. In order for us to advance in the Army of God, we must also begin at the lower rank and then we will advance as we grow or as we gain experience through our battles.

The Crucible, required by the Marines, is a 54 hour training course requiring continual movement, little sleep, and is overseen by an impossible-to-please drill instructor. Military Boot Camp is very tough training, but is it tough enough to prepare men and women to face war? No, even though they are geared to be extremely tough, it is never tough enough for what is endured in the actual battlefield. It is never tough enough to prepare our men and women for the chaos and cruelty of combat. However, without the training they would never endure one day in the field of battle. We must realize that if we want to walk this walk with God victoriously, only those willing to give it all they have will endure and live this life abundantly which will determine their life eternal.

John 10:10 (Amp) ¹⁰The thief comes only in order to steal and kill and destroy. I came that they may have and enjoy life, and have it in abundance (to the full, till it overflows).

satan is very smart. Just because he emanates evil, does not mean he is unintelligent. God created all things including satan. Prior to his fall, he was the highest ranking angel there was. I believe that satan gained that highest rank because he was far above average and willing to do all that was required. Therefore, we need to realize that he not only came to steal, kill, and destroy, but he **WILL** steal, kill, and destroy. Throughout Boot Camp, we will learn how to fight a spiritual battle. However, we need to understand that once we actually begin fighting these battles through our tests and trials, discouragement must never come. We will learn that with every test and trial we engage in through the spiritual realm, they will grow us. This is why James said to count it all joy when tests and trials come. We grow; we become stronger; our faith grows; we learn to endure; we learn how to stand; we learn to be committed, and we learn patience.

James 1:2-3 (Amp) ²Consider it wholly joyful, my brethren, whenever you are enveloped in or encounter trials of any sort or fall into various temptations. *³Be assured and understand that the trial and proving of your faith bring out endurance and steadfastness and patience.*

You will come to a place where you begin to see the gain by walking through these tests and trials. You will come to a place where you will say, *"Come on storms, my God has got this, and my gain is great!"* Maybe not exactly in those words, but I remember a time when tests came, I got excited because I knew my gain would be great. We should want more of God and that cannot come without gaining experience. Experience will not come until we look for the tests and get excited when we find ourselves in the middle of that storm. Therefore, it is up to us to engage fully equipped with the full armor of God because as our battles begin, we will start using what we gain.

Spiritual Battle

Ephesians 6:12 (ESV) ¹²For we do not wrestle against flesh and blood, but against the rulers, against the authorities, against the cosmic powers over this present darkness, against the spiritual forces of evil in the heavenly places.

Paul said we do not wrestle with flesh and blood. It is a spiritual battle which was won that day on Calvary. What makes our battles so hard is because from the time we came into this world, we have been trained to fight our battles through the flesh. The flesh will not win a spiritual battle, but we can win a spiritual battle through our minds. It is mind over matter and our minds have to be renewed to thinking like God, renewing our minds to that of Christ.

Romans 12:2 (Amp) ²Do not be conformed to this world (this age), [fashioned after and adapted to its external, superficial customs], but be

9

transformed (changed) by the [entire] renewal of your mind [by its new ideals and its new attitude], so that you may prove [for yourselves] what is the good and acceptable and perfect will of God, even the thing which is good and acceptable and perfect [in His sight for you].

To win our battles through the spiritual realm will begin with changing the way we think and aligning our mouth or words up with our renewed way of thinking. How do we do this? Well, it is not easy but definitely can be done. Military boot camps were never designed to be easy but instead to be rigid, hard, and tedious. Only those who have the mindset that they are going to conquer their battles – will win. Boot camps have never been about physical strength, even though those who are strongest will be those who survive. This is not talking about physical strength. Even in the military, those who have weak minds will be those who miss out while the strong minded will conquer. There have been many men who have engaged in boot camp with little physical strength but the determination deep within to win. In preparing their mind, they came out as winners. I can remember a time in my adolescent years where I was taught in the streets (street smarts) that if you wanted to win a fight to not focus on your physical strength, but the focus had to be in your mind. If you could talk the talk prior to the fight ever engaging, you made your opponent think you were something to fear. If you could gain this control over their mind, the battle was already won. This is done inside prison walls, in the boxing rings, and in schools of all ages. This is basically mind over matter. When you can convince someone that you are tough and when you can talk the talk enough on the streets, you begin to actually see yourself being able to take on those much bigger and physically stronger than yourself. These are not the fights or battles we need to be engaging in because our battles are not with men but with spiritual forces of darkness. However, there will be great emphasis on

10

renewing our minds. Our words we speak must line up with our thoughts and be in-line with the Word of God. As we begin training and change our way of thinking, our words will also become powerful and change the course from destruction within our lives and that of our families to a path of victory.

Finally, know that we all desire to be winners in all the attributes of our lives whether it is within our relationships, our finances, our careers, our health, etc. Having the desire to win will never bring us to that place without following a winner, and Jesus Christ has been the only winner who conquered all including conquering the grave. Therefore, our eyes must be fixed upon that which is the ultimate winner in order that we can mold our lives to fit His. In doing so, we too can become winners in all that we do.

Marines

It is not too hard to surf the web and see many blogs written by Marines who have been there and done that. What was amazing to me was how much of what is said relates to the Word of God. There are times in this book that I will use illustrations comparing the very words of a Marine to the Words of God.

A Marine said it like this... *Marine Corps Boot Camp is only as hard as you make it. If you do what you are told, when you are told with a sense of urgency, you'll have no problems.*

What are we told to do? Abide by all the commandments and statutes which are in the Word of God.

1 John 3:24 (Amp) ²⁴*All who keep His commandments [who obey His orders and follow His plan, live and continue to live, to stay and] abide in Him, and He in them. [They let Christ be a home to them and they are the home of Christ.] And by this we know and understand and have the proof that He [really] lives and makes His home in us: by the [Holy] Spirit Whom He has given us.*

If Christ is in us, should we have problems? The Word says that trouble will come. I am not trying to say that we will not have problems because the Word of God says differently. We see that Timothy talked about times ahead as the end approaches. He speaks of our world today, about people who are so absorbed in self that they are going about creating a world with much sin and with sin brings destruction.

2 Timothy 3:1-5 (The Message) 1-5Don't be naive. There are difficult times ahead. As the end approaches, people are going to be self-absorbed, money-hungry, self-promoting, stuck-up, profane, contemptuous of parents, crude, coarse, dog-eat-dog, unbending, slanderers, impulsively wild, savage, cynical, treacherous, ruthless, bloated windbags, addicted to lust, and allergic to God. They'll make a show of religion, but behind the scenes they're animals. Stay clear of these people.

Most of us either fit in one of those categories or we have been there, but the good news is that we do not have to stay there. Jesus tells us in John 16 that even though we will have trials in this world to be of good cheer because He overcame the world for us.

John 16:33 (Amp) ^{33}*I have told you these things, so that in Me you may have [perfect] peace and confidence. In the world you have tribulation and trials and distress and frustration; but be of good cheer [take courage; be confident, certain, undaunted]! For I have overcome the world. [I have deprived it of power to harm you and have conquered it for you.]*

Therefore take note, if you consider yourself a child of God, you will be able to walk through your problems when you abide by what God said. Just like in the Marine Corps, they go through boot camp in order to begin preparations on how to walk through situations. They do not let their guard down because their focus remains on those things they were taught prior to walking into the battlefield. And notice, the marine said to do those things with a sense of urgency. Why is this? I do not think battles have been won by those dragging their feet while in the midst of destruction. If we are being attacked, there is no such thing as saying, *"Wait a minute devil, I just want to finish watching this episode of my favorite sitcom."* Or an even better one would be, *"I really don't feel like battling right now because I have had a hard day and watching this program is helping to keep my mind off of my troubles."* If this is you – your troubles are only beginning. You are going to be defeated if you do not focus on what you are taught and run, rather than walk, with a sense of urgency as if your life depended on it. That is where we miss the mark. Christians today think we have tomorrow so why be hurried today. Why not put off today what can be done tomorrow? That depends on what you are facing. By no means should we run to the point that we are stressing out our physical bodies, but we must have that sense of urgency knowing that what we are doing today can mean victory and salvation for those we love dearly tomorrow. Do not waste your days doing those things which produce no fruit.

Power of the Cross

In Colossians it says that God disarmed the principalities and powers which are against us. This of course took place on

Calvary when Jesus died on the Cross in order to redeem mankind.

Colossians 2:15 (Amp) [15][God] disarmed the principalities and powers that were ranged against us and made a bold display and public example of them, in triumphing over them in Him and in it [the cross].

We must understand that the message of the Cross is not a message of defeat but rather a message of victory. It is what happened that day which changed the course for mankind and can change your course when you get this message deep inside of you. It is what happened at the Cross which gives us the victory in life today. If you lack victory, don't quit because God desires for your mind to be set free from doubt and transformed to that of Christ in order that you live the abundant life as mentioned earlier in *John 10:10*.

Let's look at this from a natural stand point. Suppose your earthly dad was a billionaire, do you think that you would ever be defeated in your finances? Of course not! I do not believe someone filthy rich would allow their own flesh and blood to do without. On the contrary, they would provide their children with the best medical attention needed, the best clothes money could buy, the best food that could be prepared, the best schools, and I could go on and on. Yet, we believe that our Father in heaven will allow us to live without. If we are living without, it is because we are not engaging. God already made things right by sending His Son to redeem His children on the Cross. If you consider yourself a child of God, you should overcome all the areas in your life where there is defeat. God owns everything we can see and the things we cannot see, why would He let us hurt for anything? God is the author and finisher of relationships, why then would He not give us what we need to have victory in our relationships? God has the power to heal, to deliver, and to transform any and all things, why then would He not equip His own children to be able to do the same? If you consider yourself a child of God, then you have rights to the inheritance of your Father. Paul sums it up in 1 Corinthians.

1 Corinthians 1:17-18 (Amp) [17]*For Christ (the Messiah) sent me out not to baptize but [to evangelize by] preaching the glad tidings (the Gospel), and that not with verbal eloquence, lest the cross of Christ should be deprived of force and emptied of its power and rendered vain (fruitless, void of value, and of no effect).* [18]*For the story and message of the cross is sheer absurdity and folly to those who are perishing and on their way to perdition, but to us who are being saved it is the [manifestation of] the power of God.*

This message of the Cross tells us that to those who are being saved, or to those who are striving to walk this walk daily, the Cross is not fruitless. If you consider yourself a child of God, the Cross is not fruitless. The Cross is not void of value and no effect. It is life to those who believe and life in abundance. Jesus sends all of us out not to baptize but to evangelize. This happens after we grow and learn of our Father. Just like the Marines, we are sent out. We train and then we go. We do not train and then spend the course of our life doing as we please, when we please, and as long as we please. You can live like that, but you will not see victory in your life. You can live any way you want, but you will see defeat in your life. The message of the Cross holds the key to living an abundant life through Christ because of the blood that was shed for mankind. The Cross at Calvary holds the power we need in order to go forth fully clothed in our spiritual armor and begin taking back everything the enemy has stolen from us and from our families. This is the power of God.

1 John 5:4 (Amp) *[4]For whatever is born of God is victorious over the world; and this is the victory that conquers the world, even our faith.*

Therefore, if we are born of God, we have the victory over this world. We have the victory to conquer, to take back ground, to win our battles, and to walk in the abundant life that was promised to us. In Boot Camp we will learn that we are all winners because we share in the crucifixion of Christ. As a winner, we will learn that we all have the power to conquer and the authority to speak to our circumstances and change the course of our life. As we see ourselves through the eyes of God, our very circumstances will begin to line up with what God has spoken over our lives not what the world speaks. As we engage in this very path chosen for each of us by our Father through the teachings and illustrations within this book, our lives will transform before our very eyes. We will never be the same again. Let me add one thing which will be emphasized more within this book. When we speak of the abundant life, do not take this to mean that God desires to give us the riches of this world. We look at an abundant life by how much stuff we acquire, but with God, there is so much more to life than things.

Maturing

A Marine said it like this... The worst part is being home sick.

There will be times that we will become home sick but that pretty much sums up to missing our old life. We are in training, and our flesh still wants to do those things we used to do. However, that home sickness will fade because as we grow up, we become stronger. As we learn, we become more confident; as we submit, we accept that which God desires instead of our own selfish desires. Then all of a sudden, we are glad we have become what Boot Camp has created us to be. In the Marines, they are known as lean killing machines but in God's Army, through Jesus Christ, we become great and powerful according to what is written.

Joel 2:11 (ESV) [11] *The LORD utters his voice before his army, for his camp is exceedingly great; he who executes his word is powerful.*

If we carry out God's Word, there will be power. How on earth could we not have victory if we became more and more like Jesus? The Word tells us that we are to imitate God as well-beloved children imitate their father.

Ephesians 5:1 (Amp) [1] *THEREFORE BE imitators of God [copy Him and follow His example], as well-beloved children [imitate their father].*

Of course, this would be fathers who were raising their children up in the ways of the Lord which we are also told to do as we see in Proverbs. And, I do not think God meant to teach them in the ways of the world but in the ways which are written in the Word of God.

Proverbs 22:6 (HCSB) [6] *Teach a youth about the way he should go; even when he is old he will not depart from it.*

Therefore, we should be imitators of God or imitators of those who are walking in the same manner which is worthy of God. I believe today there are many churches which have given Christianity a bad name where many refuse to join with the body of Christ because it is hard to tell the Christians from the non-Christians. We all seem to call ourselves Christians just because we say we believe in Jesus Christ, but how can we say we believe in someone when there is no evidence within our lives that He

17

exists? Paul and Timothy went to the church of the Thessalonians and made this statement:

*Thessalonians 1:5-6 (Amp) *5*For our [preaching of the] glad tidings (the Gospel) came to you not only in word, but also in [its own inherent] power and in the Holy Spirit and with great conviction and absolute certainty [on our part]. You know what kind of men we proved [ourselves] to be among you for your good. *6*And you [set yourselves to] become imitators of us and [through us] of the Lord Himself, for you welcomed our message in [spite of] much persecution, with joy [inspired] by the Holy Spirit;*

If we allow ourselves to be deceived by what we judge to be holy or not holy, we will miss it. We cannot afford to not be connected to a body of believers where God's Word is anointed and poured out among those present. I believe many times we go to a service expecting something extraordinary to happen and instead of listening for a Word from God, we are expecting our miracle. When our miracle does not come, we blame the church or worse, we blame God. God never changes; He is the same today as He was yesterday. There are great men and women running this race today and if we cannot imitate Jesus Christ because of not feeling that deep connection and not being able to see Him with our natural eyes, then it is time to find someone that you believe is running this race. We need to begin imitating everything we see with our natural eyes and do all that we hear from the teachings through God's Word. We will never mature in our walk with God until we allow God to transform us, and many times, He uses someone else to do just that. I would not be where I am today if it had not been for those who have touched my life and my willingness to be open-minded enough to admit, *"I was wrong Lord."* That is the first step to maturity. As parents, we can easily see the immaturity within our children, and God can also see the

18

great immaturity within us as well. Let go of your pride and become a winner today. Our pride stands in the way because we look at it as failure to admit we are wrong, but in reality, we are failures when we hold on to that pride because that is what satan will use to bring us down and destroy us. The devil not only wants to destroy you but will bring your whole family with you. Let me clarify, if you choose to follow a man that seems to be running this race, your intentions should never be to remain at that place. God desires us to grow up to the place where we develop that relationship with Him and eventually our growth comes because we are following His voice. This is just a precaution so that we do not stand before God based on our relationship through a man and not our Creator.

Hebrews 6:12 (Amp) [12]In order that you may not grow disinterested and become [spiritual] sluggards, but imitators, behaving as do those who through faith (by their leaning of the entire personality on God in Christ in absolute trust and confidence in His power, wisdom, and goodness) and by practice of patient endurance and waiting are [now] inheriting the promises.

Many men and women go off to boot camp and their parents are in hopes that they will return changed, why is this? Because parents know that there is a really good chance that the military may be what it takes to wake many young people up. Boot camp may help many realize there is more to life than the next party; there is more to life than being angry at the world, and there is more to life than living a life of destruction. Boot camp many times changes those who have the privilege to encounter something so extreme. Yes, it is a privilege and it is also a privilege to be accepted into the family of God. Jesus died for each and every one of us, but God will not force anyone to submit or to be obedient. God loves us to the extreme because He sent His Son to die for us when we did not deserve it. Boot camp is your chance to get in shape, grow up, learn obedience, gain wisdom and knowledge, and grow into your unique calling which was written just for you before you were ever born. I challenge each of you to continue in this journey to the end.

Mind over Matter

Boot camp is almost all mental and some physical. Walking this walk victoriously has to do with renewing your mind to think like God. However, there will be physical on our part but that will be much easier when we do not have to deal with a mind that thinks like the world. Your life will flow very peacefully when you do not have to deal with a mind that is worldly because when your mind is worldly, your flesh will rule instead of your spirit.

A Marine said when asked which is tougher between the mental or physical training, *"The mental training is tougher because the human mind acts in different ways when it is being pressured. When you get angry you want to hit something, you want to act out, you want to swear. But here it is teaching you how to keep your bearing and how to stay focused."*

Boot camp will teach us how to stay focused and to keep our bearing. We will learn how to overcome those urges to do things according to the ways of this world and instead will grow in a higher power of wisdom and knowledge. We will be transformed to the mind of Christ, to hold the thoughts and purposes within our heart. God will change us and with change, we will experience victory as warriors for the Most High God!

20

Chapter Two
Helmet of Salvation

Ephesians 6:17a (ESV) and take the helmet of salvation…

In putting on the whole armor of God, according to Ephesians 6, we will begin focusing on one piece of armor at a time. We will break everything down in order to clarify the meaning for better understanding. This way we will begin to apprehend the complexity of the armor and exactly how to use it to be victorious and overcome this world. We cannot expect victory if we go to battle just half way understanding how to use our armor. It is to our advantage that we prepare for battle so that we can gain ground with our enemy. In the military, a soldier learns every aspect of his battle gear. They learn the importance of wearing every aspect of their uniform from their head gear all the way down to their combat boots. Uniforms are made for either winter or summer in order to provide what protection is needed based on the terrain and climate. Included is their web gear which holds and organizes the many weapons and apparatus for easy access when needed. The men and women who go to war for our country today are equipped with night vision devices to double the field of view. They have sniper rifles, pistols, grenades, missiles, and many other offensive or defensive weapons. Our military is equipped with the finest aircraft, helicopters, battle ships, and submarines. When in Boot Camp, soldiers will learn every aspect of their clothing and all the different artillery including every tool given to them in order to be perfected in using what they have. We too will learn about each piece of armor in order that we can fully utilize every element to be effective in winning our battles in the Lord's Army. When we complete this Boot Camp, no one not even our enemy, will be able to change our thinking from the knowledge we have gained.

Physical ~ Spiritual Helmet

When Paul wrote his last letter to the church at Ephesus, it may have been addressed to that particular church at that time, but that letter was for the church as a whole. Paul was not talking to a building but rather to the body of Christ, which is the church. We are the church. Paul understood the importance of being fully equipped with the whole armor of God in order for the church to endure the end times, in order that we can endure the end times. Paul, being a Roman citizen, was very familiar with the military battle gear for that era. Paul chose to use the actual Roman armor to parallel what our spiritual armor should be. In order for us to be able to clearly visualize our spiritual armor, we must go back to biblical days in order to see all aspects of the Roman battle gear. In this chapter, we will begin by taking a deep look into the helmet and all its purposes in the natural sense as well as the spiritual sense.

The Roman helmet, generally made of bronze, had an iron skullcap inside that was lined with some type of leather or cloth in order to provide padding to the head. This helmet provided total protection in biblical days not only for the head but also the neck area of a warrior. In researching more modern head gear, there have been many designs and changes over the years. In biblical days, the helmet was extremely heavy and would weigh down the soldiers during battle. This weight made it hard in the battlefield for the soldier to move and be swift on their feet, but for that era, the helmet was much needed in order to prevent great losses. Later, the weight was taken into account where many styles of helmets or head gear were developed over the years at a lighter weight and provided even greater protection. However, the general purpose of the helmet has always been to protect the head. Besides providing protection to the head, another important aspect of the helmet was to help identify if you were the enemy force.

When we look at the purpose of the helmet in the natural sense, we have to begin to envision exactly what Paul was trying to show us in the spiritual sense. In order to do this, we must envision the actual Roman helmet. This helmet, like I said, protected the head and the neck. To go even further, what would be protected on the head? The helmet protected the eyes, ears, nose, mouth, as well as the brain and neck area. If we look at this in a physical sense, we can see that by our brain being protected, that covers our mind and the senses. The brain covers all the functions. Without our brain, we become in either a vegetative state or brain dead. Our brain is similar to a computer but much more complex. Like a computer, the brain literally stores information and retrieves the information as needed. Yet, the brain unlike the computer also acts on emotions, imagination, and common sense. There are times our emotions can get us into trouble when we are not properly lined up with the Word of God. However, we were created with all these characteristics. God designed each of us uniquely with all our emotions, imaginations, and personalities. If we go through life without this helmet on, the enemy will distort all those unique qualities in a detrimental way. He will use our emotions to bring destruction. He will use our imaginations for perversion. He will send those across our path to attack our personalities in order to make us feel unaccepted, rejected, and unsuccessful. If I had walked with satan and not God, at some point, the enemy could have persuaded me to use my gift in writing in a way to bring glory to that which is evil instead of glory

23

to God. It is important for us to remember that by putting on the helmet, we are protecting those things which are valuable to walk this walk with Christ victoriously. We are protecting those qualities for God to increase them and perfect them in positive ways. In 1 John, it warns us about the world.

1 John 2:15-17 (HCSB) ¹⁵*Do not love the world or the things that belong to the world. If anyone loves the world, love for the Father is not in him. Because everything that belongs to the world—* ¹⁶ *the **<u>lust of the flesh</u>**, **<u>the lust of the eyes</u>**, and **<u>the pride in one's lifestyle</u>**—is not from the Father, but is from the world.* ¹⁷ *And the world with its lust is passing away, but the one who does God's will remains forever.*

By this Scripture, we are able to see that without the helmet, our mind would do what the majority of people in this world do. We would spend the majority of our life gratifying the flesh, lusting after things we do not have or things which belong to someone else. Our lifestyle would be that of the world and not Jesus. By protecting our mind, we no longer long for those things we can see. Our desires begin to line up with Christ as we strive for those things above, which cannot be seen.

Let me say that it is not a bad thing to have things in this world; however, we should never get too comfortable that we are drawn to this world. The more we acquire from this world, the more we are drawn to this world. Our eyes must be trained by the renewing of our minds to see through spiritual eyes, looking at things the way that God sees them. Our ears need protection that we are able to know the voice we hear is that of our Savior. Everything is transformed by our mind and the helmet provides that form of protection because of Jesus dying for all mankind in that we are saved by the grace of God.

Message of the Cross

When we *"take"* the helmet of salvation as the Scripture says in Ephesians, we are accepting that helmet. In other words, we are accepting that free gift of righteousness which leads to salvation.

Romans 5:17-19(NIV1984)[17] For if, by the trespass of the one man, death reigned through that one man, how much more will those who receive God's abundant provision of grace and of the gift of righteousness reign in life through the one man, Jesus Christ. [18] Consequently, just as the result of one trespass was condemnation for all men, so also the result of one act of righteousness was justification that brings life for all men. [19]For just as through the disobedience of the one man the many were made sinners, so also through the obedience of the one man the many will be made righteous.

Jesus came to justify the offense of Adam. God abundantly provides grace for us and the gift of righteousness. All we have to do is receive it. God provides us with what we need in order that we are on course for salvation. There is nothing we can do to earn salvation because outside of knowing Jesus Christ, there is no salvation. We are not saved by anything we do. There are no works, no good deeds, or anything we can do in ourselves that will make us in right standing with God or lead us on that narrow path which leads to heaven. Our only way to receive salvation is through receiving the gift of righteousness first and coming to know the Father, Son, and the Holy Ghost.

God sent His Son to pay that price for our sins. Jesus redeemed mankind, and righteousness is a gift that we must accept. With any gift, it is not ours until we accept it. Therefore, we put on the helmet of salvation by simply *"taking"* the helmet as we determine in our heart that we are accepting that same course which Paul journeyed. We reach out in the spiritual realm and *"take"* the helmet from our Father and place it on our head. Throughout this book, we need to begin envisioning exactly what we are doing, such as: we *"take"* the helmet from our Father and place it on our head. It is hard to believe something when you cannot see it, but faith is believing those things you cannot see as though you can. God revealed to me some time ago that we can see faith, in a sense, if we envision that which we are believing for. In your mind, envision what you are doing. This brings it to light and makes it seem more real. It is very real but again this is a battle with our mind. In envisioning something, this helps us to be able to see it. Before going further, I want to clarify that grace is a free gift for those that believe. Being made righteous can only occur through Jesus Christ. It is this free gift of righteousness that leads to salvation. Salvation does not occur if we are not running the same race that Paul spoke of.

2 Timothy 4:6-8 (ESV) [6]For I am already being poured out as a drink offering, and the time of my departure has come. [7]I have fought the good fight, I have finished the race, I have kept the faith. [8]Henceforth there is laid up for me the crown of righteousness, which the Lord, the righteous judge, will award to me on that Day, and not only to me but also to all who have loved his appearing.

Paul knows that his time is nearing the end, but he also knows that he ran the race and he finished it well. Paul kept the faith and followed in the footsteps of Jesus Christ. We will discuss this further, but it is important to know that salvation is not just for anyone that merely asks. The Bible says we must not only ask, but we must also seek and knock. Salvation is not just words spoken. Anyone can ask and continue on their pathway which leads to hell if that is all they do. Salvation is a free gift to those that find it but it does come with a price. The cost of salvation is giving of ourselves (our life) while here on this earth.

To continue, when we think about the message of the Cross, what comes to mind? Most of us would say Jesus on the Cross. We may look at this as a defeat, but it is actually a victory. When Jesus surrendered Himself to His Father prior to being arrested, He made the choice to die for mankind.

Mark 14:36 (AMP) [36]*And He was saying, Abba, [which means] Father, everything is possible for You. Take away this cup from Me; yet not what I will, but what You [will].*

Not my will Father but Yours! Is that our life? Can we understand how to lay our life down for Christ? In order to understand the Message of the Cross, it needs to come alive within us. When I think about the Cross, I think about how Jesus died literally so that I can have a better life. I think about how Jesus went through all the suffering and persecution in order to make this world a better place for those who really love Him. I think about how Jesus' dying for me has given me a way for eternal life. I think about how Jesus' suffering paid the way for my daughter who died in 2000 to be able to suffer no more. I think about my life prior to Jesus. I think about my life prior to the Holy Spirit working in the life of my other two daughters. Let's face it – if you do not have this kind of anointing working in your life and that of your family, you are not getting the Message of the Cross. I did not deserve an innocent man suffering and paying the price for all the wrong and evil things I have done in my life time. However, God loves me and my family so much so that He believed it was worth allowing His child to die for me and my children. Why would I want to serve anything but God? Why would I want to devote my life to anything other than the ministry He has called me to? Why would I want to share anything other than my testimony with a world that is lost and going to hell? *"Lord, I am totally unworthy of everything you have done for me. Lord, there will never be anything I could do that could pay you back for all you have done for me and my family."* But, what does He want from us? God wants our obedience and our faithfulness. He wants us to love Him. He wants us to surrender everything to Him. He wants our life totally surrendered to Him. You may be thinking, *"Well, He sure wants a lot?"* But is it a lot? Is that too much to ask if He holds your life in His hands and has your life and that of your family already planned out. Is it too much to ask if His desires are in your best interest? He is our Daddy, our Father. How could we possibly love anything more than Him? He first loved us. I do not know why He loves us so much because we certainly do not deserve it. In fact, those who live disobedient are basically saying, *"God, I really do not care how much it hurt You to watch Your Son die for me. I really do not care what You think. It is all about me and not about You!"* Can you see what is wrong with this picture?

Romans 5:6-8 (NIV 1984, ©1984) [6]You see, at just the right time, when we were still powerless, Christ died for the ungodly. [7]Very rarely will anyone die for a righteous man, though for a good man someone might possibly dare to die. [8]But God demonstrates his own love for us in this: While we were still sinners, Christ died for us.

Can we not see just how much God did for mankind? Yet, we walk around with a chip on our shoulder, feeling as if the world owes us something. In reality, no one owes us anything. But, our Father in Heaven has made the way for all of us to be blessed. He has made the way for you and your family to have food and clothes, be in good health, and lack for nothing. No, we do not deserve any of this, but God desires this for all of us. If we could only wake up to see that those things we put before God are not even worth it. That sin in our life that we choose over God is not worth it. If we say that it is worth it, then our values for those things which should be important mean nothing to us. If we choose gratification of our flesh over those we love, we are missing it. Our choices in this life do not just affect us, but they affect everyone we are close to.

When we come to understand just what the Cross means to us, we are able to see that because of the shed blood on Calvary, we are saved from judgment. This is not a message of defeat but rather victory, can you see this? Jesus died for our sins; therefore, we are reconciled to God. God wanted us back. He wanted His people free from satanic forces and able to battle through everything the enemy would bring in order to go forth as a warrior winning souls for His Kingdom. God sent Jesus to pay for everything me and you have ever done wrong and everything we will do wrong.

Romans 5:9-11 (NIV 1984, ©1984) [9]Since we have now been justified by his blood, how much more shall we be saved from God's wrath through him! [10]For if, when we were God's enemies, we were reconciled to him through the death of his Son, how much more, having been reconciled, shall we be saved through his life! [11]Not only is this so, but we also rejoice in God through our Lord Jesus Christ, through whom we have now received reconciliation.

God does not bring condemnation on the world, that is satan's job. God realizes that we are far from perfect, yet He still loves us. We love our own children regardless of what they have done or will do. With our own children, we want what is best for them and it grieves our heart when they do not do what is right, but we will still love them. God also wants what is best for us, but He wants us to be obedient in order to protect us. God desires that we are

29

walking powerful in this world of darkness, and it grieves Him to see us disobey. God may still love us, but He gave us the free will to make our choices. It is not God's fault when our choices produce detrimental results in our lives. Without obedience, we open the door to satan's tactics and separate ourselves from God. Without obedience, we are no longer running the race which leads to salvation. Without obedience, none of the promises are for those that walk contrary to His Words. Without obedience, we open the door for sickness and disease to afflict our bodies and those of our children. Without obedience, we open the door which allows darkness to penetrate into our lives and those of our loved ones which ultimately will steal, kill, and destroy all of us.

Salvation

Many of us, prior to finding Jesus, looked at those living the Christian life and have had thoughts such as:

• *What a boring way to live.*

• *It has to be hard to try and live righteous, that's not for me.*

• *They all think they are better than everyone else; I don't want to be like them.*

• *I can believe in God and don't need to hang out with a bunch of hypocrites.*

When we finally do make that commitment to walk this walk with God, sometimes we conclude that it is hard to really be a Christian and much easier to just play church. Perhaps, our experience and knowledge of Christ was in a church that only believed you had to go to church once a week, give a little bit of money, live a good life by worldly standards, be a good parent to your children by worldly standards, and all was good. But in reality, if this is your strategy, it is not biblically based. Furthermore, you are probably straddling the fence. As we get further into Boot Camp, your eyes will be opened to truth that you have probably never known. As we seek deeper into the depths of God and into the spiritual realm, your spirit within will be awakened in order to see things through the spiritual realm and not through natural eyes. As long as we look upon the church through natural eyes, we will miss it. As long as we look at Christians through natural eyes, we will miss it. You have one chance at this walk with Christ and if you miss it, you will fall. If you miss it, you will not wake up in heaven. Now, I am not talking about striving to walk this walk and at times missing it. We know that as long as we live in these earthly bodies, we are going to miss it, but we must get back up. What I am talking about are those on the side lines that assume they do not have to engage. Or, those on the sidelines that judge because they do not have the truth. And then there are those on the side lines that think they see clearly and are able to determine they do not want to walk this walk because it is not real. And there are always those who believe they can just breeze through life playing church and never touching the spiritual aspects of Christianity, but all these are in for an awakening. If you fall in that category where you have judged the church, where you have judged the Christians, where you think you know all you need to know about God, you better think again. Our salvation depends on our walk with Christ. If it is not real, you will be blinded to the truth. If you are blinded from truth, you cannot see into the spiritual realm. If you are blinded from the truth, you do not know Christ and cannot understand those things which are written.

Corinthians 4:4 (HCSB) *⁴Regarding them: the god of this age has blinded the minds of the unbelievers so they cannot see the light of the gospel of the glory of Christ, who is the image of God.*

Perhaps, you found your way into a worship service where the people are really trying to live by biblical principles not that they are perfect. However, their walk seems much harder than when you just played church. The question we need to ask, *"Why do people waste years of their time going through the motions when it really means very little to them?"* If all you are doing is going through the motions, I would question my relationship with Christ. Remember, unless we are absolutely sure of our relationship with Jesus, we are not accepting that helmet from our Father. If we are not accepting that helmet, we are completely stripped of all battle gear. Without an understanding of salvation, or knowing Christ, we are not even eligible to be in God's Army. Just like when a man or woman signs up to be in the military, until they can pass all the requirements to even get in, they will be turned away. In the same sense, there will be many that the door to heaven will be shut and when they knock, God will tell them to depart.

Luke 13:25-27 (HCSB) *²⁵ once the homeowner gets up and shuts the door. Then you will stand outside and knock on the door, saying, 'Lord, open up for us!' He will answer you, 'I don't know you or where you're from.' ²⁶ Then you will say, 'We ate and drank in Your presence, and You taught in our streets!' ²⁷ But He will say, 'I tell you, I don't know you or where you're from. Get away from Me, all you workers of unrighteousness!'*

We are all unrighteous to God, and it is only by His grace through His Son Jesus that we are made righteous. If we are not running the race as Paul did, we should question our relationship. If you are basing your salvation on what a man or woman has told you rather than hearing from God, you should question your relationship with Christ. In Matthew, Jesus had asked His disciples, *"Who do you say that I am?"*

Matthew 16:16-17 (Amp) [16]*Simon Peter replied, You are the Christ, the Son of the living God.* [17]*Then Jesus answered him, Blessed (happy, fortunate, and to be envied) are you, Simon Bar-Jonah. For flesh and blood [men] have not revealed this to you, but My Father Who is in heaven.*

Who revealed to Simon Peter that Jesus was the Son of the living God? Was it a preacher or a priest? Was it a Bible school teacher or perhaps a man or woman of God? The Scripture says that flesh and blood did not reveal to Simon Peter who Jesus was. It was God the Father who revealed this to him. To continue in Matthew, Jesus responded to Peter.

Matthew 16:18 (Amp) [18]*And I tell you, you are Peter [Greek, Petros--a large piece of rock], and on this rock [Greek, petra--a huge rock like Gibraltar] I will build My church, and the gates of Hades (the powers of the infernal region) shall not overpower it [or be strong to its detriment or hold out against it].*

We are assured that our relationship is genuine when we know who Christ is because it has been revealed to us in that spiritual sense. God did not manifest Himself in the flesh in order to reveal to Peter who Jesus was. Our revelation of who Jesus is comes when we are at a place in our lives that we seek and continue to seek because we desire to know truth. Truth will never come when we continually and knowingly commit sin. Our enemy will keep us blinded as long as we are willingly committing sin. There is a huge difference in willingly committing sin and desiring deep within your heart to be free from sin in order that you find that

33

everlasting life that God's Word speaks of. For those who believe in Christ because God has revealed this to them, they will receive the truth. It is okay to come to the Lord with your life a mess. That is how we all first come to the Father. But our heart has to be at a place where we cry out to God, *"God, if you are real, please deliver me. Help me Father to know You; help me to change; I need You in my life because I cannot do this in myself anymore."* Just as Jesus told Peter He would build His church on him, He will also build on all those who walk this same walk. He will build that church within you. We come together as a body of believers, but we are the church. The church is not a building. Jesus was assuring Peter that He would build on his ministry. We all have a ministry which is our calling. If Jesus is building on you, all of Hades cannot bring you down. We put on the full armor of God because we have truth in us. We put on the full armor of God, and we walk in that armor daily because we know the truth, and it has set us free. Without truth, you will continue to sin. Without truth, you will continue to be defeated. Without truth, you will be one of those in the end who will knock and knock, and God will tell you to depart because He does not know you. If you do not know the Father, you do not know Jesus. If you do not have the truth living and manifesting in your life, you will surely die. But when you walk in that truth, you will be strong. When you walk in the truth, you will stand firm on the rock of Jesus. That will be your foundation, and you will walk as Peter walked. When you are that rock in which Jesus builds on, nothing will overpower you. Nothing will be able to tear you down, destroy that which has been given to you, and nothing will be able to come against your family, children, relationships, or finances.

According to John, Jesus came and made known the Father. Jesus came in order to not only redeem mankind but also to show us just who God is.

34

John 1:18 (Amp) ¹⁸No man has ever seen God at any time; the only unique Son, or the only begotten God, Who is in the bosom [in the intimate presence] of the Father, He has declared Him [He has revealed Him and brought Him out where He can be seen; He has interpreted Him and He has made Him known].

How did Jesus do this? Jesus shared many parables in the New Testament. Those parables were to give us insight into just who God is. God is love; God is gentle and kind; He is compassionate; He is a jealous God. And then we see Jesus. Jesus is God's Word made flesh. We are able to see God by being able to see Jesus. If we know Jesus, we know God. If we know God, we know Jesus. But primarily when we read the Word, we do not gain insight. If our eyes have been blinded, we cannot see these things. And of course, satan would like us to view God in a negative sense. Jesus prayed this to the Father about us, about those who are running the race which leads to salvation.

John 17:24 (Amp) ²⁴Father, I desire that they also whom You have entrusted to Me [as Your gift to Me] may be with Me where I am, so that they may see My glory, which You have given Me [Your love gift to Me]; for You loved Me before the foundation of the world.

We are the gifts given to Jesus. We are considered a love gift to Jesus. This is how much God loves each of us. Jesus continued praying to the Father.

John 17:25 (Amp) ²⁵O just and righteous Father, although the world has not known You and has failed to recognize You and has never acknowledged You, I have known You [continually]; and these men understand and know that You have sent Me.

Jesus is talking about His disciples, all His disciples. It did not stop with the twelve. The twelve went out and shared the gospel in order to make more disciples. This is the same today as it was in those days. But notice, Jesus said that the world has failed to recognize God. How have we failed to recognize God? This day and age, everyone rushes about caught up in their own little worlds. We are constantly surrounded by the greatness of God, yet we do not acknowledge any of His greatness. We do not acknowledge the greatness and vastness of the Universe, we do not acknowledge the miraculous miracle of a baby being born, we do not acknowledge the wonders and miracles which surround us in everything we see, touch, smell, hear, and taste. Our senses are full of exploring, discovering, creating, etc. Yet, we take for granted everything that our Father created in this world in order for us to live in the richness of all His creations. In fact, it is quite evident that our planet earth was made and formed for life to exist. If we look around and go deep beyond, we can see that everything man has built, invented, and developed would never have been possible without those things created by God. In the very beginning prior to earth, God created something from nothing. In studying the Hebrew translation for *"bara"* which was translated in English as *"create,"* actually means to fatten or to fill up. We can look at this as the earth being created to be filled. Therefore, the earth was created to be filled with living things. Man was created to be filled. Man was filled with breath, emotions, personality, etc. In a more spiritual sense, we were meant to be filled with God's Spirit, His presence. However, that which was already in existence came from something at some time which did not exist. Prior to the Universe and everything in it, the creation came from a being who always was. All things come from the Word of God and according to Scripture, the Word always was and always will be. Nothing could be in existence today without the Word of God.

36

John 1:1-3 (NIV1984) [1]In the beginning was the Word, and the Word was with God, and the Word was God. [2] He was with God in the beginning. [3] Through him all things were made; without him nothing was made that has been made.

Therefore, when we look around at everything on this planet that was created, we are able to see that the Creator took very careful attention to forming those things which would benefit life. Everything man has invented was done so using what God created. Next time you take medicine for any ailment, recognize that God purposely created those elements needed for scientist to invent medicine. Next time you dine on a fabulous meal, remember that everything you are consuming and all the comforts around you may have been invented by man yet created by God. However, even for man to invent took knowledge and wisdom which also come from God.

Jesus continued to pray to the Father.

John 17:26 (Amp) [26]I have made Your Name known to them and revealed Your character and Your very Self, and I will continue to make [You] known, that the love which You have bestowed upon Me may be in them [felt in their hearts] and that I [Myself] may be in them.

How does Jesus continue to make God known to us? After coming into the family by accepting His grace and righteousness, it is no longer Jesus who reveals the Father to us. When Jesus walked with the disciples of old, He taught and prayed to continue the work which our Father sent Him to do. Yet we see in John below when Jesus went to be with the Father, He left us a special gift.

37

John 16:7-8 (Amp) [7]However, I am telling you nothing but the truth when I say it is profitable (good, expedient, advantageous) for you that I go away. Because if I do not go away, the Comforter (Counselor, Helper, Advocate, Intercessor, Strengthener, Standby) will not come to you [into close fellowship with you]; but if I go away, I will send Him to you [to be in close fellowship with you]. [8]And when He comes, He will convict and convince the world and bring demonstration to it about sin and about righteousness (uprightness of heart and right standing with God) and about judgment:

The Holy Spirit was left with us. He is our Comforter, our Counselor, our Helper, our Advocate, our Intercessor, our Strengthener, and our Standby. We ask Jesus to come into our heart; we ask our Father to forgive us of our sins, but how can we be assured of our salvation? In Scripture we have seen that if you do not know Jesus, you do not know God and if you do not know God, you do not know Jesus. How then are we to know God so we can be assured of our salvation? Here is our answer – Jesus died for all in order to give life abundantly, and our Father in Heaven sent Him on our behalf. We cannot be saved unless we believe in the Son, but we are incapable of believing something we cannot see unless it is revealed to us through the Father. We are incapable of believing there is a God unless it is revealed to us through the Son, so how do we come to know? The conviction! When we first begin hearing a message which makes us feel convicted about the sin in our lives, it is the Holy Spirit who convicts us. He was sent on our behalf to teach us all things and remind us of all truths. It is revealed to us through the conviction we feel within our heart that there is a God and Jesus was the Son of God. At some time, every person has heard or will hear a message on salvation. When we are at the right place and allow ourselves to be vulnerable, we begin to feel that conviction upon our lives. What we are feeling is the power of God at work within us. This should reveal to us just who God is. This should show you that God sent Jesus for you, if for no one else, it was for you! If God went to all the trouble to have the Holy Spirit right there with you to put that fire under you to react to what you are feeling within, can you not see how great His love is for you? But it can't stop there, we must grow in order to know Him, really know Him!

Let me share that far too often, people feel that they can go through the motions and receive their salvation, but salvation is a process. In 1 Corinthians, Paul says, *"But to us who are being saved..."*

1 Corinthians 1:18 (AMP) [18] *For the story and message of the cross is sheer absurdity and folly to those who are perishing and on their way to perdition, but to us who are being saved it is the [manifestation of] the power of God.*

We are being saved, a process. This is also why Paul spoke of running the race. He had not ran the race but was running it, and when he knew his time was near, then he said that he knew he had ran it well. Ultimately, your salvation is determined the day you stand before the Father, and it is based on how well you ran the race. This is not to say that it is works that get you into heaven. On the contrary, how well you run the race will be determined by how well you came to know Jesus Christ. The more you know Him, the more you will become like Him. Throughout this book, you will hear me repeat this often because it needs to get deep down on the inside of you. Salvation is determined by your relationship with Christ. It is not about knowing of Him but knowing Him. The first process of salvation happens at the place of conviction. Once that conviction happens, you can bet that satan is going to be right there in hopes that you fall. satan's job is to make sure that you never grow and never really come to know God intimately. This is why it is important to

39

draw close to those that are running the race. satan is like a lion roaming to and fro seeking those he can devour. He will devour you if there is no Word in you! Many spend their whole life attending church, but they never become disciplined enough to make the effort to learn and grow. This is how the church gets a bad name and why so many walk away disappointed, feeling as if nothing is real. If all we do is play church, sit on the sidelines, and we are not players in the game, someday we will face God and will feel the shame of never really getting to know Him. You may in fact be one of those that God says, *"Depart from me, for I never knew you."* But if your walk is real, you will have a crown of righteousness which awaits you on judgment day.

Matthew 7:21-25 (Amp) ²¹*Not everyone who says to Me, Lord, Lord, will enter the kingdom of heaven, but he who does the will of My Father Who is in heaven.* ²²*Many will say to Me on that day, Lord, Lord, have we not prophesied in Your name and driven out demons in Your name and done many mighty works in Your name?* ²³*And then I will say to them openly (publicly), I never knew you; depart from Me, you who act wickedly [disregarding My commands].* ²⁴*So everyone who hears these words of Mine and acts upon them [obeying them] will be like a sensible (prudent, practical, wise) man who built his house upon the rock.* ²⁵*And the rain fell and the floods came and the winds blew and beat against that house; yet it did not fall, because it had been founded on the rock.*

Remember, when we build on the rock, nothing can come against us. Nothing can come against your family, your relationships, your children, your finances, etc. Let me add one more thing. You may say that the thief on the cross beside Jesus did not have time to get to know Jesus and of course we know the story, *"I assure you, today you will be with me in paradise."*

Luke 23:39-43 (NLT) [39]*One of the criminals hanging beside him scoffed, "So you're the Messiah, are you? Prove it by saving yourself—and us, too, while you're at it!"* [40]*But the other criminal protested, "Don't you fear God even when you have been sentenced to die?* [41]*We deserve to die for our crimes, but this man hasn't done anything wrong."* [42]*Then he said, "Jesus, remember me when you come into your Kingdom."* [43]*And Jesus replied, "I assure you, today you will be with me in paradise."*

You may question why this man went to paradise and really did not run the race well as Paul did. This man woke up in paradise because of God's grace. This man was forgiven for all his trespasses because he recognized who Jesus was. We are saved when we genuinely KNOW Jesus Christ. This man was a witness in his last breaths. This man stood up for Jesus and came against those that wronged Him. He spoke up and boldly claimed that Jesus was the Son of God. This man acknowledge his own actions and wrong doings and accepted his punishment as being just. This man sought, knocked, and asked. His relationship with Jesus was very short lived in this world, but it's not about the time invested but the investment! He could have said nothing just like most people that claim to be Christians. Most church people today say nothing when someone is wronged. Most church people today do not speak up to be heard and proclaim truth in this world. This man could have been like most of us, but he chose to speak up. He knew in his heart that this was really Jesus, the Son of the Most High God. We are told to seek Him and to keep knocking on that door. The door opens when we are genuine in our seeking. Jesus saw in this man's heart. He saw David's heart. This man, even though he was a sinner, he cried out to Jesus because he believed He was who He claimed to be. This man asked for mercy when he said, *"Remember me when you come into your Kingdom."* However, many live their lives day in and day out doing whatever it is that makes them happy. They seldom give Christianity much thought. Even those that attend church, they feel that showing up one day a week is good enough to get them into heaven, but this is where their heart is not like David's. The majority will not be fortunate enough to get it together at the last minute like the thief on the cross. The majority feel that they can live in one big party while they are young and then think about God once the clock starts ticking on by. However, it's all about the heart, and it's all about living this life seeking to find. If you never seek, you will never find and if you never find, you will never know what you missed until it is too late.

Helmet of Hope

In Thessalonians, it states that we are to put on the hope of salvation as our helmet.

1 Thessalonians 5:8 (AMP) [8]But we belong to the day; therefore, let us be sober and put on the breastplate (corslet) of faith and love and for a helmet the hope of salvation.

When we hope for something, what are we doing? We are operating in faith. Faith is the assurance of those things we hope for.

Hebrews 11:1 (AMP) [1]NOW FAITH is the assurance (the confirmation, the title deed) of the things [we] hope for, being the proof of things [we] do not see and the conviction of their reality [faith perceiving as real fact what is not revealed to the senses].

Everything we hope to accomplish, everything we strive to conquer, everything we are believing for is exercising our faith. We believe we are saved by the grace of God. We believe we will receive the promise of eternal life. When we put on our helmet of salvation, we are standing on the assurance of our everlasting eternal life with Christ. In our prayer time, when we begin to envision taking that helmet from our Father and placing on our head, we need to see how powerful this is. Our thoughts or words to our Father should be something like this, *"Father, I take this gift that you have given to me freely, the gift of righteousness through Jesus Christ. I am honored to put this helmet on my head knowing that I am saved by grace and share in the crucifixion with Christ. My faith rests in the hope of my salvation to spend eternity with You."* It does not just stop there. We should be doing this on a daily basis. We should never assume that because we are living right today that we are living right tomorrow. We miss it many times and if we take for granted that we are secure, we will miss it. If we take for granted that we have already arrived, we will fall. Christ said to always stay awake and watch.

Mark 14:38 (AMP) [38]Keep awake and watch and pray [constantly], that you may not enter into temptation; the spirit indeed is willing, but the flesh is weak.

Our intentions may very well be good; however, temptations of this world will bring us down if we are not continually walking as Christ. Putting the helmet of salvation on guards and keeps us. It keeps our mind secure in Christ and we continue walking in our hope for eternal life.

Romans 8:24 (NIV 1984, ©1984) [24]For in this hope we were saved. But hope that is seen is no hope at all. Who hopes for what he already has?

We never hope for what we already have. Just like faith cannot be seen, hope cannot be seen. Yet, I have discussed that we can envision those things we hope for. We never take for granted our salvation. Those who are backslidden in this world, they do not have the assurance of their salvation. Daily, we have the assurance of our salvation when we share in the crucifixion of Christ. Daily, we make the choice to take that helmet from our Father which gives us hope for our salvation.

Colossians 1:22-23 (NIV 1984, ©1984) [22] But now he has reconciled you by Christ's physical body through death to present you holy in his sight,

43

without blemish and free from accusation— [23] *if you continue in your faith, established and firm, not moved from the hope held out in the gospel. This is the gospel that you heard and that has been proclaimed to every creature under heaven, and of which I, Paul, have become a servant.*

There is that word, *"if!"* We are reconciled *"if"* we continue in our faith. We must continue in this walk. We continue taking that helmet daily. The helmet becomes our reminder of what we hope for, what we are believing for. This hope is not only for eternal salvation, but the grace which keeps us close to our Father even while we are here on this earth doing that which we are called to do. Our hope is for God opening and closing doors in order that our current circumstances change. We hope for that which may seem impossible, but through Christ all things are possible. It is that hope which will take us from one level to another through no other name but Jesus Christ. Are there areas in your life today that you gave up believing things could change? If God could radically change your life, what would your hopes be today?

Many of us come to the place where we feel like giving up. Many times we have no hope because our life seems hopeless. I am here to tell you today, where there is hope, there is life. Without hope, we have no life. Without hope, there is no eternal life. Without hope, there is no salvation. Without hope, we live faithless. We are not even pleasing to God if we do not have faith. Faith is our hope.

Hebrews 11:6 (ESV) [6]And without faith it is impossible to please him, for whoever would draw near to God must believe that he exists and that he rewards those who seek him.

There are times I minister to people whose lives seem hopeless, but I know there is hope! I cannot look at the circumstances because I know what my Father is capable of doing. If He can radically change my life, He can do the same for anyone. But I also know that until we let go of living in our misery, we will not rise up and start believing. If we cannot believe for something, it will never happen. Sometimes I share with people to start dreaming. We were all good at dreaming in our younger days, and I am speaking of day dreaming. Many times because life does not turn out as we had planned, we stop dreaming. But as I have said, we can see our faith if we envision it. We can see hope if we begin to envision that hope. There are those in our prison system that can tell you their life looks hopeless. I do not disagree with them. If you have never visited or seen inside the prisons, I encourage you to go if at all possible. Why? There are thousands of men and women who need a word of encouragement, a word of hope. If you are one who believes they deserve to be where they are, you should pray about it. I am not saying that they need to be out, but I am saying they deserve the same forgiveness and the same hope as anyone else. In Matthew, Jesus shared with the multitudes judgment according to God.

Matthew 5:21-22 (NLT) [21] *"You have heard that our ancestors were told, 'You must not murder. If you commit murder, you are subject to judgment.'* [22] *But I say, if you are even angry with someone, you are subject to judgment! If you call someone an idiot, you are in danger of being brought before the court. And if you curse someone, you are in danger of the fires of hell.*

I do not believe that any of us are in a place to judge those in prison. I doubt there is anyone who has not been angry with another person. I do not think any of us can say we have never spoken poorly of someone else. And it does not matter if we did not say it to their face, if the thought was in our head, we still missed it. Therefore, if our court system judged according to biblical standards, we would all have a lengthy criminal record. Sadly, we will all be judged for those things we look at as trivial, and we will also be judged for those we have judged. My suggestion to go into the prisons, is so you can see how great the hopelessness really is. If we can take our eyes off of ourselves long enough to see the pain in others, it will open up our perceptions to so many things we have taken for granted. There is a Christian song out by Matthew West, *"My Own Little World,"* which is an amazing song. If you have never heard it, I encourage you to find it. This song portrays most of America. We go about our lives which may consist of only *"me, myself, and I."* We are oblivious to the pain in this world because it is all about us. Our selfishness keeps us in bondage. Our selfishness keeps us in a state of hopelessness. It is time to begin dreaming again. I share with prisoners to dream. Dream about where you can see yourself being in this life with God. God must be in the midst of your dreams. If it is not a God-given dream, it will never happen. How do we know a God-given dream? God's will is revealed to us in His Word. When you get enough of the Word in you, you will know where you are supposed to be.

One calling that we all share which is the key to rid ourselves of the feeling of hopelessness, is to live outside of self. It is stepping out of your box and realizing that this world consists of more than just you. If you feel hopeless, give hope to someone who needs it. When we give, we receive. We are all called to go, and we are all called to make disciples.

Matthew 28:19-20 ((ESV) [19]*Go therefore and make disciples of all nations, baptizing them in the name of the Father and of the Son and of* the Holy Spirit, *²⁰teaching them to observe all that I have commanded you. And behold, I am with you always, to the end of the age."*

We are all called to give and to do so generously.

Deuteronomy 15:10 (NLT) *¹⁰ Give generously to the poor, not grudgingly, for the LORD your God will bless you in everything you do.*

When we think of poor, we always think of finances. Did you know that there are far more people in our world today who are suffering from poor in spirit than in money? We can be spiritually poor. Being spiritually poor is living in this present world without Jesus, without the wisdom and knowledge through God's Word, and without the Truth in order to live the abundant life in Christ. We are not only to give to those who are poor as in financial poverty but also to share the gospel to those who do not know Jesus. If we find ourselves in a state of hopelessness, it is time to rise up and begin to give hope to those who are less fortunate. It is time to say, *"Lord, send me, for I want to know this hope also. I will go and share, I will go and be a servant to whomever you send across my path."* I desire to be set free from those areas which have me bound. The fastest way to be set free from bondage is to give to others those things where you may lack. You will produce fruit in your life in areas where you give it away. If we give in the area of finances, we receive back in that same area. If we need hope in our lives, then we need to get God's Word implanted within us and put on that helmet and then go forth to give hope to a world that is suffering and destitute for hell. When God gives us something, He expects us to give it away. What I mean by this, if God gives us revelation in how to have hope again in our lives and we begin doing what the Word says where hope once again comes, then we go and share hope to those who have none.

47

Hebrews 6:17-19 (NIV) [17] *Because God wanted to make the unchanging nature of his purpose very clear to the heirs of what was promised, he confirmed it with an oath.* [18] *God did this so that, by two unchangeable things in which it is impossible for God to lie, we who have fled to take hold of the hope set before us may be greatly encouraged.* [19] *We have this hope as an anchor for the soul, firm and secure. It enters the inner sanctuary behind the curtain,*

Our helmet of hope is what keeps us grounded and secure in knowing we have eternal salvation. In Hebrews, it also says that because of our hope, we enter the inner sanctuary. The inner sanctuary is behind the curtain or the veil. This is our hope that we can come before God into the holy of holies. Jesus made this possible. That veil was torn away the day we came to Christ in repentance of our sins.

2 Corinthians 3:16 (AMP) [16]*But whenever a person turns [in repentance] to the Lord, the veil is stripped off and taken away.*

Arguments

I spent many years actually praying Ephesians 6 over myself but one day, God said, *"Jolene, do you really understand how powerful this is?"* Do we actually understand just what we are doing when we place that helmet on our head? The helmet, according to Thessalonians, is our hope of salvation as we have discussed. When we hope for something, we are looking forward to it or expecting it to happen.

1 Thessalonians 5:8 (NKJV) [8] *But let us who are of the day be sober, putting on the breastplate of faith and love, and as a helmet the hope of salvation.*

In Thessalonians, it is talking about being of sober mind. Most of us may have spent time in our younger days experiencing drinking and sometimes to an extent. Anytime we are making decisions but our minds are not thinking clearly due to drugs or alcohol, the result may not be what was anticipated due to not being able to see clearly. So by all means, in order to be a great warrior for God, we must be of sound mind. To clothe ourselves with all pieces of our armor, we must be sober. This does not necessarily mean to be sober from drugs or alcohol. This means that we need to really think about what we are doing. We need to envision in a spiritual sense what our battle gear is and what it does. As God brought me through weeks and weeks of revelation, I realized just how much I did not know about our armor. I realized that Christians today are defeated because they do not understand the importance of their armor. Christians are defeated today because they do not really know what each piece of armor does? Christians today do not even really know how to put the armor on, and they certainly do not know anything about the terrain they are fighting in.

If we want to win this war, we must be totally trained to know our armor, how to put it on and keep it on, how to use it, who we are fighting, and the conditions and locations of the territories where we are fighting. Without the helmet of salvation, we will not put on anything else. Without the helmet of salvation, we will not be able to go any further with Christ. We must know all there is to know about what God's Word says concerning our salvation. There must not be any argument that can convince us that our hope in our salvation can and will come to pass as we press on to the mark of the higher calling. What am I talking about when I say, no argument? What I mean is that many times we come to that place where we are walking with Christ and know we are on that same course of being saved as the disciples before us but then we miss it and fall. It's not about the fall because we will miss it, and there are times that we will fall. It is about getting back up and continuing this walk. When we get back up, too often the enemy will try to gain ground by saying, *"You are not really being saved. You are not really righteous. Look at you, if you were really right with God, you would not have done what you did."* These are arguments. These are tactics that the enemy has always used and will continue to use because they work. *"Look at you, you cannot do this walk. You cannot give up doing that, you enjoy it too much."* Arguments! We must get in a routine or discipline, where we make the decision, *"God, I will not quit! It does not matter if I miss it, I will get back up and continue this walk. I will continue to seek You and grow so that I am stronger. Lord, I will learn of You and seek You."* We must also remember that just because we are on the right course does not mean we will never miss it and mess up. God knows we are not perfect that is why He sent His Son to redeem us. However, this is no excuse to deliberately live in sin either. We need to just focus on knowing all we can about salvation so when the attacks come, no thoughts contrary to what God's Word says can convince us that we are not a son or daughter of our Father in Heaven. There is no condemnation from God. God does not condemn us, and He does not put guilt on us.

Romans 8:1(NIV1984) [1] *Therefore, there is now no condemnation for those who are in Christ Jesus,*

There is one thing I share with all the girls that God has blessed me with, my spiritual daughters. I tell them in no uncertain terms, *"Never run from me but run to me."* In other words, I do not judge or condemn you but rather when I look at you, I see who you are growing to be in Christ. Our enemy, he wants to judge and condemn us. satan wants to make us believe that God is disappointed in us. This is not true. God wants us to just simply run to Him when we miss it and just say, *"I missed it Lord, and I'm sorry."* satan knows that if we run to God, we will gain strength and continue this race. satan wants to try and keep us defeated and feeling like we are failures. But in God's eyes, He sees us as being so much more. Our life is worth so much more. I remember getting this through to one of my daughters after much time. It is harder for one of my own children to face me, but it is because of the shame they feel. Finally, one morning one of my daughters called me and simply said, *"I missed it mom."* I said, *"How do you feel?"* Her reply was, *"Horrible!"* I told her to get back up, continue going forward – No Condemnation and No Guilt! If we can just get those words in us, we can run this race and persevere to the end.

Confession of Faith

What is our confession and why is it important?

Romans 10:8-10 (Amp) [8]*But what does it say? The Word (God's message in Christ) is near you, on your lips and in your heart; that is, the Word (the message, the basis and object) of faith which we preach,* [9]*Because if you acknowledge and confess with your lips that Jesus is Lord and in your heart believe (adhere to, trust in, and rely on the truth) that God raised Him from the dead, you will be saved.* [10]*For with the heart a person believes (adheres to, trusts in, and relies on Christ) and so is justified (declared righteous, acceptable to God), and with the mouth he confesses (declares openly and speaks out freely his faith) and confirms [his] salvation.*

In order for our salvation to be real, it must be heartfelt. However, we confess with our lips what we feel within our heart. If you really believe something, you will share it. I can remember many years ago being hired to sell cars on a car lot. I remember being put in training which basically taught in-coming sales personnel how to lie to the customer in order to make sales. Even though, I was not saved during this time, I refused to be dishonest. Within just a few months, I was the top sales person and did this being honest. However, I could not sale something I did not believe in, but if I believe in something, you can bet I am going to share it with my family, my friends, and all those who God sends across my path with needs. If someone is sharing with me their difficulties and I know that I have the answer for them, I am going to bubble over with the remedy. This is what we do in this world. Everywhere you go people are sitting at tables, standing together in groups, riding in cars, and all the while they are sharing parts of their life. If Christ is real to you, you will not be able to keep Him a secret. With our mouth we speak truth, and with our lips we share faith and salvation. It goes on to show that we not only share Jesus with our words but we also use our voice to call upon the Lord.

Romans 10:11-13 (Amp) [11]*The Scripture says, No man who believes in Him [who adheres to, relies on, and trusts in Him] will [ever] be put to shame or be disappointed.* [12]*[No one] for there is no distinction between Jew and Greek. The same Lord is Lord over all [of us] and He generously bestows His riches upon all who call upon Him [in faith].* [13]*For everyone who calls upon the name of the Lord [invoking Him as Lord] will be saved.*

We cry out to God because by faith, we believe that He is God. We are exercising our faith when we put our trust in the Lord. God is faithful to those who trust and call upon Him for all things, but it goes on to ask how are we to call upon Him if we have no faith or if we do not believe?

Romans 10:14-15 (Amp) ¹⁴*But how are people to call upon Him Whom they have not believed [in Whom they have no faith, on Whom they have no reliance]? And how are they to believe in Him [adhere to, trust in, and rely upon Him] of Whom they have never heard? And how are they to hear without a preacher? ¹⁵And how can men [be expected to] preach unless they are sent? As it is written, How beautiful are the feet of those who bring glad tidings! [How welcome is the coming of those who preach the good news of His good things!]*

By faith, we share what we believe, and it is through this faith that God sends others across our path so that we are able to help them see and come to know our God. If we are not doing our part, we are in reality letting down our brothers and sisters in Christ. The Bible says that the harvest is plentiful but the laborers are few.

Matthew 9:37 (AMP) ³⁷*Then He said to His disciples, The harvest is indeed plentiful, but the laborers are few.*

Our helmet protects our mind as we renew to the things of Christ and in doing this, we share what we have been given. Our faith will increase as we use it and the best way to begin exercising our faith is with those who have little. In this I mean little spiritually.

In looking at the helmet, our mouth is one area which is protected on the Roman helmet. Our confession of faith happens as we feed on the Word of God, and that which is inside of us will be that which proceeds from our lips. Whatever we are feeding on is what we will be engaged in. The next time you are engaged in a conversation, pay attention to what your discussion is pertaining to. Far too often, we see ourselves conformed to this world because what proceeds from our mouth is no different than unbelievers. If you battle with negative remarks continually

53

coming forth out of your mouth, then you need to look at what you are putting in. If you battle with perversion, cursing, or criticism coming out of your mouth, then you need to look at what you are taking in. And, if you do not seem to be winning your battles, perhaps what is inside of you pertains to the entertainment of this world. What we feed our natural man is what we will reap. If we feed our bodies to keep the flesh satisfied, we will only reap those things of this world. If we feed our bodies to keep our spirit full, we will reap those things far greater than this world.

When we put on the helmet of salvation, we must recognize that the helmet guards our mouth from saying anything perverse, negative, evil, etc. If we desire to live a greater life free from misfortune, we must put on our helmet of salvation while understanding just what it protects. Our mouth is a vital role in who we are and who we will become. James, a servant of God, tells us that there is not an animal out there that cannot be tamed by man, but the human tongue cannot be tamed by anyone.

James 3:7-8 (AMP) *[7]For every kind of beast and bird, of reptile and sea animal, can be tamed and has been tamed by human genius (nature). [8]But the human tongue can be tamed by no man. It is a restless (undisciplined, irreconcilable) evil, full of deadly poison.*

In order to be a great warrior for Christ, it is of utmost importance that we be disciplined. Being disciplined begins with controlling our tongue. Below are some Scriptures in Proverbs which will show how our very battles will either defeat us or we will overcome them. Your destiny will depend on how much you desire to increase in the Kingdom of Heaven.

Proverbs 4:24 (NIV) *[24] Keep your mouth free of perversity; keep corrupt talk far from your lips.*

Remember, we take that helmet and we put it on. In this we are saying, *"Lord, I make the choice today to stand out and be different than the world. I make the choice to discipline my tongue and not be like the world. I choose to put that which is good within my mind so what comes out of my lips will glorify you."* This may mean separating ourselves from those who ensnare us, avoiding that which is darkness.

Proverbs 6:2 (NIV) [2] you have been trapped by what you said, ensnared by the words of your mouth.

You will become like who you associate with. When our words speak defeat, our lives will be defeated. Look at your current situations and look at how you speak over the circumstances. I have many young girls under my leadership and those who are new, their lives are defeated. They call and I minister, and their words continue to speak defeat. I tell them, your life will not change until your words change. We have to begin to see that our words speak into existence the course of our life. We will reap everything we speak. If you speak negative, you will reap a negative life and pull those you love down with you. If you change your words to positive, you also change the course for your life to be one that is blessed. Below in Proverbs 8, this is how faith talks.

Proverbs 8:8 (NIV) [8] All the words of my mouth are just; none of them is crooked or perverse.

Let me say this, if you are speaking defeat because that is what you see, it will remain as such. In other words, we must begin to speak what we do not see because faith is believing it before you see it. If you do not start speaking Proverbs 8:8, it will never manifest. Our words must be words that are just and not perverse. We cannot say, *"Lord, I will serve you once I get my life together."* You will never be walking with God if that is what you feel. You cannot do this in *"you"* because without Christ, we can do nothing. Faith speaks those things which have not happened yet but believes they are coming. Faith says, *"Lord, I thank you that the words from my mouth are just and nothing comes out of my mouth that does not bring glory to You and Your Kingdom!"* This is confessing faith and speaking faith over your life. This is speaking it before it happens. This is being able to see you as God can see you. This is who you were created to be, in the image and likeness of our God. If I want victory in a certain area of my life, then I begin to speak it first!

Proverbs 10:6 (NIV) [6] *Blessings crown the head of the righteous, but violence overwhelms the mouth of the wicked.*

I believe I have had enough violence in my lifetime and prefer to choose blessings. It is hard to do what God has called you to do when every time you turn around you are faced with heartache. I know these people well. They are the ones who continually cry out to the Lord asking, *"Why God, why me? Why does everything happen to me and my family?"* You see, God is saying to line up your mouth with good. Like I tell my spiritual daughters, change your tongue and watch your circumstances change. Do you not know why the children of Israel were defeated for 40 years in the dessert? It was because they spent 40 years murmuring and complaining about their problems. I always tell my prayer group, if you want problems to change, find people with the same problems and begin to pray with them, begin to minister Jesus to them. It is called, taking your eyes off of yourself and focusing on others which is what we are called to do. Be a servant for Christ; be an example for this world. The world is defeated and they need

Jesus. The sad part is most Christians remain defeated along with the non-believers of this world.

Proverbs 15:2 (NIV) *²The tongue of the wise adorns knowledge, but the mouth of the fool gushes folly.*

We cannot speak knowledge if we do not have God's Word in us. The knowledge of the world speaks defeat but God's wisdom and knowledge are what make us wise. This would be looking at things through the eyes of God and not our eyes which can only see as the world sees.

Proverbs 18:7 (NIV) *⁷The mouths of fools are their undoing, and their lips are a snare to their very lives.*

Rather than allowing your mouth to continue being that snare to your life as it speaks of in Proverbs 18, we should make a choice to guard our mouth, guard our tongues, make the decision to surround ourselves with those who walk faith and grow in order to be a successful Christian, not a defeated Christian.

Proverbs 21:23 (NIV) *²³Those who guard their mouths and their tongues keep themselves from calamity.*

Chapter Three
Choice

Many men and women today choose to go into the military, which leads them first into boot camp. Many times the various reasons for enlisting in the military are for opportunities, a career, an education, etc. When we make the choice to sign up with God's Boot Camp, it is because we have come to a place where we recognize that we can no longer do this life in ourselves. We come to a cross roads in our life and become tired of taking that wrong path. We make the decision to look to a greater power to lead and guide us through life. Prior to making this decision, we will come to the place where we understand salvation and know in order to cross over to God's army it becomes a way of life. There is no half way to serving God; it is either all the way or no way. Paul said it like this...

1 Corinthians 4:17 (AMP)[17]For this very cause I sent to you Timothy, who is my beloved and trustworthy child in the Lord, who will recall to your minds my methods of proceeding and course of conduct and way of life in Christ, such as I teach everywhere in each of the churches.

The choice to walk with God is a lifestyle choice where you become ready to completely renew your life to that of Christ. You will choose life and not death, light and not darkness, the Word and not the world, the Spirit and not the flesh.

1 Peter 4:1 (AMP) [1]SO, SINCE Christ suffered in the flesh for us, for you, arm yourselves with the same thought and purpose [patiently to suffer rather than fail to please God]. For whoever has suffered in the flesh [having the mind of Christ] is done with [intentional] sin [has stopped pleasing himself and the world, and pleases God]

How is it that we are to suffer in the flesh? This is where we get to the place in which Peter was referring to. At this place, we are done with living a life of intentional sin. When we choose to live for Christ, it is a sacrifice but one that will be greatly welcomed in time. When we are caught up in the sins of this world, it is hard to see beyond what feels normal to our flesh or fleshly desires. The suffering Peter speaks of is that which satisfies our fleshly desires. When we come into this world, we quickly learn what is comforting to us and what hurts. No one likes to be without and no one likes to do those things which feel uncomfortable. A baby cries to be fed, held, comforted, changed, etc. We grow from that stage into selfish people who have not had to sacrifice much in order to survive with the desires and wants of this world. It takes a lifestyle change to serve God and become Christ like. This suffering does come at a cost but the end result is far better than without.

Most of the time, people begin to seek God when there is some level of discomfort or pain in their life, and they desire something greater to bring about the necessary change to their current circumstances. However, the reason we face trials and tests to begin with is to bring us to the realization that we cannot walk in this world without going back to the root. The root in any situation goes back to the originator or creator. If you desire to fix something, you must get the manual which details that which is broken in order to make the necessary repairs. The same holds true for mankind. Although we may not even realize it, but God being our Creator is the only source where we can bring about the necessary changes to find that which will be the ultimate satisfaction. If money or things were all we needed for a life of satisfaction, we would not see so much pain in today's world. Therefore, we know finding that which will bring the ultimate satisfaction has to be something much greater than what we can see with our natural eyes. To sum this up, without God in our lives, we will continue to wander around going up and down on our roller coaster lives never fully understanding why life is the way it is because we look to all kinds of solutions to fix our problems but not back to the Main Engineer who designed us for a purpose. Therefore, once we begin to understand that there is something far greater than our minds can comprehend and we begin to transform our minds to the mind of Christ, only then will we begin to see things through the eyes of God.

Romans 6:6 (AMP) [6]We know that our old (unrenewed) self was nailed to the cross with Him in order that [our] body [which is the instrument] of sin might be made ineffective and inactive for evil, that we might no longer be the slaves of sin.

We are either bound in sin or we are bound to God. There is no freedom without God in our lives. We make that choice to meet Christ at the Cross when we make the decision that we want something far greater. Anytime we desire to gain something, there is always a cost. Yes, God's grace and mercy are free to those that find it and the gift of righteousness, but living a life with Christ and ultimately finding salvation comes with a price. It is the same price that Jesus paid for us on Calvary. We crucify our flesh and make the decision to live for Christ leaving our old self behind which was the root to sin in our lives and brought destruction into our midst in the first place.

2 Peter 1:4 (NIV) [4]Through these he has given us his very great and precious promises, so that through them you may participate in the divine nature, having escaped the corruption in the world caused by evil desires.

I can honestly say that my life today is far more blessed than it ever was when I lived in the world and actively was engaged in the sins of this world. Today, I have no desires to sin. This does not mean that I never miss it, but I desire to live a life which is holy. Today, I make the choice to obey or disobey the voice of the Holy Spirit, but when I disobey, I also make that choice to ask for forgiveness and make things right.   It is not a matter of never sinning; it is a matter of choosing to be obedient and accepting God's grace and mercy for my life. Today, my desires do not line up with what the world would consider normal, yet my life is full lacking in nothing. My life today began when I made that choice to surrender myself in order to be an heir and share in the same suffering which Christ paid for mankind. Today, I would never consider going back to my old life because I have gained so much through Christ.

Romans 8:17 (NIV) [17]*Now if we are children, then we are heirs—heirs of God and co-heirs with Christ, if indeed we share in his sufferings in order that we may also share in his glory.*

Brainwashed

Once the choice is made to walk away from your old life and to put on the new life, it is important to be fed the Word of God daily.

Ephesians 4:22-24 (NIV) [22] *You were taught, with regard to your former way of life, to put off your old self, which is being corrupted by its deceitful desires;* [23] *to be made new in the attitude of your minds;* [24] *and to put on the new self, created to be like God in true righteousness and holiness.*

Until a Christian begins to walk this path, they will never understand it. We meet Jesus at the Cross to crucify our flesh and to begin a new life with Him. The Word of God says that we put off our old self and put on our new self, but do we really do that? Do most Christians take off their old self? No, they do not. To take off the old and put on the new takes a lot of work, determination, endurance, steadfastness, diligence, etc. In other words, it means that no matter what, you want this new life God speaks of in His Word, and you will not quit until you have gained the revelation to understand how you are to do this.

In the military, months are spent renewing the minds of those sent to boot camp. In researching different military blogs, I found where a Sergeant asked a recruit, *"Who thinks they know what in the Marine Corps we feel about honor?"* The recruit replied, *"Sir, this recruit believes that honor is doing the right thing when no one is looking, sir."* In boot camp, 3 months is spent teaching the recruits over and over about values and making right decisions. Another recruit said, *"With the honor, courage and commitment, you have something that pushes you and helps you to make it every time, and is an important factor in becoming a Marine."* If you have ever known a marine, they will tell you, *"Once a Marine, always a Marine."* We may look at these techniques as a way of being brainwashed, or we can look at them as being influenced. This is what we have to see, when we come into this world, we are being influenced by day one. We are being brainwashed to believe what our parents teach us, what we learn from our friends, our teachers, coaches, employers, the media, etc. If you attend a church that believes in the spiritual gifts, speaking in tongues, and many other things which are not understood in different denominations today, you have probably heard people refer to your church as brainwashing the members. I actually love this because I teach in my prayer group to reply to these individuals and say, *"We prefer to call it influenced; we are all brainwashed and there are 3 choices in this world. You can be brainwashed to think like the world, to think like Jesus, or you can join the Marines* and be brainwashed to think like a Marine." In fact, if you are referred to as one of those "Jesus Freaks," just know that you are evidently doing something right according to Scripture.

Deuteronomy 14:2 (AMP) ²*For you are a holy people [set apart] to the Lord your God; and the Lord has chosen you to be a peculiar people to Himself, above all the nations on the earth.*

Every one of us is brainwashed today. When we first come into this world there are no perceptions to life. Everything we begin to learn from day one is someone else's philosophies, beliefs, perceptions, etc., and these are all based on the influences in their lives passed down from generation to generation. Our beliefs are formed around every single thing we encounter in our lives each and every day. How do we know then what we should believe? We all are brainwashed in either a good or bad way, who is correct? Where does our loyalty fall? Are you loyal to the world or to God? Are you loyal to the mother and father who raised you or are you loyal to the God who created you? Are you loyal to those you are closest to or does your loyalty rest with the Father of Creation. Yes, we have all been taught myths, religion, beliefs passed from one generation to the next; however, it is time for the church to grow up. Selling out to God, means the only thing that matters is that you are loyal to your Creator. The only thing that matters is that God's Word is final; there is no compromising to agree with what the world says. There is no compromising with what your family, friends, employer, or anyone else has to say. God's Word should be our final say so. In other words, if God said it – then it is final – no *"buts!"* Does it matter if you hurt someone's feelings by disagreeing? Does it matter if you are wrong and have to admit the other person is correct because God's Word backs what they said? Ask a Marine, are they willing to hurt someone's feelings or go against their drill sergeant? Does a Marine suck it up and admit they are wrong? This is Boot Camp and this is enlisting in the Army of the Most High God. I do not believe I am going to be that concerned about hurting someone's feelings when I stand before my Creator one day. I do not believe I am going to care if I have to admit I am wrong time and time again because if I am pleasing my Creator, all is good! Therefore, if you are loyal to God, then you should desire to be brainwashed to think like Jesus. Those young men and women going into military boot camp, they come out completely different. I do not think I have met any parents who have said their children came back from boot camp changed for the worse. Boot camp makes men and women out of our children that go away. God's Word when diligently fed into our spirit will radically change us for the better. If we think more like God, how can that be a bad thing?

Romans 12:2 (NIV) [2]Do not conform to the pattern of this world, but be transformed by the renewing of your mind. Then you will be able to test and approve what God's will is—his good, pleasing and perfect will.

I believe I will take my chances and engage in a church that teaches us to renew our minds to Christ, to take off the old self and put on the new self. I believe I would much rather be joined together with a group of believers that will correct me when I am wrong and push me to study and learn God's Word. We cannot go through life expecting someone else to do our studying because if we do, our relationship with our Creator is nothing more than a formality. How can we say we know God if, in fact, we spend no time getting to know Him. A relationship is built by communication, commitment, trust, and quality time spent together in order to grow and learn of each other. Remember, you cannot renew your mind to anything unless you spend time reprogramming your current way of thinking, and this is why there is Boot Camp in the military. The marines, the army, the navy, they all know when they take in new recruits, the first thing is to change their perceptions and beliefs in order to turn them into soldiers equipped and ready for war. We will only become warriors for Christ as we study to show ourselves approved and grow in that intimate relationship with our Creator.

2 Timothy 2:15 (AMP) [15]Study and be eager and do your utmost to present yourself to God approved (tested by trial), a workman who has no cause to be ashamed, correctly analyzing and accurately dividing [rightly handling and skillfully teaching] the Word of Truth.

Influence

Throughout our lives, we are continually influenced in either a good or bad way. I believe we can agree that boot camps do brainwash their recruits in order to renew their minds to become a soldier. As I have said, renewing our mind to think like Jesus can also be referred to as being brainwashed, yet I believe we can agree that this is an influence which is good. I remember reading a blog which said the preferred term to use would be persuasion instead of brainwash. We have all been persuaded to do things in our lives and sometimes those things were not good for us and sometimes they were. In each of our lives, we have had good and bad influences cross our paths. Many of us may be at a place where we are striving to go the path of righteousness but many have yet to even acknowledge there are two paths. Even if we are striving, we all have loved ones as well that are deep in that place of defeat. The influences we associate with will either lead us down the righteous path or one which is full of evil and defeat. Therefore, we can look at Boot Camp in a negative sense and remain just where we are, lacking in the knowledge of God, or we can look at Boot Camp as a method of influence which brings about a positive lifestyle. In striving for those good influences, Boot Camp will teach us how to be surrounded around those of liked minds which are traveling the road to righteousness. When this is accomplished, we will be able to actually see and touch victory in our lives daily.

The Boot Camp method has been used to take people out of their current circumstances and reprogram what they have been taught. The world's level of intelligence many times teaches or rather influences mankind to believe you are who you are. If you were fortunate to be raised according to a certain criteria accepted by the elite, you are looked up to. However, on the downside, if you were raised in situations which portrayed a level of poverty, unintelligence, lack of character, etc., you definitely did not possess anything the elite would be interested in pursuing. Those who have managed to change their circumstances from defeat to a standard of excellence, seldom share where they came from. Although, once we find truth which is in Jesus Christ, our testimonies become the very tool God uses for us to overcome defeat and also to overcome this world.

Revelation 12:11 (Amp) [11]*And they have overcome (conquered) him by means of the blood of the Lamb and by the utterance of their testimony, for they did not love and cling to life even when faced with death [holding their lives cheap till they had to die for their witnessing].*

In other words, defeat lies within the communities of the wealthy and middle class as well as those inflicted with poverty. We do not conquer and we do not overcome this world, unless we are walking with Jesus Christ and unless we have shared in the crucifixion at the Cross by means of the Blood of the Lamb. We will never overcome unless we do so by our very own testimony. No matter what class you consider yourself in today, without your testimony, you have nothing. In Scriptures, we are told that without love we have nothing. Without love you are bankrupt. Your testimony to the world shows your love for others. There are many that dare share their testimonies because they do not want others to know where they came from; however, your testimony can bring life where there was once defeat. I choose to share unashamed because I know someone out there needs to hear my testimony. Therefore, we should count it all joy for those trials we endured when we were defeated living beneath what the world considers being of significance. Yet, when we find ourselves in a place where we have walked out of our circumstances, our gratitude should go to our Father of all creation. In doing this, never forget where you were or came from and use those things God has given you to bless others. This is one piece of wisdom not found in the elite of the world but rather found in the Word of God. The influences we should strive to imitate are not those who consider themselves having achieved greater successes in this world, but rather those who are thankful for what they have endured to be that light unto the darkness in this world.

Luke 13:22-24 (NIV 1984, ©1984) The Narrow Door [22]*Then Jesus went through the towns and villages, teaching as he made his way to Jerusalem.* [23] *Someone asked him, "Lord, are only a few people going to be saved?" He said to them,* [24] *"Make every effort to enter through the narrow door, because many, I tell you, will try to enter and will not be able to.*

Jesus never said it would be easy, but what makes it a narrow door? The door is not narrow because it is actually small or because many cannot go through the door. If you research the word narrow, it can mean to restrict, limit, confine, and reduce. The reason it is hard to go through the narrow door is because it requires us to restrict our outwardly behavior as a Christian and restrict what we watch and listen to. It requires us to limit ourselves from being in situations and around people who will persuade us to go the wrong path, and it requires us to be confined from associating at certain places and with certain people. It also requires us to reduce those things we say and do that are not pleasing to God. However, God has made the door narrow for our own good. He knows that we will die a spiritual death if we allow ourselves to do any and everything just like the world. He knows that we will never grow strong and be able to rise up as a warrior if the influences in our lives are not those which help us to stay on that path God has chosen for us.

Those that will not be able to go through that narrow door never really understood salvation. They may have gone through the motions, but it never meant anything to them because they were not striving to learn of God; they were not striving to be more like Jesus; they had no desire to obey the restrictions, the limitations, the confinements, and the reductions to a certain criteria that should have been evident in the life of a Christian.

Luke 13:25 (NIV 1984, ©1984) [25] Once the owner of the house gets up and closes the door, you will stand outside knocking and pleading, 'Sir, open the door for us.' "But he will answer, 'I don't know you or where you come from.'

The owner of the house is God. Evidently, those He would not let in did not hang out with those who daily strived to be Christ-like; they did not strive to walk as Jesus walked. The world must have meant way too much to them. All those times they chose to satisfy their flesh was way too important to open their eyes to see truth and open their ears to hear.

Luke 13:26 (NIV 1984, ©1984) ²⁶ *"Then you will say, 'We ate and drank with you, and you taught in our streets.'*

Perhaps on a weekly basis, they attended a church service, perhaps they went to church socials, perhaps they put 20% into serving God, but what were they doing with the other 80% of their time?

Luke 13:27 (NIV 1984, ©1984) ²⁷ *"But he will reply, 'I don't know you or where you come from. Away from me, all you evildoers!'"*

The world categorizes sin as either a big sin or small sin. God looks upon sin as sin. Those standing before God may say that they were a good person; they may say there were times that they helped people financially, but were they sold out totally to God? There may have been times that they helped the elderly, the sick, those in need, but what about their family? Was their family in church serving God or out doing what the world does? We are all responsible for our families, which is our first ministry. If you have loved ones going to hell and you consider yourself saved, you need to start learning and growing because your own influence may be what God needs to awaken those you love. God can set in motion things to occur and not occur which can heavily weigh upon your loved ones making that decision to come to Christ, but He will not do it if you are not doing your part. He will not do it if you cannot even get out of bed to pray for those you love daily. He will not do it if you are not willing to give up your free time in order to do those things He is calling you to do.

Luke 13:28 (NIV 1984, ©1984) ²⁸ *"There will be weeping there, and gnashing of teeth, when you see Abraham, Isaac and Jacob and all the prophets in the kingdom of God, but you yourselves thrown out.* ²⁹ *People will come from east and west and north and south, and will take their places at the feast in the kingdom of God. [30] Indeed there are those who are last who will be first, and first who will be last."*

I used to strive to be the best at everything I did. In fact, I was what the world would have called OCD (Obsessive Compulsive Disorder). I literally could not sleep if everything was not perfect. I lost sleep over striving to be successful in everything that I did, but today, I am no longer concerned with what people think of me. I am no longer concerned if I am the best, and I do not care if others consider me nothing. Today, I just want to be what God wants me to be and that is totally enough.

We need to understand that the influences in our life will play a huge part on our relationship with God. He expects us to make wise choices in order to become more Christ-like. However, we need to know that the influences are not what the world would consider great influences. There will be multitudes that the world looks at as good influences that do not portray the image of Christ. To portray the image of Christ, takes perfecting the fruits of the spirit within each of us.

Galatians 5:22-23 (ESV) [22] But the fruit of the Spirit is love, joy, peace, patience, kindness, goodness, faithfulness, [23] gentleness, self-control; against such things there is no law.

When we become connected with a body of believers, it becomes evident those whose lives portray Jesus. Our influences should be those who daily are striving to walk the same walk as Jesus did. This is not to say they will not ever miss it because we all will as long as we remain in these earthly bodies; however, it is evident in the lives of those who are striving to walk a Christian walk daily. As we grow and become stronger, there will come a time that God expects us to begin giving back and being that great

71

influence in others' lives. Just because we gain wisdom and begin running that same race Paul ran toward salvation, this does not make us better than the world. We never forget our roots, as I have discussed, and our growth promotes us to the calling God has placed on mankind. Our purpose in this world has never been for our own enjoyment but to fulfill biblical prophecy. You will know when the time is right, and God will begin to send those across your path in order for your influence to make a difference in their lives.

Luke 7:34 (ESV) [34]The Son of Man has come eating and drinking, and you say, 'Look at him! A glutton and a drunkard, a friend of tax collectors and sinners!'

Jesus frequently associated with those who were not in the upper social class in biblical days. The Pharisees looked down upon Him because of the company He chose to keep. When we come to that place of growth to begin sharing our testimonies with the world, God will send those across our path which are considered the lowly of this world. To be Christ-like means that we have compassion for mankind – all of mankind! When was the last time that you associated with those who have nothing? When was the last time you ministered to the poor, the man or woman sitting behind our prison walls, or the prostitute and drug addict? We must never have the mindset that we are better than the next person. Jesus told a parable and in this teaching He said the prostitutes and the tax collectors would go into the Kingdom of God before those who think themselves better, those who think they are more spiritual, and those who think they are good.

Matthew 21:31 (ESV) [31]Which of the two did the will of his father?" They said, "The first." Jesus said to them, "Truly, I say to you, the tax collectors and the prostitutes go into the kingdom of God before you.

72

I remember one of my daughters, whose battle was drug addiction, coming to me crying and saying, *"Mother, I was in my group counseling and there was this girl there that was an addict and lived in the streets. I said to myself, 'Well God, at least I am not like her.' God began to show me that I am just like her. It does not matter if I have a place to live and food to eat; my sin is no less than her sin."* We can always learn from those who have endured great battles. I cried that day and shared this with my prayer group because this ministered to me as well. When we look upon others thinking in our heart, *"Well God, at least I am not at the place they are; at least I am doing better than them,"* we are missing it. We all miss it and we are all striving to travel this same road called life. Some of us find God sooner than others and some never find Him, but we must always remember if we want to be all God has called us to be, it begins with realizing that we are no better than anyone else. How can God use us if we think we are great just where we are? It takes God in our lives to transform us to be what He needs us to be to bring about that influence in the lives that cross our paths.

John 15:15-20 (Amp) [15]*I do not call you servants (slaves) any longer, for the servant does not know what his master is doing (working out). But I have called you My friends, because I have made known to you everything that I have heard from My Father. [I have revealed to you everything that I have learned from Him.]* [16]*You have not chosen Me, but I have chosen you and I have appointed you [I have planted you], that you might go and bear fruit and keep on bearing, and that your fruit may be lasting [that it may remain, abide], so that whatever you ask the Father in My Name [as presenting all that I AM], He may give it to you.* [17]*This is what I command you: that you love one another.* [18]*If the world hates you, know that it hated Me before it hated you.* [19]*If you belonged to the world, the world would treat you with affection and would love you as its own. But because you are not of the world [no longer one with it], but I have chosen (selected) you out of the world, the world hates (detests) you. [20]Remember that I told you, A servant is not greater than his master [is not superior to him]. If they persecuted Me, they will also persecute you; if they kept My word and obeyed My teachings, they will also keep and obey yours.*

Who was Jesus that they would persecute Him? Who was Jesus and where did He come from? In studying the Scriptures, we know that Jesus was merely the son of a carpenter. This, of course, would be His earthly father because He was and is the Son of God, who came as a mere man into our world to walk in the shoes of all who knows what it feels like to be imperfect. Jesus walked where we walk today and felt what we feel daily. Jesus came in order to show us how to overcome and how to climb far above all our situations. Joseph, His earthly father, had to work hard to make a living for his family. Jesus lived among those who had very little. He knew poverty, after all His mother gave birth in a manger among the many livestock. It was not actually a nice and cozy place to have a baby, yet Jesus grew to know how it felt to be among those who have lack in their lives.

Luke 2:7 (Amp) [7]And she gave birth to her Son, her Firstborn; and she wrapped Him in swaddling clothes and laid Him in a manger, because there was no room or place for them in the inn.

At a time when God began to increase Jesus into His ministry, we also begin to see the rejection by those who watched Him grow up as a child.

Matthew 13:55 (Amp) [55]Is not this the carpenter's Son? Is not His mother called Mary? And are not His brothers James and Joseph and Simon and Judas?

Notice the tone these words are spoken with, *"Is not this the carpenter's Son?"* We often hear that same tone used among the world today when referring to someone who does not quite fit into their class. *"Oh, he's merely a carpenter's son... we all know that he did not come from money. We all know that he was not born into a noble family or one with great influence."* Do you see the picture? God could have picked any family for His Son to be born into, but He chose a family that was below the standards of the world. Yet, we all strive to be accepted among the world's noble class. We all strive to be like those of great influence according to the world's standards. However, Jesus did not strive to be like the world but like His Father who sent Him. The good influences in our world today are those whose lives resemble the life which Jesus walked decades ago.

Motivation

Why Boot Camp? We have discussed why people enlist in the military, but why is it necessary to engage in the boot camp method to serve God? Just as the military boot camps take people away from what is normal in their life and transform them to a more productive life, enlisting with God does the same and much more. Being transformed into the image of Christ not only gives us hope for our future, it also produces specific values surrounding a culture which is abnormal to man.

John 10:7-10 (NIV 1984, ©1984) [7] *Therefore Jesus said again, "I tell you the truth, I am the gate for the sheep.* [8] *All who ever came before me were thieves and robbers, but the sheep did not listen to them.* [9] *I am the gate; whoever enters through me will be saved. He will come in and go out, and find pasture.* [10] *The thief comes only to steal and kill and destroy; I have come that they may have life, and have it to the full.*

When we come to Christ, fully engaged and entering into His salvation, we can have life and have it to the fullest. The world does not have this kind of life. It does not matter who you are in this world, without a true relationship with Jesus, you will never have life to the fullest on this earth. Jesus said that we will come in and go out and find pasture. God will lead us to solid ground. We have probably all heard the saying when someone leaves their spouse for another person: they thought the grass was greener on the other side. However, they soon find out that their same problems still exist. You may have traded in for another model, and this model may not have those same faults as the previous partner, but in time you will see they have other faults that are just as bad if not worse. However, with God we find that the pasture is greener on the other side, and it will be a place of rest through Him. We will have peace, joy, spiritual blessings, financial blessings, and total happiness in our lives when we enter through the gate Jesus speaks of.

John 10:11-13 (NIV 1984, ©1984) [11] *"I am the good shepherd. The good shepherd lays down his life for the sheep.* [12] *The hired hand is not the shepherd who owns the sheep. So when he sees the wolf coming, he abandons the sheep and runs away. Then the wolf attacks the flock and scatters it.* [13] *The man runs away because he is a hired hand and cares nothing for the sheep.*

Jesus is our Shepherd. He will never leave us or forsake us, even in times of trouble. Those people that you put your trust in, like the hired hand, the friends you think are really friends, or even family members who do not know Jesus, in time, they will let you down. Eventually, you will see the evidence of those who will really lay down their lives for you. When you are down and out and you have nothing else to give, who is going to be there to continue believing and praying for you? God will still be there.

Jesus will still be there, and all those who are really running this race as true disciples, Bible believing Christians! The real sheep will be there because they follow the Shepherd and imitate after Him.

John 10:14-16 (NIV 1984, ©1984) [14] *"I am the good shepherd; I know my sheep and my sheep know me— [15] just as the Father knows me and I know the Father—and I lay down my life for the sheep. [16] I have other sheep that are not of this sheep pen. I must bring them also. They too will listen to my voice, and there shall be one flock and one shepherd.*

You see there are many other sheep out there that have not been brought into the flock. Some of them may be people you love and have been praying and believing for God to bring in from the field. Our motivation to engage in Boot Camp and lay down our lives for Christ should be for the lost souls of our nation and other nations as well. We make the choice to lay down our lives and follow the only One that can lead us to green pastures and deliver us from the evil one, in order that we rise up as warriors taking our place in God's Army. As we engage and grow, we learn to pull down those strong holds which have those we love in captivity, and we begin to take back all that the enemy has stolen.

John 10:17-18 (NIV 1984, ©1984) [17] *The reason my Father loves me is that I lay down my life—only to take it up again. [18] No one takes it from me, but I lay it down of my own accord. I have authority to lay it down and authority to take it up again. This command I received from my Father."*

Perhaps our motivation should be the realization that all those things satan steals daily from us and those that we love, we have the authority and tools needed to drastically cause serious conflict with the demonic forces, which will be taught in Boot Camp.

Matthew 24:9-13 (NIV 1984, ©1984) [9] "Then you will be handed over to be persecuted and put to death, and you will be hated by all nations because of me. [10] At that time many will turn away from the faith and will betray and hate each other, [11] and many false prophets will appear and deceive many people. [12] Because of the increase of wickedness, the love of most will grow cold, [13] but he who stands firm to the end will be saved.

As we move farther into the end times, I believe we all know that wickedness continues to grow in this world. The evil which envelopes the nations is detrimental to the lives of every individual on this earth. Crime continually increases, cults surface, demonic activity can be seen, wars continue to be on the horizon, and even though we cannot stop prophecy from happening, we can make a huge impact on every soul we come in contact with. It is time for the body of Christ to rise up and make the bold statement, *"God, I am in for the long haul no matter what!"*

Challenge

A Marine said it like this, *"I just got out of boot camp and it was the best time of my life. It **challenged me** each and every day. My advice to anyone getting ready to go to boot camp is to **stay motivated**, **keep the end result in mind**, and most importantly **listen**. If you stay pumped up and motivated, you're set up for success. Just remember why you're there and what you want to get out of it."*

What is it that you want to get out of life? What will it take to motivate you? I knew that if something did not change with me, it would not have changed with my children and my family. I knew that if I could not walk this walk, no one following me would either. I knew every time God sent a young girl across my path for hope, my life had to speak truth in order for me to lead her in the right direction. Today, God is working in the lives of my family. Today, God is at work in the lives of my spiritual daughters. Today, God is even preparing my granddaughter for a great calling placed upon her little life. We must stay focused on the importance of life and the calling placed on each of us as children of God. The most precious gift God gives to His children, while here on this earth, is the privilege of being a parent. The only thing better than having a child of your own, is having that grandchild. Holding your baby for the first time gives you the awareness of how great and powerful love can be. The marine speaks of being challenged and in order to challenge ourselves, it begins with that motivation we just spoke about. If your motivation is anything but the love for mankind, then you need to check your heart. Our motivation should never be money or acquiring the riches of this world but rather the riches of the world to come.

Here are our challenges, take notes throughout Boot Camp in order to set goals in your life that will grow you. In staying motivated, we must keep the end result in mind. What are you expecting to get out of this? What are the desires God has placed in your heart? What are the mountains or changes which need to take place in your life? I believe this is a good start, in order to make changes we must realistically look at the whole of our lives. We must take account of our weaknesses, our faults, our strengths, our talents and gifts, in order to achieve the greatest success throughout this book. Write all of those expectations down, and write down where you would like to be with God. At the end of Boot Camp, look once again at the list you are making and see how you have grown. It is always good to be able to see progress; therefore, write it down and keep it tucked in this book.

The Marine said to just listen. Too many times we are not really paying attention to what is being said or we are preoccupied. I have learned prior to ever standing before a group and giving a word from God, I pray over the group. I pray that God opens their eyes and ears to see and hear truth, and I pray against the enemy stealing that which is planted. I think it is important to get in a habit of doing this in order for God to have your full attention. Every opportunity which presents itself, we should take advantage of learning in order to grow. Attending church services, seminars, encounters, retreats, etc. bring growth, and it is your way of saying, *"God, I lay down my flesh in order to learn of you."* Most of the time, when we do not attend a church service or another event, it is because our flesh would rather be doing something else. This is not the attitude of a warrior and will not grow the character and strength within you in order to be that victorious soldier in God's Army. It is not enough to just listen to God's Word being taught, we must be note takers. I know most of us have heard that we only retain a small percentage of what we are taught, but if we write it down, we retain much more, and if we share it with someone else, we retain even more. When we are in a service, we should have already prepared ahead of time in order to get the most of what is being taught where we are not distracted. This means, we should have already taken our bathroom break, taken care of any possible crisis so that our cell phones can be turned on silent, visited with our neighbors prior to service so we are not distracted with idle talk and conversations among those sitting next to us. This is all about showing respect for the man or woman of God who is standing before you to give you life lessons which will greatly change your life, plant seeds into your future and that of your family as well. Quite often, we take God's Word for granted. If doctors gave you a few months left to live and you were listening to someone giving you the answer to live so that you would not die, would you allow anything

80

to distract you from hearing every single word which came forth from their lips? If we took God's Word seriously, we would know that the Words being taught today are not only for eternal salvation but also for living life to the fullest while here on earth. As we draw closer to the tribulation period, many words being taught today are for survival. You may be left behind, and if so, you will need as much of the Word of God in you to be able to withstand the horror which will face this earth. If we miss it because we were preoccupied with the comings and goings of this world, we may someday face that spiritual death unexpectedly. Let's listen today as we hear God's Word being preached, and let's listen for that small quiet voice as the Holy Spirit reminds us of truths and teaches us all things.

If we stay pumped up and motivated as the Marine said, we are set up for success. We need to not think about success in the terms of this world but rather in spiritual terms. We need to have our focus on others and off, *"What's in it for me God?"* This always shows where your heart is currently, and if your motives are always about yourself, please question your walk with Jesus. God desires none would perish, and if your heart is not right, you may be in trouble. So, what areas do we need to be successful if it is not in the terms of this world? And, how do we stay pumped up? The Marine said to remember why we are here and what we want to get out of it. You should have answered those questions. The successes in this life should line up with the same desires as God. God will see to it that His people are very successful in all they set their hands to, but our desires should be for mankind. Like I have said, people should be our motivation. Sometimes we are afraid to let go of this world totally, and many Christians try to straddle the fence; however, you are never really straddling the fence. There is no grey area, only black and white. There is no half-way serving God, you either are glorifying God or giving glory

81

to satan. We do not straddle the fence. We are either on one side or the other. We must let go of self because only then will you experience real freedom.

A Marine said it like this, "*There are a few things that you need to know. This of course is in the midst of thinking you are not going to make it and you are going to die because boot camp is too hard…*

Know that in the Marines:

> 1. *They can never deny you a head call. (Bathroom break)*
> 2. *They can never deny you medical attention.*
> 3. *They can never deny you chow.*
> 4. *Always sound off loudly. (They have a motto… if they cannot hear you, they cannot help you)"*

To break this down, your basic needs will be met, and there are few things you need to know coming in. Remember, God wants to reprogram your mind so you are brainwashed to think like Jesus. If we are full of religious beliefs that are contrary to God's Word, He first has to get all the junk out and replace it with the Truth.

John 8:32 (NIV) [32]*Then you will know the truth, and the truth will set you free."*

Boot Camp is only as hard as you perceive it to be. You have to ask yourself, *"What am I willing to do to achieve a life with God?"* We work hard at things we really want. This life with Christ is all about being set free in order to live a life which is full and live eternal life thereafter. The Marine speaks of those things which cannot be denied in Boot Camp. In other words, he is trying to show that no matter how bad things get, your needs will be met, and you will not do without. God promises us these same things. He promises us that He will never leave or forsake us. He tells us not to worry about our life.

Matthew 6:25-27(NIV) [25] *"Therefore I tell you, do not worry about your life, what you will eat or drink; or about your body, what you will wear. Is not life more than food, and the body more than clothes?* [26] *Look at the birds of the air; they do not sow or reap or store away in barns, and yet your heavenly Father feeds them. Are you not much more valuable than they?* [27] *Can any one of you by worrying add a single hour to your life?"*

When I am faced with trouble upon my life, I immediately turn to the Scriptures. If I believe the Word of God, then I hold God to His Word.

Jeremiah 1:12 (AMP) [12] *Then said the Lord to me, You have seen well, for I am alert and active, watching over My word to perform it.*

It goes back to God's Word being the final say so. If He said it, then we should believe it. My trust goes in His Word and I remind Him, *"God, you said you were watching over your Word to perform it, and I know you got my back."*

The last thing the Marine said was to always sound off loudly because if they cannot hear you, they cannot help you. If we do not speak with authority, then we are not really convinced that God is who He says He is. If we do not believe what we say, why is God going to believe what we say? We will learn extensively about our words and how powerful they are, but we need to know, just like a child will listen when a parent speaks in that tone of authority, our words must speak authority as well if we expect to move mountains in our lives.

To sum it up, those things you need in order to survive physically cannot be taken from you just because you let go of the world and let go of self. However, when you do give up the world and self, you are allowing God to be in control. When this takes place, you will never hurt for those things you need or even those desires you may have in life. We were created in the likeness and image of our Father in Heaven, and if we have desires, God too has desires. It is a matter of lining those desires up with the Word and not the world and its lustful ways. Once you let go and begin to grow, your desires will change, and you will look back at your old life one day and say, *"There is nothing that would make me want to go back to that place."* So, whatever your fears for not letting go of the world or whatever you may be facing, when you become grounded and make the decision that you are standing firm no matter what the world or the enemy throws your way, God will be the one in control. And, He will hold the keys to your destiny when you are walking close to Him. I know I would rather be on the side of the army where God is my Commander and Chief instead of taking a chance with satan in charge of my life, you make that decision.

Mind of Christ

We do not function in any capacity without our brain, or we can refer to it as our mind. By protecting our brain, we do so in the sense as to have the mind of Christ.

1 Corinthians 2:16 (AMP) [16]For who has known or understood the mind (the counsels and purposes) of the Lord so as to guide and instruct Him and give Him knowledge? But we have the mind of Christ (the Messiah) and do hold the thoughts (feelings and purposes) of His heart.

Much of our battle is within our mind, and this can be our worst enemy. We have to learn to be grounded in knowing that if we are really running the same race the followers of Jesus ran in biblical days, we should have the desires to line our minds up with what God's Word says. The helmet is one of the hardest pieces of armor to put on and keep on. It says in the Word of God that we should daily die to self. *(1 Corinthians 15:31)* If we are not doing this, in reality, we are backslidden. We cannot say we are putting on that helmet, yet our minds totally line up with the world and not the Word. This would be like a soldier preparing to go to battle but his beliefs line up with that of the enemy force. If you do not share the same beliefs as your country, if you do not believe in what they are fighting for, you would not sign up to go fight a war you were against. We are against truth if we are walking in deceit. We are against that which is light if we are walking in darkness. Without your mind renewed, you become a spy helping the enemy force. We are either for God or against God. How can you go into battle to fight a war when you are associating with the very darkness you are coming against? It is like associating with the enemy by night secretly, and when daytime comes, you want to put your armor on to imitate your fellow soldiers. However, when faced with those you associate with in secret, you are not strong enough to come against them. How can you try to destroy those things you are engaged in? How can you take back what rightfully has been given to you and your family when in secret you are handing everything over to the enemy force willingly. You see, when our mind is not renewed, in secret we are handing over everything the enemy asks for. We are giving the enemy our families to destroy. We are furnishing the enemy with our finances to strengthen him. Yes, every single time you use your finances to purchase items which do not bring glory unto God, that money is landing in the hands of those that continue to strengthen the conformities of this world. Meaning, the money is going back into the powers which deceive man daily to become conformed to this world. We lay down our lives for the enemy by walking in our miseries, our sicknesses, and our struggles daily. Instead of facing the root to our problems, we put a Band-Aid on our weaknesses and continue to live like everyone else in this world that is blinded from truth. I remember one of my girls I minister to saying that it was hard for her to confront a family member with their sin, when she was also not where she needed to be with God. Of course, we are not to look at the speck in our brothers eyes when we have a log in our own; however, there is something to see by that statement.

Matthew 7:3-5 (NLT) ³ "And why worry about a speck in your friend's eye when you have a log in your own? ⁴ How can you think of saying to your friend, 'Let me help you get rid of that speck in your eye,' when you can't see past the log in your own eye? ⁵ Hypocrite! First get rid of the log in your own eye; then you will see well enough to deal with the speck in your friend's eye.

If we are engaged in sin, we are not going to confront those we love with their own sin when we are doing the same thing. It's kind of like going to your brother and saying, *"You really need to get it together and stop drinking!"* Why are you going to do that when you sit alongside your brother drinking with him? And, why would we go into enemy territory to fight for that brother trying to come against the forces that are keeping him bound when that same force has us bound as well? How can we try to stop something that we are living in? When you live in it, you are agreeing with it.

In order for marines to endure boot camp, they must be strengthened mentally as well as physically. In chapter one, we touched on the Marine which said *"The mental is tougher because the human mind acts in different ways when it's being pressured.*

When you get angry you want to hit something, you want to act out, you want to swear. But in boot camp, they teach you how to keep your bearing and how to stay focused."

What the marine is referring to is how our minds are programmed prior to boot camp. Prior to boot camp, when we get angry, we want to hit something. Prior to boot camp, when things do not go our way, we want to strike out with words and actions. Military boot camp teaches men and women how to stay calm in the midst of a storm and how to keep their minds focused on the task at hand. In God's Army, when we begin renewing our mind, we learn to stay focused on Christ. We learn to stay calm in the midst of our storms. We learn to trust and look to God's Word as the solution for any and all things.

In winning the battle over our minds, we must see that it is a matter of freeing our mind. There is a song sung by En Vogue called, *"Free Your Mind."* This song pretty much sings about the prejudices in this world. People judge without even knowing the person inside. People assume without knowing. When our minds are programmed this way, we live in bondage based on our perspectives in life. It is only when we get the Truth in us, we become free. When we are in sin, we are bound not free. In the Word, Jesus tells us to seek first God's Kingdom and all else will follow. By freeing our minds to the way God thinks, all else will follow.

John 8:36 (ESV)[36] So if the Son sets you free, you will be free indeed.

Matthew 6:33 (AMP) [33] But seek (aim at and strive after) first of all His kingdom and His righteousness (His way of doing and being right), and then all these things taken together will be given you besides.

When we win the battle over our minds, we will find ourselves free. We will find ourselves without any lack in our lives. We will find ourselves – period! We cannot even begin to know who God created us to be until we tap into the spiritual realm. This realm will never come alive to us without having the mind of Christ. Some of you may have watched the show, *"The Biggest Loser."* There was an episode where a young man won at losing the most weight ever in a season. The physical challenges were overwhelming; however, when he was interviewed on how he had achieved such a great goal, his response had nothing to do with being able to conquer the physical aspects of the challenge. This was his reply, *"The hardest part to the challenge, was simply believing in myself and keeping the faith that I could lose so much weight. It was mind over matter. I totally blocked out the limitations my mind put on myself. That is when I really felt free and the weight really started coming off."* This is exactly where most Christians are today with God. They put limitations on their lives, and they do not believe they can overcome the obstacles. Jesus said…

John 16:33 (AMP) *[33]I have told you these things, so that in Me you may have [perfect] peace and confidence. In the world you have tribulation and trials and distress and frustration; but be of good cheer [take courage; be confident, certain, undaunted]! For I have overcome the world. [I have deprived it of power to harm you and have conquered it for you.]*

Jesus overcame this world so that we too can overcome any and all things. We also see in 1 John that it shows that because Christ is in us, we have already defeated and overcame all demonic forces.

1 John 4:4 (AMP) ⁴Little children, you are of God [you belong to Him] and have [already] defeated and overcome them [the agents of the antichrist], because He Who lives in you is greater (mightier) than he who is in the world.

The reason we look as though we are losing this battle is because we willingly hand over everything to the enemy. We listen to the world instead of renewing our mind to that of Christ. Whatever we are feeding our mind, that is how we are going to think, what we are going to perceive, and how we are going to act. If we truly desire to be a warrior for Christ, it begins with our mind. The mind must line up to the Word of God before we can even go to battle.

A Marine said... Boot camp is almost all mental and some physical.

Walking this walk victoriously has almost everything to do with renewing your mind to think like God. There is the physical aspect, but that will be much easier when you are not dealing with a mind that thinks like the world. Your life will flow very peacefully when you are not dealing with a mind that is worldly because when your mind is worldly, your flesh will rule instead of your spirit.

A Marine said... Memorize your General Orders before you get to PI, know the Naval terminology, learn the Navy and Marine Corps rank structure, and practice speaking in the third person (ie Good Evening Ma'am, Excuse Recruit Rochelle, Drill Instructor Staff Sergeant Browne Ma'am. Recruit Rochelle requests permission to make a head call ma'am.) You will use that one often.

Although I was never a marine, this does show how a marine must think. A marine must reason things out; they must talk in

89

accordance with protocol, and all this training must go deep enough that they feel like a marine inside and out. To have victory, we must renew our minds so that we know exactly who we are in Jesus Christ. A marine comes out knowing they are a marine – once a marine always a marine. We have to come out knowing that God had already thought about us before He even created us. God sees what we are capable of doing and being. We are created in His likeness and image, and if we do not see and feel this, we have not had the training we need. For training, we must enlist in order to gain the Boot Camp mentality or we will never see that victory in our lives.

Below is an article written by Evan Kingsley, and was written to give a strategy in order to win the lottery. There is some insight to what Kingsley shares.

Mind over Matter Strategy to Win Lottery
By Evan Kingsley

Many writers have written about ways to win lottery. But winning lottery is not something to be fascinated about because lottery is a game of chance, and people should understand this. Luck is the major influencing factor. You can win and you can lose. But winning is a product of mind over matter technique.

Like Attracts Like
Have you read about the Law of Attraction or watched a documentary of it. The mind is a powerful essence, capable of commanding the body to do as it conceives. According to this theory what you envision over and over again is most likely going to happen because the mind tends to attract this event. In other words, the chances you'd get something increase the more you envision yourself getting it. It's true in lottery as well as any other

aspect of life. Essentially, who would not think of winning in lottery? People always hope they would win once they bought a lottery ticket. In fact, it's all about optimism. You don't always win. It doesn't mean that when you have envisioned yourself taking home the huge amount of pot money, you end up winning the next day. You can't be that lucky. But it's always better to be optimistic than pessimistic. In fact, you can employ the same attitude while playing roulette in a casino.

Mind Power

Have you experienced of thinking of a disaster and it actually took place? Many people have and it explains how receptive the mind is. It controls our decisions and behaviors more than you think it does. How you set your mind affects your attitude and outlook in life. If you're a negative thinker, you most likely envision bad events to happen-and they actually happen. Positive thinkers, on the other hand, see more good happenings. Consequently, lucky people are those who think they are lucky. Look at the disposition of winners in casinos. Do they look distraught even after a loss? The real winners have a winning attitude and they have a winning mind. So you have got to have a mind of a winner because that's the mind that wins. A positive mind has more chances of winning at a lottery or casino than a negative mind. You don't instantly become a winner, and you may not always win, but you always have the edge-whether you are to play roulette or buy a lottery ticket.

Doesn't it seem too simple?

This method seems plain but not easy because it's tough to be positive amidst existing negativity around you. If this were that easy then millions of people would've won every day because they all want to win. But it's not enough that you want to win. You have to see yourself winning; you have to feel it in your heart. Now, *thinking or envisioning that you will win is so much different from obsessing and buying too many lottery tickets at the same time. You can be positive but don't ever run short of money because you've spent every dime on lottery tickets. Mind over matter simply means that you discipline your thoughts and attitudes. This is easier said than done but you can start now.[1]*

What a powerful article. This was not even written geared towards living a life influenced by biblical standards, yet it speaks truth according to the Word of God. Our mind is powerful. Our thoughts and actions influence our attitudes and actions throughout our lives. If we are positive thinkers, we are walking by faith believing that our God is in control and we lack for nothing nor do we live in worry or fear. As the article states, it is much easier said than done. Faith is the substance hoped for and the evidence yet to be seen. *(Hebrews 11:1 KJV)*

When we live by faith, we live knowing that our God has the ultimate plan for our lives, and we trust in Him alone. We are strengthened by His might. We lack in nothing because we know that He supplies all our needs. We walk out of our homes each day knowing that whatever happens, He is in control. We do not fret or stress over any circumstances or storms faced with because we know the final outcome will be that which our God set into motion. This does not mean that we live in a box but rather that we step out of our box trusting our God and seeking Him diligently. It means that we seek daily, in order that our mind is renewed to thinking like Jesus and doing the will of our Father. We listen for the voice of the Holy Spirit and allow Him access to our lives that the cleanup process can and will happen as God transforms us to be more and more like His Son, Jesus Christ.

The Helmet of Salvation protects our head from direct blows by the enemy as fiery darts are aimed at us daily in order to cause us to doubt that God is in control. Our brain which is encased in our head is one of the most important vital organs within our body. Within our mind, our way of thinking must line up with the Word of God. The reason most people cannot live a life of positive thinking is because they continually pour negative perceptions of this world into their brain daily. Yes, it does matter what you choose to listen to and what you read. It does matter whom you hang out with because your associations will be the influences in your life. Positive people associate with positive people. When we do not line up our way of thinking with the Word of God, direct blows from the enemy forces will keep your mind defeated living in a negative world. Direct blows will cause you to become faint and waiver in what little you may have come to know about God. This is why many backslide in their walk with God. We will learn throughout this book the importance of every single piece of armor but we need to understand that without applying the Helmet of Salvation in our lives, we cannot even begin to put on any other piece of armor. The helmet is the most important piece as a new Christian. Without this first process being understood, nothing else is going to work. Salvation is the first step of beginning to know Jesus Christ. We have to have that conviction in our lives from the Holy Spirit where we come to understand the basics and that we are in a war, and we are running a race which will continue throughout our lifespan here on this earth. Without protecting our mind in order to begin growing in the Truth, we will not go any further. The military has boot camp for a reason. Without those men and women renewing their mind to think like a soldier, it would be suicide sending them into battle. They could not do it and would never believe they could do it. Dwight D. Eisenhower said, *"What counts is not necessarily the size of the dog in the fight, it's the size of the fight in the dog."* This goes back to saying that the mental strength is much more powerful than the physical strength. We are strong through Christ and without Christ, we have nothing. What size is the fight within you? If it is Christ size, you will win your battles.

Helmet of a Warrior

Ephesians 6:10-13,17a, 18 (ESV) [10]*Finally, be strong in the Lord and in the strength of his might.* [11] *Put on the whole armor of God, that you may be able to stand against the schemes of the devil.* [12]*For we do not wrestle against flesh and blood, but against the rulers, against the authorities, against the cosmic powers over this present darkness, against the spiritual forces of evil in the heavenly places.* [13]*Therefore take up the whole armor of God, that you may be able to withstand in the evil day, and having done all, to stand firm....* [17]*and take the helmet of salvation, ...* [18]*praying at all times in the Spirit, with all prayer and supplication. To that end keep alert with all perseverance, making supplication for all the saints,*

Our hope of salvation rests in the assurance that we are on the same course as the disciples in biblical days and that we remain on that course throughout our walk with Jesus Christ. In 1 Corinthians, Paul also says that he dies daily. This is taking up your cross and choosing to walk like Christ.

1 Corinthians 15:31 (AMP) [31]*[I assure you] by the pride which I have in you in [your fellowship and union with] Christ Jesus our Lord, that I die daily [I face death every day and die to self].*

Daily, we make the choice to give up self and live for Christ, or we choose to live for this world. We choose to give up all those things which gratify our flesh, in order that we are assured of our salvation. The hope of our salvation rests in the fact that we know we are living as a true disciple of Christ. Salvation is not something that we strive for and then go about living according to the gratification of the flesh. The hope of our salvation rests in the fact that we know and understand we must maintain and exercise the same discipline as the original disciples. Paul did not walk as a true follower of Jesus Christ just during the time that Jesus was with him. After the resurrection, when Jesus went to be with the Father, Paul did not decide to just go back to his old life. On the contrary, Paul continued in this walk. Daily, Paul made the choice to die to self and to live for Christ. In order to gain salvation, it becomes a daily walk; it becomes a lifestyle. It is not something that we put on and take off. When we take that helmet from our Father, we daily put it on as we choose daily to share in the crucifixion of Christ. We daily make that choice by saying, *"Father, your will be done not mine."* With every piece of armor that we should put on, we must recognize exactly what we are doing. A soldier going to battle only half-way clothed will be defeated. In order to suffice on enemy ground, we must be prepared.

Romans 8:24 (NKJV)[24] *For we were saved in this hope, but hope that is seen is not hope; for why does one still hope for what he sees?*

We believe by faith. Faith believes those things we cannot see. When we hope for something, it is for something we have yet to see. Our hope for salvation is the assurance that even though we live in these earthly bodies, we know as we take that helmet, that we are declaring to walk this walk out with Jesus Christ and live according to the Scriptures. Our hope is in eternal life with our Father in Heaven. Our time here on earth is no longer about us. Our time here is about going out as a warrior for Christ and continuing the battle which was begun with the first church and continues today. To be engaged in the Army of God, one must first take that helmet and place it on their head, so to speak. This is your confession that you understand this is a lifestyle which will continue until the day that you go to meet your Maker. This helmet is meant for those who understand salvation is real, and your life here on this earth was for a purpose and that purpose was not about you! Once we accept that helmet and make that decision that we desire to grow and learn in the truth, our lives will begin to change drastically. Most Christians, at this point, do not really ever surrender and engage in the task which lay ahead. Defeat is seen among the Christian community today because few seldom study the Scriptures to learn and grow. They do not understand their purpose. They do not have insight into the greater things, and therefore, they remain blinded. The helmet is only one aspect of our armor, and the meaning is far more detailed than just a salvation message. This will be covered in greater clarity further into this book. For now, I believe it is important for us to see that our enemy continually blinds unbelievers as well as believers, and this is a huge aspect in being able to see our struggles as Christians.

2 Corinthians 4:4 (NIV1984) [4]The god of this age has blinded the minds of unbelievers, so that they cannot see the light of the gospel of the glory of Christ, who is the image of God.

I say believers as well because many times, we may think we are believers when in reality, we have been blinded. I truly believe that we are all blinded in areas of our life because there is no way any of us have every piece of revelation there is in the Word of God. I know myself, I can read something and get great revelation from Scriptures and then go back months later and read that same Scripture only to gain more knowledge than before. As we gain truth, it is that very truth which sets us free from areas of bondage. If you ever find yourself in a place where you think you have this walk down with God, you are already deceived. None of us should ever give ourselves more credit than is due. We must remember that we are all imperfect beings, seeking Christ for that perfection.

Romans 12:3 (NIV) [3]For by the grace given me I say to every one of you: Do not think of yourself more highly than you ought, but rather think of yourself with sober judgment, in accordance with the faith God has distributed to each of you.

Chapter Four
Breastplate of Righteousness

As we begin our study into the breastplate of righteousness, we will begin with who we are in Christ. As I have said, clothing ourselves with each piece of armor is about understanding what each piece means and accepting that piece of armor for what it represents. Christians today have a hard time seeing themselves as righteous, but that is exactly what this piece of armor represents. Why is it that we cannot see who we are in Christ? It may be because we are imperfect people who do not line up to what we see as perfection. However, we must be able to see who we are in Christ, and we have to believe it with our thoughts and our words. Only then will our actions line up with the way we think and talk. Once again, this goes back to Boot Camp and our minds being transformed to that of Christ.

Areas of Defeat

Everyone has areas in their lives where they feel defeated. Many times it can be as simple as facing our defeats in order to gain insight to why we cannot overcome. In my prayer group, I give examples to show why the majority of people continue to live day in and day out in the same areas of failure. Defeat lies within the way we see ourselves. The way we see ourselves is then transformed into our thought process which will ultimately be spoken over our lives. If we continually speak negative over our situations, that is exactly what we will receive.

One of our biggest areas of defeat by far is the belief that our battles are with flesh and blood. As long as this is our perception, we will continue to fight with our spouse, our children, family, co-workers, employers, neighbors, and even complete strangers. To remain in this negative thought process will allow satan to ultimately keep you and your family bound in areas which destroy your world and everything within close proximity. We can see by the rate of divorces how prevalent satan is within our families. We can see by the increasing battle of addiction, infidelity, idolatry, and increased population within our prisons that satan hates the family unit because God ordained marriage and family. As the family unit continues to deteriorate, it is very noticeable that the welfare of our society has also continued to deteriorate. We have to be wise according to Proverbs in order to realize that this is a spiritual battle, and we make that stand to come against that which satan is using to try and destroy the family unit.

In my groups, I have had many discussions regarding problems within the marriage. There have been questions such as, *"What am I supposed to do if my spouse starts an argument with me?"* Let me clarify a few things regarding the different roles within the home. Women tend to be the complainers when they feel that their husbands are not doing their part in helping with the chores of the home and children. I speak this to myself as well as any woman out there. I was married, and I complained just like many women today. What I have shared and will continue to share is truth according to God's Word in order to bring about change that will transform our relationships. I cannot make anyone change and frankly, that is not my job. I can only be the vessel God uses to bring truth, and what we decide to do with the truth we receive is our choice. As for myself, I have had to repent many times and lay down my selfish fleshly desires because above all else, I desire to be what God wants me to be. The longer it takes me to be obedient, the longer it takes God to bring me to that place He desires me to be.

I had a young couple come to me for counseling one day and probably made a lot of points with the husband, which was not my intention, but if this can save anyone's marriage and relationship with God, then it needs to be said. As a woman, according to Proverbs 31, your role is to conform to the image of that virtuous woman. Let me add this before going further. If we study Proverbs 31, it would seem that the virtuous woman's every day chores were never ending. In America, we complain because we desire it to be easier. In America, we have become a spoiled nation who wants everything at the click of a button in order to make our lives more comfortable. Yet, in studying the virtuous woman, her life was one that was very busy doing what God considered to be a woman who was worthy, honorable, upright, and honest. I have found being in the ministry that my days are busier than ever before, yet my gains in this life have increased abundantly because instead of murmuring and complaining, I am thankful for all the many blessings God has bestowed upon myself and my family. Do I get tired and feel drained at times? Yes, but the advantages far outweigh my physical being. I am not saying that we can never rest because God expects us to rest. What I am saying is that God will provide us with the strength and stamina to take on any and all callings placed upon our lives.

To continue, the young lady that I was counseling did not have a job and was very fortunate, in today's society, to be able to stay at home with her toddler. In her eyes, she felt that her job never ended. She felt after her husband came home from working all day, he should take up the slack and give her a break from the cleaning, cooking, and taking care of their small child. This young lady's husband felt after working all day, he was entitled to sit and watch TV while she cooked and continued to take care of their child. Our role as women is not to be God or Lord over our husband but to love them and make our home one that is filled with the love of God. Our rewards for our works will be done in heaven, but if we spend our whole life complaining about how we never had any help doing what we should be doing *'in love'* for our family, then it becomes a job. If we look at our role for our families as work, we will suffer on earth as well as receive no rewards in heaven. A woman's role at home is not a job. The children we are given by God are blessings, and it is short lived. We should be thanking God daily for the children He has blessed us with, and we should take joy in the daily routine of caring for those children we love and making a home for that man we also love. Our home should be that man's castle; a loving home and one which he delights in coming to after a long day at work. On the other hand, I also shared with the man, his role is much greater. As a man, the responsibility lies on him to provide that support, security, and the spirituality within his castle. With the man, his children will only know God by how much *'God'* they see within him. With the man, his wife will come to know that *'God kind of love'* by the love and compassion he exhibits towards his wife, his children, and mankind. By no means am I implying here that the man has no responsibility towards the home and the children. If the man shows love to the wife and children according to how Jesus loved the church, he will give up himself for her.

Ephesians 5:25 (AMP) [25]*Husbands, love your wives, as Christ loved the church and gave Himself up for her,*

Jesus died a physical death for the church, and we are the church. Should we not give of ourselves also? I believe if you truly love your wife and you claim to be a Christian, your desire should be one to make your wife happy at all costs. Husbands, your rewards will also be in heaven. I remember hearing a pastor one time say that he and his wife competed at seeing who could outdo each other in pleasing and making the other happy. This sure couldn't hurt in our society and would probably build a stronger marriage. However, I believe that if the husband comes home to a loving castle, he would delight in helping with the home and children but this is not implying that it is his duty to do so.

To continue with the couple, when I asked the man if he felt he had no obligations towards helping, if she were to ask him in a different manner instead of nagging, his reply was quite different. Men do not always know what we want if we do not clarify. Women tend to believe that their husbands can automatically read their minds. Men on the other hand only know what we want by what we ask. Communication is the key to a strong marriage. I addressed the young lady after his response, and I shared, instead of complaining and nagging, a much better approach would be to say, *"Would you mind bathing the children tonight or would you mind helping me with the dishes tonight because I feel overwhelmed?"* Let's be honest, if you are feeling stressed, say so. As for those families where both parents work outside the home, talk about it and agree on how each of you can be that support system for the other. Relationships are about working together, but in order to be strong, you must have God as the center of that relationship. Time is way too short for us to always be looking for fault in those we love instead of just loving them where they are and allowing God to change them. Regardless, if the woman or the man is the stronger spiritual head of the home, our battles are not flesh and blood. If one spouse chooses not to walk with God and the other one does, the one walking with God, will eventually see the change within their spouse if they are truly allowing God to change them. The sooner we realize that God cannot do a work in those we love if we do not step back and give it to Him, the better our relationships will be, and the sooner our families will be restored to be what God intended. We must also remember that spirituality cannot be forced upon anyone, but if we work on our own relationship with God, our families will see the change within us and that is what brings about change in others.

Snared by our Words

We will continue to look at defeat based upon words and even very simple words which we speak on a daily basis.

Examples of words of defeat:

- *I have been praying and believing God for years to heal me <u>but</u> it has not happened yet!*

- *I <u>try</u> to overcome my anger <u>but</u> sometimes I get so mad I say things I later regret!*

- *I <u>try</u> to tithe or be a giver <u>but</u> there never seems to be enough finances coming in to pay bills and give to God!*

- *I really do not want to live in sin, doing those things I know are wrong in God's sight and in my mind I say I am going to overcome those things <u>but</u> I wind up doing it again and again!*

- *I <u>cannot </u>seem to overcome the feeling of depression, loneliness, etc.*

- *I know I am overweight and God has dealt with me on this issue, <u>but </u>I just <u>cannot</u> seem to lose the weight!*

- *God has dealt with me on being slow to speak and quick to listen (James 1:19) <u>but</u> I somehow keep doing these things!*

- *I <u>battle</u> with thoughts… it's as though satan tries to trip me up with putting negative or perverse thoughts in my head. I know that these thoughts are not of God. I rebuke the thoughts, <u>but</u> they continue to come back again and again. Sometimes, when I see certain people or go certain places, it's as though those thoughts come right back!*

- *I sometimes <u>battle</u> thinking too highly of myself and pray for humility, <u>but</u> why is this such a strong hold on my life? I know that I can do nothing without God!*

- *I believe everything in the Word of God, <u>but</u> sometimes, I say the wrong thing and know it is cancelling my prayers!*

Yes, cancelling your prayers is exactly what it does! We get what we say. Our words are powerful and have the means to either produce victory or defeat in our lives. What does this have to do with the Breastplate of Righteousness? If we do not see ourselves the way that God sees us, we will never be righteous in His sight. We will never overcome; we will never be able to succeed; we will never be able to do all things through Christ who gives us strength!

Philippians 4:13 (KJV) [13]I can do all things through Christ which strengtheneth me.

Notice, the words underlined in the above examples. We are not pleasing to God if we do not walk by faith.

Hebrews 11:6 (KJV) *But without faith it is impossible to please him: for he that cometh to God must believe that he is, and that he is a rewarder of them that diligently seek him.*

Faith speaks positive; faith speaks those things that we cannot see yet. For instance, faith does not say, *"I have been praying for God to heal me but it has not happened yet."* Faith says, *"I prayed for my healing and God is my healer; by faith, I am healed."* You may say, *"But, I am still sick."* And, you will continue to be sick if you cannot believe that you are healed. God wants us to exercise our faith. He wants us to step out believing for those things which may not have manifested in the natural realm but in the spiritual realm, they are confirmed. If God said it in His Word, it is done. The reason we do not conquer victories in our lives is because we do not act as victors but rather as losers. God did not make losers, and He desires for us to rise up to see ourselves through His eyes, the eyes which created each of us for something marvelous. As we begin to understand how important the way we think is to the way we talk, we will do something to change it.

If you pray and believe God to answer that which you need victory, your next step is to begin speaking that victory. Faith speaks, *"I am losing weight daily because God is moving in my life and showing me how to walk this out. A job is in my near future because God is working in my life, and He is opening a door that will produce success in my life. I have power to overcome any and all things in my life because greater is He that is in me than He that is in the world. It does not matter that I just missed it because I am stronger today than I was yesterday, and daily, God is adding to that strength. As God gives me wisdom and knowledge of this world, I have power over the enemy and able to see his tactics that I do not associate with or entertain in areas with those that would bring me down nor do I choose to go into*

106

enemy territories unprepared. I am righteous in the sight of God because I am saved by grace, and it is Jesus' blood which covers me and removes that veil so that I can come before my Father in Heaven and present my prayers at the throne of grace." This is all faith, and this is how faith speaks. Be careful when you are making a statement that you do not cancel that statement by ending with *"but."* That word *"but"* will cancel your faith and keep you walking in your defeat for years, just like the children of Israel who spent 40 years in the desert of defeat. When we say the word *"try,"* remember there is no such thing as *"trying God."* We do not test God, and we do not try God! Either you believe what God's Word says or you do not. God never changes, and if you are walking in defeat because you say that God is not coming through, it is not because God has not done His part. God is waiting on you to step up and realize who you are in Christ, so that you change things in you. The change begins with Boot Camp. The change begins with lining up your way of thinking to the way that Jesus thinks. We have an instruction manual, and it is called the Bible. It is full of knowledge and wisdom that puts scholars to shame. The world has nothing on the knowledge of God, and it is through the insight in His Word that your mind will line up with His way of thinking, and the fruit that will be produced will be that of victory and not defeat.

I believe it is important to have an accountability partner, someone that is walking this same walk with you. You can swap and share your areas of defeat, but the point in having a partner is so that you have someone to call you out, correct you, and help you to stay on that course. However, this works both ways. You or your accountability partner may see areas that the other does not see and then help to guide each other in doing what should be done to bring your thinking to that of the Word of God. An accountability partner is there to listen and see that your mouth lines up with that which is good and not evil. You will soon learn that your defeat is in your words, and many times, your area of defeat may be in the way you speak to others. Marriages today are in turmoil because satan would love us to believe that our battles are with flesh and blood as I have said. God's Word says contrary in Ephesians.

Ephesians 6:12 (NIV) *[12]For our struggle is not against flesh and blood, but against the rulers, against the authorities, against the powers of this dark world and against the spiritual forces of evil in the heavenly realms.*

If you have a close friend that desires that closer walk with God, partner up to be each other's constructive criticism partner. What I mean by this, much of our defeat lies within what we speak, and if you have someone that corrects your speech to help you break bad habits, then both of you will gain so much. Another exercise I have shared in my groups, is to practice calling God, *"Dad, Daddy, or Papa God."* The reason, sometimes this helps to develop that more intimate relationship with Him. I have raised my grandbaby calling Him, *"Papa God,"* and many times, this is how I speak also. In reality, He is my Dad. In reality, He loves me greater than any earthly father ever could. Yes, I do honor Him greatly, but also, I love Him very deeply, more so than any earthly dad or father. When my grandbaby has had a bad day at school, the first thing I ask her, *"Who is your daddy?"* Her reply is, *"Papa God."* My next response is, *"And, who fights your battles?"* You see, my grandbaby, like so many other children in this world, was cheated out of having that earthly father as a role model, one who protects, nurtures, compliments, and loves her like his little princess. However, Papa God is ever ready to fill that void in her life as well as all the other children whom do not have that earthly dad present. He will be there to heal the wounds left by all those earthly fathers who have let them down. My suggestions for all who have never had that intimate relationship with *"Father God,"* is to begin referring to Him as your *"Daddy,"* so that you can see just how much He loves and desires to fill that void left by this world. It is so important to develop that closeness and realization that He is your Dad, and He is not unreachable. God desires that intimacy with each of us individually. I have examples below of *"role play"* that you can actually do with your accountability partner.

Examples of words of victory with accountability partner:

- Partner – How are things with you and (spouse) today?
  You – They are great! My wife/husband is coming to Jesus more and more every day, and I can see an awesome change in her/him daily.
  Partner – Have you argued with her/him today?
  You – No, in Jesus name, I line up my thoughts and mouth with my God's Word!

- Partner – How is the baby doing today? Is he/she crying a lot?
  You – The baby is great, in Jesus name; he/she is a really good baby, sleeps good, etc.

- Partner – How was your day? Did you have favor with everyone you worked with today?
  You – My day was great, and it is awesome to see how people see me as confident and smart. I thank you Papa God that you are doing a work within me, and others are able to see those good works within that it brings glory to You.

- Partner – How are you feeling today?
  You – I am feeling great.

Partner – You have not been hurting?
You – In the name of Jesus, I am healed, and my body is continually lining up with God's Word. I was healed the day of Calvary, and I walk by faith and not by sight.

- Partner – Have you been defeated today?
  You – No, absolutely not! I am my Daddy's son/daughter, and there is no defeat in my life. I overcome everything by the words of my testimony that my Dad has given me and the blood that is poured over me.

- Partner – How are things between your mom/dad and you today?
  You – They couldn't be better. God has really done a great work within me and my mouth lines up with Papa God's Words not the world. I have victory in this walk because I diligently seek those things above and not beneath.

These are merely examples and may seem strange to read them, but this gives you an idea of how to line up your words where you speak things positive. There were times that God told me not to just tell my groups how to do something but to show them. Why would He have me do this? We generally learn faster by example than by mere words. This is not something that can be done overnight because it has taken us years to be programmed wrong. And, it will take time to reprogram our thought process and our words. However, this is speaking faith, and this is what is pleasing to God. *(Hebrews 11:6)*

When we are speaking faith, in the natural realm, what we are speaking may seem the complete opposite. For example, if you are sick and you have symptoms, faith speaks believing that you are well. The Word says that faith believes for what we cannot see.

Hebrews 11:1 (AMP) ¹NOW FAITH is the assurance (the confirmation, the title deed) of the things [we] hope for, being the proof of things [we] do not see and the conviction of their reality [faith perceiving as real fact what is not revealed to the senses].

It's not too hard to believe for something that you can already see, and it doesn't take faith to do that. God is a God of faith – He is faith! We are created to be like Him, and He desires that we operate in the spiritual realm, seeing in the spiritual realm. The spiritual realm is a realm which requires faith, and your faith will never increase until you exercise it. I know many people have a problem with this because they will say, *"But I am not telling the truth if I say I am healed when I still have symptoms."* Here is the thing, God says we are to believe something before it happens – how can we do that if we don't speak it before it happens? No, in reality my spouse may not really seem like he is changing for the better, but if I cannot see him changing, then he will remain just like he is. I must be able to see him through God's eyes not my natural eyes. It's up to each of us to decide what we really want out of life. If we want to remain sick in order to gain sympathy, then we can remain that way, but if we really want our healing, then it is time to believe it is happening before it shows on the surface. Faith is what moves those mountains in our lives and nothing else is going to do that for you. God wants to see His people today exercise the faith that He has given them so that it can grow. When our faith grows, those things we have believed for may actually manifest much faster.

Proverbs 6:2 (HCSB) ² you have been trapped by the words of your lips—ensnared by the words of your mouth.

We are all trapped by our words or ensnared. Whatever goes on in our lives, our words will determine the end result. Once you get the revelation that much of your defeat and victory depends on your own words, you will also recognize that you will be tested in these areas in order to grow you.

Proverbs 8:8 (HCSB) *8All the words of my mouth are righteous; none of them are deceptive or perverse.*

Let's look at two words here, deceptive and perverse. When we are deceptive, we will mislead others as well as ourselves. Someone who is deceptive is unreliable and not trustworthy. If you are going in the wrong direction, it is not because God has not given you a clear path. God does not mislead us, and He even left us with the Holy Spirit to lead and guide us safely through this life, but our words or thoughts influence our decisions we make and the actions we take. As we let go and allow the Holy Spirit to lead us, we must put our trust in God. We have spent years trusting our parents for the solution, trusting loved ones such as a spouse, trusting in our jobs to pull us through, welfare or the government, and even putting trust in that attorney to bring us a settlement that will solve all our problems. Even the dollar bill says, *"In God we trust!"* The dollar does not tell us to trust in the almighty dollar but the almighty God. This is the only One that we can put our trust in that will never let us down.

Perverse means wicked, bad, mean, vicious, etc. When we speak over someone something that is not good, we need to ask ourselves if our words were intended for good or for evil.

Ephesians 4:29 (AMP) *29Let no foul or polluting language, nor evil word nor unwholesome or worthless talk [ever] come out of your mouth, but only such [speech] as is good and beneficial to the spiritual progress of*

112

others, as is fitting to the need and the occasion, that it may be a blessing and give grace (God's favor) to those who hear it.

Are our words that we speak over someone else or even to their face ever meant to be mean and vicious? When we speak perverse things over someone else, we are bringing that judgment back upon ourselves and our own family. The adjective form of perverse is to be stubborn, obstinate, headstrong, contrary, disobedient, rebellious, and unreasonable. Do we act stubbornly because we are selfish and want our way and not God's way? Do we act contrary to what the Word of God says knowing which way we should turn but making our own decision to go against God's way because we are headstrong? Are we disobedient and rebellious towards God? We are if we are doing things our way and not God's. Was it not the disobedience of the children of Israel that led them in circles for 40 years because they were so headstrong and blinded from the truth? The end result of bad actions not only allows for ourselves to be misled and bound in an endless desert, but we are also misleading those around us. We influence those around us. Never think your actions only affect you because your choices affect those you love. Our choices affect those we would die for, our children, parents, siblings, etc. Yet, our choices also keep us in bondage along with those we love. If parents were only able to see that the world they have built for their children is far from a perfect world as long as they are doing things man's way and not God's. In fact, if we could only see as parents that we have only built a world for our children contrary to God's Word, would we awaken and repent knowing that the end result is that our own children will die a spiritual death? Would they run to God crying out for repentance in order to turn things around so that they are not bound in their own little desert along with those they love? Probably not because man from the beginning of time, has always wanted to do things his

113

own way. Man has always wanted to be in charge and the result is that we influence all those around us and they follow our same path in life instead of God's. Most today are blinded and cannot even see this and then there are those who see nothing wrong with their choices because the results are what they wanted. Yet, does God evolve in the middle? Is God the focus of your life and did you raise your children to know God as the center of their life? If not, you more than likely have followed your own path in life and not God's. Then there are families who can see that they missed it and the result upon their children's lives are not as they had hoped for. These families are in a place to be teachable in order to receive God's grace and unmerited favor?

Luke 5:32 (NLT) ³²*I have come to call not those who think they are righteous, but those who know they are sinners and need to repent."*

You see, Jesus tells us in Luke that He came for those that know they are sinners. He did not come for those that think they are righteous. Those that think they have arrived are not the teachable of this world.

We all have a chance to do it God's way and live victoriously, but there must be the decision to let go of the control by having it your way and instead, giving it to God. This is laying down our lives and becoming teachable. In order to give it to a God we cannot see, requires faith we have never gained. If you find yourself ensnared today by your own words and you have been walking in circles in your desert, it is never too late to turn to God and begin a new walk of victory. As you begin to travel this new road, your eyes and ears will be opened to a new world. As you grow in faith and righteousness, those you have influenced will also be watching the new found energy which will emanate through you.

114

Righteousness Speaks

We are beginning to learn who we are in Christ and the power through Him and the Holy Spirit that is within us. Once we gain this insight, we will begin to see how those very battles that we once looked at as huge mountains which were unobtainable, actually become just what we need to grow and increase us. Righteousness is the first place where we will begin to line up our thoughts with what the Word of God says and not what the world speaks over us. When our thoughts begin to line up with the Word, so will what we speak. As I have said, our words and thoughts must both line up with God's Word. It is amazing how our senses all go hand in hand. In other words, what we thrust our eyes upon will be what generates our thought patterns and then this is what will proceed out of our mouths. What we speak either limits our intelligence or it increases our intelligence. Of course, the world will look at this as the wisdom of the world, but on the contrary, it is God's wisdom which will increase our intelligence. The more we put in of the Word of God, the greater wisdom we will obtain and this will be what we speak. Therefore, it is correct to say that righteousness speaks righteous. In studying the Word, our aim should be to learn of God not to be able to say, *"I have read the Bible front to back."* Many people have done just that and have acquired no wisdom. The Scriptures do not come alive to those who are reading just to read but rather to those who are reading to seek truth and gain knowledge – true knowledge as they search for God. God knows His people, and those who are His, their eyes are open to see truth. In studying, we should have goals. There should be a goal to know the difference between worldly wisdom and God's wisdom; there should be a goal to know the difference between worldly love and God's love; there should be a goal to know just who we are in Christ, who we were created to be, the reason we were created, and our purpose while here on earth. These are just some of the many things which can be gained through the Scriptures, but we must know that we will never be able to see ourselves the way God sees us if we do not seek to find out just how He sees us. And, if we do not know how God sees us, our mouth will continually speak contrary to the Word of God, which is not pleasing to Him.

After working on your thoughts and those words which proceed out of your mouth, it is also a good idea to post positive statements around your home or even in your car. Put them in a place you are sure to see them daily. I have done this in my own home and still do today. We all use our mirror in the bathroom where we stand each morning and every night. The statements need to be something you battle with. If you battle with being able to see yourself as God sees you, then you need to place Scripture up that states how He sees you. Before we go any further, I have some Scriptures I would like to share so it is clear just how God does see each of us.

Jeremiah 1:5 (NKJV) [5] *"Before I formed you in the womb I knew you; Before you were born I sanctified you; I ordained you a prophet to the nations."*

God knew you before you knew yourself. You may be saying that He was just talking to Jeremiah, but let's not limit God. Remember, He is God, and if He knew Jeremiah before he was formed in the womb, do you not think that He knew you also? I remember a time when God was bringing me to the place where I needed to be able to love and forgive. These two actions go hand in hand and cannot be accomplished if we cannot first see how He loves and forgives us individually. We must be able to see that God can forgive us just as easily as He forgives someone else.

We were all created equally. God began to show me that He knew me before I was even formed in my mother's womb. I have shared with others many times how God led me back to my past. Sometimes, we need to go back – way back in order to heal and begin again. First, He brought me back to a time prior to my conception, reminding me of how many abortions my mother had because my father wanted no children. I cannot remember the exact number but to this day, I had never heard of anyone having the amount of abortions that my mother had. Finally, my mother came to the place where she did say, *"No more!"* After that place, God brought me all the way back to when I was in my mother's womb. My mother was an alcoholic and drank excessively. Of course, this was not something I knew while in the womb but something I soon experienced in life growing up. My mother died when I was a teenager, and I can remember friends of hers over the years telling me that they were surprised I was even born because of the extreme amount of alcohol she consumed while she was pregnant. After hearing these stories, I can remember, in my early 20's, standing in line to have one of my babies pictures taken, and there was this lady bragging to others about how much alcohol she consumed during her pregnancy and her child was perfectly fine. Her words sickened me because I could see my mother in her and knew what my mother's addiction had done to our family and to me personally. These are moments of unforgiveness; these are moments of hurt and pain. This is why it is important to face our past in order to heal. There is a lot of revelation God has given me in order to forgive and heal from my past, but the point I want to clarify here is that God showed me that even in my mother's womb there was a purpose, and He ultimately destined me to live. This was not the end but the beginning. After He brought me to that place, He then brought me to the place as a toddler when I died completely, and doctors brought me back to life. Again, God intervened because there was a purpose. Once again, as a teenager, I died from a drug overdose, and as I was traveling into the unknown, I was able to see my limp body below. At that moment, I cried out to God who gave me another chance at this life because there was a purpose. Never think your life does not have purpose and that God does not know you or love you. We all have a purpose, but it depends on what choices we make to ensure we walk in that path which He destined for us.

1 Corinthians 2:9 (AMP) *⁹But, on the contrary, as the Scripture says, What eye has not seen and ear has not heard and has not entered into the heart of man, [all that] God has prepared (made and keeps ready) for those who love Him [who hold Him in affectionate reverence, promptly obeying Him and gratefully recognizing the benefits He has bestowed].*

How does God see us? Scripture shows that God has prepared for those who love Him things that others will never witness or see. When we draw close to God, we grow to love Him. It will only be those who love Him that will experience the benefits that God has set aside and prepared. Recently, God has been opening my eyes to see things which only come to those who diligently seek Him. What I mean by that is, as you continue on your journey to know God to a greater degree, He faithfully opens Scripture to reveal things kept secret. I know that I was a rebel in my teens and continue to be a rebel serving Christ. Those in religious circles believe things should never be stirred up but remain in order. However, in biblical days, the disciples stirred up things every place they went.

Acts 17:4-6 (ESV) *⁴And some of them were persuaded and joined Paul and Silas, as did a great many of the devout Greeks and not a few of the leading women. ⁵But the Jews were jealous, and taking some wicked men of the rabble, they formed a mob, set the city in an uproar, and attacked the house of Jason, seeking to bring them out to the crowd. ⁶ And when they could not find them, they dragged Jason and some of the brothers before the city authorities, shouting, "These men who have turned the world upside down have come here also,*

How does God see us? He sees us as leaders not followers. God sees us as being radical when it comes to proclaiming Jesus to the world. It did not matter to Paul or to Silas what man could do to them because they had a purpose just like you have a purpose. You may have said that you have always been a rebel just like I have, but believe it or not, that can be a good thing. If we submit our will to God, there may be times that we need to be a rebel. As we can see in Acts, Paul and Silas would have been looked upon by the world as rebels. God will take that which was used for evil and turn it into good. However, the world and the religious leaders may see a rebel as being destructive and ungodly, yet God needs rebels for His cause. God will take those radical beliefs, radical visions, and radical personalities to train them for His purpose. Those who have a pioneering spirit, those that desire to continually seek for things others will not, they continually go into territories that others will not, will see things others will not. As we make that choice to say, *"God, send me; I will go where you lead even though others may criticize, persecute, and ridicule – nothing matters as long as my feet are planted on the path you choose for me,"* we will have experiences that others will not. If you desire great revelation from God, go into territories that others will not go. If you desire great wisdom and knowledge, set out to do things others will not do. If you desire more of the gifts of the Spirit to operate in your life, never be afraid to be that forerunner for God. I can remember fund raisers that I organized in order to send new Christians away to encounters to jump-start their growth. We would do car washes and bring in enough for many to attend free. It helped to know the background on those at the carwash prior to Christ or *"BC"* because I would know where to place them for a successful carwash. It was amazing that those who had been drug dealers, strippers, and hustlers, had a gift for talking to people and bringing in more funds. I would call them *"Hustlers for Christ."* Please don't get religious on me; Jesus loves the drug dealers, strippers, prostitutes, and hustlers as much as He loves you.

Isaiah 43:25 (HCSB) [25] *"It is I who sweep away your transgressions for My own sake and remember your sins no more.*

Psalm 103:12 (NLT) [12] *He has removed our sins as far from us as the east is from the west.*

How does God see us? As we draw closer to Him desiring what He desires, He sweeps away all those things we have done wrong, and He even forgets them. Does that mean God literally does not remember those bad things we have done? When God looks upon those who are His, He sees us created in His likeness and image. When He sweeps away our sins, we have a clean slate. When He looks upon us, it is as though we never did those things because He wiped the slate clean. Think about someone who has been in trouble with the law. Many times if it is your first offense, you can have the charges adjudicated which wipes the slate clean. When your charges are adjudicated, they are sealed never to be opened as long as you remain changed. This does not mean that you can continue to live a life of crime because you will fall. When we come to God for forgiveness, it is not a *"get out of jail free card."* God knows our heart, and He knows if our repentance is real or not. If you are changed on the inside, God looks at you through His eyes as who He created, His son or daughter, covered by grace – a new creation. We become our worst enemy because it is not God that sees us as being nothing, we see ourselves as being unable to overcome and change.

1 John 3:1 (AMP) [1]*SEE WHAT [an incredible] quality of love the Father has given (shown, bestowed on) us, that we should [be permitted to] be named and called and counted the children of God! And so we are! The reason that the world does not know (recognize, acknowledge) us is that it does not know (recognize, acknowledge) Him.*

How does God see us? Through His eyes, you are His child. I don't believe we really think about that. How many times as a Christian do we think, *"Wow, I am a child of the God who created everything I can see"?* I know we don't think like that because if we did, we wouldn't walk around defeated all the time. I discussed in chapter one about how your life would be different if your natural father was a billionaire. Ask yourself, if he was a billionaire, would you be living like you do right now? Yet, our Father is more than a billionaire and wants more for us. When I talk about more – where is your heart? I'm sure most would be thinking, *"Man, if my dad was a billionaire, I wouldn't be living in this house, I would be in a mansion,"* or *"If my dad was a billionaire, I would never have to work again and would be set for life."* I know most people who play the lottery have already played over and over again in their minds everything they would buy if they were to win that money. Our minds are focused on things. The Bible doesn't say that money is the root to all evil, but the love of money is the root to all evil.

1 Timothy 6:10 (NLT) [10]*For the love of money is the root of all kinds of evil. And some people, craving money, have wandered from the true faith and pierced themselves with many sorrows.*

Then you will have people say, *"Well, I'm okay because I don't love money, I just need it to live."* If you have said that, you may be wrong and unable to see it. When we are bound in something, our eyes have been blinded from the truth, and it is the truth that sets us free. What am I talking about here? We are talking about being able to see ourselves as righteous before God, but many times, there are areas that keep us from God and when this happens, we have become blinded. When we dream about having things that money can buy, those things become our idols. Yes, when those things become our idols, we have a love for money which is the root to all kinds of evil. You may say, *"Well, I'm not evil."* Why do we think our judgment is correct? If the Bible says that many will stand before God thinking that they are getting into heaven but God will say, *"Depart from me for I never knew you,"* why do we think our judgment is accurate?

Luke 13:26-27 (NLT) [26] *Then you will say, 'But we ate and drank with you, and you taught in our streets.'* [27] *And he will reply, 'I tell you, I don't know you or where you come from. Get away from me, all you who do evil.'*

This Scripture is not speaking to those in the world that we see as evil. Those who are living lives full of wickedness, they know they are not going to heaven. Therefore, it would be safe to say that God will be speaking to those who think they are not evil – yet, He declares they are evil. One area that needs to change within each of us is to understand that God's ways are not man's ways. His thoughts are not our thoughts nor are His ways.

Isaiah 55:7-9 (AMP) [7] *Let the wicked forsake his way and the unrighteous man his thoughts; and let him return to the Lord, and He will have love, pity, and mercy for him, and to our God, for He will multiply to him His abundant pardon.* [8] *For My thoughts are not your thoughts, neither are your ways My ways, says the Lord. [9] For as the heavens are higher than the earth, so are My ways higher than your ways and My thoughts than your thoughts.*

Basically, this Scripture should teach us that every thought and every way we have been programmed to believe and act upon has been man's thoughts and ways. We perceive evil as those who fit the profile according to man's beliefs, yet God's profile for evil includes those whose thoughts are unrighteous because they do not line up to His Word. When I went into homes to minister to those who never went to church, they had no problem admitting they were not right with God. Yet, most people in church believe they are right with God. Many will be surprised to see that they will not enter into heaven. I would much rather judge myself harshly than fall astray into the evils of this world and be blinded from truth. I believe it is good practice to pray daily, *"Father, test my heart that it remains pure and that there are no distractions that keep me from seeing the truth."* Then when we hear truth, instead of getting upset and saying, *"Well, that word is not for me because I am not like that,"* why can't we say, *"Father, if that is me, show me and change me?"* You see, when we are not open to changing and cannot see that perhaps we are missing it, we will fall short of heaven. If our heart is not pure, we will never make it into heaven. I know that it is hard to think otherwise, but if you all of a sudden had a billion dollars, it would probably destroy you and lead you straight to hell. You probably don't have that billion because God already knows what the consequence would be. In fact, did you know that God blocked Adam and Eve from being able to go into the Garden of Eden after their fall, not out of anger or for punishment but because He loved them and desired to give man a way out? Sometimes, we go through things for our own good just like Adam and Eve. Most of us do not realize that. How could it have been for their own good to have taken them out of paradise? You see, they ate from the tree of good and evil, but they did not eat from the tree of life.

Genesis 3:22-24 (AMP) [22] And the Lord God said, Behold, the man has become like one of Us [the Father, Son, and Holy Spirit], to know [how to distinguish between] good and evil and blessing and calamity; and now, lest he put forth his hand and take also from the tree of life and eat, and live forever—[23] Therefore the Lord God sent him forth from the Garden of Eden to till the ground from which he was taken. [24] So [God] drove out the man; and He placed at the east of the Garden of Eden the cherubim and a flaming sword which turned every way, to keep and guard the way to the tree of life.

Was God punishing man because He did not want us to have eternal life? No, on the contrary, God desires that man live forever with Him. God knew if man would have eaten from the tree of life, they would have lived forever in their sinful state. God wanted better for us; He wanted us to live forever with Him not forever in a world filled with evil, hurt, pain, rape, incest, and complete destruction. We can see by the Scripture, the reason for keeping man out of the Garden of Eden was so they would not live forever as things were. When we live our lives in sin, destruction will come. Living apart from God results in unhappiness and sufferings. If we look at Revelation, it is clear that God desires man to live forever once we overcome. To overcome simply means to replace our desires with God's desires. Remember, His ways and thoughts are not ours. In order to do good and not evil, it must line up with God's Word.

Revelation 2:7 (AMP) [7] He who is able to hear, let him listen to and give heed to what the Spirit says to the assemblies (churches). To him who overcomes (is victorious), I will grant to eat [of the fruit] of the tree of life, which is in the paradise of God.

Romans 12:21 (AMP) *²¹Do not let yourself be overcome by evil, but overcome (master) evil with good.*

How does God see us? God looks upon us with love, the same kind of love we exhibit towards our own children or spouse. The love is pure, complete, unselfish, and genuine.

1 John 4:9 (ESV) ⁹In this the love of God was made manifest among us, that God sent his only Son into the world, so that we might live through him.

How many of us would give up one of our own children to save someone we barely know? Or, how many of us would give up one of our own children to save someone we do know, but we also know that they live a life full of evil? I believe we would all say that we would not sacrifice our children for anyone on this earth. Yet, God's love for mankind is so great, that He allowed Jesus to suffer immensely for us. I'm not going to say He allowed Him to die for mankind because we all know that God raised Him from the dead; therefore, Jesus only died a physical death which we will all do in order to be raised spiritually. Still the same, God allowed Him to suffer. I think I can speak for all of us when I say, we would not sit there and allow people to torture those we love dearly, even if it meant dying to try and stop the crowds. Yet, God allowed the torment and endured what He felt as a Father knowing He could have stopped it and didn't, even when Jesus cried out, *"My God, My God, why have you forsaken me?"*

Mark 15:34 (NIV) ³⁴And at three in the afternoon Jesus cried out in a loud voice, "Eloi, Eloi, lema sabachthani?" *(which means* "My God, my God, why have you forsaken me?"*).*

125

How does God see us? He looks upon us through eyes of a loving Father always believing the best; He is long-suffering, patient and kind. He is God!

2 Peter 3:9 (AMP) *⁹The Lord does not delay and is not tardy or slow about what He promises, according to some people's conception of slowness, but He is long-suffering (extraordinarily patient) toward you, not desiring that any should perish, but that all should turn to repentance.*

God has an amazing amount of love for man-kind. We are His creation, and He desires so much more for us than we could ever imagine. How does God see us? Through the loving eyes of a Father looking down upon all of us saying, *"If you could only see just how much I love you. I knew you before you were even in the womb, and I have done everything on my part to ensure that you will live forever with Me without sin, without suffering, without pain, without fear or worries. If you would only trust Me, you will overcome!"* No, that is not in the Bible but that is God's heart, and if we studied more to really know Him, we could hear that small voice speak these very words to each of us. If we have allowed things to separate us from Christ, it is because of our choices not God's. There is absolutely nothing in this world or out of this world that can keep you from God but yourself.

Romans 8:38-39 (ESV) *³⁸For I am sure that neither death nor life, nor angels nor rulers, nor things present nor things to come, nor powers, ³⁹nor height nor depth, nor anything else in all creation, will be able to separate us from the love of God in Christ Jesus our Lord.*

I could go on and on with Scriptures that show how great our God is and how much He desires and loves us, but we will never see that until we seek Him and find Him for ourselves. As you will

126

read this more than once, but I always tell others that you cannot make it to heaven on someone else's coattail. Seeing the love that a Father has for their children, shows us how that Father sees His children. How does God see you today? God is dreaming about you today, and it is not a dream about you winning the lottery, it is not a dream about you having a fabulous career, it is not a dream about you acquiring the riches of this world, but it is a dream about the plan He has for you which was implemented before you were even born. It is up to you to decide if you want to walk down that path He designed specifically for you. I hope that you make that choice today.

Jeremiah 29:11 (NLT) ¹¹ For I know the plans I have for you," says the LORD. "They are plans for good and not for disaster, to give you a future and a hope.

Other Scriptures below that speak of the goodness of God and His desires for His children:

Luke 11:13 (NIV) ¹³ If you then, though you are evil, know how to give good gifts to your children, how much more will your Father in heaven give the Holy Spirit to those who ask him!"

The Holy Spirit is by far the greatest gift that has been given to God's children.

Luke 15:10 (ESV) ¹⁰ Just so, I tell you, there is joy before the angels of God over one sinner who repents."

Psalm 84:11 (ESV) ¹¹ For the LORD God is a sun and shield; the LORD bestows favor and honor. No good thing does he withhold from those who walk uprightly.

Romans 8:15 (ESV) [15]*For you did not receive the spirit of slavery to fall back into fear, but you have received the Spirit of adoption as sons, by whom we cry, "Abba! Father!"*

Zephaniah 3:17 (ESV) [17]*The LORD your God is in your midst, a mighty one who will save; he will rejoice over you with gladness; he will quiet you by his love; he will exult over you with loud singing.*

2 Corinthians 5:18-19 (NIV) [18]*All this is from God, who reconciled us to himself through Christ and gave us the ministry of reconciliation:* [19]*that God was reconciling the world to himself in Christ, not counting people's sins against them. And he has committed to us the message of reconciliation.*

1 John 4:16 (ESV) [16]*So we have come to know and to believe the love that God has for us. God is love, and whoever abides in love abides in God, and God abides in him.*

Isaiah 62:5 (NKJV) [5]*For as a young man marries a virgin, So shall your sons marry you; And as the bridegroom rejoices over the bride, So shall your God rejoice over you.*

Lamentations 3:22-23 (ESV) [22]*The steadfast love of the LORD never ceases; his mercies never come to an end;* [23]*they are new every morning; great is your faithfulness.*

Romans 3:22 (NLT) [22]*We are made right with God by placing our faith in Jesus Christ. And this is true for everyone who believes, no matter who we are.*

Ephesians 5:8 (AMP) [8]*For once you were darkness, but now you are light in the Lord; walk as children of Light [lead the lives of those native-born to the Light].*

Matthew 6:33 (ESV) [33] *But seek first the kingdom of God and his righteousness, and all these things will be added to you.*

These Scriptures, along with many others, are great examples to write down and tape up in various places within your home or car so that you see them often as a reminder of how God really sees you. Another way we can begin to see ourselves as God does, would be to begin stepping out of our box. Many times, we cannot see ourselves as changed because we choose to remain in our same surroundings; we refuse to do anything different. This is not about just memorizing who we are in Christ, but rather, it is about getting it inside of us enough that we actually begin to conform to be more and more like Jesus on a daily basis. This does not happen unless we are willing to do what God is calling us to do. In changing our old ways to be a better person all the way around, we have to learn to let go of what is comfortable and actually step out of our box. Now don't start panicking because this is not a bad thing. I assure you that if you listen to what I am teaching and act on what I am saying, you will see a different person in the near future. As this manifests in your life, you will begin to see a new person on the inside that will also be happier, more peaceful, and better in-tuned to God and the spiritual realm. Others will begin to also see you as different in a good way. Make this a goal but begin today. Step out of your box each day and do one thing that you would not normally do.

Examples:

• Be nice to someone that you normally are not nice to

• Do something special for someone including someone you barely know

• Take time out for someone that you rarely spend time with

• Give up something in order to bless someone besides yourself

I am sure you can think of many other things you could do, and it will actually feel good to do something different. As you begin doing these things, it will not be long until you hear that voice of God speak to you and show you His desires for your walk with Him. Many times, I have paid for someone's bill in a store when they would not have enough money; I have bought someone's lunch; I would see something in the store which reminded me of someone and would buy it for them just because I could; I have dropped everything and driven someone out of town because they had no way to get there. I could go on and on, but the main thing is that you desire to be more like Jesus and all this role play is just getting rid of those things within you which are like the world and not like our Savior, Jesus Christ.

How Great is thy Heart

The mind functions through the thought process in our brains, which is protected by the Helmet of Salvation. This works hand in hand with the Breastplate of Righteousness because our mind has to believe we are righteous and this begins to change our heart. Once we begin to see ourselves as capable of being something, our heart begins to soften and change to be more and more like Christ. Jesus had compassion which was so great for mankind, that He gave His life in order for us to live. One of the most remarkable things is to think about when Jesus was hanging on that cross being tortured, ridiculed, and tormented. He cried out to God the Father to forgive the very people who were causing all the pain mentally and physically on His body at that moment.

130

That is compassion for mankind to the greatest degree. I do not believe any of us in the midst of being tortured would be praying for the very people instigating that pain.

Applying the Breastplate of Righteousness to our lives goes beyond our reasoning unless our mind is one with God. This is a righteous act of saying, *"God, let me be all You created me to be as I give of myself for Your purpose and not mine."* Isn't that what Jesus said on the Cross at Calvary? Jesus died and gave of Himself an unselfish act which equaled righteousness. Jesus was already righteous, but He paid this price so that we could also be righteous. It is when we give of ourselves with a right heart that we become righteous in God's sight. It is when we let go of those things we desire and of our own selfish ambitions for a greater cause that we become righteous. When we begin that first step of salvation, coming to recognize and know Jesus Christ, there should be a difference which begins within. Even though our outwardly appearance may be the same, what begins to happen within should be felt. Everything begins within, and in order to be righteous in God's sight, it starts with our heart. The outwardly will never change unless the heart changes. The circumstances surrounding you will never change unless YOUR heart changes. If we are continually complaining about our lives, if we are dissatisfied about where we are today, if we can find nothing good within or without, please know that it has nothing to do with your spouse, your children, your job, or bad luck. However, it has everything to do with YOUR heart. When we first come to know Jesus Christ, our lives should feel a change deep within even if it is just to a small degree. When we come to know Jesus, our nature begins to change. The Bible speaks of this new nature as a new birth. This is where they get the saying of being born again.

Galatians 6:15 (AMP) *[15]For neither is circumcision [now] of any importance, nor uncircumcision, but [only] a new creation [the result of a new birth and a new nature in Christ Jesus, the Messiah].*

When we experience this new change within, we no longer desire that sinful nature. This does not mean we will never sin again, but we feel that change within and our desires begin to want to live more complete and holy. This of course is a gradual process just like with a new born baby, they gradually begin to learn and grow.

1 John 5:18 (AMP) *[18]We know [absolutely] that anyone born of God does not [deliberately and knowingly] practice committing sin, but the One Who was begotten of God carefully watches over and protects him [Christ's divine presence within him preserves him against the evil], and the wicked one does not lay hold (get a grip) on him or touch [him].*

If we become a child of God through the process of salvation, our blood should no longer be tainted with the blood of the first Adam but rather Jesus Christ.

1 Corinthians 15:45 (NLT) *[45]The Scriptures tell us, "The first man, Adam, became a living person." But the last Adam—that is, Christ—is a life-giving Spirit.*

We should have undergone a DNA change that says we now belong to God the Father. Realizing you are not the same person within begins to plant those seeds of righteousness. Even when we miss it, this does not mean our blood becomes tainted again. Even when we mess up, we are still God's child. God knows we must grow. He knows as we come to see who we really are, that our desires will change to want to learn more of Him. As we learn, we begin to take off the old and put on the new. This is basically getting the ugly stuff out of us and replacing it with good.

Colossians 3:5-10 (ESV) *⁵ Put to death therefore what is earthly in you: sexual immorality, impurity, passion, evil desire, and covetousness, which is idolatry. ⁶ On account of these the wrath of God is coming. ⁷ In these you too once walked, when you were living in them. ⁸ But now you must put them all away: anger, wrath, malice, slander, and obscene talk from your mouth. ⁹ Do not lie to one another, seeing that you have put off the old self with its practices ¹⁰ and have put on the new self, which is being renewed in knowledge after the image of its creator.*

However, we also need to understand that just because we have begun the process of being saved, we are still capable of back-sliding to a place that we lose our inheritance. We need to be able to see some things here. Once you become a Christian, you begin running a race in order to get to the finish.

Hebrews 12:1 (ESV) *12 Therefore, since we are surrounded by so great a cloud of witnesses, let us also lay aside every weight, and sin which clings so closely, and let us run with endurance the race that is set before us,*

When the Bible talks about laying aside every weight, a runner knows that they must be prepared for the race at hand. If there is anything that would keep you from making it to the finish line, you need to lay it aside. I know I have shared many times with those I minister to that we may have to let go of certain friends or even family members as we strive to run this race, but this does not mean that we throw them away – we lay them aside. When we lay something to the side, it remains there until we pick it up again, right? There may be a time that an old friend or those family members reach out to you because they see how your life has changed, and they have become tired of struggling in this world. So, we must see that as a runner, we remove any and everything that may get in our way. As a runner, we need to make sure that we are in good condition for the race at hand. We also need to make sure that we are physically, mentally, and emotionally ready for the race at hand. This takes discipline and sometimes hard work, but if we desire that our lives line up with God's Word, we must make that commitment to do what it takes. Why begin a race and not finish it? Yet, that is what most Christians do. They either begin the race and give up somewhere in the middle or they continue on the race at a turtles pace. We all know the story about the *"Tortoise and the Hare."* Yes, the turtle eventually won the race but that was because the hare was boastful. The hare believed it was such a joke for the turtle to even take him on and his attitude caused him the race. Yet, in reality, we are on a race, and it is a race that we run with patience keeping in mind that at the finish, we receive the prize.

1 Corinthians 9:24 (ESV) *24 Do you not know that in a race all the runners run, but only one receives the prize? So run that you may obtain it.*

Yes, in a race only one receives the prize, and this means we are to run and give it everything possible so that we gain that prize. This is not saying only one person gets the prize; this shows what our mindset should be. If we were in a natural race and knew that everyone in that race would receive a prize just to finish the race, how hard would we run? We might as well run as the turtle if all you had to do was finish. However, knowing that it is not about just finishing the race but about everything we do from the time we begin until the time we finish. You see, the hare could have won the race, except he began to think more highly of himself than he should have. We too must be careful and know that it is not because of anything we can do in ourselves that gains the prize, but it is through Jesus Christ that we are even able to run the race and finish. When we finish this race, the victor's crown of life awaits us. Yet, we can see that the man who wins this race not only finishes but does so with patience even under trials and temptations.

James 1:12 (AMP) [12]*Blessed (happy, to be envied) is the man who is patient under trial and stands up under temptation, for when he has stood the test and been approved, he will receive [the victor's] crown of life which God has promised to those who love Him.*

During our race, we must prepare, which is exactly what we are doing as we seek God in every avenue. It is not about just attending a church service once a week. If you went to school to be a doctor, could you possibly learn all that you need to know by attending school for 2 hours once a week? Absolutely not! I believe our mindset has to be where we keep our eyes fixed on the finish line or we will never make it. As we prepare to fix our eyes on striving for the finish, we will soon come to realize that we will never finish without Jesus. The hare had something within him that kept him from winning. The hare had no compassion for others but only for himself. The hare was boastful, selfish, and all about himself. As we talk about our heart, during our race we begin to see just how selfish we are. We come into this world as a baby and soon learn that it's all about what we can get. We strive day in and day out to gain the riches of this world. Yet, those things we strive to acquire will be the very things that weigh us down where we will never make it to the finish. As we begin running the race, we will soon become tired and slow down. As our pace slows down, our eyes will drift away to the riches of this world. In fact, the Scriptures even show us that many fall back into bondage.

Galatians 5:7-8 (NLT) *[7]You were running the race so well. Who has held you back from following the truth? [8] It certainly isn't God, for he is the one who called you to freedom.*

God calls us to freedom, yet even though we began the race, many will fall back. If we are not free according to Scripture, then we are bound. Once we take our eyes off of Jesus, we fall right back into the bondage we once lived. When we fall away from the truth, we accept the lies from the world and the enemy. We were accepted into the family of God, but we chose to walk away. Isn't that like a divorce? Do we divorce God and choose the world again? What does divorce cause? Ask anyone who has gone through a divorce and they will tell you it is not pleasant and the cost can be severe. Once we choose to walk away, we lose our inheritance. If we lose our inheritance, we lose the privileges that go along with being part of God's family. We lose the blessings, the peace, joy, compassion, etc. If your life is a mess, you are not living as one who is righteous. Even if you are backslidden today, you can choose to come home. God welcomes you back as a loving father would. We are given that example by the story of the prodigal son.

Luke 15:20 (ESV) *[20]And he arose and came to his father. But while he was still a long way off, his father saw him and felt compassion, and ran and embraced him and kissed him.*

You see, no matter how bad we have messed up, God still waits and waits continually crying out, *"Come home; come home."* Sometimes we think that God could never forgive us for the horrible things we have done, but that is a lie from satan. I have something I want to share at this time. I had a daughter who was the prodigal daughter, yet I continued to pray and pray for her to come home. I continued each day to wait and watch, knowing that she would return. The day came and I took her in with loving arms and welcomed her just as God welcomes us back into the family. Below, is something she wrote that God had spoken to her off and on through the years she followed her own path. One night, during the 4th night of the watch, which in biblical times would be somewhere between 3 a.m. and 6 a.m., God woke her as He began to minister to her. As she began to cry, she wrote down what I am about to share. These words are those things He had spoken to her many times during her life as she was caught up in the lies and deceptions of this world.

A Letter from God...

I know that you cry for me. I know that you think of me from time to time. I know when hands are laid upon you for prayer, you hurt and cry even more. I know why you hurt. I know you hurt because the things you do are not of me. I know you do not like the things you do. I know you do not understand why you do these hurtful things. I hear you when you cry My name. You seek me out for comfort, then go right back to your sinful ways. I know that when you are weak and on your worldly high, you feel bad and think of me. I know that when you come down off your worldly high, you are sad and cry out to me. But, after the tears are gone, you're right back to your sinful ways. I know you want to change so bad and claim you don't know how. But, that is a lie. I know that you feel trapped like there is no way out. But, that is a lie. Did you know that I cry for you too? Did you know that I love you? Did you know I am your strength when you feel weak? Did you know that I am your way out? Did you know that I wait for you? Did you know that I call your name? But, you don't turn around; you never do. Did you know that every time you cry, I cry with you?

Take a minute to let those words sink in. I know when I first read it, I cried. Do we really understand how much the God of the

Universe loves us? I don't believe we do because if so, we would turn from our sinful ways and run to Him with open arms. Yes, we will always have trouble as long as we are in this world, but the trouble doesn't have us. There is a difference. If your Daddy is King of Kings and Lord of Lords, He has the solutions to walk through every trial, test, circumstance, and trouble that comes your way. In walking through those things which concern you, you have the privilege to do so with God's peace, joy, faith, hope, and love. Begin today letting go of the junk in your life that keeps you at a place of seeing yourself as the world may see you and begin to give those things to God in order for your heart to heal. He is rising up an army of warriors today for a great battle, and it is time to choose which side you will be fighting on.

Roman Breastplate

During biblical days, common soldiers more than likely wore leather body armor with bronze or molded metal. Chainmail was another feature of biblical armor which was sometimes included. In the first diagram below, you can see the chainmail which more than likely was connected to the belt; however, chainmail was used in many areas of the armor. Chainmail was made out of small metal rings linked together to form a mesh. In biblical days, it was used in the area hanging down from the belt, it was also used for added protection in the breastplate area, and you can also find it used as a coif which was a type of covering to the head which extended down to cover the back and all sides, the neck and shoulders. When we try to gather an image in our mind of a breastplate, we must always think about what its purpose was in those days. By diagram, we know that this one piece of armor covered the heart and the lungs among other vital organs within the human body. Without this piece of armor in biblical days, soldiers would have died swiftly. With this piece of armor, most vital organs were protected in order to endure the battle at hand.

Even today, our soldiers are fully equipped with armor to protect vital organs. In fact, we even see that our police officers wear protective gear in the form of bullet-proof vests, which protects some of the same vital organs as in biblical days.

What Paul was trying to emphasize was the importance of having that breastplate and acknowledging exactly what it protected. Going into a natural battle without having the vital organs protected would basically be suicide. Our army would not last very long out in the field without proper protection. The same is true with a spiritual battle. When we make that choice to follow Christ, this is talking about getting ourselves prepared for all the tactics and strategies of our enemy. In preparation, we must know that we have the proper gear on and have learned how to use it in order to gain ground victoriously.

Standing Guard

Ephesians 6:13-14 (ESV) [13] *Therefore take up the whole armor of God, that you may be able to withstand in the evil day, and having done all, to stand firm.* [14] *Stand therefore, having fastened on the belt of truth, and having put on the breastplate of righteousness,*

Without putting on our Breastplate of Righteousness, we will never be able to stand firm. Paul spoke of standing, *"…having done all that we can do in times which are treacherous, we stand and we do so firmly."* This means, after we have done everything we know to do in the natural, we better have our battle gear on in the spiritual realm, and then, we stand and wait on God because He will come through. I cannot help but get a visual of this Scripture. It says that we take up the whole armor of God, first of all, so that we can be able to make it during the days we are living in and the days which are coming. I believe the evil days it is speaking of refer to harder times, and perhaps, it is referring to today as we are nearing the end times. It goes on to say having done all, having done all we know to do that we just stand, and we stand firm. Picture this, when you are engaged in a debate and you know you are right, what do you do? I know what we do, we cross our arms; we firmly plant our feet on solid ground, and we give our opponent that long stare which says, *"Don't go any further because I will chew you up and spit you out!"* The reason many times we come across like this is because we know we are right in what we believe, and we are willing to fight until the end to prove it. This is the mentality of a soldier. When engaged in a battle, the enemy cannot move us unless we allow it, and we allow it

140

when we begin to give up. We allow it when we begin to compromise by thinking, maybe we are wrong. However, when we know we are right and we know we are on the winning side, we stand and we do so with the authority that says, *"I am right, and I will not budge!"* You see, when we sign up to fight in God's army, we are on the winning side, and we will not lose. This mindset will only exist in those who really believe that. In the battlefield today, soldiers go through boot camp and gain this mindset, so when in the battlefield, they fight to win. That is what righteousness is all about. Righteousness believes that we really are on the winning side. Righteousness is about believing that what God's Word says is final, and there are no *"BUTS!"* Righteousness says, *"I know who I am in Christ, and I'm not going to lose because I am a winner and can do all things through Christ who gives me strength."*

Philippians 4:13 (NLT) [13] *For I can do everything through Christ, who gives me strength.*

Let me clarify, I am not speaking about trying to prove your point when you are with someone that disagrees with you. I face this situation all the time and am not going to argue with other Christians because sometimes I may be the one wrong. Here is the deal, we do not know everything in the Scriptures and your battles are not with flesh and blood but with spiritual forces. Standing your ground is about not compromising with the Word of God. This means, that you are standing for what God's Word says when the opposition is speaking what the world says or what the enemy says. I remember a pastor saying one time, to choose your battles wisely. If it is not a life or death situation, let it go. If it is not worth dying for, let it go. It doesn't matter if you believe in speaking in tongues and another Christian doesn't, let God be the one that brings truth in that situation. What I am talking about is compromising with the Word. It does matter if the opposition is telling you that God is okay with you drinking and going carousing around with those that live like the world. It does matter if the opposition is telling you that it is okay to not read your Bible as long as you are in church. It does matter if the opposition is telling you that you can watch whatever you want on television as long as you are in church. It does matter if the opposition is telling you that it doesn't matter what you do because God's grace is sufficient. It does matter if the opposition is telling you that God doesn't really mean that you can't do this or that. You better really know what the Word says instead of just agreeing with what others are telling you. All of these things are contrary to the Word of God, and all of these things will lead to a spiritual death. You must study the Word if you plan on being engaged in the battle at hand; otherwise, you are already captive to the enemy force.

If we go back to search the Scriptures, we know that Rome's military in biblical days was very powerful. Rome's military was considered very strong because they were constantly on guard day and night. This should teach us that we must also be on guard. Jesus spoke about always being on guard because no one knows the time or day when He will return, but this is not the only reason to be on guard.

Mark 13:32-36 (AMP) [32] But of that day or that hour not a [single] person knows, not even the angels in heaven, nor the Son, but only the Father. [33] Be on your guard [constantly alert], and watch and pray; for you do not know when the time will come. [34] It is like a man [already] going on a journey; when he leaves home, he puts his servants in charge, each with his particular task, and he gives orders to the doorkeeper to be constantly alert and on the watch. [35] Therefore watch (give strict attention, be cautious and alert), for you do not know when the Master of the house is coming—in the evening, or at midnight, or at cockcrowing,

142

or in the morning— [36] *[Watch, I say] lest He come suddenly and unexpectedly and find you asleep.*

In God's Boot Camp, we should conduct our everyday lives just as the military. This means, we should never let our guard down. We should always remain in close contact with God, with the Holy Spirit, and Jesus. We never take a vacation from our life source. It's funny how people go on vacation, but they leave God at home. We do not take the teachings of Christ seriously, and there will come a time when we will regret this. In order to stand and in order to remain always on guard requires that deep one on one fellowship with our Creator. It is when we drift away from God that we struggle with being able to see ourselves as righteous because there is no contact to ensure us that we are where we need to be with God. Think about it this way, if you stray away from your natural family and you do not have any contact for many years, other than maybe a phone call on occasions with just basic small talk, are those relationships very strong? No, they are not very strong because if they were, your family would be engaged in your everyday affairs. How can families care for each other when one member is down if there is little to no contact for the members to even know what goes on in each other's lives? We have all heard the saying, *"A family that prays together, stays together."* I would definitely agree and part of praying is that communication between you and God. In order for your Father in Heaven to really get to know you intimately, you must be open to allow Him an open door into your life. Yes, God knows all there is to know about us, but He will never intrude in our personal lives unless He is invited. Family members will also stay away if they do not feel that close connection to each other. Therefore, we need to remain at a place in God's army where we are in close contact with our Commander and Chief. This way, we will be more capable of

143

applying every piece of our armor in a way that will bring victory and not defeat into our life and that of our family.

Luke 11:21 (HCSB) [21] *When a strong man, fully armed, guards his estate, his possessions are secure.*

If we remain on guard, those things we have been entrusted with will remain secure. I'm not saying those things we own because we really own nothing. Everything in this earth belongs to God and the fullness of it.

Psalm 24:1 (AMP) [1] *The earth is the Lord's, and the fullness of it, the world and they who dwell in it.*

Psalm 89:11 (AMP) [11] *The heavens are Yours, the earth also is Yours; the world and all that is in it, You have founded them.*

What are we entrusted with? Our children, families, and any others we have come to love in our lives. Myself, I am grateful for not only my family but my spiritual daughters as well, and daily, I pray for each of them. When God sends people across your path that you begin to minister to and they stay and follow you, you become responsible for their spiritual being. This basically means, that you do not sugar coat anything, and what you feed them, better be truth backed by the Word of God. Not only should it be backed by God's Word, but everything we do affects all those things which concern us. I am required to not only minister righteousness to those which cross my path, but I am also required to walk it. We cannot expect others to follow us and want a deeper relationship with Jesus, if they cannot see God in us. This is why the church has received a bad name for so many years because the people on the outside witness all the wrong living among so many whom claim to be Christians, but they live no different than the world. I shudder to think of the fate of all those who proclaim to have Jesus in their lives but lead those who cross their path down the road of evil. Living a life as pure and righteous as we possibly can opens that door for fellowship with God. I know that if I am living right, God also takes care of those things which concern me. Let me also clarify that people follow God not man, but when I refer to those who are following me, it is God in me that they follow. Paul said it this way…

1 Corinthians 11:1 (AMP) *[1]Pattern yourselves after me [follow my example], as I imitate and follow Christ (the Messiah).*

It is important to see by this Scripture, we are held accountable to those who follow us.

Acts 20:28 (HCSB) *[28] Be on guard for yourselves and for all the flock, among whom the Holy Spirit has appointed you as overseers, to shepherd the church of God, which He purchased with His own blood.*

We put our armor on in order to be on guard at all times not only for ourselves but also for those God has placed in our lives. We should all be connected with other believers that are also striving to walk out this walk with Jesus. We should all be striving to live according to the principles of the Bible not just those teachings that feel good to the flesh. We should all be careful as to what teaching we are accepting and agreeing with especially in this day and time when there is so much controversy between the different denominations. If we do not know what the Word of God says, we will wind up following any doctrine and be blinded by what is truth. In biblical days, Jesus became angry when He went into the temple and saw how His Father's house had become wicked. The crowds during that time had welcomed Him into the city prior to this incident because they were looking for a Messiah to oversee them. However, when Jesus did not fit into the specifications they wanted, He was no longer welcomed. As rumors spread throughout Jerusalem, the crowds began to doubt that He was the Messiah they had longed for and as it turned out, it was the same crowds of people as well as the religious leaders who wanted Him crucified.

John 12:12-13 (AMP) [12]*The next day a vast crowd of those who had come to the Passover Feast heard that Jesus was coming to Jerusalem.* [13] *So they took branches of palm trees and went out to meet Him. And as they went, they kept shouting, Hosanna! Blessed is He and praise to Him Who comes in the name of the Lord, even the King of Israel!*

Mark 11:15-17 (AMP) [15] *And they came to Jerusalem. And He went into the temple [area, the porches and courts] and began to drive out those who sold and bought in the temple area, and He overturned the [four-footed] tables of the money changers and the seats of those who dealt in doves;* [16] *And He would not permit anyone to carry any household equipment through the temple enclosure [thus making the temple area a short-cut traffic lane].* [17] *And He taught and said to them, Is it not written, My house shall be called a house of prayer for all the nations? But you have turned it into a den of robbers.*

Matthew 27:21-23 (AMP) [21] *Again the governor said to them, Which of the two do you wish me to release for you? And they said, Barabbas!* [22] *Pilate said to them, Then what shall I do with Jesus Who is called Christ?* [23] *They all replied, Let Him be crucified! And he said, Why? What has He done that is evil? But they shouted all the louder, Let Him be crucified!*

We will never be in a different place with God if we conform to man's teachings and beliefs instead of God's. Religion will bring you to a place of bondage just like the religious leaders of that

146

day. If you desire to be in a place where you lead those you love out of sin and into righteousness, it will only happen as you draw close to the Word of God and not man's interpretations. This basically means getting to know God through Scripture personally so that you can test every spirit.

1 John 4:1 (NLT) [1]Dear friends, do not believe everyone who claims to speak by the Spirit. You must test them to see if the spirit they have comes from God. For there are many false prophets in the world.

How do we know if we are attending a church service or gathering with those proclaiming truth? One sure way to know is that the teachings you receive will be bold as those which Jesus taught. Truth many times hurts our flesh and we do not want to go back to hear a particular person teach or preach. You see, there are many things in the Word of God people do not like to hear because it ruffles their feathers and makes them feel uncomfortable. This is because that sin they are engaged in is something they do not want to let go of or change. Our natural man desires to be entertained in a way that coincides with the way we like to live. Meaning, if you enjoy living in your sin, you will feed your flesh those same evils because it is where your desires lie. On the other hand, if you desire to grow to maturity with Christ, you delight in the instructions of a man or woman of God that will teach you truth according to God's Word even if it opens your eyes to your own sins. If you continue to go to a church service which brings conviction, eventually you will begin to clean up your act because the Holy Spirit will continue to work on you to get it right. There are churches today that actually teach that every one of God's children has a ministry, and this is true. We all have a particular calling on our lives. If you are connected with other believers which believe there is more to church than just sitting on the pews, you are in a good place. We are all called, and we all have a ministry of some kind even if it is just serving. Please know, even Jesus came to serve!

Matthew 20:28 (NIV) [28] just as the Son of Man did not come to be served, but to serve, and to give his life as a ransom for many."

As we draw closer to God and develop that relationship, the Holy Spirit will begin to do a work in us and open our eyes to what we are called to do. I deeply encourage everyone to find their place in a body of believers which will help to grow you to a greater level with God. I encourage you to take every opportunity to seek small group ministries to learn more about God, more about prayer, the Holy Spirit, and every aspect of God's Word. In my prayer group, it is always evident those who truly desire to grow as a prayer warrior and be everything God intended and those who are not fully engaged. Those truly desiring a greater walk with God, continually seek a greater wisdom and knowledge which can only come by studying and time spent with our Creator. The Word says if we gain little, we are required to give back what we have gained, and if we gain much, more is required of us.

Luke 12:47-48 (NLT) [47] "And a servant who knows what the master wants, but isn't prepared and doesn't carry out those instructions, will be severely punished. [48] But someone who does not know, and then does something wrong, will be punished only lightly. When someone has been given much, much will be required in return; and when someone has been entrusted with much, even more will be required.

Do not look at this as merely financial blessings. Whatever our gain is, we are required to give back. If our gain is in knowledge, we are required to share that knowledge. God never pours out His wisdom, knowledge, and understanding for us to store it deep inside and not share with others. We will not receive more if we are stingy with what we have.

Sometimes, we do not strive to gain a lot of knowledge because we know more will be required, and we may make excuses when asked to become more involved. Sometimes, we even believe our own excuses because after all, our time is limited and this is not who we really are or what God is really calling us to do. You need to think about that if this is what you believe. God needs a mighty army of warriors, and only those who are truly ready to give whatever it takes to gain all that God desires to give them, will be successful. If you are not sure where God is calling you, then just become engaged. Step out and get involved in doing something for God. He may very well be testing you to see if you are willing to take time out of your busy schedule to help others by serving. Many times, God will not open doors until we have proven that we truly desire to give up our time.

I remember when I began pouring into God's Word, great revelation would come. The more I studied, the more I received but only as long as I was giving away what He had given to me. I have had people make comments about the great things God has shown me, and there were times people would say that they wished they could live in my home so they could learn to grow and receive from God as I was. There is no secret to receiving revelation. Anyone can receive great revelation but only if they desire it and hunger for it daily. We become too laidback in our lives and put God on the back burner instead of putting Him first. Anyone is capable of studying and seeking God to a greater degree. As you get more of Him in you, He will require you to minister to others and give back what you have learned. As you submit and are obedient in that aspect, daily you will study, you will receive, and you will share. What we feed on is what will come forth out of our mouth. If you truly desire to be a warrior, then you will learn to stand guard with your full armor on and guard not only yourself but all those souls entrusted to you. On the other hand, if you choose not to become that warrior, you will never be able to stand, and if you do not stand, you will be led away and fall from grace.

2 Peter 3:17 (HCSB) [17] *Therefore, dear friends, since you have been forewarned, be on your guard, so that you are not led away by the error of the immoral and fall from your own stability.*

You see, I cannot go back to who I was because I have people who depend on me. I must stay on guard in order to keep myself strong that I am not easily led astray by temptations. satan is always waiting for that moment when we are weak; therefore, I must use everything God has given me in order to recognize sin and remain strong. I must put on the whole armor of God each day and stand on His Word and His promises!

Fatigues of Battle

In biblical days, the Roman soldiers always carried their weapons at all times, even during times of peace. We have to understand that the Roman armor was very large and very heavy. In today's military, the uniform is nothing like that of biblical days. The uniforms today are geared for protection at a much lighter weight. Many things have been invented to not only protect but also to keep in mind durability, in terms of comfort, staying cool in extreme heat, and warm in freezing temperatures which allows less fatigue in the line of duty. Not only were the uniforms during the Roman era not designed for comfort, but the soldiers were also required to spend countless hours every day going through regiments and exercises, in order to remain in shape and to always be on guard in case war broke out. For some time, it was known that Rome's strength was in their military and all their hard work and daily routines paid off in protecting their land and people. However, even though Rome had a powerful military, all these regiments quickly began to weigh upon the soldiers, and the fatigues of battle began to be felt. There are many things we can learn from this era. Eventually, Rome fell and there were many things which contributed to their fall, but first, we need to see that some of this was due to their rigid discipline. As the military became disgruntled by what they felt was unnecessary exercises during times of peace, they began to become more relaxed, meaning they let their guard down. As Rome became slack towards their daily routines, the soldiers also came to a place where they were not as willing to continue the hard regime which had been required.

When the soldiers became more laidback from the lack of continual exercise and discipline, all of a sudden, Rome began to lose their battles. As this pattern continued, Rome no longer had a strong army to guard and protect those things which they cherished. What happens when we become lazy, uninterested in spiritual things, putting off doing what God is calling us to do, etc.? We also begin to feel that defeat in our own lives in one way or another. When we are not committed to seeking God, searching the Scriptures, studying diligently, being obedient to that small quiet voice, we become weak and feel defeated in every area of our lives. If you have ever had a strong commitment to God and spent quality time with Him, you know how it drastically changes every aspect of your life and even those around you begin to change. As soon as we become laidback, all hell begins to break loose. Those who have been in both places know this to be true, but why is it that we can know this as fact and still take a vacation from God? By this, we can see the importance of keeping our armor on at all times even when things are going great.

Let's look deeper into how we can learn from the rise and fall of the great Roman Empire. According to Paul, we put on our armor, meaning we wear it just as soldiers going to battle wear their uniform. There is a difference; one difference is in the natural realm and the other in the spiritual realm.

From a spiritual stand point, Rome was destined to fall because their treasures were stored within themselves. Having observed the Greeks intellect, the Romans applied their knowledge with action and felt they had obtained the wisdom needed to be called the elite *"Roman Empire."* The Romans stored up treasures within themselves, seeing themselves as being superior to any and every other city, culture or class of people, and they became proud and arrogant. It is no wonder that they fell. We can see by this that even if you have your armor on, it is not just about wearing it, but it is also about understanding what it symbolizes. In the natural sense, Rome became proud and felt they were superior, and this probably contributed to the soldiers attitudes of not needing to continue a daily regime of military training. Spiritually, their breastplate may have been on, but their hearts were corrupted as one who is proud and gives credit to oneself instead of God.

Proverbs 16:16-19 (NLV) [16]To get wisdom is much better than getting gold. To get understanding should be chosen instead of silver. [17] The road of the faithful turns away from sin. He who watches his way keeps his life. [18] Pride comes before being destroyed and a proud spirit comes before a fall. [19] It is better to be poor in spirit among poor people, than to divide the riches that were taken with the proud.

If you are a Christian then you should believe everything in the Word of God to be true. Paul also tells us that our battles are not with flesh and blood. Too often we try to fight our battles with our spouse, our children, our family and friends, our boss and even complete strangers. This is not our battle. If our battle is not in the natural realm, then it must be in the spiritual realm. However, we should still clothe ourselves with our armor and that is putting it on spiritually. We can see that Rome fell because they became lax and quit putting their whole armor on. By this, we know that our armor should remain on at all times. Paul teaches to keep your armor on. Jesus teaches to keep ourselves clothed and to always be on guard. When Scripture is talking about being clothed, it is referring to being clothed in a spiritual sense.

Luke 21:34-36 (AMP) [34] *But take heed to yourselves and be on your guard, lest your hearts be overburdened and depressed (weighed down) with the giddiness and headache and nausea of self-indulgence, drunkenness, and worldly worries and cares pertaining to [the business of] this life, and [lest] that day come upon you suddenly like a trap or a noose;* [35] *For it will come upon all who live upon the face of the entire earth.* [36] *Keep awake then and watch at all times [be discreet, attentive, and ready], praying that you may have the full strength and ability and be accounted worthy to escape all these things [taken together] that will take place, and to stand in the presence of the Son of Man.*

We cannot do this in the natural. We cannot keep ourselves from falling into the traps set forth by all the demonic activity which is grafted within all the self-indulgences this world has to offer. We can only be strong and stay strong as we put on our armor, which is spiritual clothing.

Romans 13:14 (AMP) [14] *But clothe yourself with the Lord Jesus Christ (the Messiah), and make no provision for [indulging] the flesh [put a stop to thinking about the evil cravings of your physical nature] to [gratify its] desires (lusts).*

153

When Jesus said to always be on guard or watching, this meant that we are to be clothed because we cannot do what God is calling us to do without our armor, and you will learn this principle throughout this book.

Matthew 25:13 (AMP) [13] *Watch therefore [give strict attention and be cautious and active], for you know neither the day nor the hour when the Son of Man will come.*

So, we stay clothed fully, even when things are going great or especially when things are going great. The enemy is always waiting for us to put our guard down, and that is when you will be attacked. Try going a few days without praying and see if you are not saying, *"Oh my, why am I going through this?"* If you have ever been consistent in prayer and then you stop, you know what I'm talking about. Now, if you have never developed that deep relationship with God, you may not know this because the devil does not see you as much of a threat and does not have to waste his time on trying to devour you. For most people that are living in sin, it is their sin that will bring destruction upon their life; satan does not really have to put forth much effort. Here is the deal, the Roman soldiers bore the fatigue of battle because they wore their gear in the physical sense. Yet, our gear has to be worn in the spiritual sense. This way we recognize when we equip ourselves with the full armor of God, that we are putting it on spiritually. We put on our armor physically when we try to do it in our natural self. This of course is trying to win a battle in our flesh and not allowing God to be our Commander and fight for us. Our strength will never be in the physical sense, and until we are able to see it has to be in the spiritual sense, we will not win our battles. In the spiritual war, it is mind over matter. This is the way that Jesus fought in the dessert. How did Jesus win His battle with satan? It was by the power of His words. Our words will either defeat us or give us victory. We should not be plagued with defeat, and we do not have to be plagued with defeat. Throughout this whole book, we must realize that every piece of armor we study is about applying this in the spiritual realm because as children of God, we were created as spiritual beings.

As Rome began to become relaxed, they also were spread so thin because many of those who had been trained to be great soldiers were no longer interested in guarding Rome. When this happened, mercenaries were hired to fill its ranks, but these were men who were not disciplined nor trained. We can see today that the majority of Christians fall into this category. God's ranks today have become thinned out as well, and those who do come forward, do not have the discipline or the knowledge to be the warriors God has called them to be. In fact, the Word of God says that the harvest is plentiful but the workers are few.

Matthew 9:37 (AMP) [37] *Then He said to His disciples, The harvest is indeed plentiful, but the laborers are few.*

Today, we can see that Christians are not disciplined as the disciples of yesterday. We do have great disciples today, but they are not the majority. God needs people to rise up and take their place in His ranks because we are entering into the end times. In addition to this, the emperors knew that their position was upheld by the army, and as the soldiers brought forth their complaints about the armor being too heavy, they were allowed to make changes to the armor where it was much lighter but less effective. Basically, they compromised to make it easier and designed more for comfort. How many times do we compromise with what the Word of God says in order to make things easier and more comfortable in our lives today? Daily, Christians compromise by their own standards or by the standards set by man. When we compromise with God's Word, we will begin to fall just like the Roman Empire fell. Once we fall, we become defeated. We cannot allow the fatigues of battle to take over where our way of thinking does not line up with God's Word. Christians do not have to feel that fatigue if they will just let go and give it to God. God does not call us to a great mission or task and not give us everything we need to accomplish it victoriously. God gives us our daily manna just like He did the children of Israel. The children of Israel had all their needs met, yet they continued to complain because it did not fit into the standards set by man. When the Word of God does not line up with our comfort level, our social status, or our financial position, we begin to either twist doctrine or make excuses to coincide with our choices. I can give many examples to this, such as:

• When something comes up that is more exciting than attending a worship service, we come up with excuses for why we cannot attend when in reality, we choose something we consider of a higher status than learning of God. *(Matthew 11:29)*

• When we see something that we feel we cannot live without but we cannot really afford it, we choose to purchase it anyway knowing that we will have to cut corners even if it includes giving of our resources to further the Kingdom of God. *(Malachi 3:8)*

• We make the choice to sign up to help with something at the church or with another spiritual organization, but when the time comes, we are exhausted from doing other things and decide we are not going to give our time. Many times, Christians do not even make the phone call to say, *"I can't come."* In reality, many times it is not because they can't come, but because they are selfish with their time. If it was something they enjoyed doing, they would be there and that is the difference. *(Titus 2:7-8)*

If we do not learn that our walk with God has to be doing it His way and not compromising with man or with the world, there are going to be many standing before God on judgment day and the question will be asked, *"What did you do with the time and the talents I gave you?"* I hate to think that in our mind will be flash backs of how we compromised again and again, in order to satisfy our own comforts, our status with society, and our financial wants not needs.

Rome fell when the Goths, the Huns, and the Alani had felt the benefits of the defensive armor and adopted this method in which Rome had once used. The stronger barbarians coming against the Roman Empire, easily overwhelmed Rome whose heads and breasts were exposed without defensive armor. They were exposed in the natural sense as well as the spiritual sense. The enemy can see that we do not have our armor on. The enemy knows when we half way put our armor on. The enemy knows when we are just partially clothed. When we are not engaged with our spiritual armor on and we do not stand firm knowing who we are in Christ, our defeat will come and our fall will be swift.

We must know and understand that Paul's message was his last message which leads me to believe it was the most important thing he could impart to the church or the disciples of Jesus Christ. Paul knew this would be his last message. Paul knew the importance of the spiritual war and the importance of being fully clothed. Paul wanted to impart to the church that we are at war, and it is a daily war in the spiritual realm. Even though, we cannot see God and even though, we cannot see Jesus or the Holy Spirit, we believe they are there. In the same sense, we should know that the war we are engaged in is spiritual, and it is all around us even though we cannot see it. In any war, the battle cannot be won by a hit and miss tactic. In fighting our battles, we must draw close to God; we must know His voice or that of the Holy Spirit, and we must remain fully clothed while standing firm. Standing firm requires endurance. Endurance means that you are not going to give up. This all goes back to knowing you are in right standing with God, and you are on the winning side; therefore, all powers of hell will not knock you off your feet. *"I will endure and continue to endure until this thing changes in my favor."* When we win, we do so in our mind, mind over matter as we have discussed in Chapter 3. A spiritual battle is won through our mind, and that requires lining our mind up with what God says not what the world says. In 2 Timothy we are told to endure suffering along with Christ.

2 Timothy 2:3-4 (NLT) *³Endure suffering along with me, as a good soldier of Christ Jesus. ⁴ Soldiers don't get tied up in the affairs of civilian life, for then they cannot please the officer who enlisted them.*

A soldier that has done well has also suffered with Christ. When we fully engage in God's army, our mind must stay renewed to His Word in order to keep us free from the temptations of life. Life will smother us and keep us in a state of defeat where we will have no peace or hope. Remember, we endure hardships. We are not of this world but of the world to come; therefore, we should not be consumed with the affairs of this world, the civilian life. We have a job to do just like Jesus did and just like the disciples of yesterday. If we are preoccupied with the things of this world, we will miss it and the enemy will bring us down. Most of our suffering today is letting go of this world and enduring those who will persecute us in order that we carry out God's will. As we get closer to the end, we will endure more suffering. Americans really do not suffer for Christ in the biblical sense or as those in other countries suffer. However, I believe there will come a time when that will all change, and it is a good thing right now to learn about endurance in order to be able to stand during harder times which eventually will fall upon all true Christians. We should be thankful for what we would consider suffering today and learn to praise God for any sufferings or persecutions to come because we are standing for something and someone we believe in enough to endure the pain! To clarify, our suffering with Christ is dying to self and living for Him. It is letting go of this world and the indulgences that this world offers. It is being conformed to the world to come and not living as those conformed to this world. It is being able to see the distinctions of those that are true Christians from those that are of this world.

Joshua 1:6-7 (Amp) ⁶Be strong (confident) and of good courage, for you shall cause this people to inherit the land which I swore to their fathers to give them. ⁷Only you be strong and very courageous, that you may do according to all the law which Moses My servant commanded you. Turn not from it to the right hand or to the left, that you may prosper wherever you go.

Here is the thing, if we are doing it God's way then we are submitting and not trying to do it in ourselves. Many times we question, *"How do we let go and let God do it? I try, but I seem to just pick it back up again and do it the same way I always have."* Do you hear what you are saying? Just as in Joshua above, we inherit that which we were destined to inherit when we abide by God's laws, His way not ours. When we do not have the victory, it is because we are doing it over and over again the same way expecting a different result but only to wind up in the same place again and again, a place of defeat! We have all heard that if you want victory, stop doing it the same way and do something different. I can guarantee you that doing it God's way will definitely be different than that of the world. If you do what He commands, you will always have the same result and that will be victory! God wants to fight for us, not against us, but He asks that we do everything through Him and that only happens when we do it His way.

Joshua 1:8 (Amp) [8]This Book of the Law shall not depart out of your mouth, but you shall meditate on it day and night, that you may observe and do according to all that is written in it. For then you shall make your way prosperous, and then you shall deal wisely and have good success.

The NLT version says the book of instructions. God's Words are our instructions to victory. God says we will have success if we do what He has given us instructions to do and that is abiding in Him. There was a time I would wonder how we were to abide in Him until God showed me that it is by doing all His commandments, His way.

Joshua 1:9 (Amp) [9]Have not I commanded you? Be strong, vigorous, and very courageous. Be not afraid, neither be dismayed, for <u>the Lord your God is with you wherever you go.</u>

When we abide in Him, we will be strong, vigorous, and very courageous. It says to not be afraid because there will be no fear if God walks with us. God is love, and perfect love casts out fear. In fact, God has not given us a spirit of fear.

1 John 4:18 (NLT) [18]Such love has no fear, because perfect love expels all fear. If we are afraid, it is for fear of punishment, and this shows that we have not fully experienced his perfect love.

2 Timothy 1:7 (NLT) [7]For God has not given us a spirit of fear and timidity, but of power, love, and self-discipline.

Our battles will not ever be won through fear, and in Timothy below, we learn that if we read our instructions, which is the Word of God, these Words are what will help us to fight well. In fact, we see that by following the instructions in God's Word, our battles are the Lord's battles. God will fight for us.

1 Timothy 1:18 (NLT) [18] *Timothy, my son, here are my instructions for you, based on the prophetic words spoken about you earlier. May they help you fight well in the Lord's battles.*

Preparation will be the key to winning any battle, just like the Roman Empire, their strength was in their military only because of all the hard work and preparation put into being strong and staying strong. If there is no preparation, there will be no strength, especially in the Lord. In order to draw strength from God, we must spend time with Him for that growth to take place and preparation to come. The Bible tells us to stand firm against the schemes of satan.

Ephesians 6:11 (NLT) [11] *Put on all of God's armor so that you will be able to stand firm against all strategies of the devil.*

satan has never fought fair and never will because he is not the author of truth but rather of lies. When you are attacked by the enemy, it will happen at a time you least expect because it will be a time you let your guard down. When things happen, they always seem to occur at a time that is very inconvenient for all parties and this is the way the enemy operates. How many times have we said, *"When things happen, it doesn't just stop there, they continue to happen?"* This is because our enemy likes to kick us even harder when we are down. We all know that a coward always strikes when your back is turned or when you are already down. satan is nothing more than a coward because he

161

knows he is already defeated; he just hopes that he can convince God's people that they are also defeated. satan desires to take as many people with him to hell. We have the options to choose and our choice depends on what we desire our outcome to be. It usually comes down to choosing life and not death, light and not darkness, good and not evil. It is your choice and this is a daily choice. It is called laying your life down at the Cross with Christ. It is called, not my will be done but yours Father. It is called, not what I want but what You want for me Lord. It is a selfless act not a selfish act, putting others needs before your own and living a life which is modeled after Jesus Christ. When we become so engaged in the affairs of this world, our guard goes down because of the distractions. Do you not think that all those distractions have been put there as temptations in order to keep God's people running around taking care of the affairs of this world to the extent that they never even stop to think about – what is life all about? What is my purpose? What is it that God created me for? satan's tactics have been working for far too long and will continue to do so until we make that choice to not succumb to the comforts of this world.

2 Corinthians 11:3-4 (NLT) [3] *But I fear that somehow your pure and undivided devotion to Christ will be corrupted, just as Eve was deceived by the cunning ways of the serpent.* [4] *You happily put up with whatever anyone tells you, even if they preach a different Jesus than the one we preach, or a different kind of Spirit than the one you received, or a different kind of gospel than the one you believed.*

The world is distracted by far and especially those living in America. America has such wealth along with every kind of pleasures available and many times just at the touch of a button. The technology age has brought us to a place that we could almost survive without even leaving our homes, but it has also handicapped us. What is this deception which Paul is speaking of? The deceptions are all the distractions which plague our world today and it is not by accident. satan is very cunning just like he was to Eve, and we are very ignorant people if we believe that we would never fall for his temptations. This world has already fallen for satan's temptations, and today more than ever, we need a wakeup call for all those who consider themselves Christians. We have become accustomed to either twisting Scripture or reading it out of context, in order to make it more comfortable for our flesh. However, the day is coming when there will be a reality check for all those who consider themselves to be Christians. When the time comes, we will all have to look deep within our own hearts to see what those things are which distract our time and our attention from Christ. I just pray that God's people do an honest assessment, in order to prepare themselves for these end times and also to be truthful with what they see. There is no time like this age to begin studying and growing in God's Word, instead of allowing the messages taught by man to be the only God you know. There are many messages today that twist the truth and many messages today that are far from the truth. I do not believe when you stand before God and say you did not know because it was what you had been taught, that God is going to say, *"That's okay my son, come on into heaven!"* It does not work that way. We are all responsible for what we know, and we cannot use the excuse that we never read that in the Word of God. The first thing God is going to ask you is, *"How many years did you have to study my Word, and you are telling me that you never read that?"* I believe we are all responsible to study and show ourselves approved by doing our own reading of Scripture and searching for truth. The importance of this is so none fall into the hands of false teachings which will lead to hell.

2 Corinthians 11:13-15 (NLT) [13]These people are false apostles. They are deceitful workers who disguise themselves as apostles of Christ. [14] But I am not surprised! Even Satan disguises himself as an angel of light. [15] So it is no wonder that his servants also disguise themselves as servants of righteousness. In the end they will get the punishment their wicked deeds deserve.

Heart of David

I love the teachings of David and decided to use this example for the most important teaching about the Breastplate of Righteousness. God refers to David as a man after His own heart.

Acts 13:22 (NIV) [22]After removing Saul, he made David their king. God testified concerning him: 'I have found David son of Jesse, a man after my own heart; he will do everything I want him to do.'

Yet, David was just like many today who struggle with sin, but they love God with all their heart. We are able to see David as just being real. David made mistakes and huge mistakes at that. David was a murderer and an adulterer, but He loved God. How on earth can anyone say they love God and do all the wrong things such as David did? I believe the story of David was to show God's children that it does not matter who you were or how bad your sins have been, you can still have a good heart and love God intimately. I always love sharing David when I am teaching. It helps to be able to see that our heart can be right; and our love for God can be pure. What makes David different than many who are living in sin? David's desires were to just do right. David's desires were to please God. David's heart cried out and yearned to be what God wanted him to be, but he was a man who

164

struggled with temptations and strong holds in his life. There were many consequences to the sins which David committed, but even with all the pain his sins brought into his life, he still loved God and desired to get things right.

You see, God knows our heart, and your relationship with God begins with having that right heart. The breastplate in biblical days protected vital organs, and the most important organ in our whole body is the heart. In fact, we are told that without love, we have nothing. The heart determines the depths of our love. On Valentine's Day, the heart is symbolized to mean love. Why is that? When we love intimately, it goes much deeper than just dealing with our thinking or our brain. When we love, it affects our whole being. When we look at the breastplate in terms of the natural realm, we know that if our heart is wounded severely, we will die a natural death. Looking into the spiritual realm, when we put on the Breastplate of Righteousness, we are protecting our heart in a spiritual sense. If our heart is dead to the Spirit, there is no connection to God. In fact, our heart not only produces life in the natural but it also produces life which connects to our Creator in the spiritual. Even when our heart is wounded emotionally, we do not function very well. When in an emotional state, we do not think clearly and we make poor decisions. I remember after my daughter's death reading a book on grief and it stressed that after the death of a loved one, you should not make important decisions due to the emotional state which affects your mind. When we have a broken heart, our mind, will, and emotions are all affected, and when we are in love, all of our senses are affected as well. However, in a state of grief, our heart is dead to being able to feel. I can remember not being able to feel the emotions I once had after the death of my daughter. I felt no joy, no happiness, no love, nothing! I literally felt dead inside. Our heart in the spiritual sense is the essence to being able to connect with God spiritually.

After dying to self and being born again into the family of God, we are meant to live spiritually. When we tap into the spiritual realm, this is the place we come alive in Christ. Yes, we may be in natural bodies, but we are capable of being able to see through God's eyes, have compassion as Christ did, feel what God feels for man-kind, conquer those things which may seem impossible, walk in the God-kind of love, acquire the peace which passes all understanding, and live and breathe for those things which are not seen with the natural eyes.

Spiritually, what is it that causes the breastplate to protect our heart? It is righteousness and that is why Paul called it the Breastplate of Righteousness. If we never feel that we are worthy to be a child of God, we will never put on our breastplate. In fact, many times in the natural we do not feel loved because we feel that we do not deserve to be loved. This all goes back to knowing that you do deserve to be loved and that you can be righteous in the sight of God. However, this is because of the great love that He had for us by allowing His son to pay that ultimate price. Righteousness is knowing that you are a child of God no matter who you are, what you have done, or how great your sins are. satan, on the other hand, loves to continue feeding you lies which say that you will never amount to anything, you will never succeed, and God will never accept you because you just aren't good enough. But, righteousness believes that Jesus died for our sins and that He paid that price totally, so that we can have fellowship with a God who loves us. You see, even though David failed time and time again, he never stopped running to God for forgiveness and crying out to God to change him. Having a heart like David, desires those same things David desired. Having a heart like David, knows that no matter what, my Dad in heaven still loves me. Having a heart like David, knows that my Dad in heaven desires that I run to Him for forgiveness and correction

166

instead of running from Him. David ran that same race in which Paul ran. The race is called running toward God not away from Him. When we begin to run the opposite direction, it is because we cannot accept that Jesus Christ paid the ultimate price in order that we are forgiven. In this day and era, the body of Christ has too much to do in preparing for the second coming of our Lord, and we are wasting time feeling sorry for ourselves because we think that God is looking down on us through eyes of judgment instead of eyes of love. Yes, we will be judged for what we have done in this lifetime, but it is being judged for our works once we have come to Christ. True disciples of Jesus Christ are forgiven and their judgment is not for their sins. We need to awaken to understand that God said that He not only has forgiven us for our sins but forgotten them. Why would He tell us in His Word that He has forgotten our sins if He still plans to judge us one day for those sins?

Hebrews 8:12 (NLV) [12] I will show loving-kindness to them and forgive their sins. I will remember their sins no more."

The Bible speaks of two separate judgments. There is the judgment seat of Christ where true Christians will stand before the Lord to give an account of what they did in order to receive their rewards. In 2 Corinthians below, Paul was speaking to the church at Corinth which were all believers of Jesus Christ. Therefore, we know that the judgment seat of Christ is meant for the church.

2 Corinthians 5:10-11 (NLT) [10] For we must all stand before Christ to be judged. We will each receive whatever we deserve for the good or evil we have done in this earthly body. We Are God's Ambassadors [11]Because we understand our fearful responsibility to the Lord, we work hard to persuade others. God knows we are sincere, and I hope you know this, too.

And there is the judgment that we are more familiar with which is the Great White Throne Judgment. This judgment is the final judgment which is spoken of in Revelation and takes place prior to the lost being cast into the Lake of Fire. *(Revelation 20:11-15)*

There are also two books that will be opened. One book gives an account of the works that Christians have done after coming to Jesus Christ, and the other one is the Book of Life which lists all the names of those that will spend eternity with the Father. Let me clarify, when we make that decision to run the same race in which Paul spoke of, it is running a race where we lay our lives at the Cross and submit to Jesus. The problem is that the church has become complacent in believing that love is not an action, but it is. You cannot claim to be a follower of Jesus Christ when you have not crucified your will in order to begin following the teachings of Jesus. There are several scriptures below in which Jesus describes the actions of those that truly love Him.

John 14:15-21 (NLT) Jesus Promises the Holy Spirit [15] "If you love me, obey my commandments. [16] And I will ask the Father, and he will give you another Advocate, who will never leave you. [17] He is the Holy Spirit, who leads into all truth. The world cannot receive him, because it isn't looking for him and doesn't recognize him. But you know him, because he lives with you now and later will be in you. [18] No, I will not abandon you as orphans—I will come to you. [19] Soon the world will no longer see me, but you will see me. Since I live, you also will live. [20] When I am raised to life again, you will know that I am in my Father, and you are in me, and I am in you. [21] Those who accept my commandments and obey them are the ones who love me. And because they love me, my Father will love them. And I will love them and reveal myself to each of them."

John 14:23-26 (NLT) [23] Jesus replied, "All who love me will do what I say. My Father will love them, and we will come and make our home with each of them. [24] Anyone who doesn't love me will not obey me. And remember, my words are not my own. What I am telling you is from the Father who sent me. [25] I am telling you these things now while I am still with you. [26] But when the Father sends the Advocate as my

168

representative—that is, the Holy Spirit—he will teach you everything and will remind you of everything I have told you.

John 21:15-17 (NLT) [15]After breakfast Jesus asked Simon Peter, "Simon son of John, do you love me more than these?" "Yes, Lord," Peter replied, "you know I love you." "Then feed my lambs," Jesus told him. [16]Jesus repeated the question: "Simon son of John, do you love me?" "Yes, Lord," Peter said, "you know I love you." "Then take care of my sheep," Jesus said. [17]A third time he asked him, "Simon son of John, do you love me?" Peter was hurt that Jesus asked the question a third time. He said, "Lord, you know everything. You know that I love you." Jesus said, "Then feed my sheep.

It will be through your actions of love and compassion that you will walk in the same footsteps in which Jesus walked. You see it is not our works which get us into heaven, but once we begin following Jesus, we will give account of what we did with what we were given. We have all been given talents and gifts in order to prepare for the second coming of Jesus Christ, and He is busy perfecting His people to have a heart like David.

Recently, I ministered to several of the homeless in my Street Ministry, and I told them that suffering for Jesus Christ does not mean that one day you will stand before the Father and say, *"Lord, I have suffered because I have lived without; I lived on the street going hungry and having nothing."*

You may be pour in the natural realm and may live without naturally, but that does not mean you are suffering for Jesus Christ. Suffering for Christ is letting go of this world and the enjoyment within in order that you use those gifts and talents to show the lost the way to the Savior that you claim to know. It doesn't matter if you do not have a dime to your name and no home, car, job, etc., you still have gifts and talents that Jesus gave you to go forth and share His name. Remember, the harvest is plentiful but the laborers are few. This is because few are willing to step out of their comfort zone and share Jesus Christ. When Jesus opens the book which gives an account for everything you have done, what will He speak about your life?

I was sitting at the drive-thru at the bank the other day when a car pulled up next to me with loud rap music. I was listening to one of my favorite Christian stations and had to turn it up a little to drown out the tunes of the vehicle next to mine. The driver of the car drove up a bit in order to get out and stand at the terminal to be able to hear the teller because he evidently did not want to turn down his music to hear what she had to say. There was another guy in the passenger seat and I could see them both very well. God showed me something that we all need to see. We can claim that we do not want to judge when in reality, we do. Immediately, my thoughts were how they must be gangsters with their loud rap music, their jeans hanging down and their black sports car. Either gangsters or drug dealers, right? Wrong – it's not for us to judge. I had 3 of my books laying on the front seat of my car when the Holy Spirit spoke to me and said, *"Instead of judging them, give them a book and let them know that I love them."* Well, the teller sent my slip to me and before I drove off, I rolled down my passenger window. The young guy looked up at me and smiled. It brings tears to my eyes right now because I think about how many times the church judges what they do not know. He was young and probably did not know that Jesus died for him. He probably did not have a clue that the God of the Universe loves him. So, I called him over and handed him one of my books. I told him that Jesus Christ loves both of them very much. He held the book to his chest hugging it and said with this huge smile, *"Are you giving me this book?"* I said, *"Yes, I wrote the book and God wants you to have it."* He said with a smile as big as can be, *"I'm going to read it, thank you!"* Now, I could have driven off thinking that they were young, dumb, and so messed up in this world that I had more important things to do than save a generation, but that is why the harvest is plentiful and the workers are few. There's way too much of that going on today within our church walls where we spend countless years ministering to the few that walk in our doors instead of the multitudes on the outside. Let's learn from this and say, "*Yes Jesus, I will feed Your lambs; I will take care of Your sheep, and I will feed your sheep!*" If we can't do this simple thing, how can we stand up in the church today and claim that we love Jesus Christ?

Matthew 25:31-46 (NIV) The Sheep and the Goats [31] *"When the Son of Man comes in his glory, and all the angels with him, he will sit on his glorious throne.* [32] *All the nations will be gathered before him, and he will separate the people one from another as a shepherd separates the sheep from the goats.* [33] *He will put the sheep on his right and the goats on his left.* [34] *"Then the King will say to those on his right, 'Come, you who are blessed by my Father; take your inheritance, the kingdom prepared for you since the creation of the world.* [35] *For I was hungry and you gave me something to eat, I was thirsty and you gave me something to drink, I was a stranger and you invited me in,* [36] *I needed clothes and you clothed me, I was sick and you looked after me, I was in prison and you came to visit me.'* [37] *"Then the righteous will answer him, 'Lord, when did we see you hungry and feed you, or thirsty and give you something to drink?* [38] *When did we see you a stranger and invite you in, or needing clothes and clothe you?* [39] *When did we see you sick or in prison and go to visit you?'* [40] *"The King will reply, 'Truly I tell you, whatever you did for one of the least of these brothers and sisters of mine, you did for me.'* [41] *"Then he will say to those on his left, 'Depart from me, you who are cursed, into the eternal fire prepared for the devil and his angels.* [42] *For I was hungry and you gave me nothing to eat, I was thirsty and you gave me nothing to drink,* [43] *I was a stranger and you did not invite me in, I needed clothes and you did not clothe me, I was sick and in prison and you did not look after me.'* [44] *"They also will answer, 'Lord, when did we see you hungry or thirsty or a stranger or needing clothes or sick or in prison, and did not help you?'* [45] *"He will reply, 'Truly I tell you, whatever you did not do for one of the least of these, you did not do for me.'* [46] *"Then they will go away to eternal punishment, but the righteous to eternal life."*

If we desire to truly be disciples of Jesus Christ, we must rethink our motivation. If we have no desire to be a servant and go through the persecution and ridicule from the world as well as the religious folks of this day, we cannot call ourselves Christians. If we desire to stand before the Father and inherit the Kingdom of Heaven, our heart must line up to that of David. Our heart must break for what breaks God's. We must have a heart for people. It's time for Christians today to rise up and stop feeling sorry for themselves and make a decision to follow Jesus Christ. Far too often, when things get tough, we quit running the race. I think most Christians which fall away into the world do so because of the guilt which satan puts on them for mistakes they make over and over again. In fact, most Christians do not believe they could ever measure up to be what God desires for them. Most Christians believe that God surely is disappointed in them when they mess up. It is easy to see why these Christians are not using their gifts and talents. If you are at this place, remember that David was at the same place in his life. David felt that he didn't measure up either. David felt that he had failed God again and again. It is our heart – either it is proud and boastful or it is humble. We become humble when we draw closer to the Lord. We become humble when we strive to be like Jesus. Being humble is accepting our weaknesses. It is okay to be weak because it is in our weakness that we gain strength from God. God desires to grow us to the place that we operate through Christ not independently. Of course, this does not happen with many today because their heart is so wounded that they cannot even forgive themselves.

Job 27:6 (NLT) [6]I will maintain my innocence without wavering. My conscience is clear for as long as I live.

After everything Job had been through, he continued to stand his ground when all his friends insisted he must have committed sin for all the suffering God was allowing him to go through. Yet, Job maintained his innocence knowing that he was in right-standing with God and his conscience would remain clear. Job was a great man of God for those who do not know the story, and then as God was bragging about how faithful Job was, satan concluded he was only faithful because God had continually blessed him. Therefore, God allowed satan to test him in every capacity but he could not take his life. Through this whole ordeal, Job never wavered or changed his heart towards God. Even though, he did not understand what this test was that he was going through, he remained faithful. Job cried out to God many times but did not hear back until his test was basically over. At the end, God blessed Job with even more than he had before. What does this tell us? Job loved God deeply, and even though he went through a period of suffering, he stayed loyal to God and totally put his trust in Him. When our heart is where it should be with God, it cries out to our Creator during times of turmoil, times of disappointment, times of sorrow, times of uncertainty, etc.

When we put on the Breastplate of Righteousness this deals in part with our mind. In fact, it takes every single piece of armor in order for our armor to work. One piece will not prepare us for a spiritual battle without all the other pieces in place. With our mind, we get our way of thinking right in order to see ourselves as God sees us. When we line up our thoughts with the thoughts of God, what comes out of our mouth will also line up. This is the righteousness that Job talked about. Job had his mind lined up with the way God thinks and therefore, in times of uncertainty or trouble, he remained steadfast in his way of thinking and nothing contrary came forth out of his mouth.

A Marine said... You have to keep a positive attitude because there will be days that you are so exhausted from training that you will just want to give up.

There is no room for negativism in the life of a true Christian. This is something that must be practiced to perfection, but it will not happen if you are not engaged in some type of boot camp. It will not happen if you do not surround yourself with positive people. You will be what you hang out with. In Boot Camp, you cannot take your closest friend with you; you cannot take that favorite cousin with you; you cannot even take your children with you. Boot Camp is you alone with God day in and day out training to get what you need to be enlisted in God's Army. If you make the decision to let go of whatever it is that is keeping you from that intimate relationship with God, those friends will follow, those cousins and family members will follow, and your children will follow. Everyone follows something, and the sad truth is that most Christians today are teaching those they love to follow the wrong leader.

I know that I have two daughters which saw me serve God diligently for 10 years and then fall away and become conformed to this world. After realizing how drastically I needed to make things right with my God, I came back home. After returning to God, I watched my girls consumed in the world. I could not blame this on anyone but myself. I had taught them all about sin, and the sad part is that destruction always follows sin. Gradually, as my girls watched my walk again with God, they began to come forward little by little. This may not happen overnight, and you cannot force anyone to develop that deep relationship with God. An intimate relationship is shared between two people, and it will only happen as we make that choice. Jesus waits on us. He is always there desiring that we come to Him. It will not happen until we choose. One of my daughters, week after week, would attend my prayer group. On the other hand, I would question why she would even attend because I could not see any change in her life or see that she was receiving anything from God. Yet, it was during these times that God would say to me, *"You may not see me working in her, but I am at work in her."* I can remember one day my daughter saying, *"Momma, I just want you to know that I have been doing what you have been teaching. I have been speaking over my situations and over myself."* I can remember this coming at a time where she cried out to the whole prayer group that she did not see herself like any of us and that she was not worthy for God to be in her life. She walked out that day. I knew because of the tears pouring down from her eyes that she deeply wanted her life to change, but her struggles were great just like David. I was surprised when she returned to my group the next week. Today, she still struggles, but she continues to cry out to God; she continues to pray; she continues to attend classes on occasions and church, but she has not fully crossed over. This is about our heart. This is about being able to see who God created us to be no matter what our struggles are. This is about wanting and desiring to change and to be what God desires of us, and this is about never quitting or giving up. Eventually, the conviction will be so great upon your life that you will be able to draw the strength needed from God to walk away from who you once were to become who you were created to be.

Remember, satan does not want us to gain strength from God. satan desires to keep us contained in our struggles and then add a huge dose of condemnation on top of what we are already battling, in order that he keeps us buried alive. Condemnation is not from God, and it is a tactic to keep us feeling guilty and keep us thinking that we will never be able to do any better. Many times when we attempt to put on the Breastplate of

Righteousness, attacks begin in order for satan to convince us we cannot do this thing. Most Christians never get past the Breastplate of Righteousness to begin to grow in depth to experience the rewards from God.

When we are talking about the heart, the heart is what carries our emotions, the way we feel, what moves us, how deeply we love, and how intensely we grieve. I can remember in my early 20's one of my much older cousins told me to always follow my heart. I never forgot her telling me that, and I made a lot of mistakes because of making choices based on what I felt instead of sound reasoning. We serve a God who has given us a book of sound doctrine. This does not mean that our heart is not important, on the contrary, God is a God of extreme emotions, yet He is also a God of great wisdom. This is the importance of all pieces of armor working together. Our mind and the wisdom gained through God must work together with our heart and emotions in order that we make those right choices in this life. However, our heart must be right, in order to even come to know our Creator. You will be able to recognize when your heart begins to change because those things which were once important in your life take a back seat to the importance of walking a more pure and holy life. When your heart gets right, you will not only hear that voice speak to you and correct you, even in small areas, but you will also be obedient. Forgiveness is one such area. When your heart is right, there will be no more holding grudges, not forgiving, getting even, being deceitful, or having any evil thoughts towards others. This ends totally. When God gets a hold of your heart, it does not mean you will not miss it, but when you do miss it, you will find yourself just like David crying out for forgiveness and mercy upon your life. I cannot tell you how many times I have found myself even in front of my group pouring out my heart in tears because my heart was crying out, *"God, please break my heart for those things which break yours; make my heart be that of David's; change my heart so my actions are like Christ."* This is making it right and desiring to be everything our Creator intended us to be.

2 Corinthians 2:10-11 (NLT) [10] When you forgive this man, I forgive him, too. And when I forgive whatever needs to be forgiven, I do so with Christ's authority for your benefit, [11] so that Satan will not outsmart us. For we are familiar with his evil schemes.

Without forgiveness and a right heart attitude towards others, we will never be able to come together and be united to form the body of Christ as a whole. We will never be able to stand together in spiritual warfare as warriors fighting for our sole purpose in life. What exactly are we fighting for? When we send men and women to war, they are fighting for our country, fighting for freedom, and everything we cherish which God has blessed this nation with. In the spiritual realm, I like to think of it in the same way. When we make that decision that we want to enlist in God's army to be all we can be through Christ who strengthens us and through the Holy Spirit that teaches us, in a sense, we are fighting for our country. I am not talking about our natural country but the place where we will soon call home. The Bible teaches us that we are not to be conformed to this world because if we are God's children, then we are of the world to come. When I put on my whole armor, I am representing the Kingdom of Heaven and all the values and everything it represents. When we enlist, we do so with all our heart and everything within our being. In taking a stand which Paul wrote in his letter to Timothy, we enlist together with our fellow brothers and sisters in Christ to run this race to the finish no matter what.

2 Timothy 4:7 (NLT) [7] I have fought the good fight, I have finished the race, and I have remained faithful.

We fight our battles side by side, united together as one body of believers because God's Word says where two or more of us come together, He is not only in our midst but He hears our prayers and answers those prayers. What we ask for is done in heaven and in earth.

Matthew 18:19-20 (NLT) *19* "I also tell you this: If two of you agree here on earth concerning anything you ask, my Father in heaven will do it for you. *20* For where two or three gather together as my followers, I am there among them."

As followers, someone who follows Jesus would be walking as He walked. There are many promises but those promises are for true believers and this is not someone who merely says they believe. Jesus shared the definition of a believer, which was given to His disciples whom followed Him.

John 14:15 (AMP) *15* *If you [really] love Me, you will keep (obey) My commands.*

Love is an action, and we will never be able to buy our way into heaven. As we run the race set before us, it will be with one aim in mind which is following Jesus. How do we follow Jesus? We give up our life and choose His ways.

Matthew 16:24 (AMP) *24* *Then Jesus said to His disciples, If anyone desires to be My disciple, let him deny himself [disregard, lose sight of, and forget himself and his own interests] and take up his cross and follow Me [cleave steadfastly to Me, conform wholly to My example in living and, if need be, in dying, also].*

Most people will live out their lives doing what they desire to do because they do not feel that they can do what it takes to be a

178

disciple of Christ. This is a lie from the enemy; however, we will never be able to die to self until we develop the intimacy toward Christ. Words mean absolutely nothing unless our actions portray what is in our heart.

John 21:17 (NIV) [17] *The third time he said to him,* "Simon son of John, do you love me?" *Peter was hurt because Jesus asked him the third time,* "Do you love me?" *He said, "Lord, you know all things; you know that I love you." Jesus said,* "Feed my sheep.

Why did Jesus ask Peter three times? We have probably heard the same question from that small quiet voice many times. There is emphasis on this question in the gospels because Jesus asked the same question three different times. The reason is simple. We are so used to saying what people want to hear or speaking without even thinking about what we are really saying. Jesus asked three times for Peter to be able to think about that question and exactly what it meant. Love is not a four letter word that we just throw out there. Love is an action. Notice that Jesus pretty much said, *"If you really love me you will feed my sheep!"* Jesus was not just speaking to Peter. Jesus was not saying, *"Peter, you are the only one that has to feed my sheep; everyone else who loves me and wants to follow me, that is not a requirement."* Jesus was speaking to everyone who calls themselves a Christian. Are you really a Christian? Are you feeding His sheep? You see David had a heart for God because he yearned to be God-like! David wanted God to be pleased with him.

Those who followed Christ in biblical days gave of themselves and died for the cause. One of my favorite things a pastor where I went for some time used to say, *"If what you are living for is not worth dying for, then it is not worth living for."* Our lives should be one as the disciples in New Testament times and our heart should

179

reflect the heart of David. When the Christian community comes to the realization that we have heart issues among us, maybe we will break down those walls enough that the Holy Spirit can come in with fire in order to do the necessary clean up to remove those things within each of us that are keeping us from being able to fall madly in love with God. We cannot do all that God is calling us to do until there is unity among those that claim to be Christians today, and this unity will never happen until God's people begin to learn how to wear their armor. The Breastplate of Righteousness is crucial to allowing a transformation within. It is crucial to coming to that place to see who we are in Christ and desiring that the selfishness, self-righteousness, self-indulgence and everything which exalts itself against the knowledge of Christ is removed from within and replaced with more of Jesus. As we are molded into His image, we come to understand the spiritual realm and who our real enemy is in order to love our fellow brothers and sisters into the fold instead of speaking evil into their lives.

2 Corinthians 10:3-5 (ASV) ³ *For though we walk in the flesh, we do not war according to the flesh* ⁴ *(for the weapons of our warfare are not of the flesh, but mighty before God to the casting down of strongholds),* ⁵ *casting down imaginations, and every high thing that is exalted against the knowledge of God, and bringing every thought into captivity to the obedience of Christ;*

Chapter Five
Belt of Truth

The Belt of Truth is vital in our walk with God. As a new Christian, your Helmet of Salvation must go on first because without understanding salvation you can do nothing else in this walk with God. In fact, without salvation, you are not even in the family. Without being a member of God's family, you have no privileges. In our earthly families, there are certain privileges we each have within that unit. Think about walking into a stranger's home, going to the refrigerator to make you a snack, plopping down on **their** couch to watch **their** TV and when the owner walks in, **you** say, *"Come on in and make yourself at home."* I don't think you would be received very well because you are a stranger and have no privileges there. In our own families, it would be nothing to go into a sibling or your parent's home and feel comfortable to do certain things. In God's family, you also gain privileges as you grow to learn what rules must be followed as you gain knowledge into your Dad's affairs. It is through the helmet, we begin to grow to the place where we see ourselves as God sees us in order to see that we are righteous in His sight. Being righteous in God's sight has nothing to do with anything we have done, but rather because Jesus bore our sins for us. Through His blood, we are redeemed. After applying the helmet and the Breastplate of Righteousness, the next step is putting on the belt. God expects us to begin to grow and that only happens by applying the Word of God to our lives. The Belt of Truth is His Word. The Belt of Truth is Jesus. According to Scripture, Jesus was the Word, and He was made flesh.

John 1:1-3 (NIV) The Word Became Flesh [1] In the beginning was the Word, and the Word was with God, and the Word was God. [2] He was with God in the beginning. ³ Through him all things were made; without him nothing was made that has been made.

More than Milk

The revelation about to unfold can be your breakthrough that brings you to the place where you can really begin to mature in Christ. We should never remain babes in Christ. With our new foundation of Christianity, we begin to take in milk just like a new born baby. In fact, there are Scriptures which talk about milk and then there are Scriptures which talk about meat.

1 Peter 2:1-3 (NIV) ¹ Therefore, rid yourselves of all malice and all deceit, hypocrisy, envy, and slander of every kind. ² Like newborn babies, crave pure spiritual milk, so that by it you may grow up in your salvation, ³ now that you have tasted that the Lord is good.

It is through taking in spiritual milk that we grow **UP** in our salvation. We cannot rid ourselves of self, meaning the producing of bad fruit such as malice, deceit, etc., without growing up. Through milk we indulge in the basics, and we cannot grow without the proper foundation. With a baby, they soon come to know who loves them and who takes care of them. It is the familiar faces that smile at them, cuddle them, comfort them, feed them, and tend to their every need. When we first gain the knowledge of salvation, we need this milk in order to develop the love relationship with our Father. Too many Christians today remain in the state of feeling inadequate, unworthy, undeserving, and unwanted. If you find yourself today feeling as though you are not good enough, you may lack in the spiritual milk needed to nurture you through the infant stage. Let me share something, as a parent and grandparent, every child is different, but I can remember the times when I have had to discipline and later having to ensure my children that I still loved them. We are no different as new born babes in Christ. When God begins to show us that we cannot do this and we cannot do that, the result many times brings out our immaturity. We begin to put on that familiar face of *"feel sorry for me!"* We begin to act up because we have been corrected. We begin to feel unworthy, undeserving, etc. This is all immaturity and God has done nothing to produce those feelings within you. A child does not remain in that place in the natural sense or at least hopefully they grow up to realize that their parents only loved them and wanted what was best when they were disciplined. As a new Christian, it is imperative in the spiritual sense that we come to know God in all aspects and this happens through stages. Just like with a newborn baby, it is through stages the child grows from infancy to the toddler stage and then from there to becoming an older child which soon grows into adolescence and then adulthood. There have been many studies aimed at how the first five years of a child's life are critical for development. One such article written states that the experiences children have in these years help shape the adults they will become. It goes on to say that babies are born ready to learn, and their brains develop through use.[1]

Through these type of studies, we are able to see the importance of children being nourished physically, mentally, and emotionally. If, as children, it is imperative to their well-being that they receive the proper nurturing in all aspects, it is even that much more important that we also receive what we need from Our Father in Heaven spiritually. We cannot slack on the nurturing stages. We cannot rush through the nurturing stages. We cannot halfway go through the nurturing stages because these are the stages most Christians never fully grasp, and it is that foundation that ensures we grow into mature Christians. We cannot become mature overnight if we are cheated out of our childhood stage.

Let me clarify something. Many times we are cheated out of our childhood and are forced to grow up too soon in the natural. This was my life, and I understand it today very well. Because of the dysfunction within my home as a child, I did not know what it was like to be dependent upon someone who loved me, nurtured me, and made me feel safe and secure. I found myself at too young of an age growing up into adulthood even though I was not ready. I found myself having to be independent before I even knew what the word meant. If I was hungry, I had to find something to eat which did not require cooking because I had not been taught much about anything. If I was lonely, I wandered the streets making friends with those who were old enough to be out at night even though I was not. If I was sleepy or tired, I made the choice when I went to bed, tucked myself in, and went to sleep in a lonely home with no one there but myself. My memories of my childhood were filled with fears, uncertainties, hurt, and pain. There were times that I was able to enjoy brief moments of my childhood, but those times were usually associated with holidays and family gatherings which were few and far between. It is through these circumstances as a child that you have adults who may be grown up on the outside but there is extreme hurt and pain on the inside. They have literally brought that little boy or girl cradled within them into the adult stages of life. These adults are thrust into a world with a lot of anger and resentment because they did not get the love and nurturing needed to grow up feeling self-worth, acceptance, and love. This becomes a cycle which is passed down from generation to generation. How can we show love and acceptance when we never had it? How can we nurture like a loving parent when we never knew what it was like? I do not believe there are bad parents; I believe there are parents who are walking around with a hurt and angry child buried inside of them. I believe this is why Peter said to rid ourselves of all malice because once we experience how good our God is, it is time to go

184

through the first stage which is milk in order to begin the healing from our past and allow that little boy or girl to heal and be released.

Being in the nurturing stage is not a stage that we remain in but a stage that we grow through. Just like an infant, they do not remain an infant forever. As a baby grows they need more solid food or they will not continue to grow. Babies eventually begin to desire something more filling and it is with more substance that they continue to develop physically. They will be irritable and fussy if their bodies are not sustained with what is needed to grow and feel satisfied. Babies grow at certain paces and no two babies are identical in that aspect. Christians also grow at different paces, and we were not created to be identical in our growth with God or any other aspect as far as that is concerned. When we continue to live off of milk, it stunts our growth and we too become dissatisfied and fussy just like a baby, but as an adult, it is seen more in not being content with what we have or do not have.

In the natural sense, we should try living off of nothing but milk for about a month to see how it feels. In my early 20's, doctors put me on a diet with nothing but unprocessed milk for one complete month to try and heal my stomach from severe problems I had been having for some time. Unless you have been put on a complete liquid diet, you cannot imagine what it is like. In those days, *"Ensure"* did not exist. There were no liquid diets which provided what you needed and nothing in the form of liquid which provided fulfillment. I literally felt as though I was being starved to death. I thought eventually my stomach would get used to not having hardly anything in it but that never happened. I stayed hungry, and I craved something more filling. I was ecstatic the day I once again could have solid food. Our natural bodies require food not just liquids to sustain us. I know there are many who are put on liquid diets for one reason or another like I was, but usually, those who are on that kind of diet are not running around burning up energy like most of this world. When I was on that liquid diet, I was still working and going to school as a student along with raising a toddler. Not that we cannot survive with liquids for some time and there are even liquids made today which will give us all the ingredients we need. However, our bodies want solid food that satisfies our appetites and sustains our bodies providing nutrients and vitamins necessary to live a healthy life to the fullest. Our bodies need the energy required to do everything we need to do to keep up with our lifestyles or the fast paced life as we know it today. In the same sense, our spiritual bodies are screaming to be fed and not just to live off of milk.

Hebrews 5:13-14 (KJV) *[13] For every one that useth milk is unskilful in the word of righteousness: for he is a babe. [14] But strong meat belongeth to them that are of full age, even those who by reason of use have their senses exercised to discern both good and evil.*

However, it is by constant use of solid spiritual food that we can distinguish good from evil. It is only through growth and understanding that comes through taking in meat that we are able to sustain as a mature Christian. We can blame the church, blame the pastor, blame our spouse, or whomever we choose for our circumstances in life, but the truth is that we can all grow into so much more with the Word of God. It is through feeding ourselves as often as possible that we change, and change within brings about change around us. Most Christians today begin attending a church and perhaps learn some of the basics, but it stops there. Christians try to live indefinitely until the day they die off of just milk. Paul wrote to the church at Corinth speaking about the issues among those who were Christians, and these same issues exist today among the Christian community.

1 Corinthians 3:2 (NIV) ^{2} *I gave you milk, not solid food, for you were not yet ready for it. Indeed, you are still not ready.*

What was the main issue among the Christian community in Corinth? I believe it is the same issue we see today. Paul continued to say...

1 Corinthians 3:3 (NIV) ^{3} *You are still worldly. For since there is jealousy and quarreling among you, are you not worldly? Are you not acting like mere humans?*

We know that we are worldly when we have not matured in Christ, and if we have not matured, we remain taking in milk because we are not ready for meat. We grow according to how much we take in and how we posture ourselves to listen and learn. Many times, we become unteachable because we believe we have already arrived. Christians will get a bit of revelation in them on occasions and then believe they know more than someone else. This is where the jealousy and quarreling comes in to play among Christians today. We become so worried about rising to a level greater than someone else that we have stopped growing. We have taken in a small amount of milk, gain a little meat, and believe we are where we need to be. Yet, we are still babes in Christ because we are not diligent in feeding our spiritual thirst and hunger in order that we grows up healthy. This was also seen with the disciples when they quarreled among themselves about whom would be greater in the Kingdom of God and Jesus intervened.

Luke 9:46-48 (NLT) The Greatest in the Kingdom ^{46} *Then his disciples began arguing about which of them was the greatest.* ^{47} *But Jesus knew their thoughts, so he brought a little child to his side.* ^{48} *Then he said to them, "Anyone who welcomes a little child like this on my behalf welcomes me, and anyone who welcomes me also welcomes my Father who sent me. Whoever is the least among you is the greatest."*

Yes, all babies grow at different paces, but it does not take a baby 5 years to become a toddler, and it does not take a baby 10 years to know what *"No"* means! Some of us desire to remain in the infancy stage because we enjoy being lazy and being spoon fed, and then others prefer to skip through the infancy stage in order to be greater than those around them. Our own children do this same thing. They get to a certain stage and all of a sudden, they know it all! As parents, we know that they do not know it all. As parents, the word *"No"* has to be enforced more directly because our children will begin to test us. Our children begin to see how far they can get with just our words; therefore, our words must be enforced with discipline. As Christians, we test God. We may have learned what *"No"* meant as a child eventually; however, we certainly do not think that applies once we are grown physically. Then, there are those who never even learned what *"No"* meant as a child because there are parents that did not enforce it. These have a hard time being obedient to God when they never were obedient as a child. Being mature with God also takes discipline. This discipline is enforced with God through stages. These stages are for our own good. These stages are the different struggles and trials we have walked through in order to mature us spiritually. However, just like our children, we handle these stages with complete immaturity. We scream and cry out to God to deliver us from our difficulties. In fact, we cry out and make deals with God. *"If you do this God, then I will do that. If you are really God, then you will take this away from me. If you are real, then you will show up. God, where are you? If you are really a God of love, then why would you allow me to go through this?"* All of these things sound just like our own children whom we say are immature. Face it, God says the same about us. We need to grow up to see that God is real; He is good; He is a God of love, and if we could only relate, we would see that it is because of His great love for us that He allows the struggles and tests in order that we mature. As parents, we desire the same thing for our own children. However, we go through our spiritual walk believing that we know so much when we don't. We want others to think that we are experts when it comes to the Scriptures. We want others to see that we know so much about Scriptures when we may not. Human nature desires to be elevated and not humbled just like the first disciples. We desire to rush through the milk stages even though we missed out on growth needed in order to gain the real meat of the gospels and gain recognition. However, those who are first will be last and the last will be first.

Matthew 20:16 (NLT) [16] *"So those who are last now will be first then, and those who are first will be last."*

The Holy Spirit daily reminds me all the time, *"Be last – be last!"* This is really hard on my flesh, especially when I'm in traffic and in a hurry, and I hear, *"Be last – be last!"* This is putting my flesh down and allowing others to go before me; it is allowing others to excel before me in the workplace; it is allowing others to go before me when I am in line at the grocery store; it is allowing others to take the credit for something that was my idea, and I could go on and on but I think you understand. Today, so many Christians live a life full of defeat because our desires are to be elevated not humbled. When I say defeat, God blesses us not man, yet we desire the blessings of man. The blessings of God are eternal, but man's blessings are worldly. This alone shows who is following God and who is following man. It is no wonder that the world looks at the Christian community and scoffs at their lives because all they see are a bunch of people calling themselves Christians, yet their lives either speak nothing but defeat or their lives say, *"I am so much greater than you!"* Why would the world

189

desire to have the lifestyle of the Christian when there is nothing visible that draws their interest? Yes, there are the few which do strive to be the disciple they were called to be; however, for those who look at others in leadership positions within the churches today and desire to be increased to that same level are doing what the disciples spoke to Jesus about. *"Who will be greater in the Kingdom of Heaven, Lord?"* It is a fine line to being humble and working towards being recognized as a great man or woman of God. As a Christian, we should all be humble. Jesus was harsh with His disciples in those days and would be with us as well.

As a new Christian, we are meant to be joined together with other believers that are running the race that Paul ran. We should be striving to drink the milk as fast as we can in order to begin taking in substance; however, it is allowing the necessary growth before we go further. My granddaughter, Charli, at one year old could put away some food. She came into this world hungry and constantly wanted milk. By the time she was 8 months old, she already had many teeth and lost interest in the bottle. When she hit the one year mark, she had a mouth full of teeth and ate any and everything including meat. It was amazing how much she could put away. At 15 months old, it was nothing for her to eat 4 slices of pizza and this was adult slices. Today, she is not obese but has the most adorable baby fat thighs. It is not that we cannot grow at a faster pace; it is that we have become a laid back nation who would rather walk this race at a slow pace instead of running the race which Paul spoke of in order to win the prize. However, for those who are running, many times the motivation is to be great in the kingdom not to show humility.

1 Corinthians 9:24-27 (NLT) [24]Don't you realize that in a race everyone runs, but only one person gets the prize? So run to win! [25] All athletes are disciplined in their training. They do it to win a prize that will fade away, but we do it for an eternal prize. [26] *So I run with purpose in every step. I am not just shadowboxing.* [27] *I discipline my body like an athlete, training it to do what it should. Otherwise, I fear that after preaching to others I myself might be disqualified.*

I'm sure most of us would say that we are constantly running to keep up with today's society, but we are walking the race when it comes to our spirituality. As I have said, babies eventually want more substance and become dissatisfied with just milk. Too many times, Christians become dissatisfied and they quit. They decide to go back into the world before they even experience the freedom from being nurtured by our Father. Many times this is because those same adults never experienced the nurturing from an earthly parent, and so, they reject any form of nurturing from God. These adults put up walls as a child and even though many may experience some degree of healing from their past once they have become an adult, they may lack seeing the value in Christianity and this will continue to keep those walls from coming down permanently. It will be through allowing our Father to nurture us, through His Word, that we grow out of the infancy stage completely and desire to continue this walk into all the different stages in which God calls us.

Hebrews 5:12 (NIV) [12] *In fact, though by this time you ought to be teachers, you need someone to teach you the elementary truths of God's word all over again. You need milk, not solid food!*

Here is the key that will drastically change your walk with God. If you find yourself defeated as a Christian, you have either remained on milk or you did not get it the first time around and quit. Yes, we are to desire solid food, but if we have not allowed God to nurture us through the infancy stage, we need to go back and learn it all over again. You may be in church but you still quit God. What I mean by this, your life shows that you have given up, and you are just going through the motions. Solid food is for the mature, but maturity will never come until you learn the elementary truths about God's Word. The elementary truths are going back into school, back to the beginning perhaps. Too often, we think we know the Word of God when we do not. Too often, even leaders go into the ministry but have skipped a very important part to that connection with God. You may know Scripture, but that does not mean you really know it. We know something by our actions. If we are not walking in what we know to be truth, then we do not really know it. Let me clarify this. If God promised us healing but it is not happening in your situation, then you do not really understand that promise. Like I said, we may know Scripture, but it is primarily by memory and that does not mean we understand what God is really saying. We will never have the understanding if we went from kindergarten to the tenth grade and skipped everything in between. You cannot successfully operate in what is taught in the tenth grade if you have no understanding. It is not just about memorizing or knowing Scripture because you have read it enough. We should put our pride down and allow God to nurture us again. Christians should be madly in love with their Father, and if you are not feeling that, you may need to allow Him to nurture you. When we have not been nurtured as a child, we grow up hard and fast. Our character paints a picture of someone who does not need anyone to tell them what to do, when to do it, or how to do it. Our dependency has always been on ourselves and the walls constructed around us do not allow for a loving God to penetrate through us. Our heart becomes cold and will not allow for God to be the center of our life. This is not a picture of someone who stands before God with Him saying, *"Well done my faithful servant, you ran the race well!"*

Let me share something that God showed me one day. My grandbaby, at one year old, she is absolutely adorable and she knows how to push your buttons. She lives with me along with her mother. Around my house, I am usually up by 4 or 5 a.m. and my daughter around 6 a.m. By 6:30 a.m., my daughter and I are waking up the girls. Some mornings we both go into the baby's room and one particular morning, she had already awoken and was standing looking at both of us with her big sleepy eyes. Immediately, we both put our arms out and were calling her to come to us. When this happens, it becomes competition between me and my daughter and a game for Charli. I can say that most of the time she reaches for her mother and on occasions, I win. This particular morning, she sheepishly grinned at her mother, knowing if she picked me and rejected her, it would stir her mother up that much more which would produce additional attention. Don't think that babies do not learn fast how to move you. Needless to say, I won that morning. That same day, God began to reveal something to me. Every single day as His children come alive and begin to go about their life, God looks down on each of us smiling with that same smile a parent gives their child daily upon arising. When Charli looks upon those who love and care for her, what does she see? She sees those who love her, cuddle her, play with her, giggle with her, feed and nourish her. You need to picture this because it portrays a love that is so great. God looks down upon you each day with this big smile that only a loving parent gives toward their child. It is in that smile that He says, *"I love you; I care for you; I believe in you; I long for you."* As His children go about their day, they forget to pray while He continues to look upon them saying, *"I love you, choose me not the world."* They continue on their way and make choices which produce unwelcomed consequences while He continues to look upon them saying, *"Don't you know that I love you, choose my ways not that of the world."* Through their day, they encounter conflicts which leave them depressed and on the verge of tears and sometimes showing deep rejection to a God that loves them while they proclaim, *"God, if you are real, where are you?"* Yet, He continues to look upon them with love in His eyes and arms outstretched saying, *"Please don't reject me, if you would just read the love letter I left for you that you call the Bible, you would know that I am here and have never left you. I love and long for you and will wipe away your tears."* Yet, they never hear the small quiet voice because their storms they face seem so great and their fears seem so real, but He continues to call out their name and cries out for them to hear Him say, *"I love you my child, do you not understand that it is through my Son I gave you freedom and a way to salvation, and it is through my Word I can deliver you from this world and all the pain which it produces."* Yet, the majority of Christians today do not know this God because they never understood the importance of being nurtured by a loving Father who longs to hold them and feed them spiritual milk that will wipe away every wound ever produced from their past.

The sad truth, Christians today seldom put on the Belt of Truth and without the belt, your walk remains consuming milk here and there with little to no growth. Without the belt, your walk with God stops with just the helmet half way on and perhaps the breastplate partially on as you have learned some basics. If you have not come to the place to put on that Breastplate of Righteousness properly, in order to see yourself as God sees you, you will never hunger for greater things. However, once you get a taste of truth within you, it will be the beginning of life and not just a mere existence. It is also not enough to begin this walk and get bits and pieces of the Word within you, this is merely walking through life improperly dressed. We have men and women today trying to enroll in God's army who are running around in circles in the battlefield, and they are being shot left and right with fiery darts

194

from the enemy forces because they are partially naked. They may be running around with their helmet half way on and their breastplate hanging on their shoulders, but there is nothing else on them. No wonder, week after week the altar is full of the same people time and time again needing prayer for everything from financial problems to health problems and marital problems to problems with their children. God is crying out to His people to *"WAKE UP!"* He has given us a book which is detailed in instructions on how to live this life to the fullest and to be strengthened through Christ fully clothed, in order to win our battles time and time again. God cannot make us put on our armor. God cannot make us study His Word. God cannot change us into people who are disciplined and obedient, and God will not change our desires for those things above instead of what this world has to offer because He created us with a free will. We must begin to get God's Word in us, the truth, in order to begin replacing the wrong way of thinking with the right way of thinking. The more of God we put in, the more of the world will be pushed out. What is in us is what will come out. Every single strong hold in our lives which keeps us bound by satan's lies can be overcome by the Word of God. God's Word is power; it is what spoke the world and all we can see into existence. As we put His Word in us, our minds become transformed into thinking like God. After all, we are created in His likeness and image; therefore, we are His children and should think like He thinks. Children who are close to a parent, they take on much of that parent's characteristics, and the same should be with our God. As we draw closer to Him, our way of thinking should line up with His ways. I do not believe I see God as being someone who is defeated, but rather, He is Lord of Lords and King of Kings. God is all powerful, and there is none like Him. I believe if we had more of Him in us and we thought more like He thinks, there is no way we would run to the altar every week because our lives WOULD NOT be defeated.

This does not mean that you shouldn't go to the altar that is not what I am saying. If you need to go to the altar for prayer, by all means do so. However, this is to open our eyes to truth in order to see that this is not the place we need to remain. If we are not satisfied with living day after day in defeat, it is up to us to discipline ourselves in order to grow to another level with God where we are the ones praying for those still taking in milk. We need to be able to see that this is a game of life, yet the Christian community no longer runs to win. Why would we not want to win? Do we believe that God will just give us the prize of eternal life just because we have done some works in His name? Every step we take should have purpose, and just like an athlete, our bodies must be disciplined to take in as much milk as possible so that we grow to that place where we are ready for more solid food. If we cannot see this, we are merely in this race for no purpose, and we may be disqualified when we come to the end of this journey.

If you are ready to run this race, know that God desires for His people to grow up. God desires that we mature. Allow God today to break away everything that keeps you from Him. Allow Him to show you that place where you welcome Him into your life to nurture you with the love and compassion you may never have felt as a child.

The Biblical Belt

Ephesians 6:13-14a (NKJV) [13] *Therefore take up the whole armor of God, that you may be able to withstand in the evil day, and having done all, to stand.* [14] *Stand therefore, having girded your waist with truth...*

In biblical days, the Roman soldier's waist was girded with a belt which was usually made of leather but was very important to the overall uniform. In those days, men wore robes in which it would have been impossible to go into the battlefield without girding up the robe. To gird something means to bind or tie it up. We also see in the American Standard Version, it says to gird up the **loins**.

Ephesians 6:13-14a (ASV) ¹³*Wherefore take up the whole armor of God, that ye may be able to withstand in the evil day, and, having done all, to stand.* ¹⁴ *Stand therefore, having girded your loins with truth...*

The loins could be referring to the upper thigh area or even the hip area. Regardless, the Scripture teaches that we are to secure the belt around our mid-section. In biblical days, the belt had many purposes all of which were extremely important. In order for a soldier to be able to fight the battle at hand, they would first have to gather the robe at the corners and tie it up under the belt securely which would make the robe look like loose fitting shorts. Without securing the robe, the soldier would easily have stumbled from tripping on the robe and the robe would have hindered movement while in battle with the enemy. This would have put the soldier in a place of disadvantage against the enemy and ultimately would have caused death.

The belt also was a support for the breastplate which was quite heavy. The belt kept part of the weight off of the shoulders and placed it more on the hip area which allowed for better movement in battle allowing the arms to move freely. It also had a sheath attached which held the sword in place and metal straps which hung down in front for more protection. Without the belt, the Roman soldiers would have been unable to endure in battle. Without the belt, soldiers would not have been able to have their weapons close at hand when needed. In those days, the belt was also an apparatus which carried the necessary weapons in battle. Even today, belts are used to secure clothing and they are also used in various areas of work. Carpenters have belts which are used to carry many tools in order to complete projects at a much faster pace, and police officers also use their belts to carry weapons needed when faced with danger just as they did many years ago.

The mid-section of our body is an area of movement. It is the core area, which means the central or innermost part that allows our bodies to have movement. It is at our waist that we are able to bend, turn, and twist. Stand up and try to walk, pick up something, sit down and see how hard it is to do those motions if you could not bend, turn, and twist. It would be very challenging to do anything adequately except to lie down or stand straight up and walking would be stiff. This is the core area of our existence, and it is the area which allows mobility in order to operate efficiently whether engaged in battle or just doing normal routine things. Our core allows us to be strong and flexible as needed.

It is also in the mid-section of our bodies where many vital organs are housed. One important organ is the stomach where food travels and literally supplies all the nutrients to all parts of the body. Just that one organ alone being critically injured would have caused death in those days. I can remember years ago when I lived out in the country, one morning we went outside and could hear a cat crying and crying in agony. We began following the sound of the cries into a wooded area. There she was under some bushes. She had evidently been run over by a car, and the whole midsection of her body had been literally crushed. I was surprised she was still alive. There was no way she could have survived and needed to be put out of her misery, which was done.

If a soldier, in those days, were to have been wounded in the mid-section, more than likely they would have never lived. There was not medical aid in those days but even today with medical aid, the organs in our mid-section are called vital organs because that is what they are. Vital means necessary for the continuation of life. There are some organs that we can sustain life without, and there are methods used today to replace certain organs, but ultimately, our organs all have a purpose and when they malfunction or are injured, it can be vital to our health and lives.

Spiritual Belt

When Paul spoke to the disciples about the Armor of God, he said to put on the Belt of Truth. To understand what the Belt of Truth means in a spiritual sense, we must first look into the natural to see the purpose of the belt for the Roman soldier. We know that the belt had many purposes as discussed above, and it is in those purposes that we can get a clearer picture in the spiritual sense to understand what Paul was trying to impart. We are going to look deeper into the mid-section of our body to understand the protection our belt has spiritually as well as in the natural.

There are a few things that we need to see by looking at this through the spiritual sense. The first one we will look at is that the waist is the center most part of our body as discussed above. It is basically the core to our existence. Our vital organs in that area are necessary to live and to live life to the fullest. We can live without some of those organs or by having implants, but in order to live life to the fullest, all those organs need to function and to do so with an outstanding performance. I don't know about you, but I like to know that all my organs are functioning to the best of their ability based on how God designed them to function. Yes, when we are sick, it affects certain organs capacity to function properly.

199

However, I am sure we would all agree that life flows much smoother when sickness subsides and everything is in proper working order once again.

Why did Paul say to put on a belt around this mid-section? Of course, we have all come to know that this is the area a belt would go, but why did Paul refer to the belt as Truth? One thing God showed me was that the Word of course is Truth, and when we study to put more and more of God's Truth in us, it replaces misconceptions and lies that we have learned over the years. Jesus was the Word, and He was made Flesh and dwelt among us. When we put the Belt of Truth on, we are actually putting Jesus on! Jesus is our healer; He is our deliverer; He is our salvation, our redemption, our solution, etc.

John 1:14 (ESV) [14] *And the Word became flesh and dwelt among us, and we have seen his glory, glory as of the only Son from the Father, full of grace and truth.*

Our Healer

Isaiah 53:5 (AMP) [5] *But He was wounded for our transgressions, He was bruised for our guilt and iniquities; the chastisement [needful to obtain] peace and well-being for us was upon Him, and with the stripes [that wounded] Him we are healed and made whole.*

Our Deliverer

1 Thessalonians 1:10 (AMP) [10] *And [how you] look forward to and await the coming of His Son from heaven, Whom He raised from the dead— Jesus, Who personally rescues and delivers us out of and from the wrath [bringing punishment] which is coming [upon the impenitent] and draws us to Himself [investing us with all the privileges and rewards of the new life in Christ, the Messiah].*

Our Salvation

Psalm 62:2 (AMP) ² He only is my Rock and my Salvation, my Defense and my Fortress, I shall not be greatly moved.

Our Redemption

Ephesians 1:7 (AMP) ⁷ In Him we have redemption (deliverance and salvation) through His blood, the remission (forgiveness) of our offenses (shortcomings and trespasses), in accordance with the riches and the generosity of His gracious favor,

Our Solution

Matthew 11:28 (AMP) ²⁸ Come to Me, all you who labor and are heavy-laden and overburdened, and I will cause you to rest. [I will ease and relieve and refresh your souls.]

When we are not walking in Truth, we are being led down a path that is full of deception and ungodliness. When we choose to walk down that path because we have not strapped on the belt, we choose to walk into darkness. When we walk into darkness, we have agreed to that sin. With sin comes every evil thing including death. I believe we could gain some wisdom from the words of James...

James 3:16 (NLT) ¹⁶For wherever there is jealousy and selfish ambition, there you will find disorder and evil of every kind.

James 4:1-3 (NLT) [1] *What is causing the quarrels and fights among you? Don't they come from the evil desires at war within you?* [2] *You want what you don't have, so you scheme and kill to get it. You are jealous of what others have, but you can't get it, so you fight and wage war to take it away from them. Yet you don't have what you want because you don't ask God for it.* [3] *And even when you ask, you don't get it because your motives are all wrong—you want only what will give you pleasure.*

James 1:15 (NLT) [15] *These desires give birth to sinful actions. And when sin is allowed to grow, it gives birth to death.*

It may not be a natural death yet, but it definitely will be a spiritual death. If you do not have Truth in you, you are slowly dying a spiritual death or maybe you already have. When we step out from under God's Truth, we have in a sense traded God for satan. Believe me, satan would love to destroy **your** world, and he will do so with **your** permission. You give him that permission when you choose not to wear your belt. God gives to all who ask, but if we never ask because we actually desire to remain in our sin, we will never receive. You bring about the consequences within your life by the choices you make.

To look at this in a natural sense, when we choose to walk down the wrong path, evil attaches itself to us. We cry out wondering why our lives are a mess, yet it was all our choosing. Stress comes, anger comes, jealousy comes, rejection, deceitfulness, and eventually, our natural organs begin to take the weight of all the stresses added by the lifestyles we have made the choice to travel. We develop stomach problems, perhaps ulcers; we begin to have problems with our pancreas, liver, and all these organs could have been protected by simply applying the Belt of Truth. Just like the soldiers, in biblical days, wore the belt in the physical sense to protect those organs from weapons which would have caused great physical wounds that could have resulted in a natural death, in the spiritual sense, when we choose not to seek and study God's Words, the result is that we become spiritually wounded and this leads to a slow natural death. Maybe you think this sounds crazy, but in reality, there are two choices in this life. One choice produces death and the other life. God's Word has the answers to whatever you face, but you will never see that if you do not seek for yourself. It does not matter what circumstances you may be facing, God has the solution. Yet, we would rather do it man's way instead of God's. His ways are not man's ways, neither are His thoughts.

Isaiah 55:8(NLT) [8] *"My thoughts are nothing like your thoughts," says the* LORD. *"And my ways are far beyond anything you could imagine.*

In Ephesians, this being the last message that Paul imparted to the church, it must have been of high priority. Today, Christians take their walk with God for granted because they choose to see their battles as natural instead of spiritual. It is much easier to walk as the world walks instead of as Jesus walked. When we cannot see something in the natural, we literally see it as non-existent. If we believe our spiritual battles do not really exist, why do we believe there is a God that we cannot see, and why believe Jesus is the Son of God when we cannot see Him? As long as we take this aspect of our Christian walk for granted, our gain for those things to come will be minimal if not non-existent for us. We will never enter into a realm with our Father in Heaven greater than what we have currently, if we cannot see past what is natural. Our God is a spiritual being, and we were also created as such, but if we only feed our natural man and not our spiritual man, we will never see anything more than what we see today. Boot Camp in God's Army can be very real and can be a huge growing experience into the spiritual realm, but we must take it as serious as the soldier takes the military uniform.

There are many things to see as to why Paul used the belt as the place to apply Truth. As I have said, our waist is the core or the center of our existence. The Word tells us that if we try to hang on to our lives and not give them up to follow Christ, we will lose our own soul. In other words, we will not see heaven.

Matthew 16:24-26 (NLT) [24] *Then Jesus said to his disciples, "If any of you wants to be my follower, you must turn from your selfish ways, take up your cross, and follow me.* [25] *If you try to hang on to your life, you will lose it. But if you give up your life for my sake, you will save it.* [26] *And what do you benefit if you gain the whole world but lose your own soul? Is anything worth more than your soul?*

Jesus should be the core to our existence. I believe that is why the belt symbolizes the Word, which is Christ. Our sole existence should be Christ; He should be the center of our lives. Without that belt on, there is no life. Jesus told Peter, blessed are you and on this rock He would build His church.

Matthew 16:17-19 (ESV) [17] *And Jesus answered him, "Blessed are you, Simon Bar-Jonah! For flesh and blood has not revealed this to you, but my Father who is in heaven.* [18] *And I tell you, you are Peter, and on this rock I will build my church, and the gates of hell shall not prevail against it.* [19] *I will give you the keys of the kingdom of heaven, and whatever you bind on earth shall be bound in heaven, and whatever you loose on earth shall be loosed in heaven."*

Understand that we are the church; it is not a building. Why was Peter blessed? He was blessed because he knew who Jesus was; he knew that He was the Son of God. Peter had his belt on!

Do you have your belt on today? Is your walk with God real today and do you really know God? Do you know Jesus? Has the Father revealed to you just who Jesus is? Now ask yourself, is Jesus your rock today? Have you made Him the center of your life? Is He the core to your existence, the reason you exist today? Remember without the core, we would be stiff and it would hinder our ability to be strong in our battles.

If your spiritual battles do not seem to be working for you, it may be that you have neglected applying that spiritual belt around your waist. To apply the belt around your waist is a very simple procedure. Our bodies let us know when they are hungry. We take in food and it travels to our stomach and then nutrients travel to all parts of the body as they flow into each vital organ and throughout every vein and capillary. We know when we begin to feel those hunger pains, and sometimes, we even begin to feel a little weak because we have not eaten in a while. In the same sense, we should be able to feel those warning signs when stress, worry, fear, or anxiety begins to flow through our bodies. Those feelings do not feel good. We have become accustomed to alleviate those feelings by supplying our bodies with drugs, alcohol, gorging ourselves with added food intake, spending countless hours in front of the TV, calling those friends for the thousandth time to pour out our problems, and we do all these things for comfort and as a means to find an easy fix to our problems. However, we will never find the solution to anything we walk through by using drugs and alcohol to numb the uneasiness within our bodies. We will never find the solution by ignoring the symptoms through different avenues of satisfying our flesh such as keeping our minds focused on television, computers, sex, or anything else that satisfies those worldly desires. We will never find the solution by pouring out our problems to any and every one that will listen. These things do not work! When we awaken the next morning, our problems still remain in the same place we left them. Our bodies are starving to be fed the Word of God which is the only solution to feeding us spiritual food which will awaken us to new heights with Jesus Christ. If we do not get the adequate nutrition needed spiritually, we will feel the stresses of this world. We need to realize, that our spiritual bodies are crying out, *"I need to be fed; I need spiritual food."* We run **from** the only One that can give us life and life to the fullest. We run from the One who has the solutions.

When I was in my teens, I was hit so hard in the stomach that I could not breathe and had to be taken to the hospital. In an actual battle, if your adversary was to hit you very hard in this area, it immediately weakens you, and you fall forward lifeless. In a spiritual battle, if our enemy can weaken us where we are not being fed properly by feeding our spirit man the nutrients it needs through the Word of God, he has won. satan's purpose has always been to destroy mankind in any way possible.

John 10:10 (AMP) [10]*The thief comes only in order to steal and kill and destroy. I came that they may have and enjoy life, and have it in abundance (to the full, till it overflows).*

If you are not enjoying life to the fullest today, you have probably not learned how to apply the Belt of Truth. Jesus came to give us life but not just any life. He came that our life would be full and not just full but that it would overflow. What is life overflowing? Have you ever met someone and they just seemed to bubble over with life? Everything about them seemed great. Their life was so filled with laughter and enjoyment that it would spill over on you. Why do people not like to be around those who are always complaining and everything in their life seems to be in turmoil? It is because we all have our own issues, and it can be depressing to continually be around someone who is always down. But, what about someone who is always up? It is like they attract people by the multitudes, why is that? It spills over on you. I know when my grandbabies are together and one of them begins to giggle and laugh, the other one joins in and soon everyone is giggling and laughing. The fun part is that when it is all over with, we don't even remember why we were laughing to begin with. This is called joy and this is something that God promises us. God wants us to be full of life so that our life overflows on others.

Romans 14:16-18 (NLT) [16]*Then you will not be criticized for doing something you believe is good.* [17] *For the Kingdom of God is not a matter of what we eat or drink, but of living a life of goodness and peace and joy in the Holy Spirit.* [18] *If you serve Christ with this attitude, you will please God, and others will approve of you, too.*

There is a saying that is spoken many times when we are faced with making a decision. That saying is that we have a *"gut feeling"* within or we consider it a *"gut instinct."* Many times people will base a decision on what they feel inside. Of course, our gut would be considered our stomach which is housed in the core or center of our body. There are times that we have flip-flops in our stomach that we relate to being in love, our stomach can begin to have a sick feeling come over us when something that produces fear happens, and then sometimes we just feel a certain way inside that influences our decisions. We are going to look more into depth at the words gut and instinct.

We will begin with the word gut. What makes the belt so vital to our Christian walk? I'm sure we have all watched boxing on television. How many times in fights does the opponent swing for the middle? This is something that God showed me. When we feed our body, our food goes into our stomach, and then the

207

nutritious supplements are dispersed to all areas of the body from the core to supply us with what we need to survive and be strong. In the natural sense, if we are hit really hard in the stomach, this weakens us for our opponent to gain ground. In the spiritual sense, satan does the same thing. satan seeks to attack us below the belt because he does not fight fair. In a boxing match, to hit in the mid-section will cause you the fight because it is not a fair fight. However, outside of the rules and regulations to an organized fight, fights have been lost because the opponent would hit in an area that would cause great injuries. satan does not care if he causes you great pain, and we need this truth in us in order to begin to win instead of losing. How does satan hit us in the mid-section? There are many ways, but the most effective way is by daily convincing God's people that it is not necessary to read and study God's Word. I have met people who believed going to church one day a week and listening to one sermon was good enough. If that is you, he has already convinced you, and you believed a lie. satan weakens us spiritually by convincing us that we do not need to apply the core of our armor. Daily, he convinces people that their walk with God is good as it is and nothing else is needed. I heard recently of a woman who wanted prayer for her wayward son, and when asked how much time she spent praying for him, her answer was none. Her reason was because she worked full time and was too busy to have time to pray. Did you know without your belt on, you won't pray. How can we possibly pray when we have no Word in us? Let me say, praying to God can merely be just talking to Him, but when you are looking for answers and want to move mountains in your life, you better have some Word in you because it's His Words that are powerful not man's.

If our adversary can convince us that we do not have time to spend studying, going to church, listening to teaching tapes, or reading a spiritual book, he has already weakened us. When we are weakened in the core of our existence, we have lost the battle. Daily, satan convinces people that it is not important to read the Word of God; he convinces them to let the pastor, preacher, or priest do the studying for them; he convinces them that if they go to church once a week that should be enough; he keeps them pre-occupied where they continually make excuses why they never have time to give to the only relationship that will drastically change their life and that is our relationship with God. These are all lies from the enemy, and as long as we walk that path, we will be living in darkness not in the light. When we are in darkness, we are bound by lies. The Bible says the path which leads to heaven is narrow and few will find it, but the path which leads to hell is wide and many will travel it. The narrow path is not because we cannot find it and travel it, but it is because we continually listen to lies from the enemy whose job is to keep us deceived and bound in order that we do not make heaven.

One more lie that Christians have listened to is that God understands when we don't have time to spend with Him. Did you know that God is a jealous God? He desires our time and attention. He wants our love. If we go day after day without giving Him much thought at all, do we really think He understands? Yes, He will forgive us, but He still wants a relationship with us. For a relationship to be good, it takes our time. When we listen to those lies and we refrain from spending time learning and growing in the spiritual realm, the enemy has hit us in the core of our existence and it weakens us. I have met people who are at a place where they have little strength to continue living this life. In their weakness they cry out to God, but the solution is to draw strength from Him. We can do nothing through ourselves but all things through Christ who gives us His strength. It is through the Belt of

Truth that we will find that strength. It is through the Belt of Truth that we will find the solution to whatever we are facing.

Philippians 4:13 (ESV) [13] I can do all things through him who strengthens me.

What happens when we do not get the truth within us? When we come to that place where there are bad feelings in our gut because of something that is going on in our lives or something we did or did not do, or perhaps something that someone else did that affected us, it will also begin to affect our health. We may begin to have that sick feeling deep within our stomach, right? Our stomach knots up, fear comes on us, worry comes and stress. We find that we cannot sleep at night. Perhaps, we are unable to eat or perhaps what soothes us is continually eating to relieve the pain within. We may find ourselves operating in unhealthy habits such as smoking cigarettes, doing drugs, or excessive alcohol use. When we are in this state, we have lost our peace and replaced that peace with fear, worry, stress, etc.

Stress is one of the major causes of health problems today. We become stressed because of how we allow situations in our lives to affect us. In other words, we allow outside circumstances to take control of our minds. Remember, we are to have the mind of Christ, and we cannot have the mind of Christ without applying the Belt of Truth. The belt of truth guards our core. That belt is not for decoration but to guard those organs which supply what is needed to the rest of the body. When our system is in an uproar, we find that we can no longer operate in a healthy way by eating right, getting enough sleep, or taking the time out for our overall health. When we are out of balance, we no longer will replace that which is good in our lives with those things harmful. It is evident that the harmful things are eating too much, smoking, drinking, doing drugs, etc. When we are stressed out totally, our body will eventually shut down. Our body begins to take on the blunt of those bad habits, and all of a sudden, we do not feel strong anymore. We become weakened to the point of giving up. You may find yourself sleeping a lot as depression sinks in, and many may find themselves at a hopeless state where life no longer seems to matter. If satan can attack our core, eventually we will die. This may not be a physical death, but what good are we if our health deteriorates? This is not to say those who live with chronic ailments are worthless, and if you are reading that into this, you are missing my point. God can turn around any situation for His good and use anyone willing to further His Kingdom. My point is simply for a generation to awaken to see their choices. If we find ourselves in a situation where our organs begin shutting down, and we find ourselves having to undergo surgery to replace or remove organs, was this what we expected for our life? When we make the wrong choice, we are hit at the core, our mid-section. It is our waist which allows us to move more freely. We can turn; we can bend down, but what if we were stiff and had no core? What if from sickness, we were left where we did not have this movement? In a physical war, the enemy would overtake those who could not move fast enough or dodge to get out of the way of danger. In the spiritual war, if we are consumed with physical ailments, how can we serve God to the fullest? How can we show the world how great our God is when we are not living an abundant life? In reality, the biblical belt used during that era protected the vital organs in the same way the Word of God protects them. Can you see the parallel? In the natural war, without the belt on, our organs could have been damaged by the tactics of the enemy, and in the spiritual war, our organs are damaged by the stresses of this world which in turn comes from our enemy. What good are we to ourselves and our families if our health deteriorates? What good are we if our organs begin shutting down and we find ourselves having to undergo surgery to replace organs or remove organs?   When our organs are affected, some are left paralytic, while others never make it and those who do survive, was it worth the suffering? Are you satisfied with where you are today? Jesus did the suffering for us; the Word of God says that He came to give us life and life to the fullest. *(John 10:10)*

We choose if we want that life more abundant based on our actions. Our choice comes down to seeking God or seeking the world. One produces life and the other produces death. When we allow situations to take over our mind, there is no peace. Without peace, we operate in what is natural to man such as fear, anger, anxiety, etc. Below is a report which shows how devastating stress is on the human body.

The American Stress Institute reports:

1. More than 40% of all adults suffer adverse health effects as a result of stress.

2. More than 75% of all visits to primary-care physicians are for stress-related complaints or disorders.

3. Stress has been linked to all leading causes of death, including heart disease, cancer, lung ailments, accidents and suicides.

4. Stress is responsible for more than half of all workdays lost annually.

5. Approximately 80% of the health-related problems in technologically-advanced countries are stress related.[2]

As I have said, when we are attacked in the core or foundation of our existence, we are weakened. However, when we replace all those negative thoughts with the Word of God, His Word will rise up in us at a time that we need it, and we will refuse to entertain those negative thoughts that the enemy brings. We refuse to trade our peace for worry and fear!

If you do a study on the meaning of instinct, you will see that it is an inborn tendency to behave in a way characteristic of a species – natural, unlearned, and predictable. Animals have instinctive behavior as well as humans, which would be classified as instinctive not learned behavior. Much of the behavior seen in animals is based on their species. Inborn tendencies found in mammals are natural behaviors and often predictable. Example - suckling is an instinct found in mammals in order to survive. This would be a natural instinct that is unlearned. Most animal's eyes are not even open when first born, yet they have that natural survival instinct to find their mother for milk. Our instinct is something which is inborn within each of us and is characteristic to human nature, race, culture, etc. It can be pretty much predictable as time goes on because we grow up doing what we have always done, when we have always done it, and in the same way as what was natural to us. Then predictable instinct is one that is acquired or learned based on the characteristics of our nature. Example – you may find yourself saying, *"I know that she or he is going to react this way!"* Our lives become predictable to those who have known us long enough. In fact, many times when we begin to put on the nature of Christ and we allow God to begin changing our predictable human nature to a more Christ-like nature, people will sometimes say, *"I know that it looks like you on the inside, but it does not act like you – who is this person that has taken over?"* This is meant to be humorous but it is very true at times. When we begin acting in a way that was not predictable and it is for the better, it often shocks others because they have never known us to act in a way that is Christ-like. It may even shock ourselves when God gets a hold of us and our character begins to completely do the opposite of what it used to do.

What I am trying to show is that we are born with certain tendencies and we react in certain ways based on those natural instincts, but we also react based on those learned instincts. We all have acquired certain instinctive behaviors based on how we were raised, things we have lived through or experienced, and things we have been taught. Regardless of our natural or acquired behavior, both can be changed. God's Word says that we are all born sinners, yet a baby is not aware of sin. In ourselves, we can never inherit the Kingdom of Heaven, yet through Christ we can. We are all born with our blood tainted with the blood of the first Adam, yet when we accept Jesus in our lives, the blood of the second Adam (Christ) cleanses and covers us.

1 Corinthians 15:45 (NLT) [45] *The Scriptures tell us, "The first man, Adam, became a living person." But the last Adam—that is, Christ—is a life-giving Spirit.*

Much of what we do just comes natural for our species and is not a learned response but an unlearned one. However, instinct can also be an acquired tendency, in the sense of how much we put into our behavior and pattern to change from our previous actions. Yes, animals have instinct and do what they have always done, but humans are not necessarily doing what they have always done. I'm sure there would be disagreement on this part, but if we believe we were created as descendants of Adam and Eve, we also know that they were created sinless prior to their fall. We certainly are not sinless today, but we cannot make the statement, *"I do what I do because it was the way I was raised, and it has always been what I have done; therefore, I cannot change this behavior because this is just the way that I am."* We can change our behavior and line our lives up to be more Christ-like to where the voice that we hear which gives us that gut feeling lines up with God's Word because we understand that the Holy Spirit is our teacher, and He was sent on our behalf.

John 14:26 (ESV) [26] *But the Helper, the Holy Spirit, whom the Father will send in my name, he will teach you all things and bring to your remembrance all that I have said to you.*

1 John 1:5-7 (NLT) [5] *This is the message we heard from Jesus and now declare to you: God is light, and there is no darkness in him at all.* [6] *So we are lying if we say we have fellowship with God but go on living in spiritual darkness; we are not practicing the truth.* [7] *But if we are living in the light, as God is in the light, then we have fellowship with each other, and the blood of Jesus, his Son, cleanses us from all sin.*

Just because we were born with instincts that are natural to the human species, does not mean that we have to remain bound in those characteristics. If we are a new creature through Christ, the old man is dead and the new man lives on. All things which are old pass away.

2 Corinthians 5:17 (ESV) [17] *Therefore, if anyone is in Christ, he is a new creation. The old has passed away; behold, the new has come.*

When we line up with God's Word, we walk according to what is natural in the spiritual realm not what is natural to man. We are capable of reprogramming our natural instincts to be one with Christ. Those instincts which become learned can become our new man created in Christ. To simplify what I am saying, our gut instincts can be learned and reprogrammed to line up with the Word of God.

215

Another definition I came across said that instinct was a psychic force or drive as in fear, love, or anger. This force is not psychic but rather spiritual. There are only two forces in the spiritual realm and one comes from the light and the other from darkness. It is not too hard to line up which force is coming at you because if it is fear, the Bible says that God has not given us a spirit of fear, and if it is love, we know that God is love. This is how we line up that voice so that we can strap on the belt of truth and put more and more of God in us, where we are able to line up the forces which attack us. Once that is done, we are able to see where it is coming from based on what we are feeling inside. satan's job today has been made easy because Christians walk out of their safe havens for the day, completely naked. We make sure we have clothes on in the natural because if we walk out without our clothes on, we know we will probably be arrested; however, we seldom give it much thought to walking out of the house spiritually naked. This is what Christians do today and that is why they are imprisoned. You see, we wear clothes in the natural to keep from going to jail, yet your spiritual man remains in jail by the enemy as long as you allow him to walk all over you. The Bible says that we are bound by lies; we are imprisoned.

John 8:31-38 (ESV) The Truth Will Set You Free [31] *So Jesus said to the Jews who had believed him, "If you abide in my word, you are truly my disciples,* [32] *and you will know the truth, and the truth will set you free."* [33] *They answered him, "We are offspring of Abraham and have never been enslaved to anyone. How is it that you say, 'You will become free'?"* [34] *Jesus answered them, "Truly, truly, I say to you, everyone who practices sin is a slave to sin.* [35] *The slave does not remain in the house forever; the son remains forever.* [36] *So if the Son sets you free, you will be free indeed.* [37] *I know that you are offspring of Abraham; yet you seek to kill me because my word finds no place in you.* [38] *I speak of what I have seen with my Father, and you do what you have heard from your father."*

To sum this up, we have studied the helmet and breastplate and now we are digging deeper into the belt. We will begin to see how these 3 pieces of armor line up in order to begin our journey to where God desires to take us. In my studies, I also found another definition for gut instinct which stated the ability to use your heart and mind to make a choice. This summed it up. Our mind is protected by our helmet and our heart is protected by the breastplate. We put both of those on, and they work together to protect our mind to the mind of Christ and our heart to remain pure; this is when our gut instinct will line up with God's Word because that is what we have been feeding on, and our choices will be those that are correct. God's will be done and not our own! It is the truth that becomes our core and our foundation.

As we study, our mind and our heart will begin to line up to God's way of thinking, but without that belt, our mind and heart will never see things through the spiritual aspect. I remember years back a cousin telling me to follow my heart. This was not good advice, especially if you are lost and your heart is not right with God. When we are not saved or even if we are saved but we have not matured in Christ, our mind will make the decision based on what the heart is feeling or based on that gut instinct. The problem with this is that if the Belt of Truth is never applied, the decisions will solely be based on what is in your heart and what your gut tells you, but it will not line up with the Word of God. A gut instinct that has been reprogrammed to line up with God's Word ties into the helmet and breastplate. When we have that deep feeling, our heart is involved along with our mind and what is deep down in our gut. However, we must understand all three pieces of armor must line up with the Word of God. Our mind will be the avenue which makes the decision or choice based on what our heart is feeling, and our heart will feel what has been stored deep within the core of our existence. We make many choices daily, and it all goes back to our mind but our mind receives the information based on what is on the inside of us. We know that our mind should have the mind of Christ, our heart should be pure, and we should be feeding our body the Word of God so that it is stored into the core of who we are in Christ.

Mind of Christ

1 Corinthians 2:16 (AMP) [16] For who has known or understood the mind (the counsels and purposes) of the Lord so as to guide and instruct Him and give Him knowledge? But we have the mind of Christ (the Messiah) and do hold the thoughts (feelings and purposes) of His heart.

Pure Heart

Matthew 5:8 (AMP) [8] Blessed (happy, enviably fortunate, and spiritually prosperous—possessing the happiness produced by the experience of God's favor and especially conditioned by the revelation of His grace, regardless of their outward conditions) are the pure in heart, for they shall see God!

God's Words are life to those who find them. In fact, we should all study the whole chapter of Proverbs 4 if we desire more wisdom.

Proverbs 4:20-23 (AMP) [20] My son, attend to my words; consent and submit to my sayings. [21] Let them not depart from your sight; keep them in the center of your heart. [22] For they are life to those who find them, healing and health to all their flesh. [23] Keep and guard your heart with all vigilance and above all that you guard, for out of it flow the springs of life.

When we choose not to walk in God's ways because we would rather walk in unrighteousness, we are making that choice to follow satan, and we will perish. When we do not put on our armor daily, we are allowing the enemy to fill our mind and heart with filth, evil, delusions, wickedness, and lies. The Belt of Truth is the core to our existence and without that belt, we will perish. Our foundation must be Christ which is Truth.

2 Thessalonians 2:9-12 (AMP) [9] *The coming [of the lawless one, the antichrist] is through the activity and working of Satan and will be attended by great power and with all sorts of [pretended] miracles and signs and delusive marvels—[all of them] lying wonders—* [10] *And by unlimited seduction to evil and with all wicked deception for those who are perishing (going to perdition) because they did not welcome the Truth but refused to love it that they might be saved.* [11] *Therefore God sends upon them a misleading influence, a working of error and a strong delusion to make them believe what is false,* [12] *In order that all may be judged and condemned who did not believe in [who refused to adhere to, trust in, and rely on] the Truth, but [instead] took pleasure in unrighteousness.*

Many today view God's Word as too restrictive and choose to walk the ways of man. The Word does restrict us but only in order to protect us from what is harmful. It is through His Word that brings true freedom; therefore, we could say that it is those things which restrict us that actually give us freedom. For those who choose to not walk according to God's Word, they have exchanged the Truth for what is a lie. The enemy daily convinces people that you really do not have to do everything the Word says; after all, God understands that we are not perfect and that we will miss it.

John 8:32 (AMP) [32] *And you will know the Truth, and the Truth will set you free.*
Galatians 5:1 (AMP) [1] *In [this] freedom Christ has made us free [and completely liberated us]; stand fast then, and do not be hampered and*

held ensnared and submit again to a yoke of slavery [which you have once put off].

We must stand firm with our belt buckled around our core section that our breastplate will be in place. Remember in biblical days, the belt assisted in holding the breastplate because of the weight. Without the belt, the breastplate would not be held in place which meant that soldiers went into battle with their battle gear half way on or not applied correctly. In the military, there are strict procedures that your uniform and all battle gear are at all times in proper order, or there are consequences. Violations of the proposed uniform standards are considered a punitive order and could be subject to prosecution under the Uniform of Military Justice.[3] If the military has strict regulations to be properly dressed, should we not take it serious to listen to what Paul was trying to teach the church in regards to our armor in God's Army?

A soldier today would never carry themselves in the manner which Christians do while being enlisted in the military. A soldier today learns respect, honor, and strives to learn and advance within the branch they are enlisted in order to gain more wisdom and knowledge to the best of their ability. Why do soldiers give the military 100%? I am sure there are many reasons from advancement to career oriented and education. Regardless their reasons, all of these things come down to the desires that a soldier strives to get more out of it than they came in with. This merely means that it is human nature that we are willing to put 100% into something where there is gain. We want something! Perhaps, it is more money that we desire, a better education, a desirable career, or status. However, most give with the attitude which says, *"What's in it for me?"* As Christians, we do not see the importance of giving all we can to advance within the Army of God because we cannot see the gain upfront! Advancement with

God is not about us but about God! The only reason we choose to give of ourselves to something when we can see no gain, is when it involves giving because we love the person or organization we are giving to. Our children and family are one example of giving and giving and giving, even when we do not receive anything for our time and effort. We will never do that as Christians until we first fall in love with our Father. We will never fall in love with our Father until we get to know Him. We will never get to know God unless we make that choice to do so. There is much gain, but that is something most will never see. If you desire today to get to know your Father to a greater degree, you must choose to put on that belt of truth daily and engage.

Being engaged means that you will never come to a place where the growth stops unless you choose to stop growing. All living things grow and when they stop being fed, they die. Our natural bodies will die if they are not fed, and our spiritual bodies will also die if not being fed the Word of God. When you choose to stop studying and learning of God, your choice makes your spirit man die – meaning it lies dormant. You will find throughout my books that I repeat myself many times and maybe say it a little different. There are reasons I do so. You can buy spiritual books from different authors which speak on the same subject and get something different from each one. Every author has gained insight into revelation based on their own experiences in life. There was a time that I told God I did not need to attend a certain class at church because I already knew about salvation, or I already knew about the infilling of the Holy Spirit. God's reply to me was, *"Are you saying that you never need to hear about that subject again because **it is My Words**?"* I never looked at it like that. Is there a certain number of times we should read about one topic that pertains to the Bible, or should we be open minded enough to continue studying more and more about each topic?

What I have learned is that every speaker has their own way of relating Scripture due to their own personalities and experiences. When we listen because we desire growth with God, we will grasp new revelation that we may not have seen before instead of having the attitude, *"I already know that."* I repeat many times because I know we need to hear it again and again. We all have areas that we are bound, and we all have areas of defeat because none of us have arrived yet. God can bring forth one Scripture and begin to show me many things not just one thing. There are many times I will use that Scripture again and again because there are many things to see. We can also read or listen to revelation from someone else and while hearing what they received from God, He begins to show us something else that was not even portrayed through what we heard. We may know a certain Scripture but if that Word is not working in our life, in reality, we really do not know it!

We need to break down those prideful spirits which want to portray how godly we are, when in fact, it is very easy to be able to see how much of God someone has in them. I have told my prayer group many times that I could spend one hour with anyone and be able to tell how much time they spend in the Word of God and also how often they share Jesus. What is on the inside of you is what will come out. If you never study and read God's Word, it will not come out because there is nothing about God in you. Yet, people today have plenty of knowledge about the top movies, the best songs, the undefeated sports teams, and all the gossip to go with it about their neighbors, co-workers, and families. We even have gossip to share about those who attend the same churches that we do. It is a shame when all we have to talk about are things of this world. The Bible says we are to think on those things above

Colossians 3:2 (ESV) ²*Set your minds on things that are above, not on things that are on earth. The Word says we are to seek those things above.*

In Psalm 141 it says that we are to put a guard upon our mouth so that we do not speak about those things as the world does.

Psalm 141:3 (ESV) ³*Set a guard, O LORD, over my mouth; keep watch over the door of my lips!*

What ties you to this world? Our ties to this world should be only those things God has called us to do, and we will never understand that until we strap that belt on daily and keep it on.

There are people who see truth as binding because it brings restrictions as I said previously. Example – the Word says, *"Thou shalt not…!"* This binds or limits the *"many"* because they desire to do what they want instead of obey the laws set down by God. However, when we look at the Word of God in this mindset, we are already deceived. God's Truth is the ultimate Truth! Regardless of what man sees as truth, if it does not line up with the Word of God, there is no truth in it. When lining up with God's Word, if that truth brings restrictions, then it must also bring freedom because the Word of God says who the Son sets free is free indeed. Jesus is the only truth that can and will set us free in any area where there is bondage.

John 8:31-36 (ESV) The Truth Will Set You Free ³¹*So Jesus said to the Jews who had believed him, "If you abide in my word, you are truly my disciples,* ³²*and you will know the truth, and the truth will set you free."* ³³*They answered him, "We are offspring of Abraham and have never been enslaved to anyone. How is it that you say, 'You will become free'?"* ³⁴*Jesus answered them, "Truly, truly, I say to you, everyone who practices sin is a slave^[a] to sin.* ³⁵*The slave does not remain in the house forever; the son remains forever.* ³⁶*So if the Son sets you free, you will be free indeed.*

Battling our Storms

2 Corinthians 10:4 (AMP) *[4]For the weapons of our warfare are not physical [weapons of flesh and blood], but they are mighty before God for the overthrow and destruction of strongholds,*

Our weapons are not carnal weapons but they are weapons of Truth. We just read about Truth setting us free. It is Truth that also pulls down the strongholds in our lives. We need to discuss the battles that we face. I like to refer to those things we walk through as the storms of life. Storms as we know them stir things up, they move things, and they swiftly travel through our lives. When great storms happen on earth which leave enormous destruction in their wake, people find them so phenomenal they discuss the effects for quite some time. When we are faced with situations that are out of our control, they can leave a path of destruction so vast that when we look upon the wake, we do so with great stress. In other words, many times we are in the midst of a storm and by looking at it through our natural eyes, everything seems hopeless. However, if my God is the God who created the Universe and all that we can see and cannot see, there is nothing too big for Him. When we are in the midst of a storm, it is time to battle through that storm.

I have been in many battles which seemed hopeless but there is one that I will share briefly because this storm happened at a time in my life when I was walking close to God, and my trust rested in Him alone. Never think that someone who is walking this walk with God does not face storms, on the contrary, satan would love to bring those down who are strong more so than those who are weak. In fact, the more you do for God and the more you know, greater will be your battles because so much more is expected of you.

Luke 12:48 (NLT) [48] *But someone who does not know, and then does something wrong, will be punished only lightly. When someone has been given much, much will be required in return; and when someone has been entrusted with much, even more will be required.*

Even though your battles may be greater, your knowledge is also greater to be able to walk through these times. This does not mean you will just breeze through because in order to continue in your growth, those tests are needed and sometimes they are very hard. We never arrive, and we always need to be tested. If we were never to face tests again once we got to a certain place with God, we would never grow past that level. Our walk with God is a continual up-hill climb, one level at a time.

Let me also say, in biblical days, great men of God faced one storm after another. In fact, Abraham learned that to be chosen meant you were not only blessed but you had to prove your faith over and over again. I continually share, many are called but few are chosen because only few choose to walk with God giving of themselves 100%. If you are walking with God and have laid your life down as many of the great men and women in biblical days and as the disciples who followed Jesus, your storms will be great. I cannot recall any who were true followers of God and of Jesus who did not face enormous battles. Today is no different. If your eyes are on those men and women today that are active in the church and their lives seem to be filled with only blessings, you should really question their walk with God. Jesus said there would be trouble. If you are faced with trouble, count it all joy as James said because you are chosen if you have laid your life down. We prove our faith again and again because God desires a people who will trust in Him and not in themselves. It is a continual conditioning of the old man and transforming that man into the new man which is the image of Jesus Christ.

The storm which stands out that I wish to share was one of my great tests, something happened that was out of my control. Inadvertently, I had actually been praying for this to happen but did not recognize it at that time. We can pray for a situation, but we have no idea what God will use to bring about the solution to our prayers. In other words, we pray for something to change, and God answers our prayer but in order for it to happen, we may have to endure a pretty big storm. The end result was what we had asked for but was not expecting the storm. Remember, the calm always comes after the storm. This is why we should never cry out to God asking to be brought out of our storm because that storm may result in answered prayer that you have been standing and believing for. We must trust that God has everything in control because He does. We should never underestimate God. When faced with a big storm, instead say to God, *"I may not understand why I am facing this, but I trust in You Lord that you will bring me through and what I gain from this storm will be worth it."* This is because whatever the reason, God had the plan. I cannot go into deep detail about the storm I faced because I wish to protect those who are innocent and involved, but I received a phone call one day which drastically changed my life. I immediately contacted a few friends whom I knew that could intervene on a decision which had been made. In the meantime, everything looked bleak and seemed that the end result was not God. I remember crying that day, but I still gave it to God. Sometimes when we are in that place, God may be working in the midst, but we are unable to see Him. Sometimes we wonder, *"Where is God,"* but, we cannot see the complete puzzle, only pieces. The following morning, as I got in my car, a song was playing about praising God in the midst of the storm. The song is called, *"I Will Praise You in This Storm,"* by Casting Crowns. I had said that I was not going to cry anymore that morning because my whole night had been filled with tears. Yet when this song played,

I broke down because God began to speak to me. It is in our storms that we must continue to praise Him because He is still in control! In our storm we cannot see Him! In our storm we cannot hear Him because our focus is on the storm.

In that small quiet voice, He began to show me how He was right there in the midst of everything which had happened the day before. What I had failed to see was the decision that had finally been made at the end of that day was not what had first been recommended. The final decision was God. The recommended decision was not God. What transpired was one of those friends I called were able to go and intervene. When she walked in, she was basically told that the decision had already been made and there was nothing she could do. Within minutes, a lady walked in the room that was in charge and happened to know my friend very well. When she heard all that was said, she changed the decision upon my friend's recommendation and against the decision of everyone else in that room. It did not take much to see God was in this, and as time went on, it became more and more evident of God's hand in the whole situation. A year later, what transpired since that day was more of the complete picture of the puzzle that God had in mind. My prayers which I had prayed for the last four years had gradually begun to unfold and almost to completion. It was evident that everything which had happened, good and bad in those last four years, were necessary to bring about the desires in my heart.

We pray for something, but we do not want to walk through a storm even if it is necessary for God to answer our prayers. We need to begin to see that those storms must happen if we desire our prayers to be answered. God is there in the midst of our storms even when we cannot hear Him. It is during those times that we should be still to witness how He is moving in our storms of life. It is especially important to praise Him for the God He is because He will bring us through each and every storm with the outcome being in the best interest of those involved.

In chapter two, we discussed that Jesus said we fail to recognize God by all the greatness He has created. This society with all of its new technology, live a fast-paced life where we are constantly running and racing to accomplish more in a day than there are hours. During all this hustle and bustle, we miss God. How do we fail to miss Him?

John 17:24-26 (AMPC) ²⁴ *Father, I desire that they also whom You have entrusted to Me [as Your gift to Me] may be with Me where I am, so that they may see My glory, which You have given Me [Your love gift to Me]; for You loved Me before the foundation of the world.* ²⁵ *O just and righteous Father, although the world has not known You and has failed to recognize You and has never acknowledged You, I have known You [continually]; and these men understand and know that You have sent Me.* ²⁶ *I have made Your Name known to them and revealed Your character and Your very Self, and I will continue to make [You] known, that the love which You have bestowed upon Me may be in them [felt in their hearts] and that I [Myself] may be in them.*

How do we fail to recognize all the magnificent wonders of this world? We have a saying, *"Stop to smell the roses,"* yet we seldom take the time to look around to see God's greatness. When you lose a loved one as I did my daughter, you become more observant to the things around you because you realize just how short life really is. Does it take a tragedy to awaken us to see God in all of His greatness? Even though our God may not be visible to the natural eye, we should be able to recognize His greatness through all of creation. We should be able to see Him in everything small and everything big. How can we deny there is a God? If we are looking, we will also be able to see Him in the midst of our storms. I was not looking for Him in the midst of the storm because I was distracted by the storm. If you have ever driven in a real storm, your focus is on that storm. Even in the storms of life, we can see how it is so easy for our focus to be on that storm, but we must take our eyes off of the storm and focus on Jesus. He will ultimately carry us through our storms, and we will be safe and secure.

During the days when I lived in northern California, I can remember not only the snow storms but I also remember the smog that would settle over the cities in the valley. There were times, literally, that you could not see anything in front of you. I remember one such time in Sacramento, where the whole day the radio station announced that the gold ball on top of the capital had been stolen, and of course, no one could see anything to know how it had happened. It was a joke, but interstates and highways had been shut down due to no visibility. It is easy to understand when we are in the midst of the storms in life that we feel God has left us there alone. I can imagine we have all been at that place in life where we felt isolated from others, and then the question becomes, *"God, where are you; why have you forsaken me?"* That sounds like what Jesus said. *"Father, why have you forsaken me?"* Jesus had to encounter what we encounter in our own storms. Jesus took on the pain of the world. He died and felt everything we feel while He hung on that cross. What Jesus experienced during that time was the feeling of abandonment. Jesus felt as though He had been isolated from man-kind, and to top that off, He felt that His Father had also turned His back on Him.

Matthew 27:46 (ESV) [46]And about the ninth hour Jesus cried out with a loud voice, saying, "Eli, Eli, lema sabachthani?" that is, "My God, my God, why have you forsaken me?"

I do not believe this is the case. God clearly says that He will never leave or forsake us.

Deuteronomy 31:6 (ESV) ⁶Be strong and courageous. Do not fear or be in dread of them, for it is the LORD your God who goes with you. He will not leave you or forsake you."

Many will say, *"But, God cannot look at sin."* This is taken out of Habakkuk I, where Habakkuk the prophet says to God, *"You who are of purer eyes than to see evil and cannot look at wrong."* Habakkuk previously asked God, *"Why do you make me see iniquity, and why do you **idly** look at wrong?"*

There is no place in Scripture where God says that He cannot look at sin or look at evil. In one breath Habakkuk states that God cannot look at wrong and in another breath he says that God looks idly at wrong. God did not say this, Habakkuk was merely crying out to God in his pain and these were his words. God is God. Of course He can look at sin. He knows when we do right and He knows when we do wrong. He is God. We cannot take things out of context. Habakkuk was crying out to God because he felt what Jesus felt on the cross. There are times when we are faced with a huge storm, and we feel that God has forsaken us. Jesus knew how this felt. Why? Because He had to go through the storm and come out on the other side just like we do. Jesus had to bear our sin and feel our pain, and in the midst of that pain because He was in a mortal body, it was antagonizing. Habakkuk could not understand why God could not just stop those that were doing evil and answer his cries. God will not always stop our storms. Finish reading the book of Habakkuk, God tells him that He is doing a work in his (Habakkuk's) day. This is a very interesting book of the Bible because it shows that God sometimes allows us to endure pain because He is doing a work in our day as well. It also shows that God desire that the righteous live by faith and wait upon the Lord. It is His timing and His will, not ours.

However, in Isaiah 2, it does say that our sin separates us from God. Sin hides God's face from us so that He will not hear our prayers. Jesus became sin for us; God looked away and did not answer Jesus when He cried out to Him. He did not desert Him but separated Himself from sin. Yes, we separate ourselves from God when we live with sin in our lives. There is a difference in separation and desertion. As Christians, we should separate ourselves from those that live sinful lives. Meaning, you have no business going into nightclubs but if someone you know that is caught up in this lifestyle comes to you, you are there for them to share Jesus. Separate from sin but not desert those that are at a place where they are ready to clean up their lives. It also says in Psalm 66:17-19 that if you have iniquity in your heart, the Lord will not hear your prayers. If there is sin in our lives, we are to clean up our lives in order that God hears our prayers. However, as soon as we ask for forgiveness, a heartfelt forgiveness, God is right there to forgive us and He will never leave nor forsake us.

Therefore, to confirm, I do not believe that God turned His back on Jesus while on the cross. Jesus had to become sin for us to redeem mankind but God was still right there. Also, when we are in the midst of our pain, in the midst of our storms of life, we cannot hear God because everything seems cloudy around us. When we are walking in fear and worry, our ears and eyes have been clouded over to where we are unable to see our answer. God is there, even when we cannot hear Him. It is at these times, we must be still to witness how He is moving in our storms of life. It is during these times we must praise Him for the God He is because He is bringing us through our storms. We go through the storms as we trust in God which is faith.

What is our weapon? Truth! We carry the Word firmly secured to our belt which is the weapon that we will fight the enemy with and conquer. We must look at all our armory in a spiritual sense. In other words, when we put on our helmet, we see that we are clothing ourselves with salvation and knowing that we are running the race which will ultimately save us to spend eternity with our Savior. We know that our mind cannot be attacked by the enemy because the helmet protects our mind. We are secure in knowing we have eternal life; therefore, no argument from the enemy or the world can change our way of thinking and believing. When we put on the Breastplate of Righteousness, we are clothing ourselves as royalty knowing that we have married into the family of royalty. We know that we have been adopted into the family of the Most High God; we are the bride. Think about the royal families in other countries, when someone marries into the royal family, they become royalty and their lives change. When we become clothed as royalty; what does that do for us? It should change us. If someone were to marry into the royal family and not make the necessary changes, they probably would not remain where they are. As a member of royalty, there are things expected of you and things you cannot and should not do because it would shame the royal family. When we become a child of God, at that point, we should have that desire to be all that He has called us to be in order to show Him glory. Clothing ourselves as royalty protects our heart because no matter what happens to us or around us, we remain who we are, royalty. We do not allow circumstances to move us because we begin to act as royalty. You would never see a prince or princess act inappropriately in public; however, God also sees us in private. A King or Queen may witness things in private through the lives of a prince or princess that others do not see, and if so, they would be corrected. In private, the Holy Spirit is our guide and teacher; He gives us Godly counsel in order to bring us to the place where we act as royalty. This is why it is important that we submit to that correction from God because He desires us to step into those shoes that He prepared for us and walk, talk, and conduct our lives as royalty. This by no means should imply we are to carry ourselves in a snobbish way or in an uncaring manner. On the contrary, we are not better than anyone else because without Christ, we are nothing and have nothing. God is King of Kings and Lord of Lords, yet He gave His Son so that we could live under grace. The grace of God gives us unmerited favor, acceptance, and undeserved forgiveness as sinners. However, God expects that we not only humble ourselves but we show honor and respect where honor and respect is due. To act as royalty means that you obey the rules and regulations set down by the King of Kings. Our rule book is not the rule book of the British Family but rather a rule book that was set in place from the beginning of time. The Word of God has all the wisdom and knowledge needed to walk in a manner worthy of royalty for God's Kingdom. Contrary to God's Word would be carrying oneself in a shameful manner. We do not start fights, and we do not even finish them; we do not offend our brothers; we do not speak harshly towards anyone; we do not gossip; we do not talk excessively, and we do not delight in doing wrong or rejoice in living a life in darkness. As royalty, our lives should be full of wisdom in order that our manner and lifestyles possess a richness of doing that which is holy unto God.

Proverbs 2:12-15 (NIV)[12] Wisdom will save you from the ways of wicked men, from men whose words are perverse, [13] who have left the straight paths to walk in dark ways,[14] who delight in doing wrong and rejoice in the perverseness of evil, [15] whose paths are crooked and who are devious in their ways.

Proverbs 2:20-22 (NIV) [20] Thus you will walk in the ways of the good and keep to the paths of the righteous. [21] For the upright will live in the land, and the blameless will remain in it; [22] but the wicked will be cut off from the land, and the unfaithful will be torn from it.

We are His children. God desires to be glorified through His children, and this will not happen if we do not conduct our lives in the manner that will bring that glory to Him. When we do not act as royalty, it not only hurts God, but it also hurts our heart. Many young people have had their hearts broken because they made the choice to step outside of the boundaries set by God and in doing so, it ultimately caused pain. In doing so, it will set you on a course for a storm in your life. When we talk about battling our storms, we must realize that our choices many times produce those storms that we face. When we engage in sex without marriage or adultery, we are actually giving a part of ourselves away and consequences are more detrimental than people may think. God intended sex to be a covenant between two people. Regardless where you are in your relationship today, when a sexual relationship begins outside of marriage, you will go through a period of hurt and pain. Relationships that subdued this period did so because the couple broke down barriers in order to forgive and be forgiven. These are storms which we produce because of disobedience to God's will. I know it is hard to wait upon the Lord many times when our emotions come into play and our desires are to have a partner in life. Yet, based on the statistics of divorce and single-parent homes, it is easy to see that man's ways will never be greater than God's ways.

Having a free will to choose our path causes us much unnecessary pain, but God allows these storms in our life to teach us valuable lessons. Myself, after making choices that affected not just my life but my children, I was done with doing it my way. Today, I do not regret where I am and who I have become because I choose His way above any other. We must know that there will always be consequences to going against God's rule book. It is not that God is a ruler over us and that He is selfish wanting us to do things His way; on the contrary, He knows that sin results in death. This of course is not necessarily a natural death. Death means opposite of life. When we are living in depression, poverty, loneliness, or whatever the case, I'm sure we would all agree that this is not life. If I desire to choose a path which produces good, I would consider that living, wouldn't you? Can those sins we choose be turned around? Yes, God can turn around any mistakes we have made, but it begins with repenting of our mistakes and then making the decision to follow Him and allow the Holy Spirit to lead us.

The Belt of Truth being applied becomes our rock and what we stand upon. There is no weapon formed against us that shall prosper.

Isaiah 54:17 (AMP) [17] *But no weapon that is formed against you shall prosper, and every tongue that shall rise against you in judgment you shall show to be in the wrong. This [peace, righteousness, security, triumph over opposition] is the heritage of the servants of the Lord [those in whom the ideal Servant of the Lord is reproduced]; this is the righteousness or the vindication which they obtain from Me [this is that which I impart to them as their justification], says the Lord.*

This means that it does not matter what the world or what the enemy does to try and bring us down, it cannot happen. God does not lie, and if He said it, that is final. If this is not working for you, then you need to look at your life. We need to get it in our head that it is not because God is not working on our behalf; it is because we are not mature enough to see the Truth. If your belt is not bringing you victory, it is probably because you are not grounded in the Word. Notice, I said **IN** the Word not **ON** the Word. God is a God of action and to serve Him requires action on our part. If we do not work, we do not eat; if we do not discipline our children, they do not grow up disciplined; if we do not get out

235

of bed, nothing gets done, and if we do not pray and study God's Word, God does not answer our prayers, and the Holy Spirit does not remind us of all Truths and teach us all things. God has never said to lie in bed or lay around the house watching TV and He will take care of you and bless you. God has never said if you go to church once a week that He will prosper and bless you. The Word says to study and show ourselves approved; the Word says to meditate on His Words day and night; the Word says to seek first the Kingdom of Heaven and then all things would be added. Our weapon is the Word of God, and it begins by applying that as our foundation, the core to our existence, by securing it like you would secure a belt around your waist. Do not let it depart from your mouth, but how will it ever come out of your mouth if you are not feeding upon it? What goes in will come out. Either defeat will be fed to your body by what you look upon and what you listen to, or victory will be fed into your life. We feed our body's filth, defeat, lies, fear, worry, and all the evils of this world by what we read and watch on TV or the internet and then we wonder why our lives are a complete mess and why our children have gone astray. If you do not pick up your weapon, which is the Bible, and begin putting in what is contrary to the world, you will not be able to battle your storms. As I have said, our battles are spiritual not flesh and blood, and the reason we cannot see that is because we feed on those things which are natural and not spiritual. We must come to that place where we make the choice, it is called a crossroads, and we either choose to believe what the world says or what the Word of God says. We either agree or we disagree, but the conclusion will always rest in what the Word of God says. Our minds must be renewed, but this will not happen until we make the choice as Peter did to build our lives on the rock of Jesus. We change because the Word shows us how to change, why to change, and the result of change. We do not compromise with the Word, we do not TRY to live by it, we either do it or we don't. It's that simple! You will either clothe yourself with the Word in order to have that spiritual weapon to win your battles or you will live in defeat.

Even as we learn to avoid the darkness, you are going to go through life storms. These grow us to be stronger and develop our relationship with God. Learning about our armor will grow us to be warriors. When I think about a warrior, I think about someone with strength and great power. I do not picture a warrior as being weak.

As I have said, it takes each piece of armor to run this race and it is a gradual process. Within each piece there is a certain amount of growth before you get to the place where you are actually ready for the next piece. In a sense, much of the armor overlaps as well. We grow in salvation when we begin to apply the helmet, but there is much to understanding the helmet. Yet while the helmet is partially on, we are also beginning to learn about righteousness and who we are in Christ. Both of these pieces of armor become areas of growth which add to the belt of truth. However, these 3 pieces of armor need to be applied securely before going to the other pieces. Without these 3 pieces being a foundation for our lives, our ministries for the lost will not be as effective. It first takes deliverance from our own pain that we gain strength through the One who has called us.

Once we become grounded in what God's Word says, we then judge according to His Word not our thoughts, feelings, or someone else's belief but ultimately God. This is the place where we really lay down our lives at the cross and choose God's way not our way. This is where we sacrifice. This is where we become teachable. This is where we are eager to learn and listen. This is a changing process and is done through the Word of God.

The Core

Let's look at what the core means. The Word of God should be the core to our existence, and the word core means the inner portion of some type of mold. Inside the mold would be hollow and would be called the core of that mold, but without the core there would be no shape. What is on the inside is what will ultimately shape any substance. What is on the inside of us will be what shapes us on the outside. Christ being our foundation will be what begins to shape us. When we first came into being, God had already called us into existence and knew us while yet in the womb. However, as a baby, there is not a lot of knowledge within us at that point, other than what it feels like to be empty inside especially when we are hungry. Babies will cry if there is something wrong and that pretty much consists of being hungry, wet, or feeling pain. A baby is content and sleeps well as long as their physical being is satisfied. As we grow, we require more to keep us content. As we continue to grow, we pretty much take in whatever is given. This means, as we begin to grow up in this world, the knowledge and the wisdom we take in is what we listen to and what we are being taught. We often hear the comments about our children being molded into images of ourselves. *"She is just like her mother; she acts like her and looks like her!"* However, our purpose in this life was not to grow into the mold or image of our parents – unless we are talking about our ultimate parent, which would be Father God! It is easy to see why our children become *"Mini-Me's."* We are normally taught according to our parent's beliefs and philosophies and not according to the

Word of God which leads to the fall of man. Predominantly, most Christian homes today are not full of Jesus!

Prior to salvation, inside each of us is our spirit man, but it lies dormant until we come to that crossroads and make the decision to accept Jesus into our lives. Prior to Jesus or BC, our influences in life pretty much consisted of our parents, teachers, neighbors, friends, and acquaintances. These influences began at an early age to shape us into the image of things in this world. When we first come to know Jesus Christ, our spirit comes alive and God begins to breathe that life in us of the Holy Spirit. As we begin to study and learn of God, those images, beliefs, and notions of this world begin to be pushed out as the images, beliefs, and truths of God's Word begins to take the place of wrong teachings. Our shape begins to change because of the inner core changing. All of a sudden, who we used to be changes into a new creation, created by our inner core being filled with more and more of God and less and less of this world. Then our outwardly appearance also begins to change. Not necessarily by physical looks although it can and will change if need be; however, what we begin to see on the outside is different. People begin to see a person who is happy as the anger, loneliness, depression, fear, worry, etc. begins to leave and is replaced with peace, trust, and a general purpose in life. Deep inside of us may have been filled with things of this world, but there were also places inside which were empty and unfulfilled. When God gets a hold of us, He not only removes those things which were destructive, but the Holy Spirit will completely fill those areas which had no purpose. We become filled with the presence of God, and a total feeling of completeness takes hold as God's Word infiltrates our whole being.

The word core has several meanings and each of these are helpful to see exactly what God's Word means as we apply it to our lives. These are the different aspects of the word core that we are going to look at: **focal point, hub, essence, spirit, soul, self, and foundation**. As we look deeper into these meanings, we will also be able to see why Paul chose the belt to represent the core as our existence.

Focal Point

Looking at the word focal point, we will be able to understand why the core is the first place our enemy attacks. satan has learned that it does not take too much on his part to be able to destroy God's people when he attacks us at the core of our bodies. In war, the focal point would be the areas to bring down in order to cripple the enemy. Anytime countries are at war with each other, they study to find those places that would be considered focal points. If a country can pin point those areas that would cripple their enemy, and they can successfully bomb those areas, they would gain an advantage and possibly win the war.

My earthly dad fought in WWII, and he kept a diary to account for every day that he flew in a mission. His group completed all 25 missions, and they were actually shot down 3 times but lived to tell about it. He was a tail-gunner in a B17 bomber. Recently, I have been reading his diary and it has been an awesome experience. Every single mission, each plane was given a target. They were to fly to the target area and as they got closer to their target, fighter planes would join them and surround them for protection so that they could make it to that target area and drop their bombs. When you start studying about the various wars that have taken place in this world, you will be able to see the revelation that God desires we come to know. We need to understand that both sides of a natural war are using the same strategies. satan every day targets areas of our lives where we are weakest in order to bring us down. However, most Christians are not trained for war and are allowing the enemy to bomb those key areas while they sit back and murmur and complain but are inactive in the fight. We too can fight this battle and be that B17 which is surrounded by fighter planes, but only if we engage in the battle from a spiritual standpoint.

God fights our battles when we walk with Him. He surrounds us with leagues of angels that battle for us in the spiritual realm in order that we can accomplish the mission that God intended us to complete. The storms that we will face, we can successfully walk through them when we come to understand the spiritual realm. This includes knowing our Father in Heaven and also knowing our enemy. No war has ever been won without knowing the enemy. This is why it is imperative to see that our focal point in our own lives must be guarded. The enemies aim is to bring us down by hitting us at our focal point and many of us do not even understand what that focal point is so they have nothing guarding that area. As we get farther into this book, we will also learn how we go forth to hit the enemy in the area of his focal point.

How do we protect that focal point? In studying history, the goal has always been to cripple the adversary in areas of strength. Those areas may be an ammunition plant, government headquarters, military stations, etc. Our enemy today is no different than what we see in the natural. In fact, satan has been playing this game far longer than man. It is through satan that evil men have used tactics throughout history in order to destroy people's lives and take away their freedoms. We live in a world which has been plagued with sin, and if we do not draw close to the light, which is Christ, we will fall into darkness. Temptation is all around us, and if we are not strong, we will give in to those enticements. Picture your life on a ship and you are in control of the course that ship takes. God allows you to choose where you sail; He will not make that choice. God desires a people who want to follow His ways and will never force anyone to do His commandments. As you guide your ship through life, you will see way out in the horizon dark and light clouds. We choose to either sail our ship into that which is light or that which is darkness. When you head into the darkness, you are sailing directly into a storm. When in the midst of our storms, many times we regret our choices, and we know those choices we made were not the path we should have taken. Many times we even think to ourselves, *"What on earth am I doing?"* Yet, we continue to sail into that storm. Why do we do this? The simple truth is because we want adventure, sensuality, and excitement, but those things which entice us are not necessarily good for us. satan did not make sin boring; on the contrary, he made it look attractive. Our strength cannot be in ourselves because it takes God's Word to battle the evils of this world. Those B17's could not have been successful in themselves alone. It took the fighter planes coming in and surrounding them to be able to complete their mission. Many men lost their lives in WWII, and today, many Christians are dying a spiritual death because we fail to understand how to allow God to be in control and lead us. Let me clarify something, I stated that the enemy's strategy was to hit areas of strength; however, in the spiritual realm, satan does this by hitting us where we are weakest. As I said, our strength never comes from us but from God. We do not have strength and the capability to win our spiritual battles without the Holy Spirit and angels encamped around about us. Put it this way, in World War II or any other war, there is no way we could have ever crippled the enemy in those areas of strength if the enemy had been prepared and had left no doors open. In other words, in the spiritual sense, when we are not prepared and we open doors to darkness by choice, our enemy is able to cripple us through our weakness' by hitting those core areas.

In the parable of the sower, it shows us that if we do not have the Word deep within, satan will come and snatch away what we do have.

Matthew 13:19 (AMP) [19] *While anyone is hearing the Word of the kingdom and does not grasp and comprehend it, the evil one comes and snatches away what was sown in his heart. This is what was sown along the roadside.*

How does the enemy focus on the focal point? satan is not really worried about people going to church or professing that they are Christians because the multitudes do this and live in defeat. satan's worries only begin if they pick up their Bible, and even worse, if they actually begin to study the Word of God. satan knows that if he can attack the focal point of our existence, we will fall. However, what's even scarier than that is the fact that most of the time he does not have to do anything. Most of the time, satan never has to do anything creative because he can just sit back and watch the Christian population destroy themselves. Every decade, satan has continued to watch man become more creative with inventions from the Agricultural Era to the Industrial Era to the Technology Era. Now that we have come so far, he can basically sit back in his easy chair while he watches man sit back in their easy chair filling their minds with pollution. As satan keeps the population so busy by working to get ahead in order to have all the latest toys and gadgets, our time becomes filled with work, work, work. I am not implying children's toys here but those toys adults will sacrifice to have. When our days begin to wind down our bodies are crying out, *"I need to rest"* in order to get what little sleep needed so that we can begin the rat race once again. However, we compromise with the Word of God by seeking our rest through material possessions.

Matthew 11:28-30 (NIV) [28] *"Come to me, all you who are weary and burdened, and I will give you rest.* [29]*Take my yoke upon you and learn from me, for I am gentle and humble in heart, and you will find rest for your souls.* [30]*For my yoke is easy and my burden is light."*

When asked about prayer and time spent with God, it is sad to say that the majority cannot seem to find the time in a day to give anything else to our Father. We make excuses in order to apply *Band-Aids* to our guilt, and we compromise as we call it a necessity. If satan already has you in the place where you have no time for prayer and no desire to study and grow, your focal point of your existence is dead. If we cannot rise up as Christians and make a stand to serve God, how can we claim to be a Christian? Is it in a name only or is there supposed to be meaning? The belt is a heart issue and ties into the breastplate. If your heart is not right with God, you will have no desire to be anything more than what you are right now. If you desire more, work on your heart and then come back to the belt.

satan knows those areas which will keep you away from being joined together with other believers, and he also knows those areas which will keep you bound. When we are bound, we are held hostage, but is it voluntary? If it is our own free will that continually chooses to not pray or to deliberately miss being joined with other believers for growth, then we are living according to our will and not God's. Remember, Jesus said, *"Father, your will not mine."*

Luke 22:42 (ESV) saying, "Father, if you are willing, remove this cup from me. Nevertheless, not my will, but yours, be done."

We choose – that simple! I had a conversation with a lady awhile back because one of her grandchildren was in ICU from trying to commit suicide. Something I shared with her had to do with a time she told me that she was attending church, but she was not connecting because she did not want *"those people"* all up in her business. I told her to just know that *"those people"* may be God's people, and when you only give so much, you are basically saying, *"God, I choose to allow YOU into my life so far – but this small part of me, no one is getting through because that is the area that I control."* This is living according to your will and not God's. The sad thing with that is God can only transform those areas you give Him access to. The sad part is that as long as you stay distant, He will also remain distant. The worst part is that as long as we hold on to that small part of us which is *"NOT GOD's WILL FOR OUR LIVES"* – we have also spoken that over our children and their children. We can pray and pray all we want to for our children and grandchildren, but until we make that blood covenant with God to give Him all of us, He will remain at a distance in our lives which consists of our prayers that go out for our families as well. You may have asked at times why God did not answer your prayers, but He may be asking you, *"Why will you not give Me access to all of your life and to your prayers?"* God only listens to those who are in right-standing with Him. He does not listen to the prayers of the sinner unless the sinner is crying out in true repentance to be saved.

Proverbs 15:29 (ESV) [29] The LORD is far from the wicked, but he hears the prayer of the righteous.

Psalm 66:16-20 (ESV) [16] Come and hear, all you who fear God, and I will tell what he has done for my soul. [17] I cried to him with my mouth, *and high praise was on my tongue. ¹⁸ If I had cherished iniquity in my heart, the Lord would not have listened. ¹⁹ But truly God has listened; he has attended to the voice of my prayer. ²⁰ Blessed be God, because he has not rejected my prayer or removed his steadfast love from me!*

This does not imply that God does not hear our prayers because we are not perfect. Yes, we all will miss it at times, but it is about the heart issue again. You can miss it or you can have a thought which is not godly, but it is what you do next. Remember, David would cry out to God when he missed it. It is called true repentance. However, we cannot justify our sin when we continually make the choice to step out in sin and run to God time and time again to repent when true repentance is not in our heart. The sinner who continues to sin chooses to do so. There is no excuse that you have an addiction and that you desire to do right but just can't. We cannot overcome sin in ourselves but through Jesus Christ. If you are not overcoming, then your relationship is not where it needs to be with Jesus.

1 John 5:4 (KJV) ⁴ For whatsoever is born of God overcometh the world: and this is the victory that overcometh the world, even our faith.

John 10:25-30 (ESV) ²⁵ Jesus answered them, "I told you, and you do not believe. The works that I do in my Father's name bear witness about me, ²⁶ but you do not believe because you are not among my sheep. ²⁷ My sheep hear my voice, and I know them, and they follow me. ²⁸ I give them eternal life, and they will never perish, and no one will snatch them out of my hand. ²⁹ My Father, who has given them to me, is greater than all, and no one is able to snatch them out of the Father's hand. ³⁰ I and the Father are one."

John 14:12 (ESV) ¹² "Truly, truly, I say to you, whoever believes in me will also do the works that I do; and greater works than these will he do, because I am going to the Father.

If we are not doing as Jesus did, we are not following but trying to lead. This is letting go of ourselves in order to walk with Jesus. True repentance means that you have a heart change and walk away from that sin. Repentance is not about going to God to say you are sorry and walking back into that same sin. Let me say that those who are new Christians, there will be a lot of testing but as long as you continually go to the Lord for direction and repentance, He will continue to change the old man into the new man.

Romans 6:5-18 (ESV) [5] For if we have been united with him in a death like his, we shall certainly be united with him in a resurrection like his. [6] We know that our old self was crucified with him in order that the body of sin might be brought to nothing, so that we would no longer be enslaved to sin. [7] For one who has died has been set free from sin. [8] Now if we have died with Christ, we believe that we will also live with him. [9] We know that Christ, being raised from the dead, will never die again; death no longer has dominion over him. [10] For the death he died he died to sin, once for all, but the life he lives he lives to God. [11] So you also must consider yourselves dead to sin and alive to God in Christ Jesus. [12] Let not sin therefore reign in your mortal body, to make you obey its passions. [13] Do not present your members to sin as instruments for unrighteousness, but present yourselves to God as those who have been brought from death to life, and your members to God as instruments for righteousness. [14] For sin will have no dominion over you, since you are not under law but under grace. Slaves to Righteousness [15] What then? Are we to sin because we are not under law but under grace? By no means! [16] Do you not know that if you present yourselves to anyone as obedient slaves, you are slaves of the one whom you obey, either of sin, which leads to death, or of obedience, which leads to righteousness? [17] But thanks be to God, that you who were once slaves of sin have become obedient from the heart to the standard of teaching to which you were committed, [18] and, having been set free from sin, have become slaves of righteousness.

We need to also understand that the church or coming together with other believers is also a focal point. Just like in war, the spiritual war is focused on the church. That can mean the individual because we are the church, but it also means the place where we all come together as one to grow. This would be a prime focus where our enemy would attack to destroy. Daily, satan sends forth demons to attack our groups and especially the true church of God. When we lack in our consistency of regularly coming together with other believers, this weakens us at the core. As we are weakened, guilt sets in for our wrong choices and we run from God instead of running to Him. This is just another tactic of satan attaching us at the core. satan knows if he can hit me where I am weak, I will feel defeated and definitely will not feel like praying. It is during these times that I have had to make my flesh pray, and it is during these times that I have had to make myself be around other believers. If we remain in this state where we are disobedient, our storms can be very fierce with no sign of a breakthrough. Just like the children of Israel, when we turn from God, we face the opposition.

In the midst of our storms, we better be speaking life and not death. How can we speak life if we quit running to the only source that will bring that life. If we get sick or face a tragedy beyond our control, and we assume that God will just understand why we quit praying and why we quit being joined with other believers because our natural bodies have been weakened from the stress or sickness, how will we pull out of that cycle? You see, if satan knows that all he has to do is put sickness and disease on your body or to bring about a huge storm in order to bring you down, you will be continually facing a storm out of your control. Some people are sick all the time, but the day may come when we are faced with a disease where there is no cure. If our faith was not strong enough for the small sicknesses and the small storms, what makes us think we will be able to muster up enough faith to heal our bodies from something that is incurable or to walk through a storm which is great? It is those very storms which are small that help us to grow our faith to a place where we can walk through the bigger storms of life. However, if every time we encounter a small storm and we retreat into our safe havens making the choice to not attend church, small groups, or fellowship with others running this race, how will we be able to battle a big storm in life when we retreated when faced with a small storm? James told us to count it joy for our storms in life, but we can't count it joy when we choose to not walk through them. *(James 1:2-3)* We never make it through a storm when we retreat. We only walk through our storms when we make the choice to face them and do as commanded. Jesus said to not forsake assembling together with others. He never said, *"But, if you are faced with a small storm, then it is okay to forsake coming together with others."* I had to come to this place myself. It is much easier to pamper your body and say, *"I am not feeling well, and I deserve to be pampered while taking it easy up in my bed not doing anything but eating and watching TV; God will understand!"* Will God understand?

Of course, this is between you and God because there may very well be times that you should not go. When I have had those times, I find an evangelist or preacher to watch on TV. We can still be fed the Word of God even if we are laid up sick in bed. Many times these are merely areas of trials that God allows us to go through to test us to see how far we have grown. If after a year, you handle sickness the same way you did the year prior, chances are you have not grown at all in that area. God desires we grow, that our belt becomes stronger as our wisdom and knowledge of Him increases. When we have grown, we will handle those areas which were once weaknesses with strengths we have acquired through the tests. It is in the midst of our tests that we should be studying and reading something which is going to bring life not death to our circumstances.

Before going further, let me say that as far as missing church or some type of fellowship, I am not trying to bring condemnation on anyone because there have been times I have had to miss, but we have to recognize it for what it is! There have been times that I did not want to attend a service, times that I felt sick and even had fever. My favorite thing is to climb up in my big bed with all my comfort food and watch a good program on television when I am not feeling well. However, satan will use things to keep us out of church or to keep us in that place where we never develop the habit of connecting to others who are strong in order that we grow. When we develop that one good habit, there's not much that will keep us away from assembling with other believers. The true body of believers comes together for God's purpose not for their own selfish desires. We come together with other believers in order to gain wisdom, knowledge, and understanding that will lead us closer to our Father.

Hebrews 10:25 (NLT) [25] *And let us not neglect our meeting together, as some people do, but encourage one another, especially now that the day of his return is drawing near.*

We will never become strengthened without the Word. The Bible says we draw strength from Him, how do we do that? We do that by His Word. It is through His Word that our strength comes. If you are defeated and weak in certain areas, it is those areas that you should study in order to replace your wrong way of thinking with God's way.

2 Corinthians 10:4-5 (NKJV) [4] *For the weapons of our warfare are not carnal but mighty in God for pulling down strongholds,* [5] *casting down arguments and every high thing that exalts itself against the knowledge of God, bringing every thought into captivity to the obedience of Christ,*

Our enemy desires to bring us down by making sure we do not empty out the garbage that is filled within our core and replace it with the ammunition it will take to gain the advantage over all demonic forces and the gates of hell!

Psalm 91:13 (KJV) *[13] Thou shalt tread upon the lion and adder: the young lion and the dragon shalt thou trample under feet.*

satan is the dragon and we have been given authority to trample over our enemy. The only power that satan has is the power that we give him.

Luke 10:19 (AMP) *[19] Behold! I have given you authority and power to trample upon serpents and scorpions, and [physical and mental strength and ability] over all the power that the enemy [possesses]; and nothing shall in any way harm you.*

satan desires that we live our lives filled with the deceit and lies that he has been planting in this world since Adam and Eve. The last thing the devil wants is for God's people to engage by getting the Truth within in order to overcome any and all things. satan already knows that he is defeated but if he can continue to convince us that we cannot overcome, he will keep us defeated.

John 16:33 (AMP) *[33] I have told you these things, so that in Me you may have [perfect] peace and confidence. In the world you have tribulation and trials and distress and frustration; but be of good cheer [take courage; be confident, certain, undaunted]! For I have overcome the world. [I have deprived it of power to harm you and have conquered it for you.]*

Do you see how we give him the power? When we give up and quit, we basically are saying, *"Here satan, this is the best I can do, go ahead and destroy my life and my family."* If you are tired of living defeated, then it is time to stand up and fight. Our attacks from the enemy will begin at the focal point; our attacks begin with our choice to either live by what the world says or study to live contrary to that of this world. This world has already been defeated in the natural by satan, but we do not have to be citizens of this world.

John 15:19 (AMP) [19] *If you belonged to the world, the world would treat you with affection and would love you as its own. But because you are not of the world [no longer one with it], but I have chosen (selected) you out of the world, the world hates (detests) you.*

If your heart's desires are to gain the riches of this world, you have chosen to remain of this world, and you will never be satisfied because you will always yearn for more. Our enemy knows where our heart is and will do everything possible to use those areas to keep us bound. If we desire to battle through our storms, it begins with learning how to outsmart our enemy. The first step we must take is one that is teachable. We cannot be taught if we think we have already arrived. It begins with being humble. It begins with admitting just where you are spiritually. It begins with confessing those areas in your life that keep you from God. Our desires should be to grow and learn of Him, and we must not forsake assembling together with other believers in order to be strong.

We must make the choice to walk according to the Word and begin to study and grow into maturity. satan knows if he can hit us at the focal point, we will fall. Whatever keeps us from not praying, studying, or attending a service with others becomes our god.

Hub

Our core is the hub of our existence. The Hub is where our heart is. There is a saying, wherever your heart is, that is where your home is. I believe that wherever our heart is will be the place we desire to be more than anything. This is something each of us has to contemplate. Our desires show where our heart is. We have talked about the heart of David. David loved God dearly even though he sinned. God knew David loved Him, and He knows if we love Him also. When we fall madly in love with God, we will chase Him. We will run after Him, asking, seeking, and knocking.

Matthew 7:7 (AMP) ⁷Keep on asking and it will be given you; keep on seeking and you will find; keep on knocking [reverently] and [the door] will be opened to you.

When I hear the word hub, I think of the hub of a city which is the heart of that city. Major cities all over America are revitalizing their downtown areas to make them the hub of that city. When visiting major cities, tourist will usually visit the downtown areas which have been set apart from the other parts of the city. I currently live in a city where the downtown area is the hub of that city. This area is distinct from the rest of the city and brings in hundreds if not thousands which frequent this area based on its attractions. The hub or downtown area basically is what makes a city unique. When we talk about core as the center, the word hub is what makes us unique inside. The hub of a city is set apart just as God has called His people out to be set apart from the world.

Ephesians 2:19 (AMP) ¹⁹Therefore you are no longer outsiders (exiles, migrants, and aliens, excluded from the rights of citizens), but you now share citizenship with the saints (God's own people, consecrated and set apart for Himself); and you belong to God's [own] household.

We are to be distinct, unique, and peculiar; we are to be a set apart people that show the world Jesus.

1 Peter 2:9 (KJV) [9] But ye are a chosen generation, a royal priesthood, an holy nation, a peculiar people; that ye should shew forth the praises of him who hath called you out of darkness into his marvelous light;

If we are not applying the Belt of Truth so that we are being filled with more of God, we will not stand out. In biblical days, those who were Christians stood out. Today, it is hard to tell the Christians from the non-Christians because they all act the same. Today, what is on the inside of non-Christians is no different than what is on the inside of the majority who proclaim to be Christians. Today, the non-Christians and those who proclaim to be Christians fill their core with the substance of this world. If people do not know that you are a Christian, I would assume that you are not applying your belt and filling your inner core with more of Jesus. What goes in will come out. If you are not putting the Word in you, then you are putting the world in you. If what comes out of your mouth is the same as what the world speaks, there is not much Word in you. I say to those I minister to that I could spend 30 minutes to an hour talking with anyone of them and would be able to see how they perceive the world, how they look at life, and how many times, if any, they spend reading and studying God's Word. Our perceptions should be different than the worlds. Our words should speak hope and not defeat, but if we have little of God in us, it will never come out of our mouth. If it's not in us, we will never share Jesus. I have shared that the Word of God in John 15, tells us that we are in this world but not of this world. We need to ask ourselves, how do we stand out? What makes us unique and different than others in this world?

Our focus should be to achieve that which is greater. Greatness will only be found in those things above not here on this earth. Our heart must line up with God's. We should strive to learn what was unique about David. God said David was a man after His own heart. Are we after God's heart? Do we desire that our heart be one with God? Or, are we satisfied with having a heart which is tainted, a heart that does not know how to love like Jesus loved? Without the heart of David, we will lack in our walk with God. Without our heart and nature changing in the spiritual realm, we will be nothing. Think of it this way, when our organs do not work properly, we may be put on life support or there may be organs that can be removed, but this can also leave us at a place where we are dysfunctional. We may still be alive where we can breathe because our heart is pumping, and we may be able to think because our brain is still intact, but we are not completely whole. We are not without blemish in the natural, and we are not without blemish in the spiritual. Yes, none of us are perfect, we all have blemishes which are imperfections, but through Christ, we are made whole. When something is whole, it is complete with nothing lacking thereof.

Colossians 2:10 (NKJV) [10] *and you are complete in Him, who is the head of all principality and power.*

Colossians 1:28 (AMP) [28] *Him we preach and proclaim, warning and admonishing everyone and instructing everyone in all wisdom (comprehensive insight into the ways and purposes of God), that we may present every person mature (full-grown, fully initiated, complete, and perfect) in Christ (the Anointed One).*

Our flaws are covered by His blood. Jesus paid the price so that we could be complete. God does not look upon us as damaged goods but rather as one who has been consecrated through Christ. To be consecrated is to be set apart, made holy, and sanctified.

*Romans 3:22-26 (NLT) *[22]*We are made right with God by placing our faith in Jesus Christ. And this is true for everyone who believes, no matter who we are. *[23]*For everyone has sinned; we all fall short of God's glorious standard. *[24]*Yet God, with undeserved kindness, declares that we are righteous. He did this through Christ Jesus when he freed us from the penalty for our sins. *[25]*For God presented Jesus as the sacrifice for sin. People are made right with God when they believe that Jesus sacrificed his life, shedding his blood. This sacrifice shows that God was being fair when he held back and did not punish those who sinned in times past, *[26]*for he was looking ahead and including them in what he would do in this present time. God did this to demonstrate his righteousness, for he himself is fair and just, and he declares sinners to be right in his sight when they believe in Jesus.*

*Colossians 1:14 (AMP) *[14]*In Whom we have our redemption through His blood, [which means] the forgiveness of our sins.*

*Hebrews 10:10 (AMP) *[10]*And in accordance with this will [of God], we have been made holy (consecrated and sanctified) through the offering made once for all of the body of Jesus Christ (the Anointed One).*

Downtowns all over this country continue to be restored in order to bring something unique to those towns and cities. When a downtown area is left to continue the downward cycle, it dries up and becomes a ghost town which has nothing to offer the community and nothing to offer tourist to venture into their city. However, when a city begins to see that their downtown can be that distinct area once it is restored, that city will have something unique for all those who happen along that path which leads into their area. When this happens, that city once again begins to thrive to be so much more than it was. As Christians, God calls us and then chooses us. Remember, all are called but few are chosen. We are all called to be those that are set apart. We are called to be those who are unique. When we submit to this calling and we begin to allow the Holy Spirit to restore us to the former condition by revitalizing us on the inside, we become those who are chosen to bring that light which will shine out those dark areas of defeat. Our former condition would be that which we were created to be prior to Adam's fall. We are all on a downward cycle until we realize that God has called us to be so much more. We are all stagnant until life is breathed into us. It takes the work of the Holy Spirit to transform us into the image of Christ and once this happens, others will stumble into our path in order to see that uniqueness which can only happen as the result of the Holy Spirit's restoration.

Essence~Spirit~Soul

Another meaning for the word core is our essence. Our essence is what identifies our nature, meaning who we are and our passions. Our essence consists of our spirit and soul. These three can all be tied in together. Our soul is our mind, will, and emotions which forms our personalities. When our core is weakened, it will affect our personalities, our emotions, and the choices we make in life. This is why when we meet people who have been physically, mentally, or sexually abused, there seems to be no life left in them. The fight which may once have been within someone is drained from the abuse and they are left depressed and oppressed, with little if any purpose to live. With the breakdown of the family unit, it is evident to see why

257

depression is so prevalent in our society. As we continue to remove God from this society, abuse, depression, addictions, divorce, and crime continues to increase. I remember when my daughter died, my life basically ended. Prior to her death, my personality was one of life even though it was not at its full potential through Christ. After her death, I no longer showed any form of life; there was nothing to smile about, no joy, and no peace. I remember crying out to God many times saying there was nothing to live for. It was a long battle and one I will never forget. Yet, I walked through that storm and came out on the other side much stronger.

Our emotions should be intact, our personalities should be thriving with love, compassion, peace, and joy but far too often, we meet people who have to put on false smiles. They will pretend that everything is okay on the outside but dare to allow you to penetrate through those walls they have built to see the inside. In reality, satan has been able to suck the life out of them. Without prayer, time spent with God or studying, we weaken our core and then as we continue to live with defeat in our lives, sickness will begin to come. Sickness can be seen mentally, emotionally, and physically.

We know that we are created to be spiritual beings, and our spirit lies dormant prior to salvation but it is still there. I remember God showing me something very valuable in my walk with Him. Prior to my salvation or B.C., there were two times in my life that I cried out to a God that I did not know in the midst of tragedy. After salvation or A.D., the growth process begins and everyone grows at a different pace but much of that depends on how fast you desire to grow. It was in one of these growth spells that God showed me that He was actually there not only during those two times but during other times in my life when I was just a small child. I asked God then, *"What made me cry out to You when I did not even know You?"* His reply to me was, *"You may not have known me but your spirit within has always known me."* That was awesome. We are created as spiritual beings whether we realize it or not. Many times people will say that they do not believe in God, but that's okay too because God believes in them and He knows them. The essence of our being is our foundation. It is who we are. It consists of our mind, will, and emotions. It consists of our personality, and it consists of our spirit within even when it lies dormant. This foundation is who we are but not necessarily who God called us to be before we were even formed in the womb. Without our foundation being Jesus Christ, we are nothing and can do nothing but merely exist. We may function but it is handicapped. We may feel in control, but we are in bondage. To be free only comes through Christ. Whom the Son sets free is free indeed!

John 8:34-36 (ESV) [34] *Jesus answered them, "Truly, truly, I say to you, everyone who practices sin is a slave to sin.* [35] *The slave does not remain in the house forever; the son remains forever.* [36] *So if the Son sets you free, you will be free indeed.*

Do you ever wonder why you do the things you are doing? I mean, there are times that I'm going through the motions of existing and I think about how easy it would be to radically change my normal routine and go about everything completely different. We usually do not do this because it does not feel comfortable. We usually have our routines that we do daily and when those routines are shaken due to circumstances, it produces stress, anger, etc. However, God did not call us to be comfortable but rather to be radical. We are not our own but we belong to Him who called us out of darkness into His marvelous light.

Years ago before Christ (BC), I can remember how I desired more than anything for my life to just be normal. However, this was not in God's plan for my life. In studying this further, I realized that He never called us to be normal but radical. What is radical? What exactly does that mean? The *"Free Dictionary"* says it like this: Departing markedly from the usual or customary; extreme or drastic; relating to or advocating fundamental or revolutionary changes in current practices, conditions, or institutions; a person who holds or follows strong convictions or extreme principles; extremist. If we were never called to be normal or to be conformed like this world, then we were called to be different. We are His peculiar people. We should be extremely different than those in this world. We should stand out. We should advocate fundamental changes and follow strong convictions and extreme principles. If we belong to Jesus Christ, we will be set apart from that which is normal!

Romans 12:1-2 (ESV) A Living Sacrifice 12 I appeal to you therefore, brothers, by the mercies of God, to present your bodies as a living sacrifice, holy and acceptable to God, which is your spiritual worship. ² ___Do not be conformed to this world___*, but be transformed by the renewal of your mind, that by testing you may discern what is the will of God, what is good and acceptable and perfect.*

Acts 17:4-7 (ESV) ⁴ And some of them were persuaded and joined Paul and Silas, as did a great many of the devout Greeks and not a few of the leading women. ⁵ But the Jews were jealous, and taking some wicked men of the rabble, they formed a mob, set the city in an uproar, and attacked the house of Jason, seeking to bring them out to the crowd. ⁶ And when they could not find them, they dragged Jason and some of the brothers before the city authorities, shouting, ___"These men who have turned the world upside down___ *have come here also, ⁷ and Jason has received them, and they are all acting against the decrees of Caesar, saying that there is another king, Jesus."*

In ourselves with all our flaws, we are not strong enough to win our battles in the natural or in the spiritual. We may live day in and day out but what is life if we merely exist? What is on the inside of us determines if we are made whole or if we are left empty. Being empty is living life without purpose, and purpose only comes through God. When we lack in areas in the natural realm, it ultimately will affect the spiritual realm. God desires that we rise up strengthened by His might not our own. Too many times we settle for where we are; too many times we accept the condition of where we are. God desires more for our lives in both realms. When we are handicapped it affects our walk with God. To be handicapped is not to imply this in a physical sense only. We can be handicapped by the way we think, what we perceive, and those things we feed upon. In fact, there are probably those who are handicapped physically who found God in the midst of their storm. Never think that it is not God to place that physical handicap upon your life in order to awaken you to something greater. However, I believe an abundant life starts with transformation inside but flows to the outside as well. Meaning, God can also take away that physical handicap especially if it hinders being able to do what He called you to do.

God wants to do a total transformation on our lives physically, mentally, emotionally, and spiritually. We must get the mindset that being handicapped in any form is not God's best and would not be what is considered being made whole or complete. In the spiritual sense, we are all capable of being whole and in order to gain strength through Christ we should all look at our flaws as a handicap that may be keeping us from winning our battles. The word handicap means a physical or mental disability and a disadvantage. Why on earth would we want to claim this for our lives? Do we really think that this is God's best? *You may say, "Well, there may be a reason that God puts on some of us a disadvantage or a disability."* As I stated above, yes, God may very well have allowed this to come upon many for various reasons, but once we get our thinking right with God and line up our lives with His Word, why would we remain there? Again, as I said above, if our physical handicap prevents us from being what God called us to be, He can very well take that handicap away. However, I will say that when Jacob wrestled with God, he was left with a limp due to his hip being disjointed. God never took that physical handicap away for it to remain as a daily reminder that our lives must be in submission to Him. The limp; however, did not interfere with doing what God had called him to do. We have to weigh out our physical handicap to see if our walk with God will remain stronger for that handicap to remain or if it will prevent us from going forward doing what we were called to do.

Remember, our storms are to teach us not to keep us in that place. We walk through our storms not remain in them unless of course they have no effect on our walk with God. I don't know anyone who would want to remain in a natural storm 7 days a week and 365 days a year. At some point we all want to be out of the storm. However, in the spiritual realm, we need to see that we remain in that place of being handicapped just as the children of Israel did for 40 years, and we do so by choice. It is our choice to either renew our way of thinking or remain in our dessert. The great men and women of biblical days did not remain who they were once God or Jesus got a hold of them. They changed physically, mentally, emotionally, etc. Yes, all of them went through storms and all suffered as being disciples of Jesus Christ, but they did not remain at a disadvantage. In biblical days, people did not pay much attention to the blind or to the paraplegic, but when they were miraculously healed, people wanted what they had. Today, I have seen many that have conquered death from cancer or some other affliction and their testimonies became a powerful tool in order to glorify God. However, this did not occur until they found an escape to go forth strong once again despite the obstacles. This goes back to the realization that the core to our existence falls on the foundation of Christ being the center of our focus. The Belt of Truth is Christ; the Word of God becomes our main focus because apart from the Word, we become separated from Christ and if separated, there is no existence other than that which is outside of God. If we truly have Jesus Christ in us, the Holy Spirit walking with us, the voice of God speaking to us, are we going to remain who we were or are we going to be changed into a new creation? Remember, old things pass away and new things begin.

2 Corinthians 5:17 (ESV) [17] Therefore, if anyone is in Christ, he is a new creation. The old has passed away; behold, the new has come.

Yes, we may walk through our troubles, but far too often, scars will be left that are carried with us throughout our lives. Wouldn't it be great to walk through our battles unscathed? We can, but that depends on what our core is made of. Our God given personalities show who we are on the inside. In other words, our soul portrays those things which please us and those things we delight in. Even though our personalities came from God, it does not mean they line up with His Word until we come to know Jesus Christ and begin to grow. I am still the same person with the same personality, but it is now used to show how great my God is instead of those desires I once put forth efforts to bring glory unto myself. All glory goes to my Father today not to me or those things which are worldly. It basically becomes lining up who you are on the inside to His Word. We do not become someone completely alien because God desires us to use our natural talents and gifts in a way that will glorify Him. However, when satan attacks our core and we are not strong because we do not pray and study the Word, it effects who we are on the inside, and it affects who God intended us to be. Our unique gifts and talents which have been tainted by satan become useless.

Once we may have struggled just trying to hold our head up while continuing in this weakened state, but soon every evil thing which satan can attach to us will come. The simple cure to our core is taking time to develop a relationship with our Father. In the midst of our storm, it is crucial to saturate ourselves with God's Word and not the world!

Self

When referring to our core, this can also be self. We either submit self to God or we continue doing things selfish and being selfish. Submitting to self is a choice. We either submit self to God or we continue doing things which gratify our flesh and we serve self. We have all come into this world living for self, but we have the choice how we leave this world. We can either change by submitting self to God, or we can continue on the same path that we began which will lead to death. On the other hand, submitting self to God assures us of life after death. We conquer the grave just as Christ did. Ask yourself where does *"self"* fit into your world? Do you increase *"self"* and elevate it above all else, or do you put *"self"* down and submit to God? Our lives daily should be His will and not ours!

What is your foundation today? Is it Christ or self? Your will be done Father, not mine! In the church today, people feel uneasy when the pastor preaches about giving more of yourself whether it is your money or your time. This feeling that comes over them is *"self."* We may as well call it what it is and that would be a spirit of self. This is not the spirit that says, *"Father, Your will be done not mine?"*

We can survive without our core being filled with the Word of God, but we will never live a life of victory. It is our choice to live life

264

with purpose or to merely exist. We have discussed how satan weakens us by convincing us that we do not need the Belt of Truth as the core of our armor. This has become a huge problem in the churches today. Most Christians will not take time out of their busy lifestyles to come pray with others. Many feel that it takes up too much time when they can just pray at home, but the problem is that if you are not connected in prayer with other believers, most will not commit to praying every single day at home. Even when we do try to commit to praying at home, many times it will be short lived because satan will make sure there is something else to take up our time. Our prayer life at home may suffer because we are always rushing trying to do 10 hours of work in 4. The American people today have placed too many obstacles within their lives and with our lives being crowded with stuff, our relationship with God suffers. This is another tactic of satan. If he keeps us overloaded, tired, run down, then our time with God is put on the back shelf and seldom even dusted off. If we desire growth and strength through God, we put God before our other obligations and work those things around Him. You may be saying, *"Well, that is easy to say but I have a job that if I am not there when I am supposed to be there, I will not have a job."* You are missing the point, we do not have to stop with OUR obligations, but we include God in those obligations. It's just like a vacation, we don't leave God at home.

Our mindset has to be one of walking as a true believer in Christ just like in biblical days. If we desire to battle through our storms and grow to be a mature disciple, it begins with working our time around God. It does not matter what your excuse, it becomes an excuse. Our storms are meant to grow us to become the army that God is building for a great battle ahead. Are you prepared today for that battle?

Acts 2:16-18 (AMP) [16] But [instead] this is [the beginning of] what was spoken through the prophet Joel: [17] And it shall come to pass in the last days, God declares, that I will pour out of My Spirit upon all mankind, and your sons and your daughters shall prophesy [telling forth the divine counsels] and your young men shall see visions (divinely granted appearances), and your old men shall dream [divinely suggested] dreams. [18] Yes, and on My menservants also and on My maidservants in those days I will pour out of My Spirit, and they shall prophesy [telling forth the divine counsels and predicting future events pertaining especially to God's kingdom]. (Joel 2:28)

*Joel 3:11-14 (NLT) [11] Come quickly, all you nations everywhere. Gather together in the valley." And now, O LORD, call out your warriors! [12] "Let the nations be called to arms. Let them march to the valley of Jehoshaphat. There I, the LORD, will sit to pronounce judgment on them all. [13] Swing the sickle, for the harvest is ripe. Come, tread the grapes, for the winepress is full. The storage vats are overflowing with the wickedness of these people." [14] Thousands upon thousands are waiting in the valley of **decision.** There the day of the LORD will soon arrive.*

Jehoshaphat means that God shall judge. Are you in the valley of decision? Are you at that crossroads in making the decision to either serve God or man? Remember, there is no straddling the fence. If we are engaged in a war and desire to be connected to the winning side, it requires our faithfulness and allegiance to God's Kingdom. Any man or woman enlisted in the armed forces such as the army, navy, marines, etc., they have given allegiance to that force. In other words, their goal is to do what is necessary to fight the good fight of faith. *(1Timothy 6:12)* God is preparing His army for the last days, and it requires that we serve Him and Him alone. Are you in a place of preparation or are you too connected to this world?

2 Timothy 2:4 (NLT) [4] Soldiers don't get tied up in the affairs of civilian life, for then they cannot please the officer who enlisted them.

If we claim to be Disciples of Christ, Christians, our connection to this world should be limited. Too much of anything this world has to offer will keep you bound and could ultimately cause a spiritual death. Too many people view the Bible as too restrictive. This is the same thing as saying that you view the truth as restrictions. This is trading the truth for a lie. When we do this, it is walking in darkness not the light. This is not true freedom, it is walking bound. People feel there are too many rules to follow in order to be a Christian, but if you feel that way, there is no relationship with God. If you feel that way, you have made God out to be some type of formality or religion that you can turn on and off as desired. That is not a relationship and truthfully, that is why many marriages do not work either. In America, we have become a selfish people who want it our way, and we want people to adhere to our philosophies not the other way around.

If we look at the laws of Moses as restrictions, we are being deceived by the enemy. There will always be laws to follow, either God's or man's laws or a ruler/dictator over a jurisdiction and even eventually a one world ruler who will dictate over all the nations according to Revelation. When we put a belt on, it does restrict just like a seat belt restricts us from being thrown from our vehicle in the event we are in an accident. But just like the seat belt, that restriction is for our own good and will save our life so that we pass over from this life to the next. God's Word restricts us from those things which will harm us. Why are there rules and laws put in place? If you have children, you should understand why there are rules and the same reason parents implement rules are the reason there are laws. This does not mean that all rules and laws are correct because they do not all line up with biblical teachings. However, the reason parents apply them to their children is because they love their children and try to keep them from harm's way. As parents, we try to protect our children from danger and making those wrong choices, but it's kind of hard to implement rules on our children's lives when we make poor decisions and go against God's rules and man's laws. Obeying rules actually gives us freedom not restrictions, and as you grasp this, you will make wiser choices.

Yes, God's Word does restrict, but so does every meaningful relationship you will ever be part of. If we cannot give unselfishly, life will always be about ourselves and no one else. Relationships that restrict us are actually in our best interest. Restrictions keep us from things which will harm us. Why do we make rules for our own children? Obeying rules actually give us freedom not restrictions. I had one daughter in her senior year who had gained my trust over the years, and I pretty much let her come and go because she was responsible. She had matured and took care of her business without me having to oversee her. If she was going to be late, she always called to let me know why. She had freedom because she had earned it, but she had earned it by proving that she was responsible. When our desires line up with God's desires, we will have true freedom because we have shown God that we understand our purpose and calling while on this earth. If we desire victory in our lives today, we must submit to every storm in our lives in a positive way. We have been given every tool and talent needed by our Father through Christ and by no means, will our God ever give us more than we can handle.

1 Corinthians 10:13 (AMP) [13] *For no temptation (no trial regarded as enticing to sin), [no matter how it comes or where it leads] has overtaken you and laid hold on you that is not common to man [that is, no temptation or trial has come to you that is beyond human resistance and that is not adjusted and adapted and belonging to human experience, and such as man can bear]. But God is faithful [to His Word and to His compassionate nature], and He [can be trusted] not to let you be tempted and tried and assayed beyond your ability and strength of resistance and power to endure, but with the temptation He will [always] also provide the way out (the means of escape to a landing place), that you may be capable and strong and powerful to bear up under it patiently.*

As we grow with God applying the belt to our lives by studying and adapting our lives to line up with the Word of God, freedom will come as our Father opens the door in areas we would have never dreamed. The men and women of God in biblical days who stepped out of their box and went to great lengths to walk in a way that was pleasing to God, experienced things and gained knowledge and wisdom in areas that most did not. Which path will you choose? The one that leads you through trials and temptations but gains the world to come or will you remain on the same path as the *"many"* trying to save their own life?

Matthew 16:24-25 (ESV) Take Up Your Cross and Follow Jesus [24] Then Jesus told his disciples, "If anyone would come after me, let him deny himself and take up his cross and follow me. [25] For whoever would save his life will lose it, but whoever loses his life for my sake will find it.

Foundation

We can all become whole through Christ but it begins with growth as I have said many times. As we grow and gain knowledge of just who God is, individually, we will be able to see what His desires are for our lives. We settle many times for where we are in life, but God sees more and He sees greater. When we settle for where we are, it is hard to convince others to follow the life we have chosen.

As we mature through Christ, we must come to the place where we can do an honest assessment of our own lives. We must ask ourselves if where we are currently is a place others would want to be. I am not talking about finances here; on the contrary, money does not buy a good life. People poor would disagree because they look at those rich and want what they have. People who are rich would disagree because they have no desire to let go of their riches. However, people who have truly found God know what true happiness really is. When people come to the place that they desire peace, happiness, and contentment, they begin to look around at those whose lives seem complete and it has nothing to do with money. In biblical days, the multitudes were curious and would travel far to see Jesus, they did not remain following Him because they never crossed over to the place of getting to really know Him. However, His walk drew the attention of the *"many."* After He went to be with the Father, people continued to follow His disciples. It had nothing to do with money; it had everything to do with something greater than anything man could buy. They did not follow those who were handicapped; they did not follow those who had leprosy; they did not follow those who had nothing to offer; however, when signs and wonders were seen among those who were Disciples of Christ, the crowds came.

Acts 2:41-47 (NLT) [41] Those who believed what Peter said were baptized and added to the church that day—about 3,000 in all. [42] All the believers devoted themselves to the apostles' teaching, and to fellowship, and to sharing in meals (including the Lord's Supper), and to prayer. [43] A deep sense of awe came over them all, and the apostles performed many miraculous signs and wonders. [44] And all the believers met together in one place and shared everything they had. [45] They sold their property and possessions and shared the money with those in need. [46] They worshiped together at the Temple each day, met in homes for the Lord's Supper, and shared their meals with great joy and generosity— [47] all the while praising God and enjoying the goodwill of all the people. And each day the Lord added to their fellowship those who were being saved.

People will follow when they see something miraculous or when they are searching for answers in their own life. Yes, people will follow those who are wealthy and in high places in this world because of the desire to gain wealth and power themselves. However, wealth and power in this world comes at a price. They basically trade their soul for something which will pass away.

Psalm 49:16-20 (NLT) [16] *So don't be dismayed when the wicked grow rich and their homes become ever more splendid.* [17] *For when they die, they take nothing with them. Their wealth will not follow them into the grave* [18] *In this life they consider themselves fortunate and are applauded for their success.* [19] *But they will die like all before them and never again see the light of day.* [20] *People who boast of their wealth don't understand; they will die, just like animals.*

Ultimately, there are two classes of people that others will follow – those with wealth and power or those whose lives portray peace and happiness. People are searching for something in this life, and if we desire to be victorious in our own battles in order to show the world something greater, it begins with us. What our core is filled with will determine who we claim our God is. Is God your salvation? Is He your deliverer? Is He your healer? Is God your comfort in times of trouble? What is your foundation made of?

We need to go a step farther and look into what the foundation of the church really is. Yes, our foundation is to be Jesus Christ, but He is what we build our churches on or those places we come to worship.

1 Corinthians 3:5-9 NLT [5]After all, who is Apollos? Who is Paul? We are only God's servants through whom you believed the Good News. Each of us did the work the Lord gave us. [6]I planted the seed in your hearts, and Apollos watered it, but it was God who made it grow. [7]It's not important who does the planting, or who does the watering. What's important is that God makes the seed grow. [8]The one who plants and the one who waters work together with the same purpose. [9]For we are both God's workers. And you are God's field. You are God's building.

Okay, let's begin to lay the foundation in order to see this more clearly. We are all workers which should be working together. We are God's field and His building. Remember when Jesus told Peter, *"I will build My church upon you!" (Matthew 16:18)*

Jesus builds upon us as we line up with God's Word. As God's field, the harvest is plentiful but the workers are few. *(Matthew 9:37)* We become that field which goes forth to share the *"Good News,"* which is Christ. Notice that we are the field and the Scripture says the harvest is plentiful. We do go forth trying to impart Truth upon the *"many."* If we are the field and the harvest is plentiful, then the Holy Spirit will convict and those who are ready will stumble into our field. However, they will not come if we are not prepared, and this is not to imply that we do not go forth. Jesus went forth but the multitudes followed Him. Those who were called out by God, the few, remained and built upon the foundation of Christ. Now let me say, this does not imply that the few should remain in YOUR field. The few do not remain in YOUR ministry in order to grow YOUR ministry to glorify YOU! The few grew and then the few went forth. Many times or most times, God is calling us to go certain places for reasons. The disciples in the New Testament continually went forth to places which needed truth, and they would remain until they taught and grew others to continue with the works they had begun. The apostles would travel from place to place to make sure that Truth was prevailing among the various places where roots had begun. Remember, some plant and some water. The apostles would correct and build up those in Christ in order to keep the Doctrine alive to glorify the Father and to keep Jesus as the head of the church and not man. The apostle's correction was to insure that there was only ONE GOSPEL being taught and not different denominations spread out among the people which would bring division. This was never the intent of true Christianity. However, man has always wanted to control and with control brought multiple denominations which instigated religion. *"If they,"* meaning that particular church, *"does not see it my way, then I will just start my OWN church."* Many churches have split today because man's personalities got in the way and man's desire to control. If Jesus is not the center and the foundation, the church is not built on HIS foundation.

WE become God's building as WE build upon TRUE Christianity. It is not a man-made building. We are the building; we are the vessel which God uses to build His church as long as Jesus Christ is the foundation and remains the head. As I said, we should be working together, yet man has institutionalized the church in the Western civilization today to become what man wanted it to be. There are so many different denominations with different beliefs and each one of them believes that they are correct. Today, I have learned that only the Word of God is correct and regardless of where I fellowship, I may grow and learn from that man or woman on the pulpit but only as I test the words which come forth as we are told to do. *(1Thessalonians 5:20-21; 1John 4:1)* I have never set foot in any church where I believed everything which was being taught. I go back to God when I question what is being said to get revelation from My Father. If we do not know the Word of God to some extent, we will buy into everything which is being taught today. There is great flaw within our *"so-called"* religious churches in America. If you don't believe me, then believe what Jesus said. From Revelation 2 to Revelation 3, we can read what was written concerning the 7 churches. Today, the 7 churches can still be seen if we look at the characteristics and nature of what we see within our institutionalized churches which are among us. There are many theories out there regarding the 7 churches written about in Revelation, and I am not here to argue on any of the different philosophies; however, I will say that if you are one to believe that the description of those churches does not apply to the churches today, you are deceiving yourself. Our churches today are not without flaw! It is far better to believe we need improvement than to believe we have already arrived. I would much rather judge myself according to God's Word prior to standing before Him at final judgment. I would far rather be hard on myself than to assume I have arrived and be one of the *"many"* whom stands before our God at the gates of heaven only to hear the words, *"Depart from me for I never knew you!"*

Before we go further, let me clarify that my outlook towards the Western Churches today is not to be critical but to bring truth in order to wake up those whom are sleeping that none would perish. My desires are not to bring condemnation but conviction, and this is not to say that I believe I have all the answers because I am far from perfection myself. It is not about being right; it is about God's Word being right. It is not about lifting ME up but about lifting HIM up! I am nothing myself without Jesus. However, we are in the last days, and there needs to be those who are willing to go forth boldly to wake up the multitudes before it is too late. God desires that none should perish but we will perish if we do not heed the instructions from the Holy Spirit. As I have said, the ministry of Jesus Christ was one that was bold and offensive. It's time church, that we put our feelings aside and cry out to God to know truth according to His Word not what is necessarily being taught from the pulpits and not what is being taught from this book. Now, let's go through these churches briefly, the first church, Jesus said...

Revelation 2:4 AMP *[4]But I have this (one charge to make) against you: that you have left (abandoned) the love that you had at first (you have deserted Me, your first love).*

The second church, Jesus said...

Revelation 2:9-10 AMP *[9]I know your affliction and distress and pressing trouble and your poverty – but you are rich! And how you are abused and reviled and slandered by those who say they are Jews and are not, but are a synagogue of Satan. [10]Fear nothing that you are about to suffer. (Dismiss your dread and your fears!) Behold, the devil is indeed about to throw some of you into prison, that you may be tested and proved and critically appraised, and for ten days you will have affliction. Be loyally faithful unto death (even if you must die for it), and I will give you the crown of life.*

The third church, Jesus said...

Revelation 4:14-16 AMP *[14]Nevertheless, I have a few things against you: you have some people there who are clinging to the teachings of Balaam, who taught Balak to set a trap and a stumbling block before the sons of Israel, (to entice them) to eat food that had been sacrificed to idols and to practice lewdness (giving themselves up to sexual vice). [15]You also have some who in a similar way are clinging to the teaching of the Nicolaitans (those corrupters of the people) which thing I hate. [16]Repent (then)! Or else I will come to you quickly and fight against them with the sword of My mouth.*

The forth church, Jesus said…

Revelation 4:20-23 AMP [20]*But I have this against you: that you tolerate the woman Jezebel, who calls herself a prophetess (claiming to be inspired), and who is teaching and leading astray my servants and beguiling them into practicing sexual vice and eating food sacrificed to idols.* [21]*Take note: I will throw her on a bed (of anguish), and those who commit adultery with her (her paramours) I will bring down to pressing distress and severe affliction, unless they turn away their minds from conduct (such as) hers and repent of their doings.* [23]*and I will strike her children (her proper followers) dead (thoroughly exterminating them). And all the assemblies (churches) shall recognize and understand that I am He Who searches minds (the thoughts, feelings, and purposes) and the (inmost) hearts, and I will give to each of you (the reward for what you have done) as your work deserves.*

The fifth church, Jesus said…

Revelation 3:1b, 3 AMP [1b]*I know your record and what you are doing; you are supposed to be alive, but (in reality) you are dead.* [3]*So call to mind the lessons you received and heard; continually lay them to heart and obey them, and repent. In case you will not rouse yourselves and keep awake and watch, I will come upon you like a thief, and you will not know or suspect at what hour I will come.*

The sixth church, Jesus said…

Revelation 3:8-11 AMP [8]*I know your (record of) works and what you are doing. See! I have set before you a door wide open which no one is able to shut; I know that you have but little power, and yet you have kept My Word and guarded My message and have not renounced or denied My name.* [9]*Take note! I will make those of the synagogue of Satan who say they are Jews and are not, but lie – behold, I will make them come and*

276

bow down before your feet and learn and acknowledge that I have loved you. [10]Because you have guarded and kept My word of patient endurance (have held fast the lesson of My patience with the expectant endurance that I give you), I also will keep you (safe) from the hour of trial (testing) which is coming on the whole world to try those who dwell upon the earth. [11]I am coming quickly; hold fast what you have, so that no one may rob you and deprive you of your crown.

The seventh church, Jesus said…

Revelation 3:15-19 AMP [15]I know your (record of) works and what you are doing; you are neither cold nor hot. Would that you were cold or hot! [16]So, because you are lukewarm and neither cold nor hot, I will spew you out of My mouth! [17]For you say, I am rich; I have prospered and grown wealthy, and I am in need of nothing; and you do not realize and understand that you are wretched, pitiable, poor, blind, and naked. [18]Therefore I counsel you to purchase from me gold refined and tested by fire, that you may be (truly) wealthy, and white clothes to clothe you and to keep the shame of your nudity from being seen, and salve to put on your eyes, that you may see. [19]Those whom I (dearly and tenderly) love, I tell their faults and convict and convince and reprove and chasten (I discipline and instruct them). So be enthusiastic and in earnest and burning with zeal and repent (changing your mind and attitude).

Okay, now let's look at this briefly. It is evident that the first church is not right with God, no need to elaborate. They have become a people who have built upon religion in order to glorify themselves and have forgotten Jesus. The second church would not be a big church but probably a small church because it says that it is in poverty yet rich. The world looks on those whom are poor as being in poverty based on the financial state. We would proclaim that a small church with a small amount of resources (money) would not be considered rich but poor. This church struggles due to lack of money. They proclaim to be poor but Jesus said that they are rich. God does not look at money as being rich but rather being poor. Rich in the eyes of God has to do with spiritual richness. We can gain all the wealth of this world and be lacking because we do not have spiritual richness.

Matthew 16:26 (ESV) [26]For what will it profit a man if he gains the whole world and forfeits his soul? Or what shall a man give in return for his soul?

We cannot buy our way into heaven. Huge glorious churches in all their richness and splendor are not assured heaven. This is not the fruit which Jesus spoke of. We are to grow in the characteristics and nature of Jesus Christ and that is gaining the fruits of the spirit which has to do with our spiritual nature. This church, the second one, is told that they are going to suffer. They are told that the devil is going to attack them; they are going to go through tests and trials, but they are told to endure. Yet, when we are going through our storms, we are murmuring and complaining to God that we don't want to be here. We are not satisfied. We are praying for God to take away the storms, but God has allowed those storms for a reason. How are we to judge God based on our suffering? Are we not to suffer for Christ? Are we not to count it joy for our sufferings?

James 1:2-4 (NLT) Faith and Endurance [2]Dear brothers and sisters, when troubles of any kind come your way, consider it an opportunity for great joy. [3]For you know that when your faith is tested, your endurance has a chance to grow. [4]So let it grow, for when your endurance is fully developed, you will be perfect and complete, needing nothing.

Remember, our storms are to perfect us. They perfect the nature of Jesus Christ within us. We want to call ourselves Christians yet we do not want to belong to that church which is suffering. We do not want to walk among those who suffer and endure many tests and many trials. We look at Abraham, Moses, Paul and many of the other great men in biblical days as great role models, yet we do not really want to follow in their footsteps because we do not want to suffer and go through storms as they did. We want to be called Christians but we want to be those who are the *"blessed Christians."* The second church was blessed. It was not the kind of blessings we desire, but it is the kind that God gives. This kind of blessing brings us closer to God where we are able to see within His heart to come to know His desires. However, we begin to look for that blessed church in order to gain the riches of this world because we dare not suffer for Christ, but that second church gains the crown of life!

I'm not going to say much about the third church because most people would say, *"Well, that's not me!"* I will say this, before you claim that this is not you, you may need to study about the teachings of Balaam and Nicolaitans. I'm sure most of us do not even know what those teachings were and if we do not know the teachings, how do we know that we do not fall into this category? Briefly, I will say that Balaam is mentioned in Numbers, Jude, Peter, and Revelation. The passages speak of the error and ways of Balaam which has to do with monetary gain. According to the Old Testament teachings, monetary gain is derived from the willingness to compromise the principles of God and teach contrary to the Word of God. This is very prevalent in our society today. There are multitudes of ministries that want your money for their monetary gain and will compromise the Word of God with every breath in order to acquire those riches. The church which looks at themselves as rich but in God's eyes they are really poor. Then we have those churches that may not be mega-churches but they still compromise the Word of God in order that they receive gain. As for the Nicolaitans, there is not enough known about them other than the meaning of the name which is a victor, conqueror over people. Therefore, the teachings of the Nicolaitans could refer to leaders over the people or the flock. When we look at leadership within the churches today, we see the vast majority of leaders being lifted up and increased in authority and rule, increased in status, fame, fortune, etc. However, when we look at Jesus Christ when He walked this earth with His followers, He came as a servant unto them not as one that ruled over them to gain the riches and fame of this world. We must be careful on both of these doctrines that what we choose to believe in is not contrary to that of the Word of God.

The forth church is not right with God and basically lives in sin to satisfy their own desires. The fifth church is dead. Let me say that this is not according to the size of your attendance. I know that the big churches believe they are alive and well with God because they have such a huge following. To be alive in Christ has nothing to do with your following. If we want to look at size, the next question is going to be, which denomination which has increased in size is correct? There are many churches out there which are huge but not all the huge churches are in agreement on doctrine. This also would be contrary to the Word of God. Our fruit is not in people but in the Fruit of the Spirit. Now, don't get me wrong, there are many small churches which are dead because the truth is not being taught and they are not walking in truth. Yet, the crowds will follow that which pleases their appetites. People want to follow what is easier. It is much easier to agree with a sermon which says that God will bless you with riches if you follow Him rather than follow a church which says that you are going to be persecuted and suffer for Christ's sake. So, when we talk about the fifth church, it is dead to the spiritual things of God. It may have some truth but not the whole truth. It may have grown to base its teachings on those which bring the crowds rather than those teachings which bring people to repentance.

I also need to add, that once you are walking according to the Scriptures and your fruit is evident according to Scripture, you will have others that want what you have. Your fruit will also be seen in those who learn and grow from you. If you are a disciple and you teach to grow others as is commanded by Jesus Christ, those teachings will begin to transform those who remain faithful to your teachings as you remain faithful to Christ. I have seen many whom call themselves leaders and have those following but yet there is not fruit of the Holy Spirit evident in that leader, nor in those following. We must look at their lives outside of church. I have actually walked into huge leader's homes only to witness the filth that they allow their children to watch on television. This is a huge problem in our society.

The sixth church is really where we should be. The second church was the testing stage but many will not endure that stage. The *"many"* will fall away or find a church that teaches that which is easier like the fifth church. But, for those who endure the second church, they really walk into that sixth church if they hold fast and remain faithful. The sixth church is for those who have endured through the testing stage. Yes, we will continue to be tested because that is necessary that our own personalities do not get in the way of being where we need to be with God. However, because of our endurance, God guards and protects us. Think about Job, He endured many storms which would have been unbearable by the *"many."* In fact, during Job's testing time, the *"many"* came to him with advice that he needed to do this or that. The *"many"* will follow the instruction of those showing an easier path because they grow weary of their storm. However, Job held fast and endured the storm and did not listen to the *"many"* but remained one of the few. Once Job got through the hardest part of His walk with God, things began to change. God did bless him and restore him. I'm sure Job had other tests but none as hard as what it took to get him where he needed to be with God. God desires that we come to the end of ourselves and our lives are submitted to Him solely! Prior to Job's afflictions was he not right with God? This is not what I am saying. Job was growing with God because he loved Him dearly. When we begin to submit to God and desire more of Him, God must begin a total transformation within our lives. That transformation cannot materialize without a storm.

The seventh and last church, which is the worst by far, is seen so prevalent in this society. This church is referred to as the church which is *"lukewarm."* This basically means that they know much of the Scriptures yet they remain in the middle by choice. They chose to be where they are. They choose to compromise because it is easier. They begin to believe a lie because they believe Jesus paid the total price for God's people and because of the price Jesus paid, the church should be blessed and not suffer. This is not biblical. In fact, we are told that we would suffer.

2 Timothy 3:12 (ESV) [12] Indeed, all who desire to live a godly life in Christ Jesus will be persecuted,

1 Peter 2:18-23(ESV) [18] Servants, be subject to your masters with all respect, not only to the good and gentle but also to the unjust. [19] For this is a gracious thing, when, mindful of God, one endures sorrows while suffering unjustly. [20] For what credit is it if, when you sin and are beaten for it, you endure? But if when you do good and suffer for it you endure, this is a gracious thing in the sight of God. [21] For to this you have been called, because Christ also suffered for you, leaving you an example, so that you might follow in his steps. [22] He committed no sin, neither was deceit found in his mouth. [23] When he was reviled, he did not revile in return; when he suffered, he did not threaten, but continued entrusting himself to him who judges justly.

In America, the church has a hard time being able to see that they could possibly be this seventh church. Instead, this church believes they have prospered because God is blessing them for their deeds. They believe that growth represents fruit. They believe that God is behind their growth even though they use worldly measures to increase their attendance. This church has to have the best of everything and is continually trying to grow their church to have more and more programs, bigger and richer buildings, the best media ministry, music ministry, etc. This church fails miserably to be representative of the church of Jesus Christ because it is not dealing with what the people coming forth need. In fact, if this church were to begin preaching the true gospel of Jesus Christ in its full entirety, they would begin to see a decrease in attendance. Jesus did not teach or preach *"feel good"* messages. Jesus was offensive in His teachings, so much so, that they crucified Him. The true church of Jesus Christ will offend the *"many."* The true church of Jesus Christ will have *"few"* followers. This does not mean that the *"many"* will not come, but it does mean that the *"many"* will not remain. These are bold statements that *"many"* would never proclaim. I do so because I have been there. I do so because I have seen from the inside what prevails among the leadership within these huge churches. I have listened to the *"do's and the don'ts"* within these churches because they dare not offend the *"many"* which would bring the attendance down. I have seen the changes implemented in order to bring in more funds to cover the financial aspects of the ministry which were shocking to say the least and were reproved by Jesus Himself in the New Testament.

Matthew 21:12-13 (ESV) Jesus Cleanses the Temple [12]And Jesus entered the temple and drove out all who sold and bought in the temple, and he overturned the tables of the money-changers and the seats of those who sold pigeons. [13]He said to them, "It is written, 'My house shall be called a house of prayer; but you make it a den of robbers.'"

Matthew 22:14 (ESV) [14]For many are called, but few are chosen."

Yet, we make excuses when it involves OUR ministry. If in fact, it is the ministry founded on the foundation of Jesus Christ, should we not endure the hard times as well as the good times and trust that God is in control? We absolutely should. If God be in control and Jesus is truly the foundation we have built upon, then we trust and endure through the testing period and suffering as God allows in order that our character is perfected. I believe there are many men and women building upon their own ministry which may truly love God, but they are blinded from seeing this truth. I believe that God is speaking to His church today to awaken. I believe that those who are listening are struggling with letting go of what they have built and allowing God to tear it down and rebuild His true church. However, the struggle within goes back to man's desire to control instead of total surrender to a power much greater. We must first become that second church and endure through our testing period counting it joy because we trust that God will ultimately prevail even if it cost us our ministry and our life.

Now let's go back to 1 Corinthians 3 once again. We left off with verse 9 where it was speaking about us being God's field and God's building.

1 Corinthians 3:10-19 NLT [10]Because of God's special favor to me, I have laid the foundation like an expert builder. Now others are building on it. But whoever is building on this foundation must be very careful. [11]For no one can lay any other foundation than the one we already have –Jesus Christ. [12]Now anyone who builds on that foundation may use gold, silver, jewels, wood, hay, or straw. [13]But there is going to come a time of testing at the judgment day to see what kind of work each builder has done. Everyone's work will be put through the fire to see whether or not it keeps its value. [14]If the work survives the fire, that builder will receive a reward. [15]But if the work is burned up, the builder will suffer great loss. The builders themselves will be saved, but like someone escaping through a wall of flames. [16]Don't you realize that all of you together are the temple of God and that the Spirit of God lives in you? [17]God will bring ruin upon anyone who ruins this temple. For God's temple is holy, and you Christians are that temple. [18]Stop fooling yourselves. If you think you are wise by this world's standards, you will have to become a fool so you can become wise by God's standards. [19]For the wisdom of this world is foolishness to God. As the Scriptures say, "He traps the wise in the snare of their own cleverness."

I am not anyone's God, and I cannot judge anyone individually. I can merely present Scripture in order to bring about clarity. We each have the responsibility to look at our own lives and our own ministry and judge it according to the Word of God. Our foundation must be built upon Jesus Christ and it must be according to the Word of God. We cannot make our own rules and laws when it comes to the architectural design of our ministry. We cannot control those who come into our field. As Disciples of Christ, we can only bring truth as it is proclaimed to us through the Holy Spirit even if that truth is offensive. The church today has come a long way since the beginning of the church in Acts, but it has not necessarily come to the correct place. I believe today that God is calling His people back to Him. I believe that God desires that we stand back and take an honest assessment of our own ministry. We must be able to see if our ministry lines up with the first church which Jesus began. We need to be able to see if our foundation is built on solid ground. Solid ground will not fall when all else around us fails. Solid ground has nothing to do with a physical building but a spiritual building. Falling has everything to do with that day we stand before our Creator. We cannot make excuses and say that this is a different time and era and what we see today as the church is due to the changes in technology and advancement within our culture. God never changes but man has remained the same in the sense of desiring to be in control. Jesus came to change man. The Holy Spirit's job is to change man. God remains the same but man must change if he desires eternal life with Jesus Christ. We see in Scripture that Jesus continually corrected man because of their desire to control. Paul continually went from church to church to correct due to man's desire to be head over the church. All the way back to the first disciples, we can see that their desires to follow Jesus were to advance in His Kingdom.

Luke 9:46 (NIV) ⁴⁶Then an argument started among the disciples as to which of them would be the greatest.

We may not voice that desire openly to be greater than others, but this is an aspect of human nature which the Holy Spirit's job is to rid us of ourselves. Why would we think that all of a sudden man's desires have changed and line up with God's desires? Why do we all believe that OUR church is the correct way a church is supposed to look? Does this not go back to man's desire to control and be the head? Why do we believe that man has built all these fabulous churches, and that we have done so in submission unto God and without reproof? I believe it is time to awaken and cry out to God to show us how our church is supposed to look. I believe that it is time for the denominations with all their rules and laws to cry out to God and allow Jesus to be the head of their churches today. I pray that each of us question our motivations, our desires, and our relationship with Jesus Christ. It is time that our wisdom is seen as foolishness to believe that we can build our churches individually and collectively

286

upon our own rules and laws which pertain to man's motivations and desires. Our desires may very well be to please God and give Him the glory, but when we do so according to our own standards, we have failed. God said, your ways are not my ways nor are your thoughts.

Isaiah 55:8 (NLT) [8] *"My thoughts are nothing like your thoughts," says the LORD. "And my ways are far beyond anything you could imagine.*

Yet today, we see that our ministries are built according to man's ways. Our ministries are built according to man's wisdom. This world has gained a lot of wisdom to know how to entice large crowds of people in order to gain riches by their commercials, advertisement, benefits, perks, entertainment, and I could go on and on. All of these techniques have been shown to work if done according to studies and the outcome brings about growth and financial benefits. Our churches today use the same methods as this world uses and the results may be the same, but we are gaining riches according to man's standards and not God's. Let's allow Jesus to be the Head and cry out for the Holy Spirit to change the way we think and our desires so that they line up with the Word of God.

One final note, there will be many say, *"God blessed the great men of Old Testament times with riches of this world and the New Testament was to add to but not take away from the OT."* This is true, but we are not men and women of Old Testament times, we are the church. The church has a different calling than those in OT times, and the blessings and riches in OT times were so that those great men of old were blessed with land and livestock to take care of ALL those in their land. Today, the church was called to go and share Jesus Christ. Jesus said that there was no man greater than John the Baptist.

Matthew 11:11 (NIV) Truly I tell you, among those born of women there has risen no one greater than John the Baptist. Yet even the least in the kingdom of heaven is greater than he.

John the Baptist shows us our mission. Jesus showed us our mission. We are to be Christ-like. Jesus came with one mission – people! If we do not have a great love for mankind as Jesus did, our heart is not right. If you have a love for people, your outlook on this life will change to where your motivations will be to go and go and go in order that others will know Your God. Our desires in this life will portray the things we really love and our actions will be for those things we desire.

Chapter Six
Gospel Shoes

As we begin to grow and mature in Christ, the time will come when Jesus will send us forth into all nations.

Matthew 28:18-20 (NLT) [18] *Jesus came and told his disciples, "I have been given all authority in heaven and on earth.* [19] *Therefore, go and make disciples of all the nations, baptizing them in the name of the Father and the Son and the Holy Spirit.* [20] *Teach these new disciples to obey all the commands I have given you. And be sure of this: I am with you always, even to the end of the age."*

This is referred to as the *"Great Commission."* A commission is when someone gives the power and authority to others in order to carry out a purpose. Jesus commissioned all disciples to go and make disciples. He told His disciples that He had been given the authority in heaven and on earth. Jesus has the authority over heaven and earth and has entrusted us with that authority to do what He did. When it talks about going into all nations, this does not necessarily mean that we all go forth to a different nation other than the nation we live in. However, there will be some that are called to go into all nations because they have been given the gift of evangelism. When it talks about all nations, Jesus desires that all nations are reached, and if every born again Bible believing Christian were to do as asked, we would be reaching all nations and all people. Like I told my sister when she got saved, God is not expecting you to quit your job and start traveling. She lives in a little bitty town up in the mountains with one traffic light in front of Wal-Mart. Of course, most of the population either works at Wal-Mart or shops there. I told her, *"God will use you right there."* Do not be surprised if He begins to send those across your path who need answers. Once you have gained some knowledge, you have graduated enough to share Jesus. It does not take much to tell those about your personal experience of how Jesus saved you. Your testimony will move mountains in other people's lives. My books are filled with my testimonies. God uses us with what we have, where we are, and what we are capable of doing.

We have discussed that if you call yourself a Christian, you are a disciple. A Christian is merely a follower of Christ. Every one of us will come to the place that God expects us to put on our gospel shoes, no one is exempt. We may make up every excuse in the book, but if we desire to walk this walk, we must talk the talk. This chapter will discuss all the aspects of our purpose in this world and how what we do in this life will determine what we do in the next.

The Great Commission

Mark 16:15-20 (NLT) [15] *And then he told them, "Go into all the world and preach the Good News to everyone.* [16] *Anyone who believes and is baptized will be saved. But anyone who refuses to believe will be condemned.* [17] *These miraculous signs will accompany those who believe: They will cast out demons in my name, and they will speak in new languages.* [18] *They will be able to handle snakes with safety, and if they drink anything poisonous, it won't hurt them. They will be able to place their hands on the sick, and they will be healed."* [19] *When the Lord Jesus had finished talking with them, he was taken up into heaven and sat down in the place of honor at God's right hand.* [20] *And the disciples went everywhere and preached, and the Lord worked through them, confirming what they said by many miraculous signs.*

I have shared that Paul's last message to the disciples was about putting on the whole armor, and with Paul knowing that he would no longer be with them, this was what he chose to impart. We must understand that if we know we are going to die, we would spend our last minutes with those we love and would use that time to impart what is in our heart. We are not going to waste precious moments talking about things that do not matter when we know we are leaving this world and those behind that we love. In the same way, Jesus knew he was leaving to ascend to His Father, and His last message to those He loved was the Great Commission. Why was this so important?

Most of us will not put forth effort in something that we do not believe in. Jesus wanted to impart our purpose in this world as believers. When we feel that we have purpose, it sets our will into motion. When we line up our will with God's will, fulfillment will be manifested in our lives. We each have a calling upon our lives which becomes our purpose, but it is perfected through Christ as our God-given personalities, talents, and gifts line up with the Word of God. There is no calling without the gospel, and there is no sacrifice without an understanding. How can we possibly sacrifice our lives if we do not understand our purpose? Man spends his whole lifetime seeking fulfillment and purpose only to come up empty handy as he takes his last breath never fully understanding the meaning to life. We will all fall short of the Kingdom of Heaven if we do not find our true purpose and fulfillment according to Scripture.

The Great Commission is the one purpose that every believer in Christ has in common. We are all expected to go forth, but how we go forth will depend on our special calling in this life and the life to come. Our feet are the instruments that God will use to take us to and fro into territories prepared for us to travel. Like the disciples before us, each had special talents and gifts, but they all had the same purpose which was sharing Jesus. We are all called to prepare the way for the second coming of the Lord just as John the Baptist's purpose was to prepare the way for His first coming, as was prophesied by the prophet Isaiah.

Mark 1:1-3 (NLT) John the Baptist Prepares the Way [1]This is the Good News about Jesus the Messiah, the Son of God. It began [2]just as the prophet Isaiah had written: "Look, I am sending my messenger ahead of you, and he will prepare your way. [3]He is a voice shouting in the wilderness, 'Prepare the way for the LORD's coming! Clear the road for him!'"

John the Baptist was a forerunner for Christ. A forerunner is a pioneer; it is someone who sees things far into the future and goes before others to help prepare the way. You will know if you have that pioneering spirit because that spirit is one like our forefathers before us, the founders of America. A pioneering spirit is one that says, *"Send me Lord for I shall go."* A pioneering spirit is someone who is willing to take risks, willing to invest their time, and willing to give up all for the purpose. Are you a forerunner for the second coming of Christ? When we fall madly in love with God, His cause becomes personal. Someone with a pioneering spirit may go where others are not willing to go, but they will also see and witness things others will never experience. Remember, Jesus said signs, wonders, and miracles would follow those who went forth in His name preaching the gospel and leading the way for others to follow. Why is the Great Commission important today? Our heart will lead and guide our feet, but if our heart is not right with God, our feet will not go into those barren places to be the voice crying out among the nations of this world. If our heart is not right with God, our feet will not engage in the greatest purpose in this life which is to lead others to still waters for His names sake. David had a pioneering spirit and in his Psalm, we can experience the heart of one who was willing to let go of this world and surrender total trust to the God of this Universe.

292

Psalm 23 (AMP) [1] The Lord is my Shepherd [to feed, guide, and shield me], I shall not lack. [2] He makes me lie down in [fresh, tender] green pastures; He leads me beside the still and restful waters. [3] He refreshes and restores my life (my self); He leads me in the paths of righteousness [uprightness and right standing with Him—not for my earning it, but] for His name's sake. [4] Yes, though I walk through the [deep, sunless] valley of the shadow of death, I will fear or dread no evil, for You are with me; Your rod [to protect] and Your staff [to guide], they comfort me. [5] You prepare a table before me in the presence of my enemies. You anoint my head with oil; my [brimming] cup runs over. [6] Surely or only goodness, mercy, and unfailing love shall follow me all the days of my life, and through the length of my days the house of the Lord [and His presence] shall be my dwelling place.

Purpose ~ To Plant or Water

Our life must be full of purpose. With each step we take, there must be purpose. We live out our lives and when we come to the end, far too often what we see was not a life that was filled with purpose. I remember after healing came from the death of my daughter, thinking about what I wanted to leave for my other children when my life was over and all would have been said and done. In reality, our lives pretty much speak of leaving our children with a legacy of how to work hard, play little, and gain much wealth. This was no longer what I wanted. I had memories of days spent with my oldest daughter, but most of those memories involved things of this world not of the world to come. I had to sit back and ask myself, *"What was the greatest legacy that I could leave my children?"* Of course, the answer is Jesus. Yes, I had raised my oldest daughter up loving Jesus, but I had failed her, by far, on walking away from the Truth when I fell from grace. As parents or anyone reading these words, please know that there is knowledge and wisdom to be gained in order to leave those we

293

love with the greatest legacy known and that is Jesus Christ. Our legacy will never be in words alone but in actions shown. Purpose with each step will reflect upon our life and the greatest memories that we can leave for our loved ones.

The question is to plant or to water. Far too many times, we plant seeds and then go back to continue watering and watering looking for that harvest. We are all called to be disciples, but sometimes, we will plant and other times we will water, and then there will be times that we plant and water. This is important to understand exactly what the Scriptures say about planting and watering in order to reap a harvest.

*1 Corinthians 3:8 (NLT) *[8]*The one who plants and the one who waters work together with the same purpose. And both will be rewarded for their own hard work.*

Notice that Paul is talking about two different people, yet they are working together. When we are talking about planting, this is referred to as planting seeds. When we share our testimony or share the gospel in any form or fashion, we have just planted a seed. We need to understand that sometimes that may be all we do. We plant the seed and wait on God to send someone else to water that seed. I will use my children for an example. Most of the time, but not always, you probably will not be the person to water the seeds you may have planted in those you love. Sometimes, you may not be the person who even plants the seeds. I know when my children were way out in the world and there seemed to be no hope to the situation, they did not want me preaching to them. Sometimes, we continually preach and preach and preach to those we love, but all we are doing is over watering, and they are drowning in our words. When we over water, they are no longer listening. Do not over water anyone. You may push your loved ones completely away and any seeds which may have been planted have rotted to the point of decay.

To understand the planting process, let's look at plants. Plants need water based on many conditions such as the temperature, climate, what type of plant, what kind of soil, etc. It is far better to under water a plant than to over water. In fact, you can over water a plant to where the plant can no longer breathe. Many times, we feel helpless because we desire for those we love to wake up, and we cannot seem to awaken them. This is not our job as Christians. Our calling is to go and make disciples, but the Holy Spirit will lead us on the correct path to do so. This path often times will not even involve those we love. When I began praying for my children to awaken, God showed me to be obedient to where He was calling me, and He would take care of those I loved. In doing this, my planting began with complete strangers, and eventually, it followed with girls that He sent across my path to water. I was obedient and left my own daughters alone. My life was transformed where they began to watch my walk. In this, I was already planting seeds simply by walking this walk. As time went on, they began to come to me and ask questions, and then more seeds continued to be planted. I began to send them to others to water only because I felt they needed a mentor, and I needed to just be their mother. Eventually, they came back to me after some growth to where they desired to follow me. Even today, I am careful how much I water them, and sometimes, I have to step back and allow God to work in them. It is really easy to grow to a place with God where you have so much knowledge that you drown every person who crosses your path. We cannot make people be Christians; we cannot make them love God; we cannot make them grow, and that is not our job. Sometimes, they may not quite be ready, and when we over water, we completely turn them to running away from anything that has to do with the Bible. In the end, God will cultivate and make those seeds grow, but we are His servants, working together to plant and water. People come to the Lord by God working in them not by anything we were capable of doing. We become obedient and serve God with purpose.

1 Corinthians 3:5-7 (NLT) *⁵After all, who is Apollos? Who is Paul? We are only God's servants through whom you believed the Good News. Each of us did the work the Lord gave us. ⁶I planted the seed in your hearts, and Apollos watered it, but it was God who made it grow. ⁷It's not important who does the planting, or who does the watering. What's important is that God makes the seed grow.*

Our mission is to increase God's Kingdom by serving with purpose. We are all joined together as a body of believers and depending on if we are the hand, the foot, the mouth, or whatever part of the body we are, determines how God will use us to plant and water those seeds.

1 Corinthians 12:12-14 (NIV) [12] Just as a body, though one, has many parts, but all its many parts form one body, so it is with Christ. [13] For we were all baptized by one Spirit so as to form one body—whether Jews or Gentiles, slave or free —and we were all given the one Spirit to drink. [14] Even so the body is not made up of one part but of many.

When we are obedient and do our part, we become the field that God can work through. As we allow God to transform us into the image of Christ, it will be through us that God can grow that which we have planted.

1 Corinthians 3:9 (NLT) [9] For we are both God's workers. And you are God's field. You are God's building.

It will never be about gaining greatness in the Kingdom or about gaining stature on this earth, increasing the Kingdom of Heaven has everything to do with saving souls. Jesus taught often seeds for the harvest. We are the laborers or servants who are called to go into the fields and plant those seeds into the Kingdom of Heaven. Jesus even showed us how to plant and water.

Matthew 9:35-38 (ESV) [35] And Jesus went throughout all the cities and villages, teaching in their synagogues and proclaiming the gospel of the kingdom and healing every disease and every affliction. [36] When he saw the crowds, he had compassion for them, because they were harassed and helpless, like sheep without a shepherd. [37]Then he said to his disciples, "The harvest is plentiful, but the laborers are few; [38] therefore pray earnestly to the Lord of the harvest to send out laborers into his harvest."

Signs and wonders will follow those who believe. Jesus planted the seeds, and He watered multitudes. Our message must have purpose and with purpose, there will be power. No one is going to follow someone who is cold and dead. If we are alive in Christ, we should be walking with life. Either we show forth life or our lives speak death.

Mark 16:17-18 (NIV) [17] And these signs will accompany those who believe: In my name they will drive out demons; they will speak in new tongues; [18] they will pick up snakes with their hands; and when they drink deadly poison, it will not hurt them at all; they will place their hands on sick people, and they will get well."

Jesus gave parables which were compared to heaven. Heaven was compared to a man who had sowed good seed into his field. There is plenty of field out there for all of us and we all have our own field, which would be the place the Holy Spirit sends us.

Matthew 13:24-30 (ESV) The Parable of the Weeds [24] He put another parable before them, saying, "The kingdom of heaven may be compared to a man who sowed good seed in his field, [25] but while his men were sleeping, his enemy came and sowed weeds among the wheat and went away. [26] So when the plants came up and bore grain, then the weeds appeared also. [27] And the servants of the master of the house came and said to him, 'Master, did you not sow good seed in your field? How then does it have weeds?' [28] He said to them, 'An enemy has done this.' So the servants said to him, 'Then do you want us to go and gather them?'

²⁹ But he said, 'No, lest in gathering the weeds you root up the wheat along with them. ³⁰ Let both grow together until the harvest, and at harvest time I will tell the reapers, Gather the weeds first and bind them in bundles to be burned, but gather the wheat into my barn.'"

Notice the Scripture says that the man planted good seed. Good seed can only come from God. Everything good is from above.

James 1:17 (NIV) ¹⁷ Every good and perfect gift is from above, coming down from the Father of the heavenly lights, who does not change like shifting shadows.

Does that mean we can also plant bad seed? Absolutely, we are continually planting seeds in others and until we line up with the Word of God, the seeds we plant are contrary to His Word. I remember being backslidden and how I touched so many lives but not in a good way. I remember that I knew so much about the Word of God, yet my life was like that of this world. All those things I imparted to others at that time were not of God. In a sense, when we plant anything contrary to God's Word, we are allowing satan to lead our steps and plant into the kingdom of this world in which he rules.

2 Corinthians 4:4 (NLT) ⁴ Satan, who is the god of this world, has blinded the minds of those who don't believe. They are unable to see the glorious light of the Good News. They don't understand this message about the glory of Christ, who is the exact likeness of God.

If we desire to impact other's lives, we must plant seeds which will take root in good soil. In looking deeper into the parable of the weeds, what the man was doing was compared to the Kingdom of Heaven. We sow good seed in a field, and we expect a harvest. We are not expecting weeds but good fruit. Yet, it goes on to say that while his men were sleeping, the enemy came and sowed weeds among the good seed. The plants came up and bore good fruit, yet there were weeds which were also present. There is something we need to see here. In Matthew, Jesus told Peter that He would give him the keys to the Kingdom of Heaven. This was given to Peter because he believed that Jesus was the Son of God. Prior to this, Jesus told him that He would build upon him, His church. We are the church. The church is not a building. If you believe that Jesus is the Son of God, then you are considered the church, and God has entrusted the church with the keys to the Kingdom of Heaven.

Matthew 16:19 (NLT) [19] *And I will give you the keys of the Kingdom of Heaven. Whatever you forbid on earth will be forbidden in heaven, and whatever you permit on earth will be permitted in heaven."*

The church has the power to use the keys to the Kingdom of Heaven to bind and loose or to permit. There is a huge responsibility on the church which is not a building, it is me and you. Yet, in every church there are good seed and there are weeds in the midst. The weeds could be characterized in two ways. Sometimes those weeds are the things which distract the Christians from drawing close to God, and then sometimes the weeds are other people who are living a double life. They may be walking among the Christian community but their lives are evil. They have no desire to lay down their own life and live for Christ. Their lives are selfish and consumed with living according to the pleasures of this world. Notice in Matthew 13, how Jesus said to let both the weeds and the wheat grow together until the harvest?

Matthew 13:24-30 (ESV) The Parable of the Weeds [24] *He put another parable before them, saying, "The kingdom of heaven may be compared to a man who sowed good seed in his field,* [25] *but while his men were sleeping, his enemy came and sowed weeds among the wheat and went* *away. ^{26} So when the plants came up and bore grain, then the weeds appeared also. ^{27} And the servants of the master of the house came and said to him, 'Master, did you not sow good seed in your field? How then does it have weeds?' ^{28} He said to them, 'An enemy has done this.' So the servants said to him, 'Then do you want us to go and gather them?' ^{29} But he said, 'No, lest in gathering the weeds you root up the wheat along with them. ^{30} Let both grow together until the harvest, and at harvest time I will tell the reapers, Gather the weeds first and bind them in bundles to be burned, but gather the wheat into my barn.'"*

The reason was to not disturb the soil in order that the wheat would be able to continue to grow. Sometimes disturbing the soil can cause a division, and there may be good wheat growing that is a new crop, yet not ripe enough to be harvested. God knows what He is doing, and it is not our job to judge who is good and who is not. We merely plant the seeds or water them and allow God to cultivate or gather the harvest.

Revelation 14:14-16 (ESV) The Harvest of the Earth ^{14} Then I looked, and behold, a white cloud, and seated on the cloud one like a son of man, with a golden crown on his head, and a sharp sickle in his hand. ^{15} And another angel came out of the temple, calling with a loud voice to him who sat on the cloud, "Put in your sickle, and reap, for the hour to reap has come, for the harvest of the earth is fully ripe." ^{16} So he who sat on the cloud swung his sickle across the earth, and the earth was reaped.

In Revelation, it shows that this is the harvest Jesus spoke of. When the time is ripe or when the earth is fully ripe and ready to be harvested, Jesus will return in all His glory. The harvest will be fully ripe when prophesy is fulfilled in that the gospel has been preached throughout the whole world.

Matthew 24:14 (NLT) ^{14} And the Good News about the Kingdom will be preached throughout the whole world, so that all nations will hear it; and then the end will come.

At that time, Jesus will come and harvest all the good wheat which will be taken up in the clouds with Him. After the wheat has been harvested, the weeds or thorns among them will also be harvested and judged by the wrath of God.

Revelation 14:17-20 (ESV) [17] Then another angel came out of the temple in heaven, and he too had a sharp sickle. [18] And another angel came out from the altar, the angel who has authority over the fire, and he called with a loud voice to the one who had the sharp sickle, "Put in your sickle and gather the clusters from the vine of the earth, for its grapes are ripe." [19] So the angel swung his sickle across the earth and gathered the grape harvest of the earth and threw it into the great winepress of the wrath of God. [20] And the winepress was trodden outside the city, and blood flowed from the winepress, as high as a horse's bridle, for 1,600 stadia.

Peter spoke about the judgment of God beginning with the house of God, the church. Again, this is not a building and does not mean that you must be in the right church in order to make it to heaven. We are all judged accordingly, and if you study the seven churches in Revelation, as was discussed in the previous chapter, it speaks about people individually. God speaks about some who are doing this and others who are doing that. We are not judged just because those we fellowship with are not living right, but judgment will come upon God's people first. I believe that the those who have matured in the fruit of the Spirit will be harvested away from those whose lives were not portrayed as living as close to holy as possible. Yes, we are all in these earthly bodies and will definitely miss it, but we all have the ability to make choices. Our choices can put us in the category of the weeds and thorns among good fruit.

1 Peter 4:17-18 (AMP) [17] *For the time [has arrived] for judgment to begin with the household of God; and if it begins with us, what will [be] the end of those who do not respect or believe or obey the good news (the Gospel) of God?* [18] *And if the righteous are barely saved, what will become of the godless and wicked?*

In order to plant and water good seed, we must first be operating in good seed ourselves. It is not possible to plant good seed if you are a weed or thorn. God knows our heart and knows if we diligently seek Him in order to be all that we can be through Christ. In Revelation, God speaks about one such church or believers who are neither hot nor cold, meaning they are lukewarm. What happened? They grew to a level with God and decided this was good enough. These are those who play church. There is no root and there is no Christian life visible. God said He would spit those who were lukewarm out of His mouth.

Revelation 3:15-16 (NLT) [15] *"I know all the things you do, that you are neither hot nor cold. I wish that you were one or the other!* [16] *But since you are like lukewarm water, neither hot nor cold, I will spit you out of my mouth!*

If our desire is to be a disciple for Christ and go into the nations to make disciples, we must totally submit to that calling which is for all believers. We must begin to be obedient in order that God can use us to plant and to water the seeds. Here is the deal, what we plant and water has the capacity to grow and grow and grow. You will never know what that one seed you plant into someone else's life will produce. Jesus told about the Parable of the Mustard Seed.

Mark 4:30-32 (ESV) The Parable of the Mustard Seed [30] *And he said, "With what can we compare the kingdom of God, or what parable shall*

302

we use for it? [31] It is like a grain of mustard seed, which, when sown on the ground, is the smallest of all the seeds on earth, [32] yet when it is sown it grows up and becomes larger than all the garden plants and puts out large branches, so that the birds of the air can make nests in its shade."

The mustard seed must have been comparable to that particular person that no one would waste their time because through the natural eye, this person seemed to be nothing in comparison to others. This person may not have had an education; they may be dirt poor; perhaps they live in the worst of neighborhoods or even out on the streets; their language and personality may be one that is offensive, or they may seem angry at the world and feel as though they deserve a handout. This is not for us to judge, but that small mustard seed may have been planted within this person just by a few words of hope or time taken to share a testimony, and then within this person, a seed might have begun to grow and grow.

If you take out time to Google, there are amazing testimonies of how God has transformed lives. I know He transformed my life, and it only happened because someone else who had a spirit-filled life within them took time out to not only plant the seeds but water them as well. The other day, I was with one of my daughters and we stopped at a traffic light. On the side of the road, there was this young boy, probably early 20's, standing with a sign that said, "Broke, need help, God bless." Most of the time when we observe those on the side of the road wanting a hand-out, we think, "They are just going to take the money and buy drugs or alcohol." That may be true, but we have judged them and that's not our job. We have probably all said, "He is just using the term 'God bless' to get money." Maybe so, but again, we judged. It's not so much about giving the money, but what else are we imparting to people? I rolled down the window and we handed him some money; God spoke to me at that moment and said, "Give him a copy of your book." I try to keep books in my car for that very reason. Wherever I go, if God sends someone across my path, I am well prepared. Sometimes, we may only be given a few seconds or minutes to impart to someone else something that would drastically change their life; however, when we are well prepared, we have the tools available for those instances where there is not much time. You see, Paul knew his time was coming to a close and his last message needed to be one that would impart something life changing to the other disciples. I believe this is why he chose to share with them the importance of clothing themselves at all times with the armor of God. Jesus, likewise, knowing He would be ascending to the Father, imparted to His followers the message to go and make disciples, but there will always be times that we only have seconds. Waiting for the light to change from red to green was all the time I had to plant a seed. Planting a seed could be giving in the natural sense because this young man was broke and had no way to eat. Yet, planting in the spiritual sense in the long run is much more meaningful. Deep inside of this young man, his spirit was dying a spiritual death and money or food for the physical body would not save him. I believe as Christians, we should always be prepared for those times when all we are given are seconds. How can you impact someone's life in a mere second? What will drastically change a life? Of course, Jesus is the answer, but how can we give them spiritual food that will awaken them? In those few seconds, I had the opportunity to bless this young man with natural food and spiritual food. I was given the opportunity to not only plant seeds but water those seeds. This was something God showed me after driving off, and I began to weep. After he thanked me for the book, he began to look at what I had given him. My daughter looked over at the young man after I had rolled up my window and began to drive away, and she said,

"Mother, he looked back at you and the look in his eyes towards you was as if he knew you really cared." Do we really care? As Christians, do we really care? My daughter and I both began to cry, and God showed me something valuable. How much is a life worth to us? How much is that complete stranger worth to us? What if because of my actions for that split second, this young man made it to heaven, and someday, when I arrive, he were to run up to me and say, *"You may not remember me, but I remember you and it was because of your actions many years ago that drastically changed my life, and I am here in heaven today because you cared."* Now, I can't save him, only Jesus can, but my actions can make the difference to someone seeing heaven or their life ending in hell. We should think about that because this is what it is all about when we plant and when we water.

We will never find our true purpose until we seek God, and our purpose will lie within the Gospel of Peace that we take to those who cross our paths.

Purpose ~ To Edify & Encourage

In fulfilling our purpose to go and make disciples of all that God sends across our path, there are many ways that we plant and water the seed in our fields. Our steps should be filled with purpose; however, our methods will be different depending on those that cross our path. We will have those that cross our paths that are not saved; some may know a little about the Bible where others may know absolutely nothing; we may have those who are Christians that need to be watered and others who need correction and guidance. As we begin our own path in obedience to our Father by submitting our lives as an example to all that cross our path, we will begin to know what Word is correct for each person individually as we listen intently for the voice and guidance of the Holy Spirit. In this section, we will discuss our purpose in edifying and encouraging the body of Christ. The body of Christ would be the church but each person individually.

Proverbs 1:3 (NLT) ³Their purpose is to teach people to live disciplined and successful lives, to help them do what is right, just, and fair.

Our purpose is to teach people to live disciplined lives. We are all called to go and make disciples, and in order to make disciples, this includes teaching them. The disciples in biblical days were taught by Christ to follow Him.

Matthew 16:24 (NLT) ²⁴Then Jesus said to his disciples, "If any of you wants to be my follower, you must turn from your selfish ways, take up your cross, and follow me.

They were also taught by Paul to do as I do as I imitate Christ. To follow someone would be to follow in their footsteps.

Philippians 3:17-20 (NLT) ¹⁷Dear brothers and sisters, pattern your lives after mine, and learn from those who follow our example. ¹⁸For I have told you often before, and I say it again with tears in my eyes, that there are many whose conduct shows they are really enemies of the cross of Christ. ¹⁹They are headed for destruction. Their god is their appetite, they brag about shameful things, and they think only about this life here on earth. ²⁰But we are citizens of heaven, where the Lord Jesus Christ lives. And we are eagerly waiting for him to return as our Savior.

We learn by example and our examples need to be biblical as we follow Christ so that others can follow in our footsteps as well. If we are not exhibiting the characteristics of Christ, in reality, we are enemies of the Cross. The only thing that makes it hard to surrender ourselves to Christ would be our not wanting to give up our own life. Edifying and encouraging others begins with lining our lives up first. How can we possibly encourage someone to walk this walk if we are doing it miserably? If we desire to be true Disciples of Christ, we will surrender and begin to do what we were commanded to do. This life is not about us; it is about others, an unselfish act. I have said many times to those I minister to that my changing place within my own life began because of the great love I have for my children and grandchildren. I remember looking back over my life after I had made a total mess of it and saw the selfishness within me. How can we claim we love our own children and would do anything for them when our own lives are filled with selfish acts that are about satisfying our own flesh not our children? I speak this to myself before anyone because when God gets a hold of your life, you begin to see just how much sin lies within. We have no right to judge others because none of our lives are pure. Even when you begin to walk this walk, you will miss it. The good part about being able to see all your own faults prior to lining up your life, is that you are less likely to judge others because you know you have been in that same place.

If we are not capable of loving complete strangers, we need to gauge our love for our own family. When our life ends and we never made the decision that Jesus meant more to us than our own selfish desires, we will have also left our loved ones nothing but natural things that will deteriorate over time. Our treasures must be stored in heaven, those things which are eternal and you cannot get more eternal than the time you put into investing in people.

Matthew 6:19-21 (NLT) Teaching about Money and Possessions
[19] "Don't store up treasures here on earth, where moths eat them and rust destroys them, and where thieves break in and steal. [20] Store your

treasures in heaven, where moths and rust cannot destroy, and thieves do not break in and steal. ²¹ Wherever your treasure is, there the desires of your heart will also be.

The greatest investment we can make while here on this earth is in people. We cannot take our money and possessions with us when we leave this earth, and even though we may leave our possessions with those we love, it is not eternal. If we desire eternal, we must find that eternal for ourselves first in order that through Christ, we are able to see things in a different sense. When we look through natural eyes, we only feel what is natural, but when we look through spiritual eyes, we will feel what Jesus felt. Jesus said in Matthew above, wherever our treasure is, there the desires of our heart would be also. Our desires should be what Jesus desired. Jesus died and paid the price for all our sins. He suffered excruciating pain for people that did not even know Him because He understood the principles of good and evil, and He knew the results of eternal life and eternal death. As we begin on this road to impart to others the principles that Jesus taught, these messages will be to edify and encourage the body of Christ.

John 14:12 (NLT) ¹² "I tell you the truth, anyone who believes in me will do the same works I have done, and even greater works, because I am going to be with the Father.

As we imitate Jesus, the works we will do will be the same works that He did and even greater works will we do as we continue to be obedient. It does not matter if we feel incapable of doing great things for the Kingdom of God, great things will manifest through us because we do all that we do through Christ. God's power will manifest in us even though we are weak because it is not through our strength that we can do anything.

2 Corinthians 12:9-10 (AMP) [9] But He said to me, My grace (My favor and loving-kindness and mercy) is enough for you [sufficient against any danger and enables you to bear the trouble manfully]; for My strength and power are made perfect (fulfilled and completed) and show themselves most effective in [your] weakness. Therefore, I will all the more gladly glory in my weaknesses and infirmities, that the strength and power of Christ (the Messiah) may rest (yes, may pitch a tent over and dwell) upon me! [10] So for the sake of Christ, I am well pleased and take pleasure in infirmities, insults, hardships, persecutions, perplexities and distresses; for when I am weak [in human strength], then am I [truly] strong (able, powerful in divine strength).

Everything we learn as we begin our journey with Christ will be what we go forth to share with others. This is why we must first begin this journey ourselves and then these things will become testimonies that will encourage others to be able to walk this walk. Our purpose in encouraging is to help those continue on their journey and not give up hope. We teach them how to walk this by example. They imitate us just as Paul taught the disciples to imitate him as he followed Christ.

1 Corinthians 11:1 (AMP) [1] Pattern yourselves after me [follow my example], as I imitate and follow Christ (the Messiah).

As children, we learn to imitate. I remember as a child trying to imitate my earthly father. I was probably about 6 years old and remember when we would sit down together to eat, I would copy what he ate. This became a game soon because my dad would figure out what I was trying to do, so he would eat faster and I would have to keep up. This was probably an awesome way to get me to eat everything on my plate and it worked. We conduct our lives daily in order to show those that we are watering, how to walk this walk especially in our storms. Even though we may come to a higher level with God, meaning we have acquired more knowledge, we still must face storms. How can we teach others by example if they never witness how we walk through the storms of life? We can't! I believe one of the greatest things we can learn is how to walk through our storms faithfully. In the midst of our storms, things may be tough, but we also have a mentor that showed us how to walk this. As Paul said to follow him as he followed Christ, he is a great mentor. We not only follow the examples of Jesus but also the examples of Paul, and as others begin to follow our example, we will be able to impart to them encouraging examples by our life and that of Paul.

Paul walked through some pretty tough storms, yet he never murmured or complained. A bad example of walking in a storm would be the children of Israel. They continually murmured and complained and the result was 40 years in their dessert. Knowing these stories which are all throughout the Bible give us tools to use when those we are watering need encouragement. It is encouraging when others that are in the midst of their storm can see two examples. One would be what happens to those who murmur and complain and the other would be an example in the Bible of someone who walked it out just like Paul and many of the disciples did. Of course, a great example is for those who are watching you to be able to see how you walk through a storm. All these examples show others that our choices have everything to do with the outcome. We can either walk as Paul did or walk as the children of Israel. One produced victory and the other defeat. The children of Israel remained in their dessert for 40 years and Paul remained in jail for less than one day. Paul walked through his storm counting it all joy and keeping his eyes fixed on what lay ahead.

Acts 16:22-24 (NLT) ²² *A mob quickly formed against Paul and Silas, and the city officials ordered them stripped and beaten with wooden rods.* ²³ *They were severely beaten, and then they were thrown into prison. The jailer was ordered to make sure they didn't escape.* ²⁴ *So the jailer put them into the inner dungeon and clamped their feet in the stocks.*

I believe we would all agree that this was a fierce storm Paul was in. Not only were they in jail bound with stocks which were small wooden boxes with a hole that your feet were secured, but they had also been beaten and stripped down. At this point, I don't believe most of us would feel like doing much of anything but crying. We murmur and complain when we have a little ailment and make up whatever excuses why we did not pray and why we did not go to church. Yet, Paul and Silas, they not only prayed, they did church within this jail.

Acts 16:25 (NLT) ²⁵*Around midnight Paul and Silas were praying and singing hymns to God, and the other prisoners were listening.*

Here they were forgetting about their pain, forgetting about not being able to even move because of their feet being anchored in the wooden box, forgetting about not being able to have good food to eat, not being able to take a bath, call their friends, watch TV, surf the web, or snuggle up in their nice soft bed. They forgot about their own life and feelings. Here they were in the midst of a great storm, ministering to the other prisoners while they were bound. Can you imagine the impact on those strangers within the jail at that time? They must have been thinking, *"These guys are crazy, how can they be so joyful when they are bruised, bleeding, and bound in stocks."* Yes, their actions impacted those in jail with them. Their actions encourage those in jail with them. You may not even realize it but when you are focusing on Jesus and not

311

your circumstances, other people are watching your actions. Here's the good news, when we are faithful and put our trust in God right in the midst of our storm, we open the door to allow God to move in our midst. The children of Israel stayed bound in their storm by focusing on the storm and not allowing God to move in their midst. You can read the full story of the children of Israel with their 40 year journey beginning in Exodus 13; however, prior to Exodus 13 there were many signs that were witnessed by God's people and yet they still doubted God was who He said He was. We should be following those disciples who have believed and trusted that God would do what He said He would do. Here is the result of Paul and Silas' actions in Acts.

Acts 16:26 (NLT) [26]*Suddenly, there was a massive earthquake, and the prison was shaken to its foundations. All the doors immediately flew open, and the chains of every prisoner fell off!*

God moved in their storm. When we begin to see how powerful our God is, we learn to trust Him and focus on Jesus and not the actual storm. God cannot move in our midst when we do not keep our eyes fixed on Jesus.

Hebrews 12:2 (NLT) [2]*We do this by keeping our eyes on Jesus, the champion who initiates and perfects our faith. Because of the joy awaiting him, he endured the cross, disregarding its shame. Now he is seated in the place of honor beside God's throne.*

It will only be through faith that we can trust that God will bring us through time and time again, and by keeping our eyes on Christ, He will initiate and perfect the faith we need to do so. Paul and Silas not only made an impact on the others who were in jail, but they also impacted the jailer's life drastically. The jailer knew he would be punished severely if not killed by allowing them to escape, this is what transpired.

Acts 16:27-34 (NLT) ²⁷ The jailer woke up to see the prison doors wide open. He assumed the prisoners had escaped, so he drew his sword to kill himself. ²⁸ But Paul shouted to him, "Stop! Don't kill yourself! We are all here!" ²⁹ The jailer called for lights and ran to the dungeon and fell down trembling before Paul and Silas. ³⁰ Then he brought them out and asked, "Sirs, what must I do to be saved?" ³¹ They replied, "Believe in the Lord Jesus and you will be saved, along with everyone in your household." ³² And they shared the word of the Lord with him and with all who lived in his household. ³³ Even at that hour of the night, the jailer cared for them and washed their wounds. Then he and everyone in his household were immediately baptized. ³⁴ He brought them into his house and set a meal before them, and he and his entire household rejoiced because they all believed in God.

Our actions during our storms will drastically change lives of those who witness how we walk through the fire. Seeds were planted and seeds were watered. Encouragement to others is not about just speaking words, it is also about action. We will show encouragement in the way we walk and endure through hard times as well as through the good times. All things work together for good even though we may not see the good at the moment we are faced with a trial.

Romans 8:28 (NLT) ²⁸And we know that God causes everything to work together for the good of those who love God and are called according to his purpose for them.

If Paul and Silas had not endured their storm, the others in jail, the jailer and his household would not have come to know Jesus. Remember, we invest our lives in those things which are eternal and people are our greatest investment. In the midst of our storm, God may have us in that place because of those lives that will be transformed as they watch our faith in operation. How great is your God? My God is great enough to move any mountain in my life, transform lives who cross my path, awaken generations, and turn cities upside down. If you believe that, allow God to use you in ways that will benefit His purpose for all those that will cross your path. In the midst of your storms, look for a greater purpose, expect a greater purpose, and ask that this purpose be to radically transform lives and awaken people to witness the greatness of our God. Paul said that he ran with purpose in every step, do you run this life today with purpose?

1 Corinthians 9:26 (NLT) [26] So I run with purpose in every step. I am not just shadowboxing.

Our walk with God will either be one that edifies and builds up the body of Christ or it will be one that portrays a life of defeat. Even though Paul endured suffering, it by no means spoke defeat but life. We need to see that those very things we endure are not necessarily speaking defeat over our lives. They only speak defeat based on how we endure. Paul endured; he was a fighter; he was a warrior. We edify and encourage others by the same messages which have been laid out for us as believers of Christ. The message has never changed. Generations have changed, technology has changed, styles have changed, culture has changed, but the message of the Cross has never changed. The storm Jesus endured for every person today spoke of one who came unselfishly, with purpose in each step, filled with love for mankind. Jesus loved greater than any man on this earth. Jesus was love, and it is through that kind of love that we find our purpose which will imitate just who Christ was.

314

1 Timothy 1:5 (NLT) ⁵The purpose of my instruction is that all believers would be filled with love that comes from a pure heart, a clear conscience, and genuine faith.

Purpose ~ Boldly Proclaim

As previously stated, our purpose is not only to edify and encourage, but it is also to bring correction and guidance to those who may be walking this walk but doing so in error.

2 Timothy 3:16 (AMP) ¹⁶ Every Scripture is God-breathed (given by His inspiration) and profitable for instruction, for reproof and conviction of sin, for correction of error and discipline in obedience, [and] for training in righteousness (in holy living, in conformity to God's will in thought, purpose, and action),

As we grow more in the wisdom and knowledge of God, our actions will become bolder. It is hard to be bold about something when you do not have enough knowledge. Usually, our actions become bold when we are sold out for a cause. Well, Jesus is our cause and when we put on those gospel shoes to go forth and make disciples, we will become like that politician that believes strongly about his campaign. We need to gain more biblical knowledge and throughout the book of Proverbs, it is full of teachings on wisdom and discipline.

Proverbs 1:1-2 (NLT)The Purpose of Proverbs ¹These are the proverbs of Solomon, David's son, king of Israel. ² Their purpose is to teach people wisdom and discipline, to help them understand the insights of the wise.

Proverbs are there for a reason. God desires as Christians, that we grow up and become wise in the things which are eternal in

315

Christ. We cannot be all God desires when our wisdom comes exclusively from man. Paul teaches us in 1 Corinthians that the wisdom of this world is foolishness.

1 Corinthians 3:18-23 (NLT) *[18]Stop deceiving yourselves. If you think you are wise by this world's standards, you need to become a fool to be truly wise. [19] For the wisdom of this world is foolishness to God. As the Scriptures say, "He traps the wise in the snare of their own cleverness." [20] And again, "The LORD knows the thoughts of the wise; he knows they are worthless." [21] So don't boast about following a particular human leader. For everything belongs to you— [22]whether Paul or Apollos or Peter, or the world, or life and death, or the present and the future. Everything belongs to you, [23] and you belong to Christ, and Christ belongs to God.*

Ultimately, everything belongs to God and the fullness thereof. A good place to begin maturing in Christ would be to learn from Solomon. The reason Paul said to pattern our lives after his or rather to follow him as he followed Christ was because sometimes it is easier to follow someone that we can actually see their walk. *(Philippians 3:17)* Of course, in all the Bible stories, we are able to see their walk because their stories are written, but it is not on a daily basis as it would be with someone you see often. However, these Bible stories are to help us see how we walk through different situations. Solomon, if you do not know the story, was David's son. After Kind David died, Solomon became his successor. One night, Solomon was visited by God in a dream.

1 Kings 3:5 (NIV) *[5] At Gibeon the LORD appeared to Solomon during the night in a dream, and God said, "Ask for whatever you want me to give you."*

Solomon had followed in the same footsteps as David in that he loved God with all his heart. When God told him that He would give him whatever he asked for, his reply was not what most of us would have asked.

1 Kings 3:6-9 (NIV) *⁶Solomon answered, "You have shown great kindness to your servant, my father David, because he was faithful to you and righteous and upright in heart. You have continued this great kindness to him and have given him a son to sit on his throne this very day. ⁷"Now, LORD my God, you have made your servant king in place of my father David. But I am only a little child and do not know how to carry out my duties. ⁸Your servant is here among the people you have chosen, a great people, too numerous to count or number. ⁹So give your servant a discerning heart to govern your people and to distinguish between right and wrong. For who is able to govern this great people of yours?"*

Solomon desired to do that which was right for the people. He desired to be wise enough to know how to judge between right and wrong; he desired to have discernment in those things which mattered in order to be fair to God's people. Solomon did not ask for riches; he did not ask for power; he wanted to know that the decisions he made were considered worthy. You may say that Solomon did not need to ask for wealth and power; after all, he was the king. Think about this, when the rich get rich, they desire to have more. Greed never ends with those who acquire great wealth. There is always someone out there who exceeds your wealth. Solomon could have asked to be the wealthiest and most powerful king of all time, but he did not do that, and in those days, there were other things which were desirable as we see in Scripture. This was God's reply in 1 Kings.

1 Kings 3:10-14 (NIV) [10] The Lord was pleased that Solomon had asked for this. [11] So God said to him, "Since you have asked for this and not for long life or wealth for yourself, nor have asked for the death of your enemies but for discernment in administering justice, [12] I will do what you have asked. I will give you a wise and discerning heart, so that there will never have been anyone like you, nor will there ever be. [13] Moreover, I will give you what you have not asked for—both wealth and honor —so that in your lifetime you will have no equal among kings. [14] And if you walk in obedience to me and keep my decrees and commands as David your father did, I will give you a long life."

You see, in those days, if Solomon could have asked for death of all his enemies, there would have been no need for war and innocent lives lost. Long life could have also been something great to ask for; how many of us would love to be granted long life? Yet, this is not what he asked for. This Scripture brings us back to the book of Proverbs, which are writings from Solomon whom there has never been nor will ever be anyone with the wisdom he acquired through God. If we truly desire wisdom, I believe saturating our minds in the book of Proverbs will result in wisdom that the world is oblivious to. Why would we not want to learn from the man who was the wisest for all time according to Scripture?

Proverbs 1:5-7 (NLT) [5] Let the wise listen to these proverbs and become even wiser. Let those with understanding receive guidance [6] by exploring the meaning in these proverbs and parables, the words of the wise and their riddles. [7] Fear of the LORD is the foundation of true knowledge, but fools despise wisdom and discipline.

When we begin to proclaim the gospel to those that cross our paths, there will be times that God will give us something that will be bold. Boldness is necessary to bring correction and discipline

318

to a generation where there is much sin today. As each era has passed to the next, we have come to the greatest era known to man with all the technology and advancement in every aspect of life. Yet, with each new invention brings new ways for satan to cleverly engage our fleshly appetites into submission through forces that are not seen, yet are very much a reality. This generation needs boldness; this generation needs clarity; this generation needs correction and discipline in order to awaken their spirit within to be able to see and hear the Holy Spirit clearly. Yes, our words should speak love because without love we are nothing, but are we not speaking out of love when we correct our children for doing wrong?

1 Corinthians 13:2 (ESV) *²And if I have prophetic powers, and understand all mysteries and all knowledge, and if I have all faith, so as to remove mountains, but have not love, I am nothing.*

Jesus said in John that he came to bring life, but satan came to steal our children, steal those we love, steal our finances, our health and in the process, he will destroy our lives and everything in close proximity.

John 10:10 (NLT) *¹⁰The thief's purpose is to steal and kill and destroy. My purpose is to give them a rich and satisfying life.*

Boldness when spoken according to Scripture is just another method in planting seeds and watering. Every individual is different, and by all means, we should love them when we are reaching out to them, but at some point, the time comes when it may take boldness to awaken them from eternal death. As we continue to receive greater knowledge on those things which are spiritual, the bolder we will become. However, we need to clarify what boldness is not. Many take offense to things spoken harshly and will use Scripture to make their point.

Romans 14:21 (AMP) [21]The right thing is to eat no meat or drink no wine [at all], or [do anything else] if it makes your brother stumble or hurts his conscience or offends or weakens him.

Romans 14:21 (NLT) [21]It is better not to eat meat or drink wine or do anything else if it might cause another believer to stumble.

These Scriptures speak of offending someone to the point that you would cause them to stumble and fall. This would mean that you are not walking what you are talking. If you are pretending to be a Christian for appearance sake only while at church, others are looking up to you as a Christian and trying to follow your example, just as Paul said to follow him as he followed Christ. While you are away from the church or other believers, you let your guard down and the pretense of walking as Christ, and then one of those following you happens to see you outside of church doing something that is wrong. In this, you are basically teaching them the old cliché, *"Do what I say not what I do."* Why on earth parents ever thought this would work is beyond me. Your children are going to do what you do; those who are following your Christian walk are going to do what you do. This is what that Scripture is speaking of, it is not talking about not speaking truth to them because of fear that you will cause them to walk away from this walk or offend them. On the contrary, Jesus expects us to correct those who are following us, but our example better be Christ-like. There are many instances in Scripture where Jesus offended His very own disciples.

John 6:60-67 (AMP) [60]When His disciples heard this, many of them said, This is a hard and difficult and strange saying (an offensive and unbearable message). Who can stand to hear it? [Who can be expected to listen to such teaching?] ⁶¹ *But Jesus, knowing within Himself that His disciples were complaining and protesting and grumbling about it, said to them: Is this a stumbling block and an offense to you? [Does this upset and displease and shock and scandalize you?]* ⁶² *What then [will be your reaction] if you should see the Son of Man ascending to [the place] where He was before?* ⁶³ *It is the Spirit Who gives life [He is the Life-giver]; the flesh conveys no benefit whatever [there is no profit in it]. The words (truths) that I have been speaking to you are spirit and life.* ⁶⁴ *But [still] some of you fail to believe and trust and have faith. For Jesus knew from the first who did not believe and had no faith and who would betray Him and be false to Him.* ⁶⁵ *And He said, This is why I told you that no one can come to Me unless it is granted him [unless he is enabled to do so] by the Father.* ⁶⁶ *After this, many of His disciples drew back (returned to their old associations) and no longer accompanied Him.* ⁶⁷ *Jesus said to the Twelve, Will you also go away? [And do you too desire to leave Me?]*

Wow, can we not see this in our churches today? Jesus spoke an offensive message and many of His disciples walked away and left Him. How many times do people hear a message in church which offends them, and they stop going? This happens so frequently that many churches will try to refrain from giving a message which may offend the people. We have become so accustomed to trying to satisfy people instead of satisfying God. We are more concerned that we may hurt someone's feelings so instead, we stop the move of God. What we fail to recognize is that the Word of God is an offensive message. In fact, many churches will refrain from teaching truth because they do not want to offend anyone. Much of this is due to churches desiring to increase in numbers rather than increase in stature. When I speak of increasing in stature, this is in achievement according to gaining those things above and not what this world has to offer.

Our achievements are weighed in accordance to what the Word of God says not according to man. God never judges by numbers or wealth achieved but by the heart of a man. It does not matter if we build the most luxurious church and have the largest attendance of any other building on this earth, in God's eyes we have gained nothing unless we have gained souls and imparted into individuals those things of importance which man cannot buy. Man's wisdom will never even come close to that of God. Of course, if we do our homework and study Proverbs in order to gain more wisdom of God and less of man, our eyes may actually be opened to the truth. According to Proverbs that which teaches people to give up their evil desires is offensive.

Proverbs 13:19 (AMP) [19]*Satisfied desire is sweet to a person; therefore it is hateful and exceedingly offensive to [self-confident] fools to give up evil [upon which they have set their hearts].*

Proverbs 15:8 (AMP) [8]*The sacrifice of the wicked is an abomination, hateful and exceedingly offensive to the Lord, but the prayer of the upright is His delight!*

To the wicked, the Word of God is very offensive. To those who enjoy living according to their own fleshly desires, the Wisdom of Solomon is offensive. To those who have no desire to change their lives and live for Christ, the teachings of Jesus are offensive. To those who seek to store up treasures in this world, the book of Revelation speaking of what is to come is offensive. To those who believe they can halfway serve God, the teachings of the Cross is offensive.

1 Corinthians 1:21-28 (AMP) [21]*For when the world with all its earthly wisdom failed to perceive and recognize and know God by means of its own philosophy, God in His wisdom was pleased through the foolishness*

*of preaching [salvation, procured by Christ and to be had through Him],
to save those who believed (who clung to and trusted in and relied on
Him). ²² For while Jews [demandingly] ask for signs and miracles and
Greeks pursue philosophy and wisdom, ²³ We preach Christ (the
Messiah) crucified, [preaching which] to the Jews is a scandal and an
offensive stumbling block [that springs a snare or trap], and to the
Gentiles it is absurd and utterly unphilosophical nonsense. ²⁴ But to those
who are called, whether Jew or Greek (Gentile), Christ [is] the Power of
God and the Wisdom of God. ²⁵ [This is] because the foolish thing [that
has its source in] God is wiser than men, and the weak thing [that
springs] from God is stronger than men. ²⁶ For [simply] consider your
own call, brethren; not many [of you were considered to be] wise
according to human estimates and standards, not many influential and
powerful, not many of high and noble birth. ²⁷ [No] for God selected
(deliberately chose) what in the world is foolish to put the wise to shame,
and what the world calls weak to put the strong to shame. ²⁸ And God
also selected (deliberately chose) what in the world is lowborn and
insignificant and branded and treated with contempt, even the things that
are nothing, that He might depose and bring to nothing the things that
are,*

With growth comes maturity and part of maturity is being able to
recognize that those things which may be offensive to us, may be
an area that God desires growth. When we choose to be
offended instead of laying down our pride and allowing God to
grow us, we will begin to slip into the trap our enemy has laid out
for us in order that we fall.

*Mark 4:17 (AMP) ¹⁷And they have no real root in themselves, and so
they endure for a little while; then when trouble or persecution arises on
account of the Word, they immediately are offended (become displeased,
indignant, resentful) and they stumble and fall away.*

When we stumble or fall away, it is because we never developed a mature root system. A strong root system, just like with a mighty oak tree, requires time to grow and mature. The mighty oak acquired its name due to the fact that it became great from a small beginning. An oak tree begins from a small acorn and grows tall and taller until it becomes great. We all start from something small and with time we grow and mature. Our growth depends on what is in our heart. We must acknowledge we have not arrived and humble ourselves in order to listen and learn. When we are easily offended, we are basically rejecting the wisdom needed to produce maturity. Like I have said, the book of Proverbs is a great place to begin to understand how God thinks versus how the world thinks. We can remain defeated throughout life by being stubborn and sure of our own wisdom, or we can acquire wisdom that is greater than man, our choice.

Psalm 119:165 (AMP) [165] *Great peace have they who love Your law; nothing shall offend them or make them stumble.*

In Psalm 119, we see that when we do not allow anything to offend us, peace will abound with us. In order to walk this out, we must love God's laws and not man's. This does not mean we do not follow man's law; this simply means that we understand that God's laws, which are His ways, are far greater than man's ways. If we become easily offended, we are not mature. If I am not where I need to be with God and it is because of something that is offensive to me, rather than become upset, maturity begins with being able to get alone with God and say, *"Lord, if this is something that is ugly within me, please show me and remove it."* I do not know about you, but I do not want to wake up one day and I almost made it to heaven, but there was this one thing that offended me and instead of making it right, I chose to hang on to it. If we want to claim to be citizens of heaven, our mannerism must be worthy of the gospel.

Philippians 1:27 (NLT) *²⁷Above all, you must live as citizens of heaven, conducting yourselves in a manner worthy of the Good News about Christ. Then, whether I come and see you again or only hear about you, I will know that you are standing together with one spirit and one purpose, fighting together for the faith, which is the Good News.*

Taking up our cross and meeting Christ begins with recognizing that we all have a purpose. Fulfilling our purpose, begins with stepping up to that plate first before Jesus can begin to transform others' lives through us. Our gospel shoes go on and then the planting and watering begin, but it will not begin until we grow and mature. Being a bold and courageous Christian begins by seeing how to put on those gospel shoes. Have you ever heard the saying, *"You don't know what they are going through unless you have walked in their shoes?"* That is so true. We may be able to plant seeds, but we will never be able to water those seeds unless we have been there. Being a mature Christian is not about arriving at the place of an abundant life. We believe we have arrived when it seems as though God is pouring out blessings our way. However, a mature Christian is one who can say, *"Wow, God so had to deal with me in that area, and let me tell you, I am so glad that I laid down my pride and allowed the person God sent across my path to be bold enough to show me the truth."* When we are mature enough to allow growth, our walk with God will take off like a rocket.

Another area of boldness that we need to see is that the church, meaning all who claim to be believers in Christ, must stand together as one. This is not happening today, but this is an area that needs to be brought forth in boldness in order for God to prepare His army for the second coming of Christ. What we speak must be spoken in love but it must be truth, and it will be received by those who are mature.

Ephesians 4:15 (NIV) [15] *Instead, speaking the truth in love, we will grow to become in every respect the mature body of him who is the head, that is, Christ.*

Notice, Paul said, when we speak the truth in love, we will grow in maturity. Remember, I said that correction spoken to our children may not come across as being spoken in love to them, but is it not love?

Proverbs 13:24 (NLT) [24] *Those who spare the rod of discipline hate their children. Those who love their children care enough to discipline them.*

We may say that we love our children, but when there is no correction or discipline, we are allowing them to grow up in a world filled with evils and act as such. Without discipline, good will not manifest through them; without discipline, love will not show through them. The same goes with us as Christians, if we say that we belong to God but we do not love as God loves, we will be judged. Only through Christ is our love perfected, and this happens as we mature but will never happen if we are offended by those words spoken boldly in order to bring about correction in our own lives.

1 John 4:17-21 (NLT) [17] *And as we live in God, our love grows more perfect. So we will not be afraid on the day of judgment, but we can face him with confidence because we live like Jesus here in this world.* [18] *Such love has no fear, because perfect love expels all fear. If we are afraid, it is for fear of punishment, and this shows that we have not fully experienced his perfect love.* [19] *We love each other because he loved us* *first. ²⁰ If someone says, "I love God," but hates a Christian brother or sister, that person is a liar; for if we don't love people we can see, how can we love God, whom we cannot see? ²¹ And he has given us this command: Those who love God must also love their Christian brothers and sisters.*

So then, are not those who bring forth words of boldness that speak correction to us not done so in love? If our brothers and sisters in Christ speak harshly in order to bring about change within us to keep us from the grips of satan, are their words not spoken in love? Are our words to our own children not spoken in love when our intent is to bring about the necessary change in order that they grow up in the admonition of the Lord?

Ephesians 6:4 (NLT) ⁴ Fathers, do not provoke your children to anger by the way you treat them. Rather, bring them up with the discipline and instruction that comes from the Lord.

Our words are not spoken in a way to provoke our children and a lot of times that is seen through control. There is a fine line here that we need to see. Words coming forth in love whether bold or merely words of comfort and encouragement should never be spoken in terms of control. How can you tell the difference? Control comes at the person in a way that you are trying to manipulate them into doing things your way only. Our words do not have to be controlling. We cannot force anyone to agree with us. We cannot force anyone to love us, and we cannot force anyone to love God. We may be able to force others to do what we say, but it does not mean they agree with you and it does not mean that they think highly of you. Control may paint a picture in your mind that portrays you as being right, but in God's eyes, you are very much wrong. We might be able to force our children to go through the motions of church, but unless your words are spoken in love, they become controlling and eventually, those you are forcing control upon will rebel. When we sit down with our children to correct them, it is done in a way that assures them we love them but want what is best. Sometimes, that boldness must come but in a way to awaken someone to the truth, and then it must not be done by control. To know our words are being spoken in love, the correction must line up with God's Word not our own way of thinking. There are times I have to stop and ask myself, *"Is this my thoughts and desires being spoken or is this what God's Word says?"* You see, maturity remembers that God said that His ways are not ours nor are His thoughts. He didn't speak this and say that some of us have arrived. None of us have arrived yet and our own desires many times get in the way. A good way to insure it is not your desires being spoken boldly and with authority to bring about change in a person is to ask yourself, *"What are you trying to accomplish in that person?"* If it is anything other than what God desires for mankind, it is not God's will. We see in Philemon, Paul shows us something valuable.

Philemon 1:8-9 (NLT) Paul's Appeal for Onesimus [8] That is why I am boldly asking a favor of you. I could demand it in the name of Christ because it is the right thing for you to do. [9] But because of our love, I prefer simply to ask you. Consider this as a request from me—Paul, an old man and now also a prisoner for the sake of Christ Jesus.

Here, Paul says he could have commanded Onesimus to do this, but Paul thought about his words. Sometimes, we need to just consider our words before we speak them. Paul went to him boldly, which is something we feel uncomfortable doing many times to those we see doing wrong. Yet, Paul went boldly and considered his words, and he knew that the way to do this was in love. When someone comes to us and speaks something in anger or demanding, our natural response is to put up our brick walls and choose not to receive what is being spoken. However, when we speak something in love, people receive it much better. So, Paul asked Onesimus to consider a request, but we must go forth boldly in order to deliver the message to those we water.

Ultimately, when we correct or discipline those we love, we do so because we love them. The Word of God, being an offensive message, is totally spoken out of love for God is love. We teach our children rules, laws, lessons, etc., in order to grow them to maturity in hopes that they eventually receive that which we have strived to impart to them. However, Christians being completely grown in the physical sense have not grown in the spiritual sense to be able to see that words of correction are for their own good. Many times those we love will choose that wrong path and there are times we must allow them to make those mistakes. Many times it is through those particular storms that God will be able to awaken them. However, if we intervene in order to prevent the storm, we may stop that which God would have used to save them.

Another area of boldness is shown in those words which are spoken prophetically. Prophesy is an area that is not taught very often in the churches, but we can see according to Scripture that we are all to desire to prophesy.

1 Corinthians 14:1 (NLT) [1]Let love be your highest goal! But you should also desire the special abilities the Spirit gives—especially the ability to prophesy.

In the last days, as we prepare for the second coming of Christ, the Holy Spirit has been poured out on those who are considered Disciples of Christ. With the outpouring which began at Pentecost *(Acts 2:1-4),* men and women have prophesied for years and continue to do so.

Acts 2:18 (AMP) [18]*Yes, and on My menservants also and on My maidservants in those days I will pour out of My Spirit, and they shall prophesy [telling forth the divine counsels and predicting future events pertaining especially to God's kingdom].*

Prophesy brings forth divine counsel and predicts future events that pertain to the Kingdom of Heaven. We are all to desire the ability to prophesy. Prophesy takes boldness. When you are speaking a Word from God, it takes boldness.

Acts 4:13 (ESV) [13]*Now when they saw the boldness of Peter and John, and perceived that they were uneducated, common men, they were astonished. And they recognized that they had been with Jesus.*

When the anointing of God falls down on those who are obedient, many times the words coming forth are very bold and sometimes may not be what others desire to hear. We have become accustomed to receiving a *"feel good"* message at our places of worship, going home to enjoy the rest of our day, and doing our normal routine all week long until time to get another message that feels good to our flesh. The *"feel good"* messages may be for encouragement and uplifting which are needed at times, but the prophesies must be welcomed if we are going to turn cities upside down and bring about a revival that is anointed by God. Paul and Silas operated prophetically and told of future events. Their teachings turned the world upside down and those who were religious wanted to put them away.

Acts 17:6 (ESV) [6]*And when they could not find them, they dragged Jason and some of the brothers before the city authorities, shouting, "These men who have turned the world upside down have come here also,*

We all need to be honest and ask ourselves, do we fall in the category of being radical like Paul and Silas or do we fall into the category of being like the religious leaders of that day? The *"feel good"* messages may be good for a time, but this world needs to be turned upside down if the Christian community wants to impact the Nations. Nice, sweet, sugar coated messages are not going to bring about correction or discipline needed to a world that is filled with corruption. I have been told by some that they were not ready to hear such teachings because it produced fear, and of course, as we have already determined in Scripture above *(1 John 4:18)*, fear is brought about because of not really experiencing God's love. When we really don't know God, we fear punishment because we are not living right. Fear ultimately comes from satan, and he uses that strong hold in many Christian lives in order to keep them from receiving messages spoken in boldness. We need to grow up today and realize that our world as we know it is in trouble, and if we desire to be a spokesperson for God, He needs warriors, not the Easter bunny bringing a fluffy *"feel good"* message. Yes, prophesy is in love! Prophesy is about waking up a generation before it's too late. Prophesy is about waking up our children to keep them on a path that is Godly and not worldly. If these messages produce fear, does that mean they are not God? Remember the Scripture in 1 John 4 says perfect love casts out fear?

If we are walking with Christ and know that we are right with God, there is no fear. For those that receive fear from a spoken word from God, it is a fear that should be produced to bring about change. The kind of fear God does not give is that which man initiates. Man and this world will try to produce fear in order to keep you bound in lies. Even when Peter and John were threatened because of their boldness, they prayed to God to see them through.

Acts 4:29 (ESV) [29] *And now, Lord, look upon their threats and grant to your servants to continue to speak your word with all boldness,*

This was the type of fear that man tries to intimidate upon people. Did Peter and John choose fear? No, they chose to keep their eyes on Christ. We do not receive the spirit of fear that the enemy will try to put on us, but we do receive the God-kind of fear that keeps us on the right track. There are two kinds of fear with one bringing about harm that we overcome and the other is detrimental and should be looked at through the eyes of wisdom. Those who are wise according to God's standards understand that there is a good fear that keeps us from falling away from God. I do not want to miss heaven, and if I looked at every word coming at me in a negative way, I cannot grow. Instead, words need to be looked at in a constructive way in order to bring about change that helps me to walk closer to the way Jesus walked. We make choices; Peter and John had a choice and they took it to God. They refused to receive the fear man was trying to provoke in them and instead chose to walk fearless among their enemies. They knew that man could do nothing to them if God were for them.

Romans 8:31 (ESV) [31] *What then shall we say to these things? If God is for us, who can be against us?*

Psalm 118:6 (ESV) [6] *The LORD is on my side; I will not fear. What can man do to me?*

Psalm 56:11 (ESV) [11] *in God I trust; I shall not be afraid. What can man do to me?*

Prophesies go forth in order to strengthen, encourage, and bring comfort. We know how an encouraging word sounds but

332

sometimes it may have the sound of boldness, especially to make a point. If I were to minister to someone who was doing something contrary to God's Word in which the consequences to their choice was not going to have a good ending, it may take my correction to show them an alternative to their choice in order to produce a better outcome. I have walked through many things, and many times, I am able to use those areas and bad choices to show others that their old way does not work. It may not be what they wanted to hear, but when I am able to show that I chose God's way and the result was significantly different, is that not encouraging? Is it not encouraging when someone says, *"The reason things never work for you is because you are doing it contrary to God's Word, but I can show you how to do things differently in order to gain a different result."* Is that not showing the world that their result can be great if they do it God's way? Even if the tone becomes one like when we speak with that voice of authority to our children to get them to move in the right direction, is it not still encouraging? Even if we need to show them the end result if they do not change and that takes us to the prophecies in Revelation. Is Revelation not part of God's Word? Should we refrain from teaching Revelation because it produces fear? If that fear is necessary to bring about change in a person in order that they get on the right path which leads to heaven, is that fear not spoken in love for that person? Maybe, we would look at it as a method to strengthen and if so, in the end, there will be encouragement when the result is satisfying.

1 Corinthians 14:3 (NLT) [3] But one who prophesies strengthens others, encourages them, and comforts them.

In truth, God desires that we awaken from our sinful ways in order that we have life to the fullest and then life eternal with Him. He desires that none of us live bound in wickedness and end in eternal death.

Ezekiel 33:11 (AMP) [11] *Say to them, As I live, says the Lord God, I have no pleasure in the death of the wicked, but rather that the wicked turn from his way and live. Turn back, turn back from your evil ways, for why will you die, O house of Israel?*

As our faith grows in God, our boldness will also grow. We can see examples all through the Old and New Testament of the Bible of great men and women who were not only faithful but bold in their Christian walk. An area which needs to be touched on, in order that our Christian walk can be extended past the walls of our buildings we choose to worship, is one that takes boldness. As I have stated, if you find yourself offended, that is a lack of maturity and what I am about to share may be offensive to some. However, if we are going to rise up as one body, we need to do so in one accord.

Christ never meant for there to be churches on every corner; He never meant for the church to be in competition with each other; He never meant for there to be so many different beliefs. I don't know about you, but do you ever wonder what denomination is correct? I've come to realize that they are probably all correct in some areas and all wrong in some areas, after all, they are being run by man and man is not perfect. However, according to Philippians 1:27 which was discussed above, the church should be standing together in one spirit with one purpose.

The way I see it, we must put our differences behind us and join together to fight this fight as one body. Boldly speaking, nothing else really matters. What really matters is that there is only One God and One Purpose! We either all believe that Jesus is the Son of God and the purpose is to win souls for the Kingdom of Heaven, or our life really has no purpose. In these end times, God is shaking the church today and preparing warriors for His purpose. Those who do not fall in line with the teachings of Christ will fall, but it will not be in line with Christ. God is going to bring down denominational lines and that includes non-denomination. Just because a church concludes they are non-denomination, does not mean they are not a denomination. A denomination is basically a group of people who come together in agreement with those of liked minds, sharing in the same faith, conducting business in a way agreed upon; therefore, the non-denominational people do the same thing as the denominational people, yet they claim they are not a denomination. I am not coming down on the non-denomination exclusively because I have been a member of several non-denominational churches in my life-time. This message is for all denominations! There is not a church out there today that is perfect, but we need to be able to see that we need each other. I believe there are those within every denomination that really love God. I believe that we will see people from all denominations in heaven. Why can we not just come together and agree on what matters and lay everything else aside? I am ready to see Jesus come back, but He needs warriors to rise up together for His Purpose, and it is not going to happen unless we lay our differences aside and join as one united in one faith for one purpose.

Our choices we make each day will determine our decision to either stand up in unity with our brothers and sisters in Christ or agree with our enemy to be divided among other Christians. God is building an army and this whole book is about becoming that warrior He desires you to be. We must go forth together in this battle because if we all believe in One God, One Son, and One Holy Spirit and if we believe there is only one purpose, then we should march forth together bold as a lion in order to begin to take back what rightfully belongs to the Church!

Proverbs 28:1 (ESV) 28The wicked flee when no one pursues, but the righteous are bold as a lion.

Purpose ~ Glorify our Father in Heaven

The last purpose we will discuss is to glorify our Father in all that we do. When we go forth as warriors in our gospel shoes, our actions should bring glory to God. It really does not matter if we walk in this purpose or not, God's plan will ultimately take place without us, but if we desire to be faithful to the purpose, it includes being diligent in our walk. Our steps are with purpose; our steps are to plant and water; our steps are to edify and encourage others; our steps are to speak forth boldly, and our steps are to show glory to God. It's about His purpose not ours.

Proverbs 16:4 (NLT) ⁴ The LORD has made everything for his own purposes, even the wicked for a day of disaster.

All the purposes we have discussed to this point, glorify God. When we are doing all the other things we are called to do, we are glorifying God. However, we need to look at glorifying God specifically. Even when we make our own plans, God works around them. None of us are perfect and most of us do not consult God in our every move, yet God already has accounted for every plan we will make, and His purpose will still prevail.

Proverbs 19:21 (NLT) ²¹ You can make many plans, but the LORD's purpose will prevail.

How do we glorify God? How do we show glory to anything? By acknowledging how great it is; by bragging about it; by putting every spare moment into those things we consider priority, and we could probably think of many other ways. As a grandmother, I love my grandchildren and constantly talk about everything they do, everything they say, and I even showcase all the amazing pictures. I had always said that I was not going to be that type of grandmother, but to my surprise, I am exactly that type of grandmother. My children are amazed when I begin pulling up pictures to complete strangers, but they are used to it by now. God wants the glory. When I can show off my grandchildren, it brings glory to me. It's like, wow – look at how amazing these beautiful little girls are, and they belong to me (so to speak). In reality, our children do not belong to us, they belong to God, but this is to give you an example of how we give glory. However, God is the same way, and in fact, God likes to brag about His children, as well, in order to get the glory.

Job 1:8 (AMP) [8] *And the Lord said to Satan, Have you considered My servant Job, that there is none like him on the earth, a blameless and upright man, one who [reverently] fears God and abstains from and shuns evil [because it is wrong]?*

Here God is carrying on a conversation with the devil. Isn't it awesome when our children follow the paths we know bring good things, and how completely phenomenal it would be to stand before those who try to convince them otherwise and be able to say, *"It doesn't matter what you try to do to bring them down, they are good children and obedient to the ways I have shown them!"* This is exactly what God was doing; He was bragging to satan about how awesome His servant Job was. It did not matter what satan wanted Job to do, Job was obedient to God. Yes, we love to brag about our children because after all, we are created in the likeness and image of God. God loves to brag on those who are doing well; He loves to point out how awesome we are when we do great things for Him. All those things we do that are for good and not evil, all those things we do expecting nothing in return, all those things we do to help others, all those things we do to exalt our God, they all show glory to our Father in Heaven.

1 Thessalonians 2:4 (NLT) *⁴ For we speak as messengers approved by God to be entrusted with the Good News. Our purpose is to please God, not people. He alone examines the motives of our hearts.*

We go forth as messengers for the cause. Our purpose is to please God not man, and God alone knows our heart and what our true motives are. When we truly die to self, our motives will be for Christ. Our motives will never be for the same things Jesus lived and died for unless our heart has been completely transformed to that of Christ. When we die to self, our lives will be one for people. Jesus walked this earth and died a horrible death for people. His motivation was for people. Our motivation will be for people when we are able to see life through God's eyes and not man. The way we think has taken years and years of being programmed to think like the world, and it will be through time spent in God's Word to begin changing the way we think. The disciples had years with Jesus to learn of a new way to think, and many thought His way of thinking was strange. It was strange! If you are accustomed to things a certain way and all of a sudden, someone comes along and tells you all your ways are wrong and now you have to re-learn them a new way, would you not think that was absurd? However, it may sound absurd, but that is only because it is new. As we grow up in Christ, we will begin to see things differently, and it will make more sense. God desires that we all grow up in the Truth, and with Truth, He knows that our lives will change for the better.

Jeremiah 32:39 (NLT) [39] And I will give them one heart and one purpose: to worship me forever, for their own good and for the good of all their descendants.

I know that I desire what is best not only for my children but also for my grandchildren. We have touched on division within the churches, and the book of Jeremiah is a perfect example of why we should all be joined together with one heart and one purpose. There should not be division among our brothers, but how can we not see there is division? How is it that the churches today believe they are not the ones living in division? If we are not joined together in one heart with one purpose, then we are not joined but divided. God desires that we worship Him forever and with that, it shows Him glory. Yet, as long as the churches remain divided, how will we ever come together in one purpose? United, we should serve one God and win souls for the Kingdom. Being joined together in one heart connects us to the one God we serve, and the purpose is winning souls for God's Kingdom not for mankind. In Acts, it states that God's purpose is for the nations to seek after Him.

Acts 17:27 (NLT) [27] "His purpose was for the nations to seek after God and perhaps feel their way toward him and find him—though he is not far from any one of us.

When we seek after God, all other things will follow. In Matthew, Jesus taught about seeking God first and all things would be given besides.

Matthew 6:31-34 (AMP) [31]Therefore do not worry and be anxious, saying, What are we going to have to eat? or, What are we going to have to drink? or, What are we going to have to wear? [32] For the Gentiles (heathen) wish for and crave and diligently seek all these things, and your heavenly Father knows well that you need them all. [33] But seek (aim at and strive after) first of all His kingdom and His righteousness (His way of doing and being right), and then all these things taken together will be given you besides. ³⁴ *So do not worry or be anxious about tomorrow, for tomorrow will have worries and anxieties of its own. Sufficient for each day is its own trouble.*

When I speak this Scripture over myself, I always add, *"Thank you Lord that as I seek You first, all things will be added according to Your will."* You see, far too often, people look for scriptures to pray over their situation because they are seeking answers to a particular circumstance. For instance, I need a job, so I will claim this Scripture that as I seek God, He will provide me with a job. I'm not going to say if He will or will not provide you with that job; however, it is not necessary to pray for what God already knows you need. If you develop that intimate relationship with God, then you know Him. If we have a great relationship with our earthly dad, do we not know him better than someone else would? Of course we do! I do not want to miss it with my Father in Heaven, and I want to glorify Him in all that I do; therefore, I want it to be His will not my own. Is that not what Jesus prayed? Why do we believe we know better than God? Suppose I choose what I want but it was not what God wanted for me, and then suppose He let me have what I wanted but it was not His best? If my desires line up with God's desires, and I truly seek those things above rather than those things which are on earth, why would I ask for those things on earth? If I spend my time with God asking for those things which are of this earth, how can I say that I am seeking the Kingdom of Heaven first? I know that my Father already knows what I need so why would I be anxious for things needed? Why not trust instead that my God has what I need in His hands? I believe we miss it here because our heart is not right. I believe we miss it because our desires do not really line up with God's desires. You may say, then how can I be what God desires me to be? This is merely by seeking Him and His righteousness; it is by seeking Him and His wisdom, His knowledge, and His understanding. We grow more and more into His likeness and image as we seek Him, and then we will see Him bragging about us to our enemy, satan. The real test will be when you can endure those storms in your life. We really show God glory when we are able to say, *"Father, I may not understand why I am at this place in my life, but I trust You and know that You will bring me through. I will count it all joy in the midst of this test in order that I grow to be more like Jesus, fully able to crucify my flesh in order to bring You glory." (James 1:2-4)*

1 Peter 5:12 (NLT) Peter's Final Greetings [12] I have written and sent this short letter to you with the help of Silas, whom I commend to you as a faithful brother. My purpose in writing is to encourage you and assure you that what you are experiencing is truly part of God's grace for you. Stand firm in this grace.

Even when we do not understand, we stand firm. Think back to the time that you endured a really traumatic time in your life. Now think about how you eventually got through that time. If you are currently in a time of stress, think back to a time that has passed, and you made it through. You may be saying that you did not really get through it, but you are still alive to talk about it today. So in a sense, you did get through because today is another day. We allow things to cripple us when we do not have to allow it. It is our choice the final outcome. So, it set us back financially, or maybe it costs us something very dear or even someone. We still choose the final outcome. Even with my daughter's death, I chose the outcome ultimately. I had the choice to either allow her death to cripple my life or to find something good from the experience. You may say that there is nothing good from the experience, but that is where you are wrong. We choose! If you make the decision to allow a loved one's death to cripple your life then you also are allowing your choice to affect all those you love that are still living. I believe that is one thing that really affected me. I did not want my depression or my outlook on life to spill over on my other children. My other children already were dealing with the death of their sister, whom they loved dearly and her death was far too much to put on her younger siblings, but it happened. Our choice is to see that we do not have to remain feeling that there is nothing to live for because this life is not what we should be living for to begin with. What we should be living for is seeking God first so that we can begin to really understand life. God made life, we did not! How can we possibly understand life when we did not create it? So then, no matter what we have walked through, we have come through it one way or another. We may not have walked through it victoriously, but we did walk through it. Today is a new day, and we have a lot to be thankful for and no matter what we have faced or will face, our choice is to trust God and show Him glory by accepting whatever it is we must walk through. Yes, count it joy because ultimately, we will gain something from whatever we walk through. They are all learning experiences. My daughter's death was such a learning experience. I learned how to love greater. Yes, I did! We take life for granted, and we even take those we love for granted. I learned that sometimes we do need to stop and smell the roses because if we did just that, we might be able to stand still and see all of God's glory in everything that He has created. Life is not about this body, this life, this career, this earth, or whatever we give all our time and talents to. Life is about people and about God. It is about seeing God's glory, and we can experience that by having a heart changing attitude in order to see how great it is to serve Him and His people. Life is about giving and giving and giving and giving and never expecting anything in return. Isn't that what Jesus did?

John 15:5-17 (NLT) *⁵ "Yes, I am the vine; you are the branches. Those who remain in me, and I in them, will produce much fruit. For apart from me you can do nothing. ⁶ Anyone who does not remain in me is thrown away like a useless branch and withers. Such branches are gathered into a pile to be burned. ⁷ But if you remain in me and my words remain in you, you may ask for anything you want, and it will be granted! ⁸ When you produce much fruit, you are my true disciples. This brings great glory to my Father. ⁹ "I have loved you even as the Father has loved me. Remain in my love. ¹⁰ When you obey my commandments, you remain in my love, just as I obey my Father's commandments and remain in his love. ¹¹ I have told you these things so that you will be filled with my joy. Yes, your joy will overflow! ¹² This is my commandment: Love each other in the same way I have loved you. ¹³ There is no greater love than to lay down one's life for one's friends. ¹⁴ You are my friends if you do what I command. ¹⁵ I no longer call you slaves, because a master doesn't confide in his slaves. Now you are my friends, since I have told you everything the Father told me. ¹⁶ You didn't choose me. I chose you. I appointed you to go and produce lasting fruit, so that the Father will give you whatever you ask for, using my name. ¹⁷ This is my command: Love each other.*

Do we remain connected to the vine? If we say we are Disciples of Christ, then our life should not matter. We look at this Scripture and what probably stands out to many is that if we do as Christ said, He would give us whatever we ask, but if our heart is one for people, whatever we ask would be motivated by what we love. If we love people, would our asking not be like that of Solomon? Solomon could have had anything, we have studied this, yet he wanted more wisdom in order to do right by the people that he was responsible for. Jesus shows us in this Scripture above that when we do all that He has commanded and we abide in Him, we will be showing glory to His Father. If you are not abiding in the Son today, it may be time to lay down your life to live for Christ in order that your purpose in this life brings glory to our Father in Heaven.

Roman Soldiers Sandals of War

In biblical days, the Roman soldiers wore sandals into battle. That would probably not be sufficient in war today; however, in those days, that was just about as good as it got. During this era not everyone had shoes or sandals, but in war times, they were able to see the importance in having some type of protection for their feet. The sandals in those days were made with either leather or wood for the sole at the base of the foot, and they were tied on with thongs which were made of leather. John the Baptist had declared that he was not worthy to even untie the thong of Jesus' sandals.

John 1:27 (NASB) ^{27} It is He who comes after me, the thong of whose sandal I am not worthy to untie."

We are able to see that the sandal was held on with thongs and tied onto the feet. When a soldier wore the sandals it was a sign that they were ready to go into battle. On the sandals of the soldiers, there were nails attached to the bottoms in order to have traction for gripping the ground to keep from being knocked over or sliding off of an incline. When in battle, it was important that the soldier was swift with his feet in order to fight the hand to hand combat which was normal during those times. Equipped with their sandals on, they were able to endure the battle for longer periods of time and to move faster and farther than would have been possible with no protection at all to the feet. When in combat, a soldier could stand his ground by digging in with the nails at the bottom of the sandal and remain standing in order to overtake his opponent.

344

Spiritual Boots of War

Ephesians 6:11-15 (KJV) [11] Put on the whole armour of God, that ye may be able to stand against the wiles of the devil. [12] For we wrestle not against flesh and blood, but against principalities, against powers, against the rulers of the darkness of this world, against spiritual wickedness in high places. [13] Wherefore take unto you the whole armour of God, that ye may be able to withstand in the evil day, and having done all, to stand. [14] Stand therefore, having your loins girt about with truth, and having on the breastplate of righteousness; [15] And your feet shod with the preparation of the gospel of peace;

What was Paul trying to impart to us when he told us to shod our feet with the preparation of the gospel of peace? Using the Roman soldier's sandals as a reference to the gospel of peace, this is the place we come as we grow in maturity, and the time comes when we hear that voice say, *"Go, make disciples of all nations."* The gospel of peace is sharing the complete Bible. It is taking Jesus to the world. We cannot go if our feet do not take us, and our feet will not go unless our mind tells our feet to go. All pieces work hand in hand. As we mature, it is time to share Jesus because without the Word of God, there is no peace. Peace that passes all understanding is something that people would buy if it were that easy.

Philippians 4:7 (ESV) [7] And the peace of God, which surpasses all understanding, will guard your hearts and your minds in Christ Jesus.

This is what the world would give everything to have but it cannot be bought. Peace at all times, peace when troubles come, peace when faced with uncertainty, peace upon waking and lying down at night, peace in the midst of every storm in life, and upon understanding this kind of peace, it guards our hearts and our

345

minds that we do not lose that peace. What would we give for that kind of peace? Yet, if we are true Disciples of Christ, this peace is ours. Therefore, we should be able to walk consumed in peace daily. Remember, we make those choices, and in making choices, it is our decision what we allow to steal or take away our peace. What steals your peace today? Whatever you have allowed in your life to steal your peace, you should take it back and hold on to it, don't compromise with this world! As we take the gospel of Jesus Christ to the world, we take them peace; we take them hope; we take them the assurance of life after tomorrow, and this is something that is given free through Jesus Christ but it does come with a price. The cost is making the choice to die to self. Once you have decided that you choose Christ totally, then it is time to go with your gospel shoes on into the world and share everything that God has given to you. You impart to others all the revelation, the testimonies, the wisdom and knowledge that has been freely given to you. This is what is expected after you make the decision to become a warrior in God's army. It is about applying your complete armor daily to your life.

As a believer, we need special shoes that we put on daily just as the Roman soldier did to prepare to go into battle. It is a sign of readiness. In biblical days when the soldier was ready to go into battle, they put on their sandals. Today, as we seek God and begin to grow, the day comes that we are ready to begin going and giving back those things we have matured in. Our training is not over with but any boot camp will tell you that it does not matter how much training you get while there, it will never be enough to prepare you for the battlefield. The rest of your training will come fast and hard but will be done in the battlefield. It is time to rise up and begin running this race while enduring all that you can endure in order to grow into areas which are greater. If we never make it to the battlefield as a Christian, we have missed out on the race. The race begins when we step out putting our gospel shoes on. Then we go forth to take the Good News to all that God sends across our path in order to begin planting and watering seeds. This will be a testing period but as we are faithful, more tests will come as our attitude becomes one that takes joy in every test because these are the tools needed to shape us. As a believer, we grow to know that our hearts are guarded and our minds are protected to what we have learned thus far. We will not lose it as long as we hold on to it. There is no going backward unless we chose to go there. From this day, it is moving forward with purpose which we have discussed above. We stand firm on what we believe in not moving unless God moves us. We understand that our God prevails over everything and we are on the winning side. As we submit to God's will and no longer our own will, our feet become prepared and His Words begin to burn within us with the desire to go forth and awaken a generation to truth.

Psalm 18:33 (AMP) [33] He makes my feet like hinds' feet [able to stand firmly or make progress on the dangerous heights of testing and trouble]; He sets me securely upon my high places.

No matter what we face, no matter what the terrain is like, He makes our feet able to stand firm against any and everything. Our feet are to the body what our will is to our soul. Without our feet, our body can go nowhere and the same with our will. If our will is not His will, our desires will not be one to go. Remember, our soul houses our desires and emotions. Without lining our will up with God, our desire will never be to win people to Jesus. If our desire is not for people, we are not really Disciples of Christ and if not disciples, we perish. Our choice must be to seek God in order that we grow up fully matured in the things that are eternal. The only thing that keeps Christians from crossing this line is the devil, yet the Word says that if we resist, he flees.

James 4:7 (AMP) [7] *So be subject to God. Resist the devil [stand firm against him], and he will flee from you.*

Do not allow strong holds to keep you from God. I remember there have been times that my grandbaby would tell me that the devil made her do it. Of course, this does not work. I remind her that she can resist the enemy and rebuke him from her life. It again is our choice. We either remain in our sin because we choose to or we make the decision to come against temptation and resist evil. If we resist, he will flee because there is no sense in satan sitting around watching us be obedient to God. That would have to be depressing on his part to see us do good and not evil, so why would he remain?

It is through the gospel that our will is set in motion. The Word of God gives us our purpose and our focus as the message goes deep within our being and the meaning to life becomes evident where nothing else will ever seem to matter again. We apply our spiritual shoes to ready our feet by studying to show ourselves approved. Once approved, we are ready to get our feet dirty so to speak. It is time to move forth allowing our feet to carry us on the journey of our life doing what we were meant to do from the beginning.

Preparation of the Gospel of Peace

As God brings forth people across our path, we become equipped with our armor and time spent seeking the Kingdom of Heaven, in order to go forth to do all we are called to do. Preparation brings us to that place where we are ready to begin a long journey with the Lord. I cannot think of a more fulfilling journey than one that is filled with the presence of God in my life on a daily basis. This was the intentions when God created man. We were to walk with Him daily in fellowship as Adam and Eve did; however, today we can have that same fellowship through Jesus Christ.

1 John 1:2-3 (NLT) [2] This one who is life itself was revealed to us, and we have seen him. And now we testify and proclaim to you that he is the one who is eternal life. He was with the Father, and then he was revealed to us. [3] We proclaim to you what we ourselves have actually seen and heard so that you may have fellowship with us. And our fellowship is with the Father and with his Son, Jesus Christ.

As we study and prepare, here was something a Marine said.

A Marine said... Believe it or not, you will have a little fun in boot camp if your platoon ever learns teamwork.

I know many times we believe that being a Christian is no fun, but if that is how we feel, we have not really walked the life of a true disciple. Just like the Marine, believe it or not, there is a little fun in Boot Camp, and I would go on to say that it can be extremely exciting and fun walking this walk out. This Marine talked about teamwork. I remember my pastor talking about teamwork quite a bit. If only one person is engaged there is only so much that can be accomplished, but when we work together as a team, we can conquer a lot of ground. This all goes back to being connected to others who are walking this walk with you through Boot Camp. It is great if you have friends or family members or even those in the church that desire to really walk this walk, and you join together to do so. The Marine went on to say...

...and you will make friends that you will keep in touch with throughout your career.

There is only one career, and it begins with doing it God's way. You may have plans and dreams, but until you latch onto those

God given dreams, which He does plant in you, only then will you see true victory in your life. Once you have latched onto the truth, your career will take off because you are where God wants you. You will meet people along your path, and those you meet which are your brothers and sisters in Christ, they will be your true friends that stand beside you through all things. Your spiritual brothers and sisters in Christ will become your family because you will endure together in all things. One day, when we all get to heaven, we will look around to see many of those who endured the battle beside us. When I look at my brothers and sisters in Christ, many times I envision that day when we will have finally arrived after such a long journey that we faced together. In biblical days, the disciples became as brothers or as one just as we do today. They lived together and died together; they endured good times and hard times; they fought side by side for the same purpose and died for the same cause. I know that I cannot make it without my brothers and sisters in Christ. I know that they need me, and I need them. If I am in a battle, which we all are, I want to know that those standing with me are of liked mind. I want to know that they are willing to give up this world in order to gain the next. Daily, we are in a battle, and we need to find our spiritual brothers and sisters in order that we remain as one strengthened by His might.

The Gospel of Peace is critical to the Full Armor of God in Spiritual Warfare. Paul gives us a picture of our feet shod for readiness in order that we take peace to the world. Have you ever wondered why the gospels, which are the books of the Bible which recount the life of Jesus, are referred to as the gospel of peace when in fact, the contents speak of so much more than just peace? In fact, within the gospels, Jesus tells us that the two greatest commandments were to love God and to love our neighbors.

Matthew 22:36-39 (ESV) [36] *"Teacher, which is the great commandment in the Law?"* [37] *And he said to him, "You shall love the Lord your God with all your heart and with all your soul and with all your mind.* [38] *This is the great and first commandment.* [39] *And a second is like it: You shall love your neighbor as yourself.*

However, the gospels are known as the Gospel of Peace not the gospel of love. Why is that? We know that God is love and Jesus came so that through Him we are able to connect to the Father.

1 John 4:8 (ESV) [8]Anyone who does not love does not know God, because God is love.

John 14:6-7 (ESV) [6]Jesus said to him, "I am the way, and the truth, and the life. No one comes to the Father except through me. [7]If you had known me, you would have known my Father also. From now on you do know him and have seen him."

We are able to know the extent of God's love through Jesus because if God is love, Jesus is also love. By knowing Jesus, we know God. Yet, the gospels are called the Gospel of Peace. Peace can only be found through Jesus, and we cannot give peace if we do not have peace. The gospels are referred to as the Gospel of Peace because it is through Jesus that we can obtain peace and no other way. Jesus was peace and if we want to obtain that peace, it will be through Him.

John 14:27 (ESV) [27]Peace I leave with you; my peace I give to you. Not as the world gives do I give to you. Let not your hearts be troubled, neither let them be afraid

Peace is one thing that every person wants in their life. Think about it, without peace you really have nothing. People live day in and day out knowing love to some extent because if nothing else, we love. We love our families, our children, our spouse, but peace is something we have to struggle to have. You may be in a relationship that seems good by the world's standards where you are in love, but if your life is continually in turmoil for whatever reason that you have no peace, you will be miserable. We desire peace but the peace that Jesus gives us is not the peace that can be obtained within this world. It does not matter what we do to obtain peace, it will never be the kind of peace that is acquired through Jesus. If we do not learn about this peace, how can we take the Gospel of Peace to the world? Is your life today saturated in the peace Jesus speaks of? If not, you have more homework to do. This will only come with time spent in your relationship with God the Father and Jesus the Son. Nothing can bring this kind of peace into your life except the Son.

When our enemy offers false ways to peace, as soldiers that have matured, we are able to stand firm against him. Daily, satan gives the world false perceptions of peace as he continually destroys our world. As he persuades our focus to be on the concerns of this world, instead of peace, we buy into that false perception and the result eventually will produce fear, worry, anger, etc. When we take our eyes off of Christ, we place them on the things of this world which satan uses to entice us to fall away instead of standing firm on the teachings of Christ. Our peace is taken when we agree with sin or false perceptions.

Matthew 10:13 (ESV) [13] *And if the house is worthy, let your peace come upon it, but if it is not worthy, let your peace return to you.*

We must judge ourselves. We know if we are living worthy. No, none of us are worthy but we know if we are striving to live righteous. Yes, we will miss it but that is why Jesus came in the first place. It is about having that heart of David and God knows our heart. As we strive to be what God called us to be, our peace will remain unless we become distracted and fall into a trap set by our enemy. As we please and glorify God in all that we do, our peace will continue day in and day out. Jesus spoke to His disciples in John so that they would understand it is through Him that we have peace.

Luke 2:14 (ESV) [14]*"Glory to God in the highest, and on earth peace among those with whom he is pleased!"*

John 16:33 (ESV) [33]*I have said these things to you, that in me you may have peace. In the world you will have tribulation. But take heart; I have overcome the world."*

Even though there will be tribulation, we do not have to lose our peace. Jesus' walk on this earth was not filled with completely tranquil days, on the contrary, there was much tribulation, but He endured all of it to show us how. Just because we go through things does not mean we have to lose our peace. If He overcame, we too can overcome as we remain in Him and He remains in us. We walk through differently than the world in order that we are able to take peace to the world. It is easy to show others how to walk in peace when all is going well, but that is not what the world needs. They need mentors that are able to show them how to remain in Christ even through those tough times so that they do not lose heart. With God our lives do not have to be a roller coaster where one day things are good and the next they crash. I remember the times in my life when I was not walking close to God. I remember crying out, "Why is my life such a roller coaster?" This is how it feels. Yet, when you draw close to Him, He draws close to you.

James 4:8 (ESV) [8]*Draw near to God, and he will draw near to you. Cleanse your hands, you sinners, and purify your hearts, you double-minded.*

Many Christians take on certain battles before they are ready. There are times and seasons for everything. There is a time to prepare. God's grace will take you through those times of trouble as God is preparing you for the place He desires you to be. However, remember His promise to you.

1 Corinthians 10:13 (ESV) [13] No temptation has overtaken you that is not common to man. God is faithful, and he will not let you be tempted beyond your ability, but with the temptation he will also provide the way of escape, that you may be able to endure it.

Jesus also spent time preparing. We may not realize that, but His early days were a time of growing and learning. It was after His baptism by John the Baptist that the Holy Spirit ascended upon Him, and then He went into the dessert to defeat satan. After His desert experience, His ministry began. Jesus' time of preparation had taken many years to grow and mature to the place God desired before His days began on the battlefield. We too have a period that requires preparing for the path God has laid out for us to walk. During all these growing and learning years, we will continually endure times of trouble that will actually produce good fruit within us in order that we grow to the place to being fully equipped for the battle at hand. Jesus was equipped with the Holy Spirit which teaches us all things. The fruits that need to be perfected within us are the fruits of the Spirit, which are love, joy, peace, patience, kindness, goodness, faithfulness, gentleness and self-control. *(Galatians 5:22-23)* As we endure battles, we grow in the fruits because we learn to be more like Jesus. When we learn to count it all joy for all tests and trials, we have begun to learn how to operate in these fruits. If we fully operate in each of these fruits, our lives become more and more like Christ. All of a sudden, we have made satan's work really hard because if he cannot produce the opposite of the fruits within us, he has failed, and we have become victors. If I refuse to hate, I remain in love.

If I refuse to allow anything to take away my joy and peace, I have overcome just as Jesus did. *(John 16:33)* We do not murmur and complain but count it joy because God is perfecting those fruits needed in order to be victorious on those paths laid out for us to travel.

Daily, count it joy for the trials and tests as we put on our gospel shoes standing ready for the task at hand. Without these tests, we will never be ready and equipped with what we need to suffice in battle. Notice that Jesus sent disciples to make disciples. This is all about preparing our feet to take us where our mind is set on going.

Luke 10:1-12 (NIV) [10]*After this the Lord appointed seventy-two others and sent them two by two ahead of him to every town and place where he was about to go.* [2]*He told them, "The harvest is plentiful, but the workers are few. Ask the Lord of the harvest, therefore, to send out workers into his harvest field.* [3]*Go! I am sending you out like lambs among wolves.* [4]*Do not take a purse or bag or sandals; and do not greet anyone on the road.* [5]*"When you enter a house, first say, 'Peace to this house.'* [6]*If someone who promotes peace is there, your peace will rest on them; if not, it will return to you.* [7]*Stay there, eating and drinking whatever they give you, for the worker deserves his wages. Do not move around from house to house.* [8]*"When you enter a town and are welcomed, eat what is offered to you.* [9]*Heal the sick who are there and tell them, 'The kingdom of God has come near to you.'* [10]*But when you enter a town and are not welcomed, go into its streets and say,* [11]*'Even the dust of your town we wipe from our feet as a warning to you. Yet be sure of this: The kingdom of God has come near.'* [12]*I tell you, it will be more bearable on that day for Sodom than for that town.*

We are sent out as lambs among wolves; however, as God calls us to go, the Holy Spirit walks with us. God will take care of those who are doing the same works which Jesus did. What you give will be given back to you. Our life while here on earth accounts for where we will be when we leave these bodies and enter into the eternal. It is not about this life but this life will determine the life to come. We all desire heaven if given a choice, and the choice is ours based on our actions while here. Paul tells us in Philippians that given a choice, it is much better to be with Christ than here on this earth, yet Paul chose to stay awhile in order to do more work which needed to be done to make disciples.

Philippians 1:22-26 (NIV) ²² *If I am to go on living in the body, this will mean fruitful labor for me. Yet what shall I choose? I do not know!* ²³ *I am torn between the two: I desire to depart and be with Christ, which is better by far;* ²⁴ *but it is more necessary for you that I remain in the body.* ²⁵ *Convinced of this, I know that I will remain, and I will continue with all of you for your progress and joy in the faith,* ²⁶ *so that through my being with you again your boasting in Christ Jesus will abound on account of me.*

Paul lived unselfishly on account of people. His purpose was the same purpose Jesus came and died for. This is our sole purpose and determines our outcome for the next life. Depending on where we plant seeds will determine how we spend eternity.

Revelation 22:12-15 (NIV) ¹² *"Look, I am coming soon! My reward is with me, and I will give to each person according to what they have done.* ¹³ *I am the Alpha and the Omega, the First and the Last, the Beginning and the End.* ¹⁴ *"Blessed are those who wash their robes, that they may have the right to the tree of life and may go through the gates into the city.* ¹⁵ *Outside are the dogs, those who practice magic arts, the sexually immoral, the murderers, the idolaters and everyone who loves and practices falsehood.*

We cannot play church. Our rewards begin with our accomplishments here on earth. We are not rewarded for playing church; we are not rewarded because we attended church services on a weekly basis. This is not the kind of servant Paul was and not what Jesus commanded those who chose to follow Him.

Matthew 28:19-20 (ESV) [19] *Go therefore and make disciples of all nations, baptizing them in the name of the Father and of the Son and of the Holy Spirit,* [20] *teaching them to observe all that I have commanded you. And behold, I am with you always, to the end of the age."*

We are rewarded based on our works here on earth. No, our works will not get us into heaven, only through Jesus can we obtain eternal life, but those things we do once we have come to know Jesus Christ will determine where we spend eternity and how we will spend eternity.

John 8:31 (AMP) [31] *So Jesus said to those Jews who had believed in Him, If you abide in My word [hold fast to My teachings and live in accordance with them], you are truly My disciples.*

It is not just about following the commandments; it is about obeying and living by all that Christ taught. This is our example; Jesus is our example; Paul is our example; those you know within the church that are walking this out, they are your example.

John 21:17 (NLT) [17] *A third time he asked him, "Simon son of John, do you love me?" Peter was hurt that Jesus asked the question a third time. He said, "Lord, you know everything. You know that I love you." Jesus said, "Then feed my sheep.*

If we are not feeding His sheep, how can we consider ourselves His sheep? If we are His sheep, we feed other sheep. If Jesus is our shepherd, we are His sheep and will do what He commanded us to do.

Matthew 25:31-37 (NIV) [31] "When the Son of Man comes in his glory, and all the angels with him, he will sit on his glorious throne. [32] All the nations will be gathered before him, and he will separate the people one from another as a shepherd separates the sheep from the goats. [33] He will put the sheep on his right and the goats on his left. [34] "Then the King will say to those on his right, 'Come, you who are blessed by my Father; take your inheritance, the kingdom prepared for you since the creation of the world. [35] For I was hungry and you gave me something to eat, I was thirsty and you gave me something to drink, I was a stranger and you invited me in, [36] I needed clothes and you clothed me, I was sick and you looked after me, I was in prison and you came to visit me.' [37] "Then the righteous will answer him, 'Lord, when did we see you hungry and feed you, or thirsty and give you something to drink?

Our inheritance has already been prepared for us since the creation of the world. As we travel down the chosen paths that God has ordained for each of us, are we observant of much work that must be done in order for Christ to return? Jesus said, *"The harvest is plentiful but the workers are few." (Matthew 9:37)* We need to pray for laborers, those willing to walk this walk with us in order that we feed His sheep, clothe those who need clothes, feed those who are hungry, and give drink to those who are thirsty. This is not just about natural food and water but spiritual food and water as well. Are you prepared today to equip yourself for this long journey in order that you run with purpose the race set before you and impart to others everything freely given to you?

2 Timothy 2:12 (NLV) [12] *If we suffer and stay true to Him, then we will be a leader with Him. If we say we do not know Him, He will say He does not know us.*

Paul said in 2 Timothy, that as we suffer and are faithful to Jesus, we will reign with Him in the world to come. As we endure hardships for Christ's sake, we will also be rewarded in the next life. If you have not made this step today, apply your gospel shoes in order that your steps are with purpose in order to gain souls for tomorrow and bring glory to our Father.

Chapter Seven
Order of Importance

Ephesians 6:10-20 (NKJV) [10] *Finally, my brethren, be strong in the Lord and in the power of His might.* [11] *Put on the whole armor of God, that you may be able to stand against the wiles of the devil.* [12] *For we do not wrestle against flesh and blood, but against principalities, against powers, against the rulers of the darkness of this age, against spiritual hosts of wickedness in the heavenly places.* [13] *Therefore take up the whole armor of God, that you may be able to withstand in the evil day, and having done all, to stand.* [14] *Stand therefore, having (1) girded your waist with truth, having (2) put on the breastplate of righteousness,* [15] *and having (3) shod your feet with the preparation of the gospel of peace;* [16] *above all, (4) taking the shield of faith with which you will be able to quench all the fiery darts of the wicked one.* [17] *And (5) take the helmet of salvation, and (6) the sword of the Spirit, which is the word of God;* [18] *praying always with all prayer and supplication in the Spirit, being watchful to this end with all perseverance and supplication for all the saints—* [19] *and for me, that utterance may be given to me, that I may open my mouth boldly to make known the mystery of the gospel,* [20] *for which I am an ambassador in chains; that in it I may speak boldly, as I ought to speak.*

When I began this series on teaching my prayer group to be warriors, at one point, I prayed and sought God because I desired to know why Paul placed each piece of armor in the order that was listed. Was this just random and there was no specific reason, or was there a greater purpose that we have not seen? The pieces of armor which Paul lists are not by chance but rather these pieces are listed in their order of importance. These pieces have practical reasons for their order in regards to the spiritual battles that we fight. This chapter will look at each piece and why it should be applied in the order Paul gave.

Belt of Truth (1)

Ephesians 6:10-14a (NKJV) [10] *Finally, my brethren, be strong in the Lord and in the power of His might.* [11] *Put on the whole armor of God, that you may be able to stand against the wiles of the devil.* [12] *For we do not wrestle against flesh and blood, but against principalities, against powers, against the rulers of the darkness of this age, against spiritual hosts of wickedness in the heavenly places.* [13] *Therefore take up the whole armor of God, that you may be able to withstand in the evil day, and having done all, to stand.* [14a] *Stand therefore, having* **(1)** *girded your waist with truth...*

When we talk about order of importance, we would assume since Paul spoke of putting on the Belt of Truth first that this would be the most important piece of armor. What we need to see is that it takes all pieces to be an effective warrior and there is no piece that is more important than another. However, the Belt of Truth will be the most important piece that we will ever apply to our lives. Understand that this piece alone will not make a warrior, and we are all called to walk this walk out which cannot be accomplished without engaging in this battle.

Paul used the belt to symbolize the Word of God. We have discussed what a belt does in the natural. A belt keeps things in place; it helps to secure something or hold it together. A belt also can complement an outfit. When we look at this spiritually, the Word of God keeps our perspective for life in place, it keeps us secure and grounded in truth which produces life and not death, it holds us together where we are joined to the body as one, and it adds to us by creating within us something that is unique and more perfected through Christ. The belt is put on first because it is the core to our existence. We cannot fight the enemy without truth. We cannot go forth in battle and operate effectively if we do not first have the Truth. It is the Truth that defeated satan in the desert.

Matthew 4:1-11 (NIV) Jesus Is Tested in the Wilderness [1] Then Jesus was led by the Spirit into the wilderness to be tempted by the devil. [2] After fasting forty days and forty nights, he was hungry. [3] The tempter came to him and said, "If you are the Son of God, tell these stones to become bread." [4] Jesus answered, "It is written: 'Man shall not live on bread alone, but on every word that comes from the mouth of God.'" [5] Then the devil took him to the holy city and had him stand on the highest point of the temple. [6] "If you are the Son of God," he said, "throw yourself down. For it is written: "'He will command his angels concerning you, and they will lift you up in their hands, so that you will not strike your foot against a stone.'" [7] Jesus answered him, "It is also written: 'Do not put the Lord your God to the test.'" [8] Again, the devil took him to a very high mountain and showed him all the kingdoms of the world and their splendor. [9] "All this I will give you," he said, "if you will bow down and worship me." [10] Jesus said to him, "Away from me, Satan! For it is written: 'Worship the Lord your God, and serve him only.'" [11] Then the devil left him, and angels came and attended him.

We know that Jesus was the Word and the Word is Truth, and the Word dwelt among us. It was God's Words spoken over and over again while temptation came, and in the dessert Jesus continually proclaimed, *"It is written!"* Victory was won in biblical days in every circumstance when God's Words were used. The result of His Words and not man's words were miraculous healings, extraordinary signs and wonders, and multitudes saved, restored, and transformed. Christ was revealed as who He was because the Truth always prevails. Today, we put on Truth in order to prevail. Without the Belt of Truth, Jesus does not abide within us.

John 14:16-21 (ESV) ¹⁶ *And I will ask the Father, and he will give you another Helper, to be with you forever,* ¹⁷ *even the Spirit of truth, whom the world cannot receive, because it neither sees him nor knows him. You know him, for he dwells with you and will be in you.* ¹⁸ *"I will not leave you as orphans; I will come to you.* ¹⁹ *Yet a little while and the world will see me no more, but you will see me. Because I live, you also will live.* ²⁰ *In that day you will know that I am in my Father, and you in me, and I in you.* ²¹ *Whoever has my commandments and keeps them, he it is who loves me. And he who loves me will be loved by my Father, and I will love him and manifest myself to him."*

Without Jesus in our lives, we have no victory and there is no eternal life in heaven. Without Jesus, we have nothing, can do nothing, and will be nothing. You may survive and be breathing, but without Jesus what you have right now is all you will ever have and when you die, you have nothing because you stored up nothing for the next life in eternity. Do not think it just ends there, on the contrary, we all will live eternally, but where we live depends on what is secured around our waist.

Matthew 25:46 (AMP) ⁴⁶ *Then they will go away into eternal punishment, but those who are just and upright and in right standing with God into eternal life.*

When I began teaching the armor to my prayer group, I applied the helmet first because if you have not come to the place where you believe that Jesus is the Son of God, and if you have not taken that first step towards salvation, you cannot go any further. In fact, without your spirit inside awakening to conviction of just who Jesus Christ is, there will never be another piece of armor applied. When we first come to the place where we hear the message of the Cross and where we feel the conviction inside by the Holy Spirit, at this place is where we make a choice to follow

364

Jesus or continue on the path of this world. This is called salvation. It is your salvation but it is a lifetime journey that begins when you make that choice. As discussed earlier in this book, after beginning your salvation journey, you must know who you are in Christ, and you must know that you are in right standing with God. If we cannot get that on the inside of us, we will never grow from that point. Next, we must put the belt of truth on in order to begin the growth process that we absorb any and everything that has to do with God. Once we begin getting the truth in us, God will expect us to prepare our feet with the preparation of the Gospel of Peace by taking Jesus to the world. As we share the gospel, we are giving and giving and all those things we give are given back to us, and this is where the battle begins so that we raise our shield and sword as warriors.

However, Paul taught this message not to the lost but to those who had accepted Jesus into their lives and were on their salvation journey. They were called disciples. We are called Disciples of Jesus Christ when we come to know who He is and His agenda becomes our life. Yes, those who are lost, must first apply that helmet to know about salvation, but for those who are already on this journey, their belt is the first thing that should be applied upon rising each day in order that they have Jesus on before they walk out into this world. The helmet is put on much later for a reason and will be discussed, but as Christians, the most important piece of armor is Jesus. Our belt is our foundation; it is the rock of Jesus, and daily we should speak this over our lives and live it knowing that we go nowhere without Christ as the center of our being.

Breastplate of Righteousness (2)

Ephesians 6:10-14 (NKJV) *[10]Finally, my brethren, be strong in the Lord and in the power of His might. [11] Put on the whole armor of God, that you may be able to stand against the wiles of the devil. [12] For we do not wrestle against flesh and blood, but against principalities, against powers, against the rulers of the darkness of this age, against spiritual hosts of wickedness in the heavenly places. [13] Therefore take up the whole armor of God, that you may be able to withstand in the evil day, and having done all, to stand. [14] Stand therefore, having (1) girded your waist with truth, having (2) put on the breastplate of righteousness,*

As we have studied, the Breastplate of Righteousness protects many of our vital organs, including our heart. When we live a righteous life, we are protecting our heart. Our heart is the most important organ in our body. When we do those things which are contrary to God's Word, we open the door for an attack on our heart. We have determined that the belt is the most important piece of armor because without Jesus we can do nothing, but right behind the belt would be our heart.

The enemy would love to keep all of us from coming to know Jesus, but if he fails in that area and we begin to grow and learn of Christ, the next area of attack will be our heart. It is hard to operate when our heart has become wounded. I cannot think of anything more debilitating than being in a broken state and unable to function. I remember many times being in this broken state, but the time that was far worse than any other was when my daughter died. I literally felt dead inside with no reason to live. Was I able to make good decisions? Absolutely not, I lived in a state of depression unable to even see things which were happening all around me. Would the Breastplate of Righteousness have made it different? Yes and no! When we are faced with a hard tragedy,

God designed our bodies to be able to walk through these times; however, we must still walk through them. This means, there is a time for healing. Our bodies shut down for a time and feel numb, but this is part of being able to handle the pain inside. However, with the breastplate, it assures us that we will get through. I cannot imagine going through what I did and not knowing God. The book of Job was my comfort. Even though it still hurt, being able to see that Job did get through gave me hope. I also knew that God was there with me, and this did make it easier to endure. What is the outcome? We bounce back and stronger than ever. Many people do not bounce back and many are never the same again due to tragedies, but it does not have to be that way. Our Breastplate of Righteousness ensures us of who we are and that God has an ultimate plan which will happen regardless of what we may think. God may love us, but He is not moved by tears alone. Our tears many times are to manipulate but God sees through them. Like I said, there is a time for healing, but it does not drag on in order that those tears and depression keeps others in a place where they feel sorry for us. I can remember way too many times people telling me that they felt sorry for me. My response was to please not feel sorry for me; my God had brought me through and who I am today is a result of everything I have lived through. I do not want to go back and relive any of it or change it. If I am assured that I will be with my daughter someday, why would I want to drag her back into this life if she is in a much better place now? If we cannot believe that, we really do not believe God is who He said He is. You may have lost someone and be saying, *"How do I know they will be in heaven someday?"* My answer is that you don't know, but you have to make that decision to either go forward with God or to go forward with satan. There is no in between. We either serve God or satan, that simple.

Like I said, when we are wounded inside, it affects our ability to think or reason, and our mood changes drastically to the point of depression far too often. Any time in my past, if the enemy could bring about a broken heart, I was useless. Even though we may have that belt on and have begun to saturate our lives in God's Word, if we are not fully grounded, we are still capable of falling. I was a strong Christian for 10 years and fell from grace because my heart became so wounded that I could not function, and this was prior to my daughter's death. I said it affects our ability to think and reason. If we cannot think straight, how are we going to remember what God's Word says about our situation? It is imperative that we learn the importance of the Breastplate of Righteousness which is the second most important piece of armor to become grounded.

Many Christians today live with a broken heart, and many live with a damaged heart because of wrong images spoken over them that they are not able to see themselves as righteous. When we have not learned how important this piece of armor is, we can walk around never growing to be all that God called us to be. If satan can keep us in this state, it does not matter that we have the belt on because we will never be able to advance any further into the spiritual realm.

As the second piece of armor, we must get it down deep in our heart just how important we are to God and how much He loves us. I know growing up as a child, most of us knew our parents really loved us even when we messed up. This is the mind set we must have with God. This piece like the other body pieces all fit together and work together, but it does not matter if we have it in our mind that yes, this is who I am in Christ, we must have it in our heart. Our heart will never believe that God is who He says He is; our heart will never believe that God will do what He said He would do, and our heart will never believe we are capable of any and all things, if it is not grounded in His Word. Therefore, as we study by applying our belt to know the Word of God front and back, we must also study righteousness in order that we truly desire to be righteous and see ourselves as such.

Gospel Shoes (3)

Ephesians 6:10-15 (NKJV) [10] *Finally, my brethren, be strong in the Lord and in the power of His might.* [11] *Put on the whole armor of God, that you may be able to stand against the wiles of the devil.* [12] *For we do not wrestle against flesh and blood, but against principalities, against powers, against the rulers of the darkness of this age, against spiritual hosts of wickedness in the heavenly places.* [13] *Therefore take up the whole armor of God, that you may be able to withstand in the evil day, and having done all, to stand.* [14] *Stand therefore, having (1) girded your waist with truth, having (2) put on the breastplate of righteousness,* [15] *and having (3) shod your feet with the preparation of the gospel of peace;*

The Gospel Shoes are the third most important piece of armor to apply. Like I have said, all pieces work together and all are important. Why would we shod our feet with the preparation of the Gospel of Peace prior to the other three pieces? We can surely understand why the belt would go on first and the breastplate second, but why the shoes third? There is more than one reason, but there is only one that I can share at this time without jumping ahead. Think about it this way, if you are getting dressed to go into the battlefield, before you would pick up any weapon or put on your helmet, you naturally would put your clothing on which would be the belt and breastplate and then you are going to put your shoes on before anything else. Furthermore, how would you bend down to pick up your shoes and tie them to your fee with a heavy helmet on and weapons in your hands? This is the logical reason and probably a good one; however, spiritually, our feet will lead us where we need to go. Our feet carry us to our purpose. Every step we take should be with purpose, and we normally do not walk out the door without being clothed. If we are not grounded in God's Word and in righteousness, our feet will probably not go in the right direction either. Our feet will carry us where our heart leads them; therefore, it is also extremely important thus far, that the other pieces have been applied in the correct order.

As we have discussed previously, we are all called to go and make disciples. How can we impart to the world how great our God is if we are not first putting truth in us and second being able to see ourselves as righteous? Those first two things must be grounded within us in order to be strong enough to take it to the world. When I have new girls that I am watering or ministering to, it is imperative to let them know that they are not strong enough to go out into this world of darkness and begin sharing the gospel to any and all that cross their paths. This does not mean they cannot share Jesus, but it is important where they go in order to do so. Prior to becoming a Christian, we all had strong holds and some stronger than others. If there are areas of weaknesses, satan will use those areas to try and bring you back down where you fall from grace. The easiest way he can do this is through others who are living in those same weaknesses as you once were. I remember telling my daughter, you are not strong enough to take this to your friends who are still living in those same strongholds you once were. I would tell her that she could send them across my path, but it was not her place to go into darkness in order to shed light just yet. Although, she decided one night that she was strong enough, so she went and she relapsed. Thankfully, she was at the altar the very next morning crying out to

God. It was all good, sometimes we must relapse to grow stronger, and this taught her that mom was right but actually, it was God that was right. He has never told us to go into darkness to minister. We do not send someone who had an alcohol problem prior to Jesus into bars to minister, and we do not send someone who had a gambling problem into casinos. This is ludicrous, and I was not talking about my daughter going into an establishment as such, but into the home of a friend that had the same stronghold that she did. It is not about staying away from going into places that are obviously darkness but also visiting those who struggle in those same areas you once did. Eventually, we become strong, but we still have no business going into certain places. Myself, I am strong enough to go into bars and casinos, but why would I do that? There are plenty of people who are lost that live in the bars and casinos that cross our paths daily without having to go into their territory. God will send them across our path if we are obedient and faithful to be bold when they come.

This is the third piece of armor and the third area that satan will use to bring you down if you do not become grounded in the first two pieces of armor. As I have said, this does not mean you cannot share Jesus but allow God to bring those you are to minister to across your path because He will. If satan knows that he cannot bring you down in the area of the belt because you are determined to seek God with all your might and grow and mature, then he will go to the second piece of armor. If satan cannot bring you down in this second area because you know God intimately and know that all things work for good no matter what your tests and trials, then he will go to the third area.

Romans 8:28 (NLT) [28]*And we know that God causes everything to work together for the good of those who love God and are called according to his purpose for them.*

When satan goes to this third area, we must be wise enough to know that we are not strong enough yet. This is part of being humble and an area of the heart. If our heart has not matured because we have not studied enough of the Word (belt), then we become boisterous in believing we have arrived when we have not.

Romans 12:3 (AMP) [3] For by the grace (unmerited favor of God) given to me I warn everyone among you not to estimate and think of himself more highly than he ought [not to have an exaggerated opinion of his own importance], but to rate his ability with sober judgment, each according to the degree of faith apportioned by God to him.

A good place to keep your thought process would be to know that until Jesus comes back, you have not arrived and you are not wiser than anyone else; you are not more spiritual than anyone else, and you are not more powerful or anointed than anyone else. This is just a good place to be. It is better to be humble than to think more highly of yourself. It is about coming to that place where we crucify our flesh or our self and allow Christ to reign in our lives. It is all about Him and not about us. We decrease as He increases and only then will we be productive in this life as we apply our Gospel Shoes in order to take us on that journey of our life. Purpose with each step is what we strive for on a daily basis, and we will not find that purpose in life until we have stepped into the book that God wrote about us, our own story. We will not start walking through our chapters of life until we secure ourselves with the Word and Righteousness.

The belt, breastplate, and feet are prior preparations for the battles we face each day. These three pieces of armor begin our preparation for the battlefield. The good part of the Gospel Shoes, once we are at that place because we have endured Boot Camp, we walk forth into the field to give. This becomes our purpose to give all we receive. We cannot out give God! This is not just about resources such as money and material things, but it is about imparting to others wisdom and knowledge and giving of our time. Whatever we desire more of, give it away and you will receive more. Give joy away, peace, patience, etc. Our cup will runneth over as our heart becomes one of giving. Below is Psalm 23, the book that most Christians are very familiar. It is the *Psalms of David*. Remember, we have talked about having the heart of David and here it is. Right now, I want you to read this but do not just read it because you know the words. We need to read this slow, and allow it to sink deep inside so that we really understand what David was saying.

Psalm 23:1-6 (AMP) [1] *The Lord is my Shepherd [to feed, guide, and shield me], I shall not lack.* [2] *He makes me lie down in [fresh, tender] green pastures; He leads me beside the still and restful waters.* [3] *He refreshes and restores my life (my self); He leads me in the paths of righteousness [uprightness and right standing with Him—not for my earning it, but] for His name's sake.* [4] *Yes, though I walk through the [deep, sunless] valley of the shadow of death, I will fear or dread no evil, for You are with me; Your rod [to protect] and Your staff [to guide], they comfort me.* [5] *You prepare a table before me in the presence of my enemies. You anoint my head with oil; my [brimming] cup runs over.* [6] *Surely or only goodness, mercy, and unfailing love shall follow me all the days of my life, and through the length of my days the house of the Lord [and His presence] shall be my dwelling place.*

Does your cup runneth over today? If it doesn't, it's not God's fault. He assures us that if we allow Him to be over our lives, our lives will runneth over. If we allow the Lord to guide us as we go forth to share Jesus and we humble ourselves knowing that this is about God, all things will go according to His plans which are far better. As we put on our Gospel Shoes, we are changing people's lives because this *"God over the Universe"* actually chose us to do something more miraculous than anything else in this world. Through us He saves people; through us He restores lives; through us He heals wounds, and because of our obedience, He ensures us that goodness and mercy will follow us, love will follow us, and we shall dwell with Him forever. It is awesome to be at this place of giving and the benefits are extraordinary!

Luke 6:38 (AMP) *[38] Give, and [gifts] will be given to you; good measure, pressed down, shaken together, and running over, will they pour into [the pouch formed by] the bosom [of your robe and used as a bag]. For with the measure you deal out [with the measure you use when you confer benefits on others], it will be measured back to you.*

Shield of Faith (4)

Ephesians 6:10-16 (NKJV) *[10]Finally, my brethren, be strong in the Lord and in the power of His might. [11] Put on the whole armor of God, that you may be able to stand against the wiles of the devil. [12] For we do not wrestle against flesh and blood, but against principalities, against powers, against the rulers of the darkness of this age, against spiritual hosts of wickedness in the heavenly places. [13] Therefore take up the whole armor of God, that you may be able to withstand in the evil day, and having done all, to stand. [14] Stand therefore, having (1) girded your waist with truth, having (2) put on the breastplate of righteousness, [15] and having (3) shod your feet with the preparation of the gospel of peace; [16] above all, (4) taking the shield of faith with which you will be able to quench all the fiery darts of the wicked one.*

The fourth piece of armor Paul said to apply was the Shield of Faith. Why would we lift our shield before putting on the helmet? I guess it could make sense in the natural to put on the helmet first

374

before picking up your weapons, but we are not going to look at this in the natural, even though, we could argue that it would be possible to lift your shield and then put your helmet on next with one hand but maybe not probable. We are going to look at this in the spiritual. I noted above there were other reasons that the shoes were put on prior to the helmet and the weapons, the main reason is because it is imperative that the helmet goes on right before we pick up that last weapon. For now, we will discuss why the shield is fourth.

As we know, once we have secured ourselves with God's Word (belt) and the breastplate by developing that deep heartfelt relationship with God, we applied our shoes in order to get our feet wet so to speak. With the Gospel Shoes on, we have walked into the battlefield to be attacked. We may not have walked into the field expecting to be attacked, but we will be attacked even before we are fully trained. Remember, I have taught that no matter how tough a boot camp is nothing will prepare you for what is to come in the actual battlefield, and anytime we walk out into a battlefield, we will be attacked. You may say, well I prefer to stay on the sidelines instead of going where I know I will be attacked. However, it is in the battlefield that we really mature by falling and getting back up. With all things that grow, they must endure a period of transformation. Even babies will fall in order to grow stronger. Plants and trees go through a process where they are weak before they gain strength. A warrior is grown in the battlefield not prior. You will never be a true warrior until you have learned how to fight, and you will never learn how to fight until you learn how to endure. What is enduring? Enduring is being able to take the heat. Enduring is running this race even though you are being knocked down. Enduring is getting back up again and again and not quitting. Endurance grows patience, temperance, tolerance, and we could go on to include all the fruits of the spirit.

A true fighter is one who does not quit and learns to endure through hardships and times of trouble. In order to get our feet wet in the battlefield, we begin to endure the attacks. In fact, once you grow to the place that you put on the shoes to go and make disciples, all hell will break loose. You have now stepped out of your box to be a true disciple, and the enemy will increase the pressures in order to bring you down before you mature to the place where demons will tremble when you awaken each day. I remember someone sending me something through Facebook which said, *"When I awaken each day, the enemy says, 'Oh crap, she's up!'"* This is how it should be, that demons tremble when we awaken and they flee when we walk into a room. In fact, James said that if we resist the devil, he will flee from us.

James 4:7 (ESV) ⁷ Submit yourselves therefore to God. Resist the devil, and he will flee from you.

We discussed above that we are to be aware of those places we choose to go witness Jesus until we become strong, but we have no say so about where we will tread in the spiritual realm. You need to know that once you begin sharing Jesus, spiritual forces of darkness will try to stop you. satan may have hated you before, but now you are targeted. However, we need not be afraid because once we have grown to that place with God, we also have leagues of angels and the Holy Spirit on our side. You must have grown in the belt and the breastplate because if you have not grown to where you know who you are in Christ, you will be knocked off your feet continually. When this happens, instead of standing up and fighting for your purpose, you will be running backwards to your spiritual leader crying because it is tougher than you thought. Here is the deal, God desires warriors and warriors must become tough. We endure to the end but our prize awaits us in heaven as we continue running the race Paul spoke of.

1 Corinthians 9:24-27 (ESV) ^{24} *Do you not know that in a race all the runners run, but only one receives the prize? So run that you may obtain it.* ^{25} *Every athlete exercises self-control in all things. They do it to receive a perishable wreath, but we an imperishable.* ^{26} *So I do not run aimlessly; I do not box as one beating the air.* ^{27} *But I discipline my body and keep it under control, lest after preaching to others I myself should be disqualified.*

As we step out into the field, our faith will grow because we will be tested, tried, and then we will become triumphant as our faith grows. At this point, instead of running backwards, we will begin to lift that shield. When we pass the test and endure the trials, we will triumph over our enemies and death will not keep us down.

Romans 8:2 (AMP) ^{2} *For the law of the Spirit of life [which is] in Christ Jesus [the law of our new being] has freed me from the law of sin and of death.*

Romans 8:11 (AMP) ^{11} *And if the Spirit of Him Who raised up Jesus from the dead dwells in you, [then] He Who raised up Christ Jesus from the dead will also restore to life your mortal (short-lived, perishable) bodies through His Spirit Who dwells in you.*

Deuteronomy 28:7 (AMP) ^{7} *The Lord shall cause your enemies who rise up against you to be defeated before your face; they shall come out against you one way and flee before you seven ways.*

The battlefield makes boys into men, and God will make Christians into Warriors. It is grow up time; it is no more feeling sorry for yourself; it is no more tucking your tail and running to that person who understands you with tears in your eyes. This is do or die time! Yes, maybe I sound like a drill sergeant, but if we do not get to this place, we will never grow up and mature. Our military sergeants do not baby our men and women, and we would be appalled if we heard them do so. We do not want babies in the battlefield fighting for our freedoms, and God does not want babies fighting for souls.

The good news is that as we spend day in and day out in the battlefield, our faith is continually exercised and God is looking down upon us saying, *"Good job; keep it up!"* I want God on my side, don't you? I want to be all that God called me to be, and in order to do that, I must begin to believe every single thing that is in the Word of God. It will be His Words that grow me into the image and likeness of my God who created me. When things get tough, we get tougher, and it is at this place that we understand we needed that Shield of Faith on before the Helmet. The helmet may be good to protect many things, but prior to being fully trained in order to fight, we need protection.

Yes, our helmet will protect us in the battle and it is powerful, but once we put on the Gospel Shoes, all hell will break loose. We need the shield to stop the fiery darts of the enemy immediately. Yes, I said we are to expect to be attacked, but that does not mean we are to just lay there and take it. We are to fight back but until we grow and learn how to fight, the shield will help to guard us. In fact, if we really believe God is who He says He is and we are who He says we are, then our shield of faith should be strong enough through Christ to protect us and those we love from the powers of darkness.

Let's look at this scenario in the natural and then in the spiritual. In the natural, before we leave our safe havens, which would be

378

our homes, we get dressed first. After we clothe ourselves, our bodies, we begin to pick up those things we would normally take with us. If you are a woman, you would grab your purse and a man would pick up his wallet. We get our car keys and head for the door. Draw a visual in your mind. Look at your purse or wallet as your shield. You are fully clothed with your belt, breastplate, and shoes. You pick up your shield which is what you need for defense. It contains your Driver's License if you get pulled over; it contains your insurance card if you were to be in a wreck, and it contains your checkbook, cash or credit cards to keep from running out of gas. Our keys would be the source or power used to take us from one destination to another as compared to our gospel shoes. Our keys take us each step with purpose. If we never put on our shoes, we would never go into those places we are called, and we will never grow or experience what God intended us to experience. Without the keys, we would be on foot; without the keys, life would be extremely harder; without the keys, life would be very treacherous. Yes, years ago there were no cars but with new technology, we are able to go further and do more than in biblical days. And, if we use the resources we have been given today in order to glorify God, much can be accomplished. Therefore, the key is essentially what is needed for success, meaning our gospel shoes. We can gain all the knowledge and wisdom through God's Word, and we can know who we are in Christ, but until we step out of our box and go, we will never be true disciples.

Taking all the necessary things needed in our purse and wallets are equivalent to picking up our shield with all the tools we have grown in through the Word of God and going forth in our Gospel Shoes by faith. Without faith, we know that we are not even pleasing to God. Without faith, we are saying, *"God, I believe in you and I believe in Jesus, but I don't really believe you are who*

379

you say you are and I don't believe you are capable of doing *everything your Word says."* Without faith, we really do not believe at all. Without our shield, it is like walking into the battlefield and lying down on the terrain and saying, *"satan, come and get me because I am defeated."* This is not a soldier mentality. If we lack faith, we need to go back to applying our belt and our breastplate. We can put on the gospel shoes but without being grounded in the Word and Righteousness, we are merely walking into the battlefield naked, and the attacks will knock us completely down where we fold under the pressures and live a life of defeat instead of victory.

The last thing to recognize is that if the enemy cannot succeed in keeping us from putting on our belt, we know he will attack us in the heart area as discussed above. Then we know that if he is unsuccessful in attacking our heart, he will work on trying to cause us to fall once in the battlefield after we have applied the shoes. If we are grounded with the belt and the breastplate, we will be able to endure the attacks in the battlefield. As we endure in the midst of our storms, we will grow in faith. If all seems to be going great as we endure, satan will continue to attack us in the area of faith. Never get to the place where you think, *"Okay, all is good, I got this!"* It is when we become too confident that we let our guard down. What we are really doing is letting our shield drop down because the battles begin to seem easier. satan will continue with the attacks and he will be watching for the time you become over confident and let your guard down. It is at these times we fall.

Another way satan will beat us down is by continually attacking us trying to wear our natural bodies down. How many times in the midst of a battle do we tire? I know myself that it is not so much the battle as it is my physical body becoming drained. Anytime our military are at war, time goes on and the battles continue, they naturally become tired and weary. Until we begin to see victory in a battle, it's as though our efforts are seemingly unsuccessful. This is enduring the battle. As we engage with the shield, faith will grow, but sometimes the battles continue and continue until we grow weary and with weariness, the sense of giving up comes. This is an important lesson and one that will be discussed further in the Shield of Faith chapter, but endurance means we do not quit. Faith grows greater in time. If we quit, we basically never believed.

If satan cannot cause us to fall with the belt, breastplate, or shoes, he will continue with one storm after another in our life trying to cause us to put our shield down and give up. When this happens, we walk off the battlefield. We become weary and feel as though all efforts to win souls have not been successful, so we back down and quit! This can occur even as we witness to those who cross our paths. We watch those that we have planted and watered do well and then fall back into the world. Sometimes no matter how much effort we give, it will seem as though we planted, watered, and became excited as we watched souls grow only to see them backslide. This can make us feel as though we did not do something right and then we become discouraged. This is where we have to understand that God cultivates; we only plant and water. Never become discouraged because if you planted and watered, even though they may have fallen, some eventually come back. I know this for certain. I have seen it time and time again especially in my daughters. I went through times of believing, this time they are sold out only for them to fall and return to the world. My part is to just plant and perhaps water if needed, then allow God to do the rest. If it did not take, then it is given to God. We only do our part and we do not try to be God. Once I know that I have done all required of me, I merely say,

"God, I give them to You." Of course, we continue to pray for all those we have ministered to.

Helmet of Salvation (5)

Ephesians 6:10-17 (NKJV) [10] *Finally, my brethren, be strong in the Lord and in the power of His might.* [11] *Put on the whole armor of God, that you may be able to stand against the wiles of the devil.* [12] *For we do not wrestle against flesh and blood, but against principalities, against powers, against the rulers of the darkness of this age, against spiritual hosts of wickedness in the heavenly places.* [13] *Therefore take up the whole armor of God, that you may be able to withstand in the evil day, and having done all, to stand.* [14] *Stand therefore, having (1) girded your waist with truth, having (2) put on the breastplate of righteousness,* [15] *and having (3) shod your feet with the preparation of the gospel of peace;* [16] *above all, (4) taking the shield of faith with which you will be able to quench all the fiery darts of the wicked one.* [17] *And (5) take the helmet of salvation,*

The helmet, which is the fifth piece of armor, protects our brain or it can be referred to as our mind. This is the next to the last piece of armor to apply. I remember during this study asking God, *"Why would it be almost last?"* As I am about to share the importance of this piece of armor with you, you may be asking the same thing I asked God some time ago. If this piece is so important, why was it placed almost last? I have said that all pieces are important but they are applied as matter of importance based on the battle we face. This is not about importance but about what needs to be on first, second, and so forth due to this spiritual battle we endure on a daily basis. All things arranged in the proper order also have to do with our own Christian walk and what needs to be strengthened before attempting another piece of the armor. Just like in military boot camps, they train them in certain areas first before they go to areas which may actually be more important but useless if they were not perfected in other matters first. In this we would understand that it may not be what is actually the most important but what is important for today. It would kind of be like putting the cart before the horse. We cannot begin to pull a cart behind a horse if we are not trained in knowing all details about the horse first. Same with the armor, Paul knew we had to grow up in other areas before we could actually become warriors that were ready for full-fledged war. When Paul put them in order of importance, it was what is important first in order to transform us into the image of Christ. If you knew nothing about Jesus, how could you understand faith when you do not even know Christ? If you do not know anything about the Word of God, how could you understand applying the Gospel Shoes?

Therefore, the helmet must go on right before picking up the sword for a reason, yet it is extremely important. Once we pick up the sword, we know we are walking forth to battle forces of darkness yet to be understood. Yes, we picked up the shield; however, the shield protects and the sword destroys. Therefore, we can defend before actually destroying. This will be discussed further in the shield and sword chapters, but for now, we need to see why the helmet is vital to put on right before stepping out with our sword into spiritual battle.

Remember, Paul was speaking to those who were disciples, they understood salvation. So, the helmet did not need to be applied first in that case. However, even though we may have come to recognize just who Jesus is, this does not mean we fully understand salvation. Much of what I teach today in regards to the helmet is to go much deeper into just what salvation means. I remember sharing that many times, just because we believe that we are saved, we feel that we do not need to study salvation. This is ludicrous. Salvation is the most important thing we can gain in wisdom, knowledge, and understanding because without knowing it fully, we may miss eternal life. Why would we not want to know all there is to know about salvation? After all, it is only through salvation that we will make it to heaven, but Christians are boisterous when it comes to studying this in depth. I believe satan is behind this in order to keep Christians in the dark. If the only way to make it to heaven is through salvation, then I want to thoroughly study this just so that I am assured I am truly saved and not blinded in any area. This should be our mindset. Remember, we should never think we have arrived. After all, Jesus even said that few would actually find heaven yet most believers or church goers think they will be there. There is something terribly wrong with this picture, and I believe it is something to contemplate.

Matthew 7:14 (AMP) ¹⁴ But the gate is narrow (contracted by pressure) and the way is straitened and compressed that leads away to life, and few are those who find it.

Salvation becomes our way of life. This is about being saturated in the love of Christ. This is about being brainwashed or influenced by the Word of God as discussed in chapter 3. This is one of the hardest pieces of armor to put on and keep on. Paul noted in 1 Corinthians, that he died daily to self. Paul did so in order to acquire fellowship with Christ.

1 Corinthians 15:31 (AMP) ³¹ [I assure you] by the pride which I have in you in [your fellowship and union with] Christ Jesus our Lord, that I die daily [I face death every day and die to self].

If our desire is fellowship with Christ, we give up our life, our way of living, our lifestyle because if we are not doing that, in reality, we are in a backslidden state. We cannot straddle the fence. We either love God and His way of life or we love the world.

Romans 8:5-8 (TNIV) *⁵ Those who live according to the sinful nature have their minds set on what that nature desires; but those who live in accordance with the Spirit have their minds set on what the Spirit desires. ⁶ The mind controlled by the sinful nature is death, but the mind controlled by the Spirit is life and peace. ⁷ The sinful mind is hostile to God; it does not submit to God's law, nor can it do so. ⁸ Those controlled by the sinful nature cannot please God.*

God's way of life should spill over into our life. Our way of life lines up with the way Jesus lived and the apostles lived. Paul shows us this way of life through Christ.

*1 Corinthians 4:17 (AMP)¹⁷For this very cause I sent to you Timothy, who is my beloved and trustworthy child in the Lord, who will recall to your **minds** my methods of proceeding and course of conduct and **way of life** in Christ, such as I teach everywhere in each of the churches.*

The way Jesus taught, we should teach. There should be nothing held back and our life should be an example for those who choose to follow. Our choices in this life should be to choose life and not death, light and not darkness, the Word and not the world, and the Spirit and not our flesh. When we choose all those things which bring life, we choose to crucify our own flesh and allow Christ to live through us.

Romans 6:6 (AMP) ⁶We know that our old (unrenewed) self was nailed to the cross with Him in order that [our] body [which is the instrument]

385

of sin might be made ineffective and inactive for evil, that we might no longer be the slaves of sin.

Prior to lifting the only offensive weapon and actually fighting, we cover our head with the helmet. When we fight offensively, we begin to take back what is rightfully ours. Our defensive weapon is our shield and our offensive weapon is our sword. Prior to going into battle with the sword, we will apply the piece of armor, the helmet, to protect us throughout the battle no matter how great. The helmet becomes a check point to make sure we are ready before entering enemy terrain.

I like to call the helmet our pep-talk. If we look at a boxing match or even a football game, right before a boxer goes into the ring or the players in the football game begin their play, there is pep-talk. The football team all huddle together for encouragement, motivation, strategy, tactics, and to celebrate. Usually the leader of the huddle may be the team captain, but the huddle is necessary in order to drown out the high level of noise during a game when the field communication can be difficult. The same with a boxer, the coach will gather around him as he puts in the mouth piece, wipes the sweat from his forehead and all the while he is encouraging him and giving him pointers. These pep-talks are done in order to achieve success. Prior to us going into enemy terrain to fight the good fight, we need to be completely prepared and we will see that our helmet does just that. Jesus is our team captain when the noise level of demonic activity is such that we are unable to focus or see clearly through the storms. This is where our helmet comes into play. Knowing that we are a child of the most High God and Jesus is our Captain, we understand that we have a right to our inheritance of a sound mind, peace, power, and anointing from on High.

However, the helmet in biblical days actually protected much more than just our mind. We discussed in the helmet chapter briefly about what was protected but will emphasize this in this chapter due to the great importance of this one piece of armor. As we study this, we will understand how the helmet becomes our pep-talk. The helmet not only protected the mind but also, the eyes and ears, the mouth, the neck and the actual air which we breathe in. We will look at each of these areas.

Mind of Christ (5a)

We are at the place of being brainwashed as discussed in chapter two. Dealing with our mind, it is the centralized location of our thoughts, beliefs, concepts and the area which controls our choices in life. The brain is crucial to our existence as it controls our voluntary and involuntary movements. The voluntary movements are those movements that we control such as using our arms, legs, etc., and the involuntary would be areas such as breathing, blinking, our heart beating, etc. Without our brain we do not exist and without it performing accurately, we would not be whole and sound.

René Descartes, a 17th-century philosopher, said, *"I think, therefore I am."*[1] In Proverbs it says that what we think in our heart, this is who we are. Our mind does the thinking but our heart will persuade our mind. In other words, if we do not feel strongly about something, we will cast it aside. It becomes those things that we value and trust that persuade our lives.

Proverbs 23:7 (KJV) [7]For as he thinketh in his heart, so is he: Eat and drink, saith he to thee; but his heart is not with thee.

387

It is through our brain that we feel emotions, personalities develop, and memories are made and stored. Our brain consumes enormous amounts of oxygen every second and fuels energy even while sleeping as the involuntary activities continue. Our brain continues to change even as we age; therefore, it does not matter what our age, where we came from, or what has been spoken over us, our brain is capable of change. However, the brain does not work alone but is the central part of the nervous system. Spiritually, we do not work alone either. Our brain may be the key to what controls our lives in the natural, but in the supernatural, our brains or mind can be renewed to that of Jesus Christ.

Ephesians 4:23 (AMP) [23] And be constantly renewed in the spirit of your mind [having a fresh mental and spiritual attitude],

In order for our mind to be protected, we apply the Helmet of Salvation. The helmet is crucial in order to protect one of the most vital organs within the human body. Why is it referred to as salvation? It is referred to as salvation because without understanding and knowing salvation as we have discussed, we can go no further. Without running towards Jesus Christ for our salvation, we cannot have the mind of Christ.

1 Corinthians 2:14-16 (ESV) [14] The natural person does not accept the things of the Spirit of God, for they are folly to him, and he is not able to understand them because they are spiritually discerned. [15] The spiritual person judges all things, but is himself to be judged by no one. [16] "For who has understood the mind of the Lord so as to instruct him?" But we have the mind of Christ.

Without the mind of Christ there is no renewing our minds to think differently from the world. We would continue to think as this world which is destined to die in their sin; therefore, there is no hope. Jesus said in Luke that we are to be careful how we listen or how we perceive something. If we do not have an understanding of salvation, our knowledge will not be spiritual and those things we assume are correct based on worldly knowledge will be that which is false. This is not a win-win situation. When we do not have spiritual knowledge, we lose everything.

Luke 8:18 (AMP) [18]Be careful therefore how you listen. For to him who has [spiritual knowledge] will more be given; and from him who does not have [spiritual knowledge], even what he thinks and guesses and supposes that he has will be taken away.

Unless we saturate our lives in Jesus Christ, our thinking will be immature.

1 Corinthians 14:20 (AMP) [20] Brethren, do not be children [immature] in your thinking; continue to be babes in [matters of] evil, but in your minds be mature [men].

There are many brain cells which can divide and grow but with billions of brain cells within the human body, much of the function remains a mystery to man. Man will never understand the complexity of the mind because only a being that is complex in nature knows all the mysteries of this intricate organ. God knew the complexities of the mind of Jesus because He is the Creator of all things. We have the mind of Christ when we line up our thinking with God's Word and not the world.

1 Corinthians 2:16 (AMP) [16] For who has known or understood the mind (the counsels and purposes) of the Lord so as to guide and instruct Him and give Him knowledge? But we have the mind of Christ (the Messiah) and do hold the thoughts (feelings and purposes) of His heart.

It is through running this race while continually seeking more wisdom and knowledge of the Word of God that our thoughts line up with Jesus' thoughts and our purpose becomes His purpose. This organ alone, (the brain) if lined up with God's Word, will line our steps up daily on the path chosen for each of us. However, when we choose not to apply our helmet in order to protect our mind, our thoughts, feelings, and purposes, then our lives will line up with the world and this will be our fall from grace.

Revelation 2:23 (AMP) [23] *And I will strike her children (her proper followers) dead [thoroughly exterminating them]. And all the assemblies (churches) shall recognize and understand that I am He Who searches minds (the thoughts, feelings, and purposes) and the [inmost] hearts, and I will give to each of you [the reward for what you have done] as your work deserves.*

Our mind is the hardest thing to bring into alignment with the Word of God and is protected by the helmet. We battle within our minds daily. Our mind can be our worst enemy and would probably be the cause of most of the defeat within our lives. Our mind will be the area hardest to train, conquer, and tame. When we applied our belt and our breastplate, we began bringing our mind into subjection to the Word of God; however, there is much work there and a lot to see. Once we apply God's Word through the belt, and we know who we are in Christ with the breastplate, our minds should desire to line up with the Word of God. We gain knowledge and wisdom through the Word of God when we study, and when we step out into the battlefield as a disciple, we begin to gain more wisdom through our actions and those experiences we triumph through. When we do not count it all joy for the storms of life, we have gained no wisdom. Wisdom happens as we walk through storms victoriously and this deals with how much time we have spent applying the Word to our lives in order to gain the wisdom. This is important that you understand this. All pieces work together as I have said over and over again. We will never gain knowledge without reading and studying. We read to KNOW something – knowledge! We gain knowledge by reading the whole Word of God and also we can gain wisdom by focusing on the Book of Proverbs. The Book of Proverbs is the book of wisdom. We should conduct our lives according to living as spoken in Proverbs. You cannot live part of it and not all of it. We either apply all the Word of God to our lives or the outcome will not be God's best. However, as we study God's Word, we should take that knowledge along with wisdom from Proverbs into the battlefield. Knowledge and wisdom can be gained by reading but both can also be acquired by living what you have read.

Let's look at knowledge first. Have you ever heard of firsthand knowledge? Firsthand knowledge comes by seeing or living something. We have all heard the saying, *"seeing is believing."* Firsthand knowledge is stored much deeper within our heart than just reading about something. When we were in school, we learned many things in order to pass tests but today, we probably would not remember most of what we studied. When we walk through those things we have read, it becomes experiences. Through experiences, we gain a wealth of knowledge. There is no knowledge like knowledge we have lived through. You cannot ever fully understand what it is like being in a hurricane unless you lived through one, and you will never understand what it is like to give birth to a baby unless you have given birth. You are able to say, *"I know what it feels like to have a baby,"* and *"I know what it is like to be in a hurricane."* It does not matter how many times you study it or hear about it, it is not the same as firsthand knowledge.

The second thing is wisdom. As we come to know something not just from reading about it, we gain wisdom. Wisdom comes as we learn to walk through a situation that we have knowledge in. We cannot gain knowledge without reading and then we learn to take that knowledge into our battles and walk it out, and Proverbs is a great place to study in order to see if we did well as we face our own battles in the battlefield. Once we have achieved the knowledge and begin to gain wisdom, the last thing needed would be to have the understanding. To explain understanding, suppose you had the wisdom and were walking through a storm, you did everything according to God's Word. You kept your joy and peace; you were patient and continued on the course allowing God to walk you through that storm. After the storm was over with, you felt pretty good because you never got angry or upset, you did not lose your peace, and you continued to have faith God was in control. So, after the storm died down, did you understand why it happened to begin with? Many times you will not understand; however, you followed God through the course. It is only through God that we receive the understanding, and when we do, it all makes sense. However, most of the time the understanding will come right away because God desires to grow you; understanding is delayed when it deals with a much greater piece of the puzzle, and the timing is not right at that moment.

Proverbs 4:1-7 (NIV) Get Wisdom at Any Cost [1] *Listen, my sons, to a father's instruction; pay attention and gain understanding.* [2] *I give you sound learning, so do not forsake my teaching.* [3] *For I too was a son to my father, still tender, and cherished by my mother.* [4] *Then he taught me, and he said to me, "Take hold of my words with all your heart; keep my commands, and you will live.* [5] *Get wisdom, get understanding; do not forget my words or turn away from them.* [6] *Do not forsake wisdom, and she will protect you; love her, and she will watch over you.* [7] *The beginning of wisdom is this: Get wisdom. Though it cost all you have, get understanding.*

When there is a much bigger picture, we may not receive the understanding in a timely manner, or we may not receive the understanding because of an action on our part. In other words, we may think we have done well when; in fact, there may be an area that God is dealing with that we have not seen. Whatever the reason, we must trust that He holds the end result in His hand. So now, we can see that understanding will not come until our minds are subjected to the Word of God. We cannot receive understanding without first receiving the wisdom and knowledge, and it takes discipline on our part if we are ever going to grow to be all God desires. We are acquiring discipline by being in the battlefield, but all areas must line up with God's Word. We can have all the wisdom and knowledge, but until we have the understanding in those areas that we need to grow, we have grown to a degree but there is still so much more. It will be through the understanding that much revelation is gained, and we also must see in order to gain this understanding through God's Word may cost us everything. At what cost are you willing to give in order to gain?

For the helmet to protect our mind to keep it pure, takes understanding the power of lust. Lust is an area that affects our mind and results in our heart not being pure. We cannot keep a pure heart when we allow our mind to be influenced by lust.

1 Peter 4:1 (AMP) [1]*SO, SINCE Christ suffered in the flesh for us, for you, arm yourselves with the same thought and purpose [patiently to suffer rather than fail to please God]. For whoever has **suffered in the flesh [having the mind of Christ]** is done with [intentional] sin [has stopped pleasing himself and the world, and pleases God]*

How do we suffer in the flesh? This is by letting go of self; it is a sacrifice. When we begin to think like Christ, it becomes a lifestyle. You may say this is too hard, but once you completely climb over that fence instead of straddling it, it will become a choice that you would never go back to the other side of the fence to become who you once were.

The helmet is vital to protecting our mind that we do not lust within our mind. Our mind must be renewed daily or continually to the Word of God. Our thoughts must be pure if we desire to live a life with Christ. There may be times that thoughts come which are not pure, but it is not about the thoughts that come but rather what we do with the thoughts when they come. We will all have thoughts that are not pure, but we do not have to receive those thoughts. We have a choice to either cast down those thoughts or meditate on them.

Corinthians 10:3-6 (NKJV) [3] *For though we walk in the flesh, we do not war according to the flesh.* [4] *For the weapons of our warfare are not carnal but mighty in God for pulling down strongholds,* [5] *casting down arguments and every high thing that exalts itself against the knowledge of God, bringing every thought into captivity to the obedience of Christ,* [6] *and being ready to punish all disobedience when your obedience is fulfilled.*

When we apply the helmet we are actually guarding our mind because once we understand salvation and choose to run the same race as Paul, we should also come to know who we are in Christ. We should become grounded in God's Word and fully activated in sharing Jesus with the world. We understand that we are on the winning side. Being on the winning side, we never let our guard down because our enemy will try to attack us even once we have come this far. Remember, never think you have arrived.

394

satan is not stupid; in fact, he is very smart but he was not smart enough to keep from being cast out of heaven. However, he will continue to cause Christians to fall, and we must be on top of all of his tactics and strategies. Being grounded in God's Word means never to slack in the areas you have already triumphed through. We never come to the place where we can take a vacation from God's Word. We never come to the place where we are not meditating on those Scriptures that taught us who we are in Christ, our purpose in this life, and our daily battles. Like I have said, this becomes a lifestyle. We are on the winning side and remain victorious unless we allow the guard to be taken off of our mind.

2 Corinthians 4:4 (AMP) ⁴For the god of this world has blinded the unbelievers' minds [that they should not discern the truth], preventing them from seeing the illuminating light of the Gospel of the glory of Christ (the Messiah), Who is the Image and Likeness of God.

Many times people will run and run this race until they become burned out. This happens when there is no balance. satan looks for opportunities in order to steal, kill, and destroy. *(John 10:10)*

I know how easy it is to fall from grace, but this only happens when we are not diligent in our walk and maintaining our armor. The tactics and strategies of our enemy most often focus on our mind. satan knows if he can cause us to slip in our mind, he can continue to knock us down. When Eve fell from grace, it began with the thoughts she meditated on that satan had spoken. *(Genesis 3:1-5)*

Eve could have cast aside those thoughts but instead, she dwelt on them just like we do. It was through thoughts that I fell from grace many years ago. satan will come at us by using others to speak negatively over us, or he may bluff us in areas where we are weaker. When I think about the word bluff, I think about a card game. How many times are card games won by a bluff? satan can use people you are close to in order to get you to agree to something you normally would not have agreed because that person is working to convince you that it's not what you think it is. You listen and listen until you are worn down and give in. I can give an example such as someone that knows you are trying to walk this walk with God and they influence you to go somewhere or do something that you would never have done, but they wore you down until you gave in and felt guilty afterwards. The enemy will work on you even when you may be doing something for God, but you begin to listen to the wrong voice that convinces you to keep on and keep on when God may have been saying, this is as far as you go. However, when you keep on and on until you are at a place of exhaustion, you become drained by doing it in your own strength and not God's. Anytime we are burned out, we are using our own strength and not allowing God to work through us, especially in battles. If God is fighting for us, why would we operate in fear, worry, or allow stress to take over?

*Philippians 4:7 (AMP)[7]And God's peace [shall be yours, that tranquil state of a soul assured of its salvation through Christ, and so fearing nothing from God and being content with its earthly lot of whatever sort that is, that peace] which transcends all understanding shall garrison and mount guard over your **hearts** and **minds** in Christ Jesus.*

We can see that the heart and mind work together. We are assured through salvation or by applying the Helmet of Salvation that we should fear nothing; we should be content and at peace within our whole being. Understand that salvation does not mean just eternal life. Salvation is an assurance that we are joined together with Christ and being joined, we have a purpose while here on earth as well. Prior to coming to know Jesus, there was a veil which separated us from God. However, we still remain separated when our heart remains hardened. With a hardened heart, we have placed a barrier or wall around us that keeps God out. A hardened heart puts us at a disadvantage because we are unable to be taught. If we do not allow God to break through the hardness and heal whatever needs to be healed, the veil will remain on our heart just as in Old Testament times, and we will continue to be separated from God. The veil is only lifted as we grow to understand the Truth and then the Truth will set us free. In fact, when the veil is lifted, we gain back the power to understand.

*2 Corinthians 3:14 (AMP)[14]In fact, their minds were grown hard and calloused [they had become dull and had lost the power of understanding]; for until this present day, when the Old Testament (the old covenant) is being read, that same veil still lies [on their **hearts**], not being lifted [to reveal] that in Christ it is made void and done away.*

We are judged according to the law when we have not made the choice to accept Jesus Christ. Therefore our battle within our mind deals with our thoughts and determines where we are in our walk with Christ. Many claim they are a Christian, yet their actions are contrary to someone who is genuinely a Disciple of Christ.
This seems right that the Helmet of Salvation would be applied right before the last piece of our armor because our mind is the hardest thing to bring in alignment with the Word of God. Prior to walking forth into the battle, the helmet actually reminds us of many things in order to persevere in the battle.

Matthew 13:13-17 (ESV) [13]This is why I speak to them in parables, because seeing they do not see, and hearing they do not hear, nor do they understand. [14] Indeed, in their case the prophecy of Isaiah is fulfilled that says: """You will indeed hear but never understand, and you will indeed see but never perceive." [15] *For this people's heart has grown dull, and with their ears they can barely hear, and their eyes they have closed, lest they should see with their eyes and hear with their ears and understand with their heart and turn, and I would heal them.'* [16] *But blessed are your eyes, for they see, and your ears, for they hear.* [17] *For truly, I say to you, many prophets and righteous people longed to see what you see, and did not see it, and to hear what you hear, and did not hear it.*

We are reminded that the helmet protects not only our mind to understand but also our eyes and ears that we are not blinded from truth.

Eyes & Ears Open to Truth (5b)

In biblical days, the Roman soldiers wore a helmet which not only covered their head but also the whole face, to include the neck. Therefore, the Helmet of Salvation covers our eyes and our ears as well. It is through Jesus Christ that we are saved and through walking out our salvation, our mind is renewed to think like Christ and our eyes and ears are open to Truth. When we are not walking with Christ, our eyes and ears are blinded from the Truth. If we are living any lies, according to Jesus, our father is the father of lies.

John 8:38-44 (NLT) [38] *I am telling you what I saw when I was with my Father. But you are following the advice of your father."* [39] *"Our father is Abraham!" they declared. "No," Jesus replied, "for if you were really the children of Abraham, you would follow his example.* [40] *Instead, you are trying to kill me because I told you the truth, which I heard from God. Abraham never did such a thing.* [41] *No, you are imitating your real father." They replied, "We aren't illegitimate children! God himself is our true Father."* [42] *Jesus told them, "If God were your Father, you would love me, because I have come to you from God. I am not here on my own, but he sent me.* [43] *Why can't you understand what I am saying? It's because you can't even hear me!* [44] *For you are the children of your*

398

father the devil, and you love to do the evil things he does. He was a murderer from the beginning. He has always hated the truth, because there is no truth in him. When he lies, it is consistent with his character; for he is a liar and the father of lies.

As we walk this walk and obtain the knowledge and understanding needed to be fully clothed in the Armor of God, our eyes and ears will continually be open to Truth and we shall live a life which is blessed.

Matthew 13:16 (NIV) [16] *But blessed are your eyes because they see, and your ears because they hear.*

We touched on lust above when we were studying about protecting our mind with the helmet. Lust is a huge strong hold that has probably affected every single Christian today and many continue to remain bound by this spirit. We will discuss spiritual forces in another chapter in more detail. However, when we think about lust, we think about it in a sexual perspective, but lust is far more than just sexual. When someone lusts, they have a strong desire for those things which are of this world. John warns us strongly about engaging in lust.

1 John 2:15-17 (HCSB) A Warning about the World [15]*Do not love the world or the things that belong to the world. If anyone loves the world, love for the Father is not in him. Because everything that belongs to the world* [16] *the **lust of the flesh**, **the lust of the eyes**, and **the pride in one's lifestyle**—is not from the Father, but is from the world.* [17] *And the world with its lust is passing away, but the one who does God's will remains forever.*

Lust actually begins with our eyes and ears. This warning is spoken to Christians. The world could care less about what John had to say, but this is addressed to those who are followers of Christ. It is detrimental that Christians are careful about what they listen to and what they gaze upon. We have no business as Christians listening to music or anything else which is contrary to the Word of God, and we have no business entertaining our senses with images that conflict with the lifestyle of Jesus. If we cannot imagine Jesus sitting down watching the filth on our televisions today and listening to the degrading music, then we have no business engaging in those things either. What we fail to see is that these things are tactics of the enemy to keep us bound in areas so that we will never rise above where we are currently and advance in the wisdom, knowledge, and understanding only given to us by God. When we willingly make the choice to step outside the boundaries outlined in the Word, God will allow our eyes and ears to be closed to Truth.

2 Corinthians 4:4 (ESV) ⁴In their case the god of this world has blinded the minds of the unbelievers, to keep them from seeing the light of the gospel of the glory of Christ, who is the image of God.

The next time you are in a storm and cannot seem to focus in order to walk through victoriously, look around at your lifestyle and see if it would be a lifestyle that Jesus would engage in. I have said this and will say it again, we want to run to church for prayer when the storms get tough. We desire to run to God to pull us out of those dark places. When I am approached by someone in a dark place and I have seen that their walk in the world is no different than the world, I cannot stand and believe for them that God is going to miraculously pull them through. Sometimes it takes that strong word from another Christian to tell you that God wants you to clean up your lifestyle, and He may allow you to remain in that dark place to awaken you. Yes, when we first come to know Jesus, He just wants us to come as we are and He will begin the cleanup process afterwards. However, Jesus never meant for you to come and remain as you are. We come to Christ because we desire our lives to change for the good, but sometimes our lives will remain in a filthy mess because we choose to remain living a filthy lifestyle. Our Helmet of Salvation is basically saying, *"Lord, I put on this helmet of salvation that it protects my mind to the mind of Christ that I hold His thoughts, His purposes within my heart; it protects my eyes and ears to Truth that I refrain from all ungodliness; therefore, my eyes and ears are continually open to Truth and I am set free from all areas that I have been bound!"*

John 8:31-32(ESV) The Truth Will Set You Free [31] So Jesus said to the Jews who had believed him, "If you abide in my word, you are truly my disciples, [32] and you will know the truth, and the truth will set you free."

This is what the helmet does. This is what our journey of salvation should look like. We either desire this or as the Scripture said above, we enjoy living in our sin and our father is the father of lies because we have chosen to listen to a lie instead of live a life of Truth!

In protecting our mind, eyes, and ears from lust, we refrain from filling our mind with the things of this world. If we love things in this world more than God, it becomes lust to us. If we choose a pleasure of this world over being a true disciple, we have chosen to engage in lust. Our mind cannot be filled with lust unless we feed it. The mind has no opening, and in order to feed it, the openings are through our eyes and ears. What we feed our eyes and ears go into our mind, and when we continually day in and day out feed our mind the lusts of this world, it begins to be stored in our heart. Remember the Scripture we discussed, as a man thinks in his heart, so is he? When we continually feed this into our bodies, it builds up in our heart, and we become that which has been stored within our heart. Prior to Jesus, if you struggled with strong holds in this world and you were delivered, go back to living like the world and see how long it takes for those same feelings, thoughts, doubts, and afflictions to come upon your life once again. We will never be like Jesus if we fill our mind with the world, and if we fill our mind with the world, Jesus said that your father is not God.

Our eyes and ears should be open to those things above and not deceived by the lusts of this world. Our eyes should never lust for those things we see because this world is temporal and will pass away. Where are you storing your treasures today? Most store their treasures in things of this world not things above. Our mind encases all our senses, what we feel physically, what we smell, what we see, and what we hear. All these senses can be transformed into the image of Christ that our will and all our emotions and desires become God's will not our own. As we line up to the Word, we begin to be able to see things through our spiritual eyes, and this is with understanding. We see the way God sees through and by faith.

Luke 10:23 (HCSB) *23 Then turning to His disciples He said privately, "The eyes that see the things you see are blessed!*

Luke 2:30 (HCSB) *30 For my eyes have seen Your **salvation**.*

It is not through the natural eyes that we will see those things which are a mystery to man but through the spiritual eyes. It was the disciples in that day whom were blessed. It was the disciples whom continually sought out Jesus and became accustomed to His lifestyle that were able to see those things most will never see because they were able to see things through the eyes of God. You may be saying, *"How were they blessed?"* After all, according to the Bible, the disciples that followed Jesus, they died for the cause; they were continually persecuted and hated by those in the world; they lived from place to place just like Jesus with no place to call their home. So, how were they blessed?

John 15:18-19 (ESV) The Hatred of the World [18] *"If the world hates you, know that it has hated me before it hated you.* [19] *If you were of the world, the world would love you as its own; but because you are not of the world, but I chose you out of the world, therefore the world hates you.*

Matthew 8:19-20 (ESV) [19] *And a scribe came up and said to him, "Teacher, I will follow you wherever you go."* [20] *And Jesus said to him, "Foxes have holes, and birds of the air have nests, but the Son of Man has nowhere to lay his head."*

It's very easy to see that the world we live in would say those men lived in poverty; they had no worldly possessions; they were nothing more than what we call the homeless today. No wonder the world hated them; the world today judges and hates those who live in poverty. Perhaps the word *"hate"* is too harsh, but even though we may not say the word *"hate,"* when we judge others harshly according to the world's standards, we do not accept them. If we do not accept someone, isn't that the same thing as disliking them? We can sugar coat the words all we like, but let's call it like it is. If you do not like someone, you certainly could not say that you love them. Biblically speaking, there are no gray areas; it is either black or white. We either like something or we don't like it. Now you may like something or someone more than someone else, but it is still like or dislike, no in between. Jesus gave us a new commandment to love others, and this includes those we would consider our enemies.

John 13:34 (ESV) [34] *A new commandment I give to you, that you love one another: just as I have loved you, you also are to love one another.*

Luke 6:27 (ESV) Love Your Enemies [27] *"But I say to you who hear, Love your enemies, do good to those who hate you,*

Jesus never said we are to like them but love them. He doesn't even consider that there is like and there is love. The Word talks about love and the Word talks about hate. We call it like and we call it dislike, but it is love and hate. We are to love all regardless of who they are, if they are homeless, poor, or anything else that does not fit into our worldly standards. The problem is that we have become accustomed to living like the world and not like Jesus or the disciples lived. Please, do not put words in my mouth because I am not telling anyone to go and sell their homes and live on the street. Yes, this is a different era, but the Word of God has never changed. If we cannot let go of our lives enough to walk as Christ did by giving and giving and giving and loving those less fortunate and falling down on our face before God and crying out for Him to forgive how we have judged others harshly, do we honestly think we are going to be one of the few who make it to heaven?

Matthew 7:12-14 (ESV) The Golden Rule [12] *"So whatever you wish that others would do to you, do also to them, for this is the Law and the Prophets.* [13] *"Enter by the narrow gate. For the gate is wide and the way is easy that leads to destruction, and those who enter by it are many.* [14] *For the gate is narrow and the way is hard that leads to life, and those who find it are few.*

Matthew 7:21-23 (ESV) I Never Knew You [21] *"Not everyone who says to me, 'Lord, Lord,' will enter the kingdom of heaven, but the one who does the will of my Father who is in heaven.* [22] *On that day many will say to me, 'Lord, Lord, did we not prophesy in your name, and cast out demons in your name, and do many mighty works in your name?'* [23] *And then will I declare to them, 'I never knew you; depart from me, you workers of lawlessness.'*

This is all seen through spiritual eyes and many of us are blinded where we are unable to see what God sees, and we are deaf to where we are unable to hear what God hears. Can you hear the cries of the hungry or perhaps those who are suffering from the afflictions of this world such as poverty, sickness, or disease? Are you able to feel what God feels? Let's ask ourselves again, how were the disciples blessed? I will tell you how they were blessed. They had eyes that could see greater than those who look with mere natural eyes, and they had ears that could hear much greater than the world that hears through natural ears. They were able to see what God sees, hear what God hears, and their heart was able to break for those same things that Jesus' heart broke for. We need to look at this picture because there is something wrong when our desires are for more of the world and not more of God.

Not to discourage anyone because it would be easy to feel as though you are not capable of being able to do this. You are absolutely right. We are not capable of loving like Jesus did and does, but by faith, we believe that one step at a time God transforms us more into His image. The battles in this world are all spiritual and the strongholds in your life did not happen yesterday. God knows this. God knows that satan has had a long time working on you and your desires. However, if we really desire to be at a different place with God, we gradually begin by letting go of this world. We begin as we walk by faith and not by sight, trusting that God is doing a work within us. Our battles will be won when we stop seeing as the world sees and begin to see as God sees. We cannot see what God sees without understanding and that only comes after we acquire the wisdom and the knowledge. We do not battle in the natural realm but in the spiritual. Even those who do not know Jesus, daily they are battling in the spiritual realm, but they do not live victoriously in those battles because they have no wisdom, knowledge, or understanding. You may know people or even yourself at a time when you did not believe in Jesus, and you thought your life was okay because it may have seemed that way in the natural realm; however, battles are not always won even though your natural mind may have thought you won a particular battle. We are not winners just because we win an argument; we are not winners just because we got our way; we are not winners just because things have gone according to our own selfish plans. This is wisdom according to the world, but this wisdom is foolishness and will pass away.

When our ears are closed, we are not able to even hear the voice of our Shepherd or the Holy Spirit. It is only those who are diligently following Christ that know His voice and follow Him.

John 10:27 (ESV) ^{27}*My sheep hear my voice, and I know them, and they follow me.*

Those in this world that do not have that heartfelt relationship with God, they have no understanding what it is like to even know Jesus intimately. These continually day in and day out live according to the world's standards and their own standards. If your eyes and ears do not see and hear, your heart has grown cold. Until you are humbled, you will not know Jesus and will not receive the inheritance due for those who are His true disciples.

Matthew 13:15 (HCSB) ^{15} *For this people's heart has grown callous; their ears are hard of hearing, and they have shut their eyes; otherwise they might see with their eyes and hear with their ears, understand with their hearts and turn back— and I would cure them.*

Mark 8:18 (HCSB) ^{18} *Do you have eyes, and not see, and do you have ears, and not hear? And do you not remember?*

Everywhere we look, there are multitudes going to and fro yet there is no purpose. They live to gain and live to acquire and live to leave it all with those they leave behind that they loved. Yet, they never lived for God, Jesus, or the Holy Spirit. The sad truth is that they never knew the only person that was worth dying for. In old age, they reminisce over all the years and look for meaning. Some may find the true meaning to life during this time, yet most will die and never really know God. All the years of running to gain and store up treasures for those they leave behind has been wasted with nothing to show for their life. Someday, after their own children have grown old and their grandchildren have their own families, all that is left of what was stored up may be a few old pictures that will eventually be thrown out because no one alive even knew who they were. An even sadder truth, they leave behind those they loved a legacy. We all leave a legacy even if it was not a good legacy. A legacy is anything we leave behind, it may be possessions and it may be our way of life, what we taught and handed down to our children and the cycle continues. If we are honest, we would say that if we were to die tomorrow, the legacy we are leaving those we love are some possessions and maybe we taught how to live a life that is worthy to our social standards. Those we leave behind only know what we imparted to them before we left this world and the cycle continues. The problem with this is that the only legacy that will ensure our loved ones make it to heaven is a legacy where they not only heard us speak of how to walk as a Disciple for Christ but seeing us walk as a Disciple for Christ. Our hope should be in reaching this world before it is too late to awaken generations to Truth in order to save multitudes from the Lake of Fire.

Our eyes and ears must be open and this happens as we come to understand the Helmet of Salvation and the importance that we apply it every day in order that temptation does not overcome us in our choices of what we gaze upon and listen to. People choose evil over good daily which closes their eyes and ears to Truth leaving their heart hardened. All it takes is obedience. All it takes is awakening and crying out to God for repentance in order to receive Jesus and pray that the God of the Universe would begin to open your eyes and ears to Truth that you are no longer deceived.

John 12:40 (ESV) [40] *"He has blinded their eyes and hardened their heart, lest they see with their eyes, and understand with their heart, and turn, and I would heal them."*

Ezekiel 12:2 (HCSB) [2] *"Son of man, you are living among a rebellious house. They have eyes to see but do not see, and ears to hear but do not hear, for they are a rebellious house.*

Lips Protected (5c)

As discussed, the Roman soldier's helmet also covered their lips or mouth. This is another area which desperately needs protection. These all tie in together beginning with what we watch and what we listen to which goes into our mind and is stored deep within our heart. What you take in will eventually come out of you. Everything we take in will come out. If we take in evil, evil will come out; if we take in corruption, corruption is going to come out of us. If we take in lust, it will come out. This is why there is a saying, *"Birds of a feather flock together."* Who you choose to hang out with will be who you become. When you hang out with someone who curses like a sailor *(excuse the saying because this is not intended to speak against sailors),* you can be assured it is going to come out of your mouth as well. When we watch or listen to things contrary to God's Word, eventually, our speech and actions will be just like what we are pouring into our bodies. Yes, we do have to live in this world until we are called home, but it does not mean the world has to live in you. It is through obedience of continually putting more and more of God in that your heart is protected and the good remains there. When we continually put the world in us and not God, we cannot walk as Christ walked. How can you imitate someone when you barely know who they are? We grow up to be like our parents regardless how many times we may have professed, *"I will never be like my dad; I will never be like my mother,"* yet, we become the image and likeness of what we experienced for years. It takes years again to reprogram what we have become.

Our mouth will make us or break us. We must learn that we have power over our actions by reprogramming in order to speak that which is good and not evil. When I pray this, I ask the Lord, *"Father, I put on my Helmet of Salvation that it protects my mouth that nothing precedes but those things which bring **You** glory, and those things which are acceptable to **You**."*

Proverbs 10:32 (AMP) *[32]The lips of the [uncompromisingly] righteous know [and therefore utter] what is acceptable, but the mouth of the wicked knows [and therefore speaks only] what is obstinately willful and contrary.*

It is easy to see how important it is to clothe ourselves daily with the full armor because without it, there is no way we can live righteous being acceptable to God. I do not want to be wicked or live wicked. I believe the world categorizes what is wicked but even that is contrary to God's Word. According to the Word, someone who is wicked follows the world and not the Word of God. This would mean the majority of the people today are considered wicked according to God. Yes, we are all sinners, but we do not have to live as a sinner. We cannot make excuses for our choices that do not line up with God's Word. We cannot say, *"Well, God knows that this is just who I am and this is the best I can do."* Try that when you stand before God someday and see if He says, *"It's okay, you can come on in."* No, He will not say that because He knows how many years you have had to study His Word. He may say, *"That's no excuse, you have had 50 years to read My Word, yet you do not even know what it says regarding your sin?"* Jesus paid the price for our sin, and we can choose to live a life that is righteous. Righteousness is the desire to live according to Christ and striving to get there. We are not punished when we miss it as long as we are striving to live right, and God knows if you are striving. Striving is not coming home each day and plopping down in front of the TV to fill ourselves with more of the world instead of seeking to know more about God and His Word. This all goes back to our heart. God knows your heart. We know if deep inside we truly desire to let go of those sins that keep us from God. If we truly desire to live without sin, we turn to God to show us how. Man cannot do it in himself because we do not have the strength within ourselves to overcome.

1 John 5:1-4 (ESV) Overcoming the World 5 Everyone who believes that Jesus is the Christ has been born of God, and everyone who loves the Father loves whoever has been born of him. ² By this we know that we love the children of God, when we love God and obey his commandments. ³ For this is the love of God, that we keep his commandments. And his commandments are not burdensome. ⁴ For everyone who has been born of God overcomes the world. And this is the victory that has overcome the world—our faith.

There is also no straddling the fence as I have said. We can put a lot of God in and a lot of the world trying to have the best of both worlds. The problem with this is that you cannot love mammon and God both.

410

Matthew 6:24 (ESV) [24] *"No one can serve two masters, for either he will hate the one and love the other, or he will be devoted to the one and despise the other. You cannot serve God and money.*

You will eventually come to love one and not the other, and the love of the Father is not in you when you are trying to play church. God knows your heart. I know people who live this lifestyle. I see their walk. They go to church and outside of church they associate with the world and the things in the world which gratify the flesh, yet they speak as though they are Christians when they are around Christians. Jesus had this to say about those people.

Matthew 12:34 (AMP) [34]*You offspring of vipers! How can you speak good things when you are evil (wicked)? For out of the fullness (the overflow, the superabundance) of the heart the mouth speaks.*

God sees your heart. God knows if you truly love Him and desire to follow Him because Jesus said if you were truly His disciple, you would follow Him, follow in His ways not the ways of this world. It takes denying your desires and your free will, meaning you take up your own cross. You must bear the burden of losing your own life just like Jesus did for us.

John 8:31 (NLT) Jesus and Abraham [31] *Jesus said to the people who believed in him, "You are truly my disciples if you remain faithful to my teachings.*

Matthew 16:24-25 (ESV) Take Up Your Cross and Follow Jesus [24] *Then Jesus told his disciples, "If anyone would come after me, let him deny himself and take up his cross and follow me.* [25] *For whoever would save his life will lose it, but whoever loses his life for my sake will find it.*

When we love God, it will come out of our mouth. Our lives will be changed and others will be able to see the love of God within us. There is this lady that works at a department store named Linda; I love being in her line at checkout. There is no questioning her life with God; you know that she loves the Lord deeply. Once you are close enough in line for her to check you out, you can understand her words, but even from way back, you can tell she is quietly singing praises to God. When I am fortunate to be in her line, I can feel the anointing of God flow from her body. It is a joy to be touched by such a beautiful lady with such a precious spirit. This is what comes out of our mouths when we are full of God. Even Linda cannot hold in what she is full of, which is Jesus Christ.

Psalm 145:21(AMP) [21]My mouth shall speak the praise of the Lord; and let all flesh bless (affectionately and gratefully praise) His holy name forever and ever.

When you are full and you continually put more in, you will be overflowing. When we overflow, it spills out and touches other people.

Luke 6:45 (AMP) [45]The upright (honorable, intrinsically good) man out of the good treasure [stored] in his heart produces what is upright (honorable and intrinsically good), and the evil man out of the evil storehouse brings forth that which is depraved (wicked and intrinsically evil); for out of the abundance (overflow) of the heart his mouth speaks.

Throat Protected (5d)

Another area protected by the Roman soldier's helmet was the throat. The helmet in those days completely covered the throat area front and back. When I think about the throat, I think about how many times people have been killed through strangulation. If we are being choked, we cannot breathe and eventually will lose consciousness and die. In the natural sense, our throat sustains life as it is an avenue that our food and water must travel in order to go into the other organs and be distributed throughout the body. It also sustains life as it is the avenue air travels, whether it is breathed through our nose or mouth. Oxygen is carried into our lungs and again distributed to other parts of the body.

There are many ways that we can die when the throat area is cut off. It can be from choking on food, injuries sustained, and as previously mentioned by someone actually choking us to our death. I'm sure many of us could remember a time when we have choked on food and some of you may have actually had something lodged in your throat that someone had to perform the Heimlich maneuver in order to save you. It is imperative to see that our enemy would also like to choke the life out of us in order to keep us in a state of lifelessness spiritually even if we do not die a natural death.

In the spiritual sense, when we take in spiritual food by what we choose to read with our eyes and listen to with our ears, the life of the Holy Spirit breathes life within us. Our bodies, instead of being lifeless, are filled with spiritual food which sustains us. Jesus tells us that it was better that He went to the Father so that He could send the Comforter, which is the Holy Spirit.

John 16:7 (AMP) ⁷ But I tell you the truth, it is to your advantage that I go away; for if I do not go away, the Helper (Comforter, Advocate, Intercessor—Counselor, Strengthener, Standby) will not come to you; but if I go, I will send Him (the Holy Spirit) to you [to be in close fellowship with you].

John 14:26 (AMP) ²⁶ But the Helper (Comforter, Advocate, Intercessor—Counselor, Strengthener, Standby), the Holy Spirit, whom the Father will send in My name [in My place, to represent Me and act on My behalf], He will teach you all things. And He will help you remember everything that I have told you.

The Holy Spirit's job, as we know, is to be our teacher and to remind us of all truths. When we feed on the Word of God, spiritual food travels throughout our body just like natural food.

John 4:31-33 (AMP) *[31]Meanwhile, the disciples urged Him saying, Rabbi, eat something. [32]But He assured them, I have food (nourishment) to eat of which you know nothing and have no idea. [33]So the disciples said one to another, Has someone brought Him something to eat?*

This seemed strange to the disciples when Jesus spoke these words, but we understand this when we look at what food does to the natural. When we eat natural food, our bodies grow naturally. When we go to school and begin to listen and learn according to the standards of this world, the knowledge taught by man, again we grow in wisdom and knowledge in the natural. So, it is easy to see that our spiritual being must also be nurtured. As we have discussed, our bodies consist of the soul which is our will and emotions, our spirit which is the part that connects to God or to the spiritual realm, and then the body houses those components. We were created to be spiritual beings and this part lies dormant, in a sense, until we find Jesus. As we feed the spiritual man, it grows and matures in the things of God. Even Jesus, had to be nurtured spiritually.

Matthew 3:16-17 (ESV) *[16]And when Jesus was baptized, immediately he went up from the water, and behold, the heavens were opened to him, and he saw the Spirit of God descending like a dove and coming to rest on him; [17]and behold, a voice from heaven said, "This is my beloved Son, with whom I am well pleased."*

It was at that moment that the Holy Spirit consumed Jesus and His ministry began at that time. In fact, to be more precise, Jesus began as a child to learn God's Word when he would spend days in the temple. The Holy Spirit ascended upon Him at baptism and

414

then He was led into the desert where He began His spiritual battle with the enemy. At that place, His natural body was weakened due to fasting from food but His spiritual body was strengthened being totally dependent upon God through His Spirit. His ministry to the world began once He walked out of that dry place and He overcame all obstacles presented as He glorified His Father through every trial and test bearing the burden of constant pain and suffering which ultimately led to His crucifixion in which the battle was finally won. satan was once and for all defeated. This is the ministry of Jesus Christ! This is the ministry that we are to walk in if we call ourselves His Disciples!

So, just as we go to school to learn how to read and write along with many other things, we must also tune in to our spiritual teacher, the Holy Spirit in order that our spirit man in nurtured in the same way that Jesus was. It is through spiritual growth that we learn our purpose and are able to please God.

John 4:34 (AMP) ³⁴*Jesus said to them, My food (nourishment) is to do the will (pleasure) of Him Who sent Me and to accomplish and completely finish His work.*

We all have a purpose to fulfill. Just like John the Baptist, his purpose was to prepare for the coming of Christ, and we are to prepare for the second coming. Each one of us has a specific job to do, and it is through growing and maturing that we come to know our special gifts and skills in order to step out and do the perfect will of God for our lives.

John 6:27 (AMP) ²⁷*Stop toiling and doing and producing for the food that perishes and decomposes [in the using], but strive and work and produce rather for the [lasting] food which endures [continually] unto life eternal; the Son of Man will give (furnish) you that, for God the*

Father has authorized and certified Him and put His seal of endorsement upon Him.

Life is not about living to eat but rather about eating to live in the natural, and in the spiritual as well. In the natural, with all the fine restaurants and thousands of different cuisines, it is easy to become a lover of foods, but food in the natural realm will never produce life. We must have food in order to live, but we should never live just to eat. Yes, I believe that God desires that we enjoy His world that He created for us, but we can get to a place where our enjoyment of such delicacies become lust to our eyes and to our tastes. Our cravings should instead be for the food Jesus spoke of. The food of life that truly gives everlasting life is the Word of God. This is the only food that will truly satisfy our appetites and sustain us for eternity. Jesus was in fact called the Bread of Life.

John 6:55 (AMP) [55] For My flesh is true and genuine food, and My blood is true and genuine drink. (bread of life)

John 6:57 (AMP) [57] Just as the living Father sent Me and I live by (through, because of) the Father, even so whoever continues to feed on Me [whoever takes Me for his food and is nourished by Me] shall [in his turn] live through and because of Me.

John 6:58 (AMP) [58] This is the Bread that came down from heaven. It is not like the manna which our forefathers ate, and yet died; he who takes this Bread for his food shall live forever.

The Breath of Life (5e)

The last area that the helmet protects is the very breath that we breathe in. Breathing is an involuntary action which occurs by impulses that the brain sends out. Breathing is an area we seldom think about, yet if we were to stop breathing, we would die. We do not have to think in order to breathe because our brain is wired to control our breathing and also to monitor the levels of carbon dioxide in our blood stream which can kill us at high levels. Therefore, our brain also controls the rate of breathing to eliminate too much carbon dioxide. Most of us are not even aware of this, and we just go about our day as if all is in control within our bodies. We have faith that God made our bodies to function with little problems, and in the event a problem does occur, then our faith goes in the direction of the doctors to fix us.

Genesis 2:7 (ESV) [7] then the LORD *God formed the man of dust from the ground and breathed into his nostrils the breath of life, and the man became a living creature.*

In the spiritual sense, the majority of Christians probably never even consider the breath of life which sustains us spiritually, in order that we live in this world abundantly and continue over into the next life with Christ. In order to live a life of abundance, the Holy Spirit was left with us as our teacher and instructor. Just as God breathed life into man as a living creature, Jesus breathed life into His disciples in order that they would be able to carry out the calling which is also placed on all believers.

John 20:21-22 (AMP) [21] Then Jesus said to them again, Peace to you! [Just] as the Father has sent Me forth, so I am sending you. [22] And having said this, He breathed on them and said to them, Receive the Holy Spirit!

2 Timothy 1:8-14 (ESV) [8] Therefore do not be ashamed of the testimony about our Lord, nor of me his prisoner, but share in suffering for the gospel by the power of God, [9] who saved us and called us to a holy calling, not because of our works but because of his own purpose and grace, which he gave us in Christ Jesus before the ages began, [10] and which now has been manifested through the appearing of our Savior Christ Jesus, who abolished death and brought life and immortality to light through the gospel, [11] for which I was appointed a preacher and apostle and teacher, [12] which is why I suffer as I do. But I am not ashamed, for I know whom I have believed, and I am convinced that he is able to guard until that Day what has been entrusted to me. [13] Follow the pattern of the sound words that you have heard from me, in the faith and love that are in Christ Jesus. [14] By the Holy Spirit who dwells within us, guard the good deposit entrusted to you.

This was not the breath of life naturally; they were already living creatures that breathed in order to live a physical life. This breath of life was the Holy Spirit that filled them with a different kind of life that is only found spiritually. In the natural we can do very little, but in the spiritual, all things are possible. Yet, we are incapable of living a spiritually sound life without the Holy Spirit within us. When Christians live in this world without the infilling of the Holy Spirit, they live a life that is dead or dried up. Just as the Holy Spirit ascended upon Jesus after Paul the Baptist baptized Him in the Jordan River, He will also ascend upon all those that truly desire to walk as Christ fulfilling all we are called to do. Yes, Jesus was led into the desert, and we will also have our own desert experiences which will grow us to be all that God called us to be. Just as He defeated the enemy, we too will also have victory over that which is evil. In Scripture, we see that as disciples, we are to do those same things that Jesus did and even greater as we come into these end times.

John 14:12 (ESV) [12] *"Truly, truly, I say to you, whoever believes in me will also do the works that I do; and greater works than these will he do, because I am going to the Father.*

Below, we see that the Lord spoke to Ezekiel and told him to prophesy to dry bones.

Ezekiel 37:4-6 (AMP) [4] *Again He said to me, Prophesy to these bones and say to them, O you dry bones, hear the word of the Lord.* [5] *Thus says the Lord God to these bones: Behold, I will cause breath and spirit to enter you, and you shall live;* [6] *And I will lay sinews upon you and bring up flesh upon you and cover you with skin, and I will put breath and spirit in you, and you [dry bones] shall live; and you shall know, understand, and realize that I am the Lord [the Sovereign Ruler, Who calls forth loyalty and obedient service].*

This is not about just being able to breathe in the natural but also in the spiritual. God was speaking about dried up bones that needed life. He was not talking about a natural life but spiritual. When we have breath and spirit enter us, we rise up with life – God breathed life! Once we come alive with God's Spirit in us, we not only live but we have knowledge and understanding of who God really is and how great He is. This brings about a change within us of loyalty and obedience. Christians today are not obedient or loyal to the purpose of going forth to make disciples. We are not obedient or loyal because we lack the *Breath of Life* within our mortal bodies, and we are all dried up. We can walk in many church services today and they have either become so structured that the Spirit of God cannot flow through them, or they are dried up and dead with no life. Yet, God called out to Ezekiel hundreds of years ago to prophesy to that which was dead and to speak life into it. In the Scripture above, Jesus breathed the Holy Spirit into His followers, He told them that as the Father had sent Him to go forth, He was sending all that follow Him to go forth.

419

We have been given everything we need to rise up and speak to that which is dead and call it to life. As we go forth full of the Holy Spirit, we need to speak life into those things which are dead and call them to life. You may be saying that you are not a prophet, yet Paul tells us that we should all desire to prophecy. We should all pray that we prophesy. There is the gift of prophecy and then there is prophecy that is given to all those who diligently seek and ask for it. Paul said we should all pursue the gift of prophecy.

1 Corinthians 14:1-5 (ESV) Prophecy and Tongues 14 Pursue love, and earnestly desire the spiritual gifts, especially that you may prophesy. ²For one who speaks in a tongue speaks not to men but to God; for no one understands him, but he utters mysteries in the Spirit. ³On the other hand, the one who prophesies speaks to people for their upbuilding and encouragement and consolation. ⁴The one who speaks in a tongue builds up himself, but the one who prophesies builds up the church. ⁵Now I want you all to speak in tongues, but even more to prophesy. The one who prophesies is greater than the one who speaks in tongues, unless someone interprets, so that the church may be built up.

Below in Revelation, John fell down at his feet to worship but was restrained because this was a mere servant of God's. We fall at the feet of God to worship Him, but what we need to see in this Scripture below is that the Truth which has been revealed to us by Jesus Christ is the Spirit of all prophesies. The Holy Spirit is our teacher and counselor; it is He who fills us and in that breath, all inspirations come alive that we stand up to teach, preach, and interpret the divine will and purpose of God the Father.

Revelation 19:10 (AMP) ¹⁰Then I fell prostrate at his feet to worship (to pay divine honors) to him, but he [restrained me] and said, Refrain! [You must not do that!] I am [only] another servant with you and your brethren who have [accepted and hold] the testimony borne by Jesus. Worship God! For the substance (essence) of the truth revealed by Jesus is the spirit of all prophecy [the vital breath, the inspiration of all

420

inspired preaching and interpretation of the divine will and purpose, including both mine and yours].

As we apply the Helmet of Salvation, it is through salvation that we come to know the Holy Spirit and as He breathes in us, that breath has purpose. Daily, I pray that as I put on the Helmet of Salvation, that it protects the very breath that I breathe in, and in that breath comes life to my mortal body that it is quickened to the things of God. The Breath of Life ties in to the mouth. Our enemy would love to choke out the very life that we breathe in, and most of the time, he is successful because we walk around living defeated. We must make that choice that our bones will not be dead but will be awakened by the breath of the Holy Spirit. We must speak to our bodies as Ezekiel spoke to the dry bones and command them in the name of Jesus to awaken and produce life. The Holy Spirit is the ingredient that will sustain our life until the second coming of Christ. If you are a deadbeat Christian only watching the game of life on the sidelines and not participating in the game, rise up and call yourself to life. Rise up today, and pray that the infilling of the Holy Spirit will engulf your very body and bring it to life.

To tie in all elements of the helmet, again it is what we gaze upon and listen to that feed our mind, and as we continually put corruptness within our bodies, it stores down deep within our heart that eventually those things within our heart will come forth out of our mouths. As we speak evils out of our mouth, they choke all life out of us that when looked upon in the spiritual realm, all that can be seen are dry dead bones. Our life is sustained by the spiritual food we consume and the air which we breathe. As I take in air daily, I will speak and thank God that the air I am consuming is the *"Breath of Life"* and it continually is filling me that my cup runneth over.

421

Psalm 23:5(ESV) [5]You prepare a table before me in the presence of my enemies; you anoint my head with oil; my cup overflows.

Remember, Paul share great wisdom with us in order that we continue on the race set before us. Paul was convinced that nothing could separate him from the love of Christ, are you?

Romans 8:31-39 (ESV) God's Everlasting Love [31]What then shall we say to these things? If God is for us, who can be against us? [32] He who did not spare his own Son but gave him up for us all, how will he not also with him graciously give us all things? [33] Who shall bring any charge against God's elect? It is God who justifies. [34] Who is to condemn? Christ Jesus is the one who died—more than that, who was raised—who is at the right hand of God, who indeed is interceding for us. [35] Who shall separate us from the love of Christ? Shall tribulation, or distress, or persecution, or famine, or nakedness, or danger, or sword? [36] As it is written, "For your sake we are being killed all the day long; we are regarded as sheep to be slaughtered." [37] No, in all these things we are more than conquerors through him who loved us. [38] For I am sure that neither death nor life, nor angels nor rulers, nor things present nor things to come, nor powers, [39] nor height nor depth, nor anything else in all creation, will be able to separate us from the love of God in Christ Jesus our Lord.

Sword of the Spirit (6)

Ephesians 6:10-20 (NKJV) [10] Finally, my brethren, be strong in the Lord and in the power of His might. [11] Put on the whole armor of God, that you may be able to stand against the wiles of the devil. [12] For we do not wrestle against flesh and blood, but against principalities, against powers, against the rulers of the darkness of this age, against spiritual hosts of wickedness in the heavenly places. [13] Therefore take up the whole armor of God, that you may be able to withstand in the evil day, and having done all, to stand. [14] Stand therefore, having (1) girded your waist with truth, having (2) put on the breastplate of righteousness, [15] and having (3) shod your feet with the preparation of the gospel of peace; [16] above all, (4) taking the shield of faith with which you will be able to quench all the fiery darts of the wicked one. [17] And (5) take the helmet of salvation, and (6) the sword of the Spirit, which is the word of God; [18] praying always with all prayer and supplication in the Spirit, being watchful to this end with all perseverance and supplication for all the saints— [19] *and for me, that utterance may be given to me, that I may open my mouth boldly to make known the mystery of the gospel,* [20] *for which I am an ambassador in chains; that in it I may speak boldly, as I ought to speak.*

We are at the last piece of armor that Paul spoke to us about. Why would you think this piece would be the last piece of armor to apply? Remember, it's not about this piece being of least importance because all pieces are valuable, and they are all needed to effectively win our battles. However, why would this one piece have been the last on the list? There is more than one answer to that question. If we are looking at this in the natural standpoint, prior to lifting your sword for battle, you would be heading out to battle or already in the battlefield. Soldier's in biblical days, kept their swords close at hand but did not have them in their hand. A police officer has their gun close at hand, but they do not carry them around in their hand. The soldiers were fully clothed when they went into the field but had not necessarily lifted their sword until they were ready to fight their enemy. The same for police officers, they may be ready at any moment to use their weapon if need be, but until that time, it is not in their hand even though they are fully clothed in the uniform. Another reason, the sword would have been their offensive weapon. As an offensive weapon, it is only used when you are planning to attack someone or something. The sword was the last thing to apply to your life because it was not necessary unless you were in a battle.

On a spiritual level, Paul used the sword to represent the Word of God. Now notice, our belt is described as the Belt of Truth, correct? The Belt of Truth is also the Word of God, so what was Paul trying to say here? When we apply the Belt of Truth, this is at the stage where we are growing to gain knowledge and wisdom in order to be ready to step out and be that disciple that we are all called to be. As we study to show ourselves approved, we are clothing ourselves with all Truth in order that we walk out into this world in the likeness and image of Christ. We are representing Jesus when we go and begin to share the Gospel of Peace. Remember, the gospels represent peace and share the life of Christ. However, when we first walk out into the field to harvest, remember the harvest is plentiful with souls, we are rookies. As a rookie, we just came out of Boot Camp and have proceeded to get our feet wet. As we learn to endure the battles, God will not allow us to go through what we are not capable of at that time, our battles will get tougher but we will be stronger through Christ. The day comes that it is no longer just about sharing Jesus, now it becomes about fighting the fight at hand in order to take back what is rightfully ours. We will discuss this further when we talk about the shield and sword, but for now, when we begin to lift our sword, we have become stronger that our sword becomes sharper than any two-edged sword, dividing the soul from the spirit.

Hebrews 4:12 (ESV) [12] *For the word of God is living and active, sharper than any two-edged sword, piercing to the division of soul and of spirit, of joints and of marrow, and discerning the thoughts and intentions of the heart.*

With the belt, we acquired knowledge and wisdom and when we put our shoes on, we acquired firsthand knowledge and wisdom by action, living through what we preach. When we lift our sword, we understand that the Word of God has the power to do all we are called to do. This is a spiritual battle that is only fought in the spiritual realm. This battle is only fought as you line up your life to become that warrior God intended you to be. When we lift that sword, we intend to fight; otherwise, we do not lift that sword. In volume 2 of this series, we will go much deeper into the sword and the purpose of this weapon.

End Note

We have covered the basic armor to become grounded in the Word of God. Volume 2 of this series will lead you deeper into the actual spiritual battle and the weapons which we use. God always intended His people to be prepared for every battle at hand. In doing so, we must not only study to show ourselves approved but we should also strive to develop that intimate relationship with our Father in Heaven. I pray that these words within this book leads those to know God deeper, has placed a hunger to search further, and a desire for His wisdom, revelation and above all the understanding.

Volume 2 of this series will be released fall of 2016

~~~~~~

References

Chapter 3 – Choice

1. Mind Over Matter Strategy to Win Lottery.
http://ezinearticles.com/?Mind-Over-Matter-Strategy-to-Win-Lottery&id=4610138

Chapter 5 – Belt of Truth

1. Child Development the First Five Years
http://raisingchildren.net.au/articles/child_development.html

2. Stress - A Main Cause of Illness
http://www.energeticforum.com/paths/7162-stress-main-cause-illness.html

3. Line of Departure
http://www.lineofdeparture.com/2012/03/07/armys-top-nco-talking-radical-reforms-to-uniforms-grooming/

Chapter 7 – Order of Importance

1. New Learning Transformational Designs for Pedagogy and Assessment
http://newlearningonline.com/new-learning/chapter-7/descartes-i-think-therefore-i-am

www.ingramcontent.com/pod-product-compliance
Lightning Source LLC
Chambersburg PA
CBHW060236100426
42742CB00011B/1544